STUDIES IN THE HISTORY
OF CHRISTIAN MISSIONS

R. E. Frykenberg
Brian Stanley
General Editors

STUDIES IN THE HISTORY OF CHRISTIAN MISSIONS

Boone Aldridge
*For the Gospel's Sake: The Rise of the Wycliffe Bible Translators
and the Summer Institute of Language*

Alvyn Austin
China's Millions: The China Inland Mission and Late Qing Society, 1832–1905

Chad M. Bauman
Christian Identity and Dalit Religion in Hindu India, 1868–1947

Michael Bergunder
The South Indian Pentecostal Movement in the Twentieth Century

Judith M. Brown and Robert Eric Frykenberg, *Editors*
Christians, Cultural Interactions, and India's Religious Traditions

John B. Carman and Chilkuri Vasantha Rao
Christians in South Indian Villages, 1959–2009: Decline and Revival in Telangana

Robert Eric Frykenberg
*Christians and Missionaries in India:
Cross-Cultural Communication Since 1500*

Susan Billington Harper
*In the Shadow of the Mahatma: Bishop V. S. Azariah
and the Travails of Christianity in British India*

D. Dennis Hudson
Protestant Origins in India: Tamil Evangelical Christians, 1706–1835

Patrick Harries and David Maxwell, *Editors*
The Spiritual in the Secular: Missionaries and Knowledge about Africa

Ogbu U. Kalu, *Editor,* and Alaine M. Low, *Associate Editor*
*Interpreting Contemporary Christianity:
Global Processes and Local Identities*

Donald M. Lewis, *Editor*
*Christianity Reborn: The Global Expansion of Evangelicalism
in the Twentieth Century*

Jessie G. Lutz
Opening China: Karl F. A. Gützlaff and Sino-Western Relations, 1827–1852

For the Gospel's Sake

*The Rise of the Wycliffe Bible Translators and
the Summer Institute of Linguistics*

Boone Aldridge

WILLIAM B. EERDMANS PUBLISHING COMPANY
GRAND RAPIDS, MICHIGAN

Wm. B. Eerdmans Publishing Co.
2140 Oak Industrial Drive N.E., Grand Rapids, Michigan 49505
www.eerdmans.com

27 26 25 24 23 22 21 20 19 18   1 2 3 4 5 6 7 8 9 10

ISBN 978-0-8028-7610-2

Library of Congress Cataloging-in-Publication Data

Names: Aldridge, Boone, 1962– author.
Title: For the Gospel's sake : the rise of the Wycliffe Bible Translators and the
    Summer Institute of Linguistics / Boone Aldridge.
Description: Grand Rapids : Eerdmans Publishing Co., 2018. | Series: Studies in the history of
    Christian missions | Includes bibliographical references and index.
Identifiers: LCCN 2017041267 | ISBN 9780802876102 (pbk. : alk. paper)
Subjects: LCSH: Wycliffe Bible Translators—History. | Bible—Translating—History. |
    Summer Institute of Linguistics—History.
Classification: LCC BV2370.W93 A43 2018 | DDC 266.006/01—dc23
    LC record available at https://lccn.loc.gov/2017041267

Contents

Foreword

God is committed to communicating with his creation—men, women, and children with whom he wants a relationship. He does this consistently through the translation of his Word, the Bible.

To do this, time and again throughout history, God has chosen to work through people with strengths and weaknesses, flaws and shortcomings that from a human perspective should have held them back, people like Abraham, Isaac, Jacob, Moses, Rahab, David, Paul, and so many others. These men and women were not perfect, but God, in his sovereignty, used them anyway. Each faced harrowing external trials. As Joseph tells his brothers near the end of his story in Genesis 50:20, "You intended to harm me, but God intended it all for good."

The book you hold in your hands is a part of this story of God's faithfulness to his Word. Sometimes difficult to read, it recounts the history of SIL and Wycliffe Bible Translators grappling with our complex family of organizations and our past. In these pages Fredrick "Boone" Aldridge intimately addresses the linguistic, anthropological, and theological trials we have faced over the past seventy-five years. What this book makes clear is that God has been in control to keep the work going, using people who were faithful to him.

The story continues to be written as we move toward the finish line, what one of our founders, William Cameron Townsend, saw as the completion of the task—the day when God's Word would blanket the whole earth and every tongue, tribe, and people group would have access to and be able to engage with

God's transformative Word of life. As the future unfolds, it is comforting to be reminded of God's sovereignty throughout our past. None of us, whether individually or together, could have achieved what God has accomplished through Wycliffe and SIL.

BOB CRESON
President and CEO
Wycliffe Bible Translators USA

Preface

When research for the present volume on the development of the Wycliffe Bible Translators (WBT) and Summer Institute of Linguistics (SIL) International was initiated in 2006, I had already completed nearly a decade of service with both organizations in the United States and Africa. The roots of this present study can be traced to my varied reactions to the organizations' unique strategies, which elicited emotions ranging, at times, from puzzlement to surprise, and at other times from annoyance to admiration. As my questions multiplied, and with the answers seemingly buried under accumulated layers of belief, habit, and myth, an examination of the organizations' histories seemed to offer the most logical line of inquiry for understanding the sometimes enigmatic character of WBT and SIL.

The fact that I am a member of both organizations offered unparalleled opportunities during the course of this wide-ranging inquiry. While researching this volume, I was afforded unrestricted access to the organizations' archives, and to their personnel, both retired and in service, for interviews. As an insider, I did not encounter the same level of mistrust that an outsider might have confronted. Moreover, there is perhaps no better way to acquire an overall sense of the organizational culture than to work for the entity one hopes to study. The status of an insider served me well over the past few years of research and reflection on WBT and SIL, and I am grateful for the fortunate circumstances in which I found myself. Some members of WBT and SIL might sense that, for an organizational insider, I have been overly critical. Others will perhaps believe that an injustice has been done to William Cameron Townsend, affectionately known as "Uncle Cam" by those who knew him well and served in his era. Others still will perhaps complain that more emphasis is placed on the twists and turns of controversial events than on Bible translation, the organizations' bread and butter. All these complaints, it must be admitted, contain at least a modicum of truth. Such are the hazards of critical historical investigation and, as well, of the necessity of crafting the narrative around turning points and the resolution of conflicts in order to illuminate the subject in a somewhat concise fashion. To the historian also falls the thankless task of puncturing myths, some of which are the very stories that sustain us and reassure us in troubled times. I can only hope that, in narrating what is surely a most remarkable and fascinating story, I have accomplished the task with equal measures of critical insight and sympathetic perception, for this delicate balance was all along my highest aspiration. Any blame for missing the mark rests on my shoulders alone.

Acknowledgments

In the course of researching and writing this book, I benefited from the assistance of a long list of Wycliffe Bible Translators and SIL International members, all of whom generously gave of their time and candidly shared their experiences. I wish to thank SIL anthropologist Karl Franklin, who read the entire manuscript more than once and offered many insightful comments. To SIL anthropologist Tom Headland goes particular appreciation for his commentary on an early version of the manuscript, encouraging me along the way, providing documents, and answering questions. Likewise, I am indebted to Cal Hibbard, the archivist for the Townsend Archives, for his help on numerous occasions. Hibbard's labors collecting, organizing, and preserving Townsend's voluminous correspondence and other documents of historical interest over the past several decades have provided historians a veritable gold mine. SIL's Vurnell Cobbey, who has labored for a number of years organizing the Kenneth L. Pike papers, provided help along the way and was a constant encouragement to me during my research. And I am especially grateful to WBT and SIL for offering me complete and unfettered access to the organizations' archives and for permitting me the freedom to follow the organizations' development wherever the sources led.

This present study was originally conceived as a doctoral dissertation. Therefore I wish to extend my profound appreciation to Professor David W. Bebbington, who deserves credit for making postgraduate study not only a rigorous undertaking but also an enjoyable and fascinating process. To Bill Svelmoe I owe a debt of gratitude, for it was he who encouraged me to pursue postgraduate studies that ultimately led to this project. My appreciation also extends to both Prof. Brian Stanley and Prof. Robert Eric Frykenberg for their many helpful comments and suggestions along the way.

And finally, to my endearing wife Julie is owed an outsized share of the credit for completion of this volume, for without her support and constant encouragement it would never have come to fruition.

Abbreviations

Archives

BGA	Billy Graham Center Archives
CAA	Central American Mission Archives
GIAL	Graduate Institute of Applied Linguistics
MBA	Mexico Branch of the Summer Institute of Linguistics Archives
PSC	Kenneth L. Pike Special Collection
LCA	SIL International Language and Culture Archives, Dallas, Texas
TA	William Cameron Townsend Archives
UOA	University of Oklahoma Archives
WSA	WBT-SIL Corporate Archives

Organizations

AAA	American Anthropological Association
ABS	American Bible Society
AIM	Africa Inland Mission
APRA	American Popular Revolutionary Alliance
BIOLA	Bible Institute of Los Angeles
BTL	Bible Translation and Literacy
CAM	Central American Mission
CAMF	Christian Aviators' Missionary Fellowship

CIM	China Inland Mission
COD	Church of the Open Door
ECOSOC	United Nations Economic and Social Council
EFMA	Evangelical Foreign Missions Association
FAP	Fuerza Aérea del Perú
GARB	General Association of Regular Baptists
GILLBT	Ghana Institute of Linguistics, Literacy and Bible Translation
GMU	Gospel Missionary Union
IFMA	Interdenominational Foreign Mission Association
ILC	International Linguistic Center
ISO	International Organization for Standardization
IVCF	InterVarsity Christian Fellowship
IWGIA	International Work Group for Indigenous Affairs
JAARS	Jungle Aviation and Radio Service
LAIM	Latin American Indian Mission
MAF	Missionary Aviation Fellowship
NACLA	North American Congress on Latin America
NAE	National Association of Evangelicals
NBTO	National Bible Translation Organization
NGO	nongovernmental organization
NSD	National Security Doctrine
PMA	Pioneer Mission Agency
RBI	Robinson Bible Institute
SIL	Summer Institute of Linguistics
SIM	Sudan Interior Mission
SVM	Student Volunteer Movement
TSC	The Seed Company
UCLA	University of California at Los Angeles
UND	University of North Dakota
UNESCO	United Nations Educational, Scientific and Cultural Organization
USAID	United States Agency for International Development
UTA	University of Texas at Arlington
WA	Wycliffe Associates
WBT	Wycliffe Bible Translators
WBTI	Wycliffe Bible Translators International
WCC	World Council of Churches
WGA	Wycliffe Global Alliance
YFC	Youth for Christ

Introduction

The Wycliffe Bible Translators (WBT) and Summer Institute of Linguistics (SIL) combination is a paradox that begs for an explanation.[1] This dual-structured mission—essentially sister organizations constituting a single institution—was one of the most controversial, fastest-growing, and largest evangelical missions of the twentieth century. This strikingly unconventional mission was formed in the mid-1930s and officially incorporated in 1942 under the direction of William Cameron Townsend, a former Central American Mission (CAM) missionary. In the early 1930s, it was Townsend's twofold objective to train missionary candidates in the rudiments of descriptive linguistics and then to send the graduates of his summer course into anticlerical Mexico, where they would take up Bible translation among the nation's indigenous peoples. To gain access to Mexico, Townsend established SIL as a scientific and humanitarian organization. Since a number of highly placed Mexican government officials were eager to employ SIL's missionary-translators in indigenous language development and social uplift projects, they permitted SIL to enter Mexico under government sponsorship as a scientific organization, while also allowing Townsend's young recruits to pursue Bible translation. SIL was not the sort of missionary institution that most North American evangelicals would understand or support. Therefore, WBT was created to relate to evangelicals at home as an expressly religious mission. The WBT-SIL combination was an elegant solution to the

1. Wycliffe Bible Translators was originally formed as a US corporation. In 1980 WBT in the United States became a member organization of Wycliffe Bible Translators International, which today is doing business as Wycliffe Global Alliance. The Summer Institute of Linguistics is today known simply as SIL International.

thorny problem of relating to two entirely different publics. If the dual strategy was ingenious, it was nonetheless provocative. To more than a few observers, ranging from Christian fundamentalists to secular anthropologists, WBT-SIL was nothing more than a pretense to conceal a hidden agenda. For several decades the organization had to contend with a nearly unceasing stream of criticism from one quarter or another. Why, then, did WBT-SIL enjoy nearly unparalleled growth to become one of the twentieth century's largest independent, nondenominational faith missions?

The Historical Missionary Context of the Study

The mission historian Andrew Walls has convincingly argued that the "voluntary society" arose in the early part of the eighteenth century in response to the "consciousness of individual responsibility," which was a cardinal characteristic of Enlightenment thought.[2] The rationalization of missionary activity along individualist lines rather than under the aegis of the state church was ideally suited to an entrepreneurial approach to missions, especially among British and American boards. "The principle of the voluntary society is," Walls explained, to "identify the task to be done; find appropriate means of carrying it out; unite and organize a group of like-minded people for the purpose."[3] Acting upon Enlightenment assumptions, missionary societies from the eighteenth century took on qualities that resembled those of a commercial enterprise. In the early to mid-nineteenth century, the business-like practices of many voluntary missionary societies came in for reproach from opponents who had been affected by Romantic sensibilities. Of these critics, the Church of Scotland minister Edward Irving was the first and most important. Irving sermonized against caution and planning in missionary activity, and urged instead that missionaries should depend on supernatural protection and spiritual intuition. What Irving preached, the minister and orphanage founder George Müller put into practice by never asking for money. Following the trail blazed by Irving and Müller, faith mission advocates, such as the China Inland Mission (CIM) founder Hudson Taylor and the American Presbyterian minister and missions promoter Arthur T. Pierson, forsook salaries and shunned solicitation in favor of trusting God

2. Andrew F. Walls, "The Eighteenth-Century Protestant Missionary Awakening," in *Christian Missions and the Enlightenment*, ed. Brian Stanley (Grand Rapids: Eerdmans, 2001), 29–30.

3. Andrew F. Walls, *The Missionary Movement in Christian History: Studies in the Transmission of Faith* (Maryknoll, NY: Orbis, 1996), 229.

alone to supply their financial needs.[4] In a word, the rise of the faith mission movement was a Romantic reaction to the Enlightenment-styled voluntary society model of missions. Perhaps more than any other missionary organization of the twentieth century, the WBT-SIL enterprise was, as will be seen, an innovative combination that was equally influenced by the spirit of both the Enlightenment and Romanticism.

As with numerous other independent missions, WBT-SIL was conceived as a faith mission after the pattern of Hudson Taylor's CIM. Taylor created CIM in 1865 after failing to convince the denomination to start missions in the interior of China, beyond the established coastal mission stations.[5] The "faith mission" nomenclature derived from the practice of not soliciting funds. Rather, as Taylor himself once put it, financial support was expected to appear miraculously "as an answer to prayer in faith."[6] Keswick holiness teachings were another important aspect of the faith mission enterprise. The Keswick movement emphasized the consecrated Christian life and spiritual power for Christian service. The movement's teachings were well suited to the faith mission endeavor, since the leaders of independent missions sought candidates who possessed the spiritual mettle required for pioneering missionary service but who would also humbly submit to direction from mission boards that paid no salaries.[7] Faith missions also exhibited a particular concern for saving souls, and these institutions therefore poured a greater part of their energies into evangelization than into educational or social activities.[8] The appearance of faith missions was accompanied by the proliferation of independent Bible institutes. These new educational institutions instructed potential missionaries in the ways of Keswick spirituality and equipped them with the minimal Bible knowledge necessary for rapid evangelization. Indeed, in many Bible colleges spiritual vigor was prized above scholarly attainment.[9] The faith mission movement constituted a methodologically pragmatic, spiritually vigorous, and exceptionally energetic effort to evangelize all parts of the world in the shortest possible time.

4. David W. Bebbington, *The Dominance of Evangelicalism: The Age of Spurgeon and Moody* (Downers Grove: InterVarsity, 2005), 185–90.

5. Klaus Fiedler, *The Story of Faith Missions: From Hudson Taylor to Present Day Africa* (Irvine, CA: Regnum, 1994), 32–34.

6. James Hudson Taylor, *Retrospect* (London, 1894), 95, quoted in Fiedler, *Story of Faith Missions*, 24.

7. Joel A. Carpenter, "Propagating the Faith Once Delivered: The Fundamentalist Missionary Enterprise, 1920–1945," in *Earthen Vessels: American Evangelicals and Foreign Missions, 1880–1980*, ed. Joel A. Carpenter and Wilbert R. Shenk (Grand Rapids: Eerdmans, 1990), 117–22.

8. Carpenter, "Propagating the Faith," 125–27.

9. Virginia Lieson Brereton, *Training God's Army: The American Bible School, 1880–1940* (Bloomington: Indiana University Press, 1990), 87–103.

Initially evangelical faith missions were envisaged as supplementing the work of existing denominational boards, but over the course of the twentieth century they became the dominant form of North American missionary enterprise. By the early 1980s, about 91 percent of the thirty-five thousand Protestant North American missionaries serving abroad belonged to an evangelical mission.[10] This restructuring of North American missions was closely related to the emergence of fundamentalism and to midcentury developments within evangelicalism. Into the early part of the twentieth century, despite the differing perspectives on missionary thought and practice between denominational mission boards and independent faith missions, there was general agreement that Protestant Christianity was the one and only true religion and that making converts to the Christian faith should be the primary aim of missions. As some liberal mission thinkers and missionaries in the 1920s and 1930s began to take a more charitable view of the major non-Christian world religions and to stress the social dimension of Christianity over conversion, fundamentalists appeared on the scene defending the uniqueness of Christianity and the centrality of evangelism.[11] The close relationship between fundamentalism and faith missions was on display at the World Christian Fundamentals Association inaugural meeting in 1919, where seven of the main speakers were members of the conservative Interdenominational Foreign Mission Association, which had been founded in 1917 in response to the perception that liberalism was increasingly prevalent among denominational missions.[12] By the 1930s, the typical North American faith mission differed from its denominational counterpart in a number of respects. In faith mission circles, spiritual zeal was valued over educational criteria for missionary candidates; the faith method of no solicitation was favored over structured budgets and fund drives; premillennialism was generally the only acceptable eschatology; and a narrower focus on evangelization was strongly preferred over a broader socioreligious missiology. Put concisely, by the 1930s many independent faith missions were of a part with North American fundamentalism.

10. Robert T. Coote, "The Uneven Growth of Conservative Evangelical Missions," *International Bulletin of Missionary Research* 6, no. 3 (July 1982): 118.

11. William R. Hutchison, *Errand to the World: American Protestant Thought and Foreign Missions* (Chicago: University of Chicago Press, 1993), 125–75; James Alan Patterson, "The Loss of a Protestant Missionary Consensus: Foreign Missions and the Fundamentalist-Modernist Conflict," in Carpenter and Shenk, *Earthen Vessels*, 73–91.

12. Edwin L. Frizen Jr., *75 Years of IFMA, 1917–1992: The Nondenominational Missions Movement* (Wheaton, IL: Interdenominational Foreign Mission Association, 1992), 85–96; *God Hath Spoken* (Philadelphia Bible Conference Committee, 1919), 5–6, 17, 23–26, cited in Carpenter, "Propagating the Faith," 100.

Introduction

Evangelicalism and Fundamentalism

A considerable amount of ink has been spilled attempting to define evangelicalism and fundamentalism. Evangelicalism is perhaps most easily described by what has become something of a standard definition. David W. Bebbington, a historian familiar to students of Anglo-American evangelicalism, has provided a fourfold definition of the evangelical movement, which was a form of Protestantism that originated during the transatlantic revivals of the 1730s. Conversionism, activism, biblicism, and crucicentrism are the four essential characteristics singled out by Bebbington. Evangelicals have long insisted that the gospel should be widely and passionately preached, since individual conversion was considered the only remedy for sinners. Once they experienced conversion, evangelicals have demonstrated a propensity to become active in seeking to lead others to conversion. Among evangelicals, the Bible has always been held in high regard, since they believed it alone presented a truthful account of the gospel message. Finally, the cross has held a special place for evangelicals, for upon it rests the doctrine of atonement.[13] While a more detailed definition might be preferred by some, Bebbington's "quadrilateral" defines evangelicalism with sufficient precision while not becoming unwieldy.

The term "fundamentalism" first appeared in the widely read Baptist paper the *Watchman-Examiner* in 1920, when the paper's editor, Curtis Lee Laws, defined "fundamentalists" as Christians prepared "to do battle royal for the Fundamentals."[14] Laws took the term from a series of publications, *The Fundamentals*, which appeared under the sponsorship of California oil millionaire Lyman Stewart from 1910 to 1915. Published in twelve volumes, *The Fundamentals* comprised a large number of articles by well-known Bible teachers all aimed at buttressing the "fundamentals" of the Christian faith; with Stewart's financial backing, a vast number of copies were sent to pastors, missionaries, theological students, and others all over the English-speaking world.[15] The language that originally connoted conservative evangelicals who were militant antimodernists and ecclesiastical separatists has over the past few decades been used to describe militant and separatist movements within Islam, Judaism, Hinduism, and Buddhism, to name but a few. These movements, as well as others, are examined at length in the massive five-volume Fundamentalism Project, which was published in the early 1990s under the editorship of Martin E. Marty and

13. David W. Bebbington, *Evangelicalism in Modern Britain: A History from the 1730s to the 1980s* (New York: Routledge, 1989), 2–17.

14. George M. Marsden, *Fundamentalism and American Culture: The Shaping of Twentieth-Century Evangelicalism, 1870–1925* (New York: Oxford University Press, 1980), 159.

15. Marsden, *Fundamentalism and American Culture*, 118–23.

R. Scott Appleby. The appearance of this voluminous body of research furnishes sufficient evidence of just how extensively applied the term "fundamentalism" has become.[16] In this present work, the term "fundamentalism" is restricted to that subgenre of North American evangelicalism that appeared in the late nineteenth century. Perhaps the most suitable approach to describing this form of fundamentalism is to borrow a convention employed by the well-known scholar of North American fundamentalism, George Marsden, who made a practice of referring to "tendencies" that characterized the movement.[17] In the broadest sense, fundamentalists were militant antimodernists and ecclesiastical separatists. Most fundamentalists also exhibited a marked tendency to emphasize doctrinal orthodoxy, scriptural inerrancy, premillennial dispensationalism, and creationism. This cluster of traits typified what might be loosely referred to as classical fundamentalism.

Fundamentalists have often been caricatured as backward and uncouth, while their antagonists are taken as virtuous defenders of progress. If some of the more outspoken fundamentalists swung rhetorical punches at theological liberals, the latter had their own pugilist in the ring. In a paroxysm of wartime patriotism coupled with progressive theology, Shailer Mathews and Shirley Jackson Case, of the University of Chicago Divinity School, on more than one occasion accused the fundamentalists of anti-Americanism and conspiring with the Germans during World War I. What had aroused their ire to the point of spinning conspiracy theories? Many fundamentalists were exponents of premillennial dispensationalism, a theological view that tended to take a dim view of the potential for human progress, which the faculty at the divinity school read as unpatriotic and anti-American at a time of national crisis.[18] By pointing out that both sides of the fundamentalist-modernist controversies traded blows, I strike a cautionary note. A significant theme in this volume is the attempt to situate WBT-SIL in the evolving landscape of mid-twentieth-century evangelicalism. It should therefore be stated at the outset that an attempt has been made to see these varied cultural and religious movements as objectively as possible from within their historical contexts. Put another way, even though WBT-SIL will be shown to have been more broadly evangelical than strictly fundamen-

16. All five volumes of the Fundamentalism Project were edited by Martin E. Marty and R. Scott Appleby and were published by the University of Chicago Press. They bear the following titles: *Fundamentalisms Observed*, vol. 1 (1991); *Fundamentalisms and Society: Reclaiming the Sciences, the Family, and Education*, vol. 2 (1993); *Fundamentalisms and the State: Remaking Polities, Economies, and Militance*, vol. 3 (1993); *Accounting for Fundamentalisms: The Dynamic Character of Movements*, vol. 4 (1994); and *Fundamentalisms Comprehended*, vol. 5 (1995).

17. Marsden, *Fundamentalism and American Culture*, 6 and passim.

18. Marsden, *Fundamentalism and American Culture*, 145–48.

talist, mounting this argument in no way implies a negative judgment of the fundamentalist movement in its various permutations.

WBT-SIL in Context

After completing a year of service in Guatemala as a colporteur with the fundamentalist Bible House of Los Angeles, Cameron Townsend joined the Central American Mission (CAM) in 1919. Cyrus Ingerson Scofield, a prominent fundamentalist and the editor of the immensely popular *Scofield Reference Bible*, founded CAM as a faith mission in 1890. Townsend thus came of age as a missionary in a fundamentalist setting. Moreover, Townsend dropped his Presbyterian denominational membership in 1921 and joined the fundamentalist Church of the Open Door, located in Los Angeles. When he formed his own mission, it too had strong ties to the fundamentalist network. For example, in the years before the official incorporation of WBT-SIL in 1942, the Pioneer Mission Agency (PMA), which was essentially an arm of American Keswick, served as the fledgling organization's home office.[19] To the casual observer in the 1930s and 1940s, WBT-SIL would have appeared as just another faith mission that was part of the fundamentalist network.

Appearances in this case were somewhat illusory. While the PMA, and later WBT, presented to the North American Christian public a conventional faith mission image, abroad SIL engaged in a remarkably progressive style of missionary activity. In Mexico, SIL collaborated with the revolutionary government in indigenous education. In Peru, SIL not only cooperated with the government on education but also regularly served the Peruvian armed forces and Roman Catholic missionaries by transporting their personnel in SIL aircraft. In addition, after the organization moved its linguistic summer school to the University of Oklahoma at Norman in 1942, nonevangelicals and Catholics were permitted to study alongside SIL's evangelical students. In short, the dual-organization strategy opened up opportunities for WBT and SIL to pursue two very different courses of action. SIL, with its quasi-secular scientific status, engaged in projects of social uplift while, at the same time, WBT maintained all the trappings of a faith mission. WBT-SIL was following Townsend's pathbreaking effort to overcome the obstacles of established tradition. "I yearn," he once wrote, "for

19. The Keswick movement was inaugurated in 1875 at Keswick, England. Annual conferences were held that taught that holiness was achieved not by personal effort but by letting go and trusting Christ for sanctification. Conferences of the American arm of the movement were held at Keswick, New Jersey.

other organizations to begin to break loose from the time-honored shackles of churchianity and become all things to all men for the Gospel's sake."[20] The dual-organization strategy was a brilliant concept, but it was also replete with contradictions. The interplay between the two sides of the organization, the innovations the dual strategy spawned, and the confusion and exasperation it engendered are all themes that will occupy a central place in this study.

At midcentury, when WBT-SIL was striking out in a progressive direction abroad under the banner of SIL, North American fundamentalism was itself experiencing a transformation. During the fundamentalist-modernist controversies of the 1920s and 1930s, some of the most outspoken fundamentalist leaders tarnished the movement's public image. In a 1928 sermon entitled "Why I Am a Big F. Fundamentalist," the well-known Baptist pastor and evangelist John R. Rice announced that "Fundamentalism is not only what you believe but how strong you believe it," and, he added, "if necessary, offending and grieving people and institutions."[21] A younger generation of less militant and more progressive fundamentalists, such as the evangelist Billy Graham, set out in the 1940s and 1950s to reform this strident brand of fundamentalism and to reengage mainstream culture through a renewed focus on social issues.[22] Evangelical scholarship had also suffered from the anti-intellectualist tendencies within the fundamentalist subculture, and Fuller Seminary was established in 1947 in an effort to reclaim lost intellectual ground for North American evangelicalism. A lion's share of recent historiography has focused on the establishment of the seminary as the seminal event in the intellectual revival of fundamentalism.[23] In his 1987 account of Fuller Seminary, George Marsden narrated the seminary's struggle to restore evangelical scholarship to respectability.[24] His account is of particular interest to the study of WBT-SIL, since he provides an analogous account of a progressive fundamentalist institution. Yet Fuller Seminary dif-

20. Cameron Townsend, "Discussion of the Wycliffe Policy of Service," March 1956, 1, TA 12104.

21. John R. Rice, "Why I Am a Big F. Fundamentalist," *Fundamentalist*, March 2, 1923, 3, quoted in Barry Hankins, *God's Rascal: J. Frank Norris and the Beginnings of Southern Fundamentalism* (Lexington: University Press of Kentucky, 1996), 44.

22. Joel A. Carpenter, *Revive Us Again: The Reawakening of American Fundamentalism* (New York: Oxford University Press, 1997).

23. John D'Elia, *A Place at the Table: George Eldon Ladd and the Rehabilitation of Evangelical Scholarship* (New York: Oxford University Press, 2008); Gary Dorrien, *The Remaking of Evangelical Theology* (Louisville: Westminster John Knox, 1998); George M. Marsden, *Reforming Fundamentalism: Fuller Seminary and the New Evangelicalism* (Grand Rapids: Eerdmans, 1987); Rudolph Nelson, *The Making and Unmaking of an Evangelical Mind: The Case of Edward Carnell* (New York: Cambridge University Press, 1987); Garth M. Rosell, *The Surprising Work of God: Harold John Ockenga, Billy Graham, and the Rebirth of Evangelicalism* (Grand Rapids: Baker Academic, 2008).

24. Marsden, *Reforming Fundamentalism*.

fered in some notable respects from WBT-SIL, and these points of departure will be highlighted in subsequent chapters. Although it was never WBT-SIL's explicit intention to reform fundamentalism, the remarkably progressive path taken by the organization naturally situates the present study within the body of established literature on the emergence of the new evangelicalism (alternatively named neo-evangelicalism).

WBT-SIL's global reach and its work among indigenous peoples attracted an outsized share of criticism from anthropologists, especially in the years after the social upheavals of the late 1960s. These adversarial treatments of WBT-SIL have proved effective in shaping perceptions of the organization over the past three decades; this is especially the case with David Stoll's 1982 work entitled *Fishers of Men or Founders of Empire? The Wycliffe Bible Translators in Latin America*.[25] By relying on Stoll's polemical analysis in his important 1992 social history of Catholicism in Peru, the Jesuit historian Jeffrey Klaiber wrongly concluded that SIL "refuses all contact with the Catholic church" in the Amazonian region.[26] Klaiber's assertion, as will become evident, is without merit. Another fitting example is the 1996 work entitled *Exporting the American Gospel: Global Christian Fundamentalism*, in which authors Steve Brouwer, Paul Gifford, and Susan D. Rose were mistakenly convinced by Stoll's analysis that WBT-SIL was committed to "dispensationalist thought," and that the organization was therefore a purveyor of North American fundamentalism abroad.[27] The influence that Stoll and other critical interpretations have had on the historiography of WBT-SIL invites closer examination.

Although the two organizations were individually incorporated in 1942, the membership roster of the two entities was identical, as was the board of directors. Furthermore, each side of the organization shared an overarching common purpose in Bible translation. Thus, unless the subject matter demands explicit reference to either WBT or SIL, the two sides of the dual organization will be treated as a single hyphenated organization.[28] When examining the organiza-

25. David Stoll, *Fishers of Men or Founders of Empire? The Wycliffe Bible Translators in Latin America* (Cambridge, MA: Cultural Survival, 1982).

26. Jeffrey Klaiber, *The Catholic Church in Peru, 1821–1985: A Social History* (Washington, DC: Catholic University of America Press, 1992), 328.

27. Steve Brouwer, Paul Gifford, and Susan D. Rose, *Exporting the American Gospel: Global Christian Fundamentalism* (New York: Routledge, 1996), 185.

28. From about the middle of the 1970s, the leaders of WBT-SIL began to place greater stress on the organizational duality, and in 2006 the two organizations were disentangled by establishing fully separate boards of directors and by appointing separate executive directors. Therefore, it would be inappropriate to utilize the hyphenated acronym after 2006, but in the time frame covered in the present study, it accurately conveys the nature of dual organization.

tion abroad or when exploring its linguistic nature, SIL will naturally come into focus. On the other hand, WBT will take center stage when considering the North American evangelical context. Confusing matters somewhat is the fact that the organization's linguistic school was referred to as Camp Wycliffe in its first decade or so of existence. The linguistic school was eventually absorbed into the SIL side of the organization. Therefore Camp Wycliffe should rightly be considered a part of SIL. What is important to keep in mind is that WBT-SIL, in the period under consideration in this volume, was effectively a single mission with two corporate identities that were designed to relate to different publics.

Organized into six main chapters, this study is an attempt to account for WBT-SIL's remarkable growth in the face of persistent criticism. At the same time, this work also endeavors to explain the strategies and policies of this complex and often confusing missionary organization. Chapter 1 traces Cameron Townsend's life from his California roots to his efforts in the early to mid-1930s to establish WBT-SIL in Mexico. The primary aim of this chapter is to illuminate the character of Townsend's mind, for it above all else shaped the contours of WBT-SIL. The next four chapters investigate various aspects of the organization thematically from roughly the late 1930s to anywhere between the 1960s and the early 1980s. Chapter 2 is an account of SIL's development as a linguistic organization and how it became a recognized scholarly institution. Chapter 3 examines the organization's Bible translation strategy, as well as developments in the area of translation theory and practice. Chapter 4 examines SIL in the Peruvian context, which provides an exemplary case study of the ultimate development of Townsend's innovative ideas. Chapter 5 turns to North America, where WBT publicized the efforts of SIL to both evangelical and nonevangelical audiences. Chapter 6 examines WBT-SIL's overall organizational development from the mid-1960s down to the early 1980s and its encounters with anthropologists on the political left during this same period.

CHAPTER 1

Pioneering and the Progressive Ideal

Cameron Townsend was by nature and experience endowed with a frame of mind that knew few limitations to his pioneering missionary strivings or to his progressive ideals for the social uplift of the world's indigenous peoples. More an entrepreneur in some ways than a conventional missionary, Townsend struggled to comport himself after the fashion of a typical faith missionary. Born into a family that had traversed the country from Pennsylvania to Kansas to Colorado and finally on to California in search of a better life, the young Cameron Townsend was himself an expression of this American peripatetic urge; it was an impulse that, when combined with more than a touch of idealism, imagined something bigger and better just over the horizon. Therefore, as a missionary he was instinctively drawn to pioneer where other missionaries had yet to tread, and as a progressive-minded idealist, he strove tirelessly to conquer social injustice. Discovering that language was perhaps the greatest barrier to effective evangelization and to realizing his dream of social justice for Latin America's indigenous peoples, Townsend reordered the missionary endeavor by locating Bible translation, literacy, and education in the forefront of his strategy. His unbounded vision often bumped up against the narrower conception of missionary activity pursued by the Central American Mission (CAM) in which he served during the 1920s and early 1930s. Suffused with an irrepressible determination, he launched his own venture. With the help of a former missionary and energetic preacher, Leonard Livingstone Legters, Townsend took his radical concept of missions into anticlerical Mexico, where the WBT-SIL dual-missionary organization first took shape. To understand WBT-SIL, then, it is necessary to appreciate something of the extraordinarily creative mind of Cameron Townsend as it developed over the course of his youth, his first decade of missionary service in Guatemala, and his initial forays into Mexico.

Cameron Townsend came of age during the high tide of the American Progressive movement. Although little concrete evidence indicates a close correlation between the ideology of the Progressive movement and Townsend's approach to missions—after all, he was not given to studied reflection or detailed elaboration on the origins of his often imaginative ideas—it nonetheless remains, whether by natural inclination or by direct influence, that his outlook bore a striking resemblance to the ideals of this early twentieth-century sociopolitical movement. As the narrative unfolds, it will be seen too that Townsend, unlike most faith missionaries and fundamentalists, was often on the same side of the fence as the purveyors of the Social Gospel, a religious movement that shared many features with American sociopolitical Progressivism.

From about 1900 to 1920, Progressives sought to lessen economic inequity in America by attacking political corruption and curbing unrestrained capitalism. Hiram Johnson, a California Progressive and the state's Republican governor from 1911 to 1917, is a fine example of the Progressives' stress on political reform. In his 1911 inaugural, Johnson intoned that "the first duty that is mine to perform is to eliminate every private interest from the government and to make the public service of the State responsive solely to the people."[1] Newly elected president Woodrow Wilson not only pledged to effect a return to "equality" and "justice" in his March 1913 inaugural, but he also promised to protect American citizens "from the consequences of great industry and social processes which they cannot alter, control, or singly cope with."[2] Progressives insisted that reformed government had a central role to play in achieving social justice for American citizens at a time when many of them were struggling to adapt to the industrialization and urbanization of America.

The idea of progress was clearly manifested in this early twentieth-century reform movement. "In the struggle [for] equality of opportunity," President Theodore Roosevelt declared in a 1910 speech at Osawatomie, Kansas, "nations rise from barbarism to civilization, and through it people press forward from one stage of enlightenment to the next."[3] The Progressive's reformist "vision," wrote prominent economist John Bates Clark in 1913, is an "Eden . . . that he can seriously expect to reach." Bates said this achievement was "practicable for all

---

1. Quoted in Walter Nugent, *A Very Short Introduction to Progressivism* (New York: Oxford University Press, 2010), 69.

2. Woodrow Wilson, "An Inaugural Address," March 4, 1913, in *The Papers of Woodrow Wilson*, ed. Arthur S. Link et al. (Princeton: Princeton University Press, 1966–1994), 27:151.

3. Theodore Roosevelt, "The New Nationalism," in *The Works of Theodore Roosevelt: National Edition*, ed. Hermann Hagedorn, vol. 27 (New York: Charles Scribner's Sons, 1926), 5.

humanity."[4] This sentiment was also unmistakably on display when Wilson, in 1889, insisted that "it should be the end of government *to assist in accomplishing the objects of organized society*." Wilson went on: "Every means, therefore, by which society may be perfected through the instrumentality of government, every means by which individual rights can be fitly adjusted and harmonized with public duties, by which individual self-development may be made at once to serve and supplement social development, ought certainly to be diligently sought. . . . Such is the socialism to which every true lover of his kind ought to adhere with the full grip of every noble affection that is in him."[5] In other words, it was considered possible for the modern state to bring about a more perfect, if not perfected, social order. With much the same logic and spurred by his own Wilsonian tendencies, Townsend would harness his own mission to the state-making process in Latin America. Beginning in Mexico and continuing in Peru and beyond, the Summer Institute of Linguistics, under his direction, functionally became an extension of the state and took a hand in these nations' ambitions for effecting their own progressive social transformations.

Purveyors of the Social Gospel were affected by the same intellectual currents that influenced the Progressives. Walter Rauschenbusch, perhaps the Social Gospel's leading figure, wrote in 1914 that "there are two great entities in human life,—the human soul and the human race,—and religion is to save both."[6] Many conservative evangelicals, especially those in the premillennial-dispensational camp, disagreed. Society was, according to many fundamentalists, ultimately doomed, and only individual souls could be saved.[7] The closer the Social Gospelers came to historicizing Christianity as the outworking of God immanent in society, the more fundamentalists de-emphasized social concerns and stressed evangelism aimed at rescuing individual souls from the present age. Historians have referred to the fundamentalists' shying away from

4. John Bates Clark, "Reform or Revolution," January 27, 1913, quoted in Martin J. Sklar, "Capitalism and Socialism in the Emergence of Modern America," in *Reconstructing History: The Emergence of a New Historical Society*, ed. Elizabeth Fox-Genovese and Elisabeth Lasch-Quinn (New York: Routledge, 1999), 318.

5. Woodrow Wilson, *The State: Elements of Historical and Practical Politics* (Boston: Heath, [1889] 1909), 631–32, quoted in Trygve Throntveit, "'Common Counsel': Woodrow Wilson's Pragmatic Progressivism, 1885–1913," in *Reconsidering Woodrow Wilson: Progressivism, Internationalism, War, and Peace*, ed. John Milton Cooper Jr. (Baltimore: Johns Hopkins University Press, 2008), 28.

6. Walter Rauschenbusch, *Christianity and the Social Crisis* (New York: Macmillan, 1907), 367.

7. George M. Marsden, *Fundamentalism and American Culture: The Shaping of Twentieth-Century Evangelicalism, 1870–1925* (New York: Oxford University Press, 1980), 62–68; Timothy P. Weber, *Living in the Shadow of the Second Coming: American Premillennialism, 1875–1925* (New York: Oxford University Press, 1979), 82–104.

social reform (which had loomed large in nineteenth-century evangelical-ism) between about 1900 and 1930 as the "Great Reversal."[8] The way in which Townsend navigated this particular aspect of the religious milieu was strikingly uncommon for an evangelical in the interwar period, and in doing so he set the stage for how he would eventually shape his own mission.

Cameron Townsend's Early Life

Cameron Townsend was born in an old farmhouse on July 9, 1896, in Eastvale, California. In his junior year of high school, the family moved forty miles west to Clearwater, closer to Los Angeles. The home in which Townsend grew to maturity was a deeply religious one. His father, William Hammond Townsend, was a devoted Presbyterian who led daily devotions in the home and saw to it that the family was in attendance at the Clearwater Presbyterian Church on Sundays. Cameron Townsend later recalled that the church was rather "life-less."[9] Thus, according to his brother Paul, it was their father's influence that primarily shaped their religious character. William Hammond taught his children to trust in God and stressed absolute honesty and personal integrity, but his admonitions were not aimed at inculcating any kind of dogmatic religion or procuring conversionary experiences in his children.[10] It comes as no surprise then that Cameron Townsend could never recall having been "born again."[11] Perhaps the most telling evidence that he did not hail from a narrow religious setting was his taking a Roman Catholic girl on a date when in high school.[12] Cameron Townsend's religious upbringing was broadly evangelical and not overly doctrinaire.

The Townsend family had high hopes for their eldest son's advancement off the farm. His mother was especially resolute that Cameron, who had four elder sisters and a younger brother, would attend college. Graduating at the top of his class in high school intimates that his family's expectations were well founded.[13] With ambitions of becoming a minister, another idea earnestly

8. Marsden, *Fundamentalism and American Culture*, 85–93.

9. Cameron Townsend, Hefley interview, c. 1970, p. 2, TA 43654.

10. Cameron Townsend, Hefley interview, June 1970, pp. 4–5, 7, TA 43635; Paul Townsend, Hefley interview, c. 1970, pp. 6–7, TA 43505; Paul Townsend, interview by Ethel Wallis, January 1987, pp. 41–45, TA 43778.

11. Cameron Townsend, Hefley interview, c. 1970, p. 5, TA 43637.

12. Cameron Townsend, Hefley interview, c. 1970, p. 3, TA 43637.

13. Cameron Townsend, Hefley interview, c. 1970, p. 4, TA 43637; Paul Townsend, Hefley interview, c. 1970, p. 2, TA 43505.

fostered by his mother, Townsend enrolled at Occidental College, located near Los Angeles, in the fall of 1914.[14] Occidental was a Presbyterian institution offering a broad liberal arts education, where the sciences were coupled with traditional subjects such as Greek, Latin, philosophy, and Bible study. Bowing to the winds of progressive educational reforms, the college withdrew from Presbyterian oversight in 1910 while remaining evangelical in religious temperament.[15] A number of Townsend's essays written while at Occidental are reflective of the school's intellectual atmosphere. In his sophomore year he read the noted philosopher William James's essay "The College Bred." Townsend agreed with James that a college education should prepare students to recognize, as he put it in his own 1915 essay, "the highest ideals, the best in art and literature, and the greatest in science."[16] It is difficult to imagine Townsend reading James had he attended, for example, the nearby and recently established Bible Institute of Los Angeles (BIOLA). Bible schools such as BIOLA largely forsook a liberal arts "education" for a narrower focus on Bible-based "training," which aimed primarily to prepare students for evangelizing lost souls. Virginia Lieson Brereton, in researching the Bible school movement, correctly observed that "brevity, practicality, [and] efficiency were summed up in the word 'training.'"[17] Occidental attempted to broaden students' intellectual horizons rather than to narrow them. Therefore Townsend was expected to make some effort at cultivating the life of the mind rather than simply picking up practical pastoral or missionary skills.

Lofty Jamesian ideals soon faded, and by his third year in college Townsend had grown restless; he was coming to the conclusion that he was not particularly suited for the intellectual life or the tedium of seemingly abstract academic study. While he earned top grades in Bible and history, his performance was merely adequate in other subjects. It is somewhat ironic that this future Bible translator earned his lowest marks in Greek and Spanish.[18] Later in life Townsend recalled that he became "quite discouraged in college."[19] He was especially dispirited if his efforts produced no immediate and tangible results other than a good mark. "I was tired of working to get good grades," he com-

14. Cameron Townsend, Hefley interview, c. 1970, p. 5, TA 43637.

15. Robert Glass Cleland, *The History of Occidental College: 1887–1937* (Los Angeles: Ward Ritchie Press, 1937), 11, 40, 46–47.

16. Cameron Townsend, "Recognizing the Best," February 26, 1915, TA 115.

17. Virginia Lieson Brereton, "The Bible Schools and Conservative Evangelical Higher Education," in *Making Higher Education Christian: The History and Mission of Evangelical Colleges in America*, ed. Joel A. Carpenter and Kenneth W. Shipps (Grand Rapids: Eerdmans, 1987), 115.

18. Cameron Townsend's Occidental College transcript, 1914–1917, TA 42061.

19. Cameron Townsend, Hefley interview, c. 1970, p. 5, TA 43637.

plained, "but not really retaining what I was studying."[20] In a December 1915 essay on Christian faith, Townsend offered up some indications of his heart superintending his mind. "It is with the heart that man believes unto salvation. This is not the Devil's brand. His believing is of the head and does not point to life. Intellectual belief is merely one step towards faith." Perhaps thinking of his own future beyond the confines of the academy, he added that "faith . . . produces a change in a man's life whereby he feels in his heart toward certain hopes and expectations held forth by Christianity as toward realities either present or to be fulfilled."[21] Townsend also found his fellow aspiring ministers rather dull company. He therefore joined the Student Volunteer Movement (SVM), where he discovered a group of missionary-minded students who, as he described it, "had life and a lot of enthusiasm."[22] Townsend was not dim-witted, but he was restless and frustrated with studies that, to him, seemed disconnected from the life of action he craved.

At his first SVM meeting, Townsend was asked why he wanted to be a missionary. Having joined for the camaraderie as much as anything else, he stood up, lamely stated, "I don't know," and promptly sat back down.[23] Despite signing the SVM pledge in 1915 and expressing a vague unease over not doing enough to witness for his faith, there is little evidence that Townsend aspired to missionary work.[24] In fact, he was restless enough to have joined the California National Guard just before the United States entered World War I. He was therefore expecting to be called up for wartime service when he spotted an advertisement placed in a local newspaper by the Bible House of Los Angeles in 1917 seeking college students to volunteer as colporteurs selling Bibles in Latin America. He impulsively grasped at this missionary opportunity. While Townsend awaited a call to active duty, the Bible House offered him a place in Guatemala. Faced with conflicting commitments, he managed to secure a military deferment, which he sought only after a furloughing missionary matron referred to him and a friend as "cowards" for avoiding missionary service by marching off to war.[25] With the expectation that he would return home after a year of missionary service, Townsend dropped out of college at the end of his third year.[26] Not for the last time

20. Cameron Townsend, interview by Betty Blair, December 3, 1980, p. 4, TA 43737.

21. Cameron Townsend, "Christian Faith: Have It?," December 3, 1915, pp. 1–2, TA 108.

22. Cameron Townsend, Hefley interview, c. 1970, p. 5, TA 43637.

23. Cameron Townsend, Hefley interview, c. 1970, p. 5, TA 43637.

24. Cameron Townsend's Student Volunteer Movement for Foreign Missions form, May 31, 1915, TA 900113.

25. Cameron Townsend, Hefley interview, c. 1970, pp. 14–15, TA 43637.

26. Cameron Townsend, Hefley interview, c. 1970, pp. 1–2, TA 43737.

did he leap where others might have engaged in a protracted struggle with self-doubt. Indeed, it could almost be said that the twenty-year-old Cameron Townsend who boarded a ship bound for Guatemala in the fall of 1917 was an accidental missionary. This young man who would one day become the founder of the world's largest faith mission seemingly embarked for the mission field as much to escape the drudgery of college as to fulfill any kind of heartfelt missionary calling.

The Education of a Trailblazer

The Bible House of Los Angeles was a small, independent mission that primarily focused on the distribution of Spanish Bibles and tracts in Latin America. It was founded and directed by an inveterate fundamentalist, R. D. Smith, who also sat on the board of the Central American Mission (CAM). Smith placed Townsend under the direction of Albert E. Bishop, a veteran CAM missionary serving in Guatemala.[27] Although supervised by Bishop, the young colporteur was largely self-directed since his backcountry excursions carried him far from CAM territory. Townsend had barely set foot in Guatemala when he became aware of the plight of the country's indigenous peoples. While making arrangements for his travels in early October 1917, he decided, on Bishop's advice, "not to get pack mules but to walk and let [a] native worker carry my pack not to exceed one hundred pounds." Uneasy with the bargain, he recorded in his journal that it seemed "cruel."[28] During a visit to a *finca* (a coffee plantation) in Alotenango, he was distressed when he realized that the Indians were often held in debt peonage. Observing their shabby quarters on the edge of town, he remarked that Alotenango was "the most miserable little city I've seen in these parts."[29] After a weekend of preaching, the beleaguered inhabitants had endeared themselves to Townsend, who penned in his diary that "it was kind of hard to say goodbye to the Indians."[30] Incidents of this nature made a deep impression on the young Cameron Townsend, leaving him with an enduring empathy for the downtrodden indigenous peoples of Latin America.

Townsend was not simply overreacting to an unfamiliar situation, for there were in fact profound social inequalities. Indians of Mayan descent constituted a majority of Guatemala's inhabitants, but the minority of mixed-blood *ladinos*

---

27. Cameron Townsend, Hefley interview, c. 1970, p. 5, TA 43630.
28. Cameron Townsend, "Diary," October 3, 1917, TA 151 and TA 152.
29. Cameron Townsend, "Diary," October 27, 1917, TA 171.
30. Cameron Townsend, "Diary," October 28, 1917, TA 172.

controlled the levers of power.[31] In Guatemala, as elsewhere in Latin America, the indigenous peoples were generally held in contempt and occupied the low-ermost rung in the social hierarchy. In the nineteenth and early twentieth centuries, social Darwinism seemed to offer the elite classes a suitable ideological explanation for the "inferior races."[32] The inherent racism of social Darwinism, especially when coupled with laissez-faire capitalism, was a particularly devastating combination for Guatemala's indigenous peoples. Legislative Decree 243 of 1894, still in force when Townsend arrived in Guatemala, was a typical example. This law gave extraordinary power to employers over their peasant laborers, and local authorities were obliged to arrest workers who failed to meet their nearly impossible obligations. Debt peonage was part and parcel of this exploitative system, and Indian laborers were therefore indentured essentially in perpetuity.[33] In effect, Indian labor was considered a low-cost commodity to be exploited.

Townsend's choice of an indigenous Cakchiquel Indian as a traveling companion also shaped the contours of his thinking. Although he worked with a number of Guatemalan nationals, the thirty-five-year-old Francisco (Frisco) Díaz was his most frequent companion on the trail. Townsend displayed an uncommon degree of humility toward Díaz, as well as other Guatemalan nationals. "I am going to learn a lot from them," he recorded in his journal in October 1917.[34] When Díaz's efforts surpassed his own in October 1918, he was quick to point out that "Frisco sold more testaments than I did today."[35] The two men shared equally in the evangelistic work and the miseries of backcountry travel.[36] Often isolated from mission stations, Townsend was educated less by expatriate missionaries than by his Indian friend, guide, and "mentor," and as a result he was afforded more than a few opportunities to observe the world from the indigenous point of view.

It did not take long for Townsend to encounter Roman Catholic opposition in Guatemala. Liberal governments in Guatemala since 1871 had imposed severe restrictions on the Catholic clergy and had confiscated the church's property.

31. *Ladinos* were the Hispanicized upwardly mobile class in Central America, especially in Guatemala.

32. Magnus Mörner, "Historical Research on Race Relations in Latin America during the National Period," in *Race and Class in Latin America*, ed. Magnus Mörner (New York: Columbia University Press, 1970), 223–24.

33. Richard Newbold Adams, *Crucifixion by Power: Essays on Guatemalan National Social Structure, 1944–1966* (Austin: University of Texas Press, 1970), 176–77.

34. Cameron Townsend, "Diary," October 23, 1917, TA 165.

35. Cameron Townsend, "Diary," November 8, 1918, TA 524.

36. Cameron Townsend, "Diary," December 21, 1917, TA 214; "Diary," January 23, 1918, TA 345.

However, the few remaining clergy were still influential, and Catholic ritualism was combined with traces of Mayan religious custom into an ardently held folk Catholicism.[37] Time and again Townsend recorded that a town was "fanatical," signifying that its inhabitants held tenaciously to their religion.[38] He and his various traveling companions were sometimes refused food or lodging after it was discovered that they were Protestant *evangelistas*, and tracts handed out in their proselytizing efforts were often torn to shreds.[39] By the time he completed his year of itinerating, Townsend was well versed in Latin America's Catholic-Protestant antagonisms. If he felt like lashing out at religious intolerance, he discovered that doing so would likely cause more harm than good. On at least one occasion he was threatened with jail for proselytizing.[40] In another instance, he observed a fellow missionary upbraid an irate plantation owner who was beating an indentured Indian. The missionary's interference resulted in his permanent disbarment from preaching on that plantation. From such confrontations Townsend learned that it was better, as he put it, "simply [to] stand and be concerned" but not to "say anything." "I had to be careful [and] . . . respect their customs and not be independent about it," he later recalled.[41] This attitude toward deep-rooted social and religious realities that Townsend developed in 1917 and 1918 would prove to be a key factor in how he later approached similar situations; rather than confronting adversaries directly, he would deploy more nuanced tactics when attempting to overcome social injustice or religious intolerance.

Treading softly on foreign soil did not indicate that Townsend had become less headstrong. His sister Ethel once recalled that her brother "had a determined mind," emphasizing that "if he thought something should be done, he was going to do it."[42] Apparently this drive to set events in motion included co-opting others to attain his objectives. "He would manipulate even in high school," his brother Paul related in an interview, adding that "I can remember him manipulating things around and getting things his way."[43] By April 1918, Townsend had decided that completing his college education was out of the question. "I would never feel right in going to

---

37. Adams, *Crucifixion by Power*, 278–79; Kay B. Warren, *The Symbolism of Subordination: Indian Identity in a Guatemalan Town* (Austin: University of Texas Press, 1978), 43–50, 87.

38. Cameron Townsend, "Diary," May 13, 1918, TA 400; "Diary," May 15, 1918, TA 402; "Diary," November 5, 1918, TA 521.

39. Cameron Townsend, "Diary," October 22, 1917, TA 164.

40. Cameron Townsend, "Diary," November 5, 1918, TA 521 and TA 522.

41. Cameron Townsend, Hefley interview, c. 1970, p. 15, TA 43737.

42. Ethel Townsend, Hefley interview, c. 1970, p. 4, TA 43502.

43. Paul Townsend, Hefley interview, c. 1970, p. 11, TA 43505.

school," he wrote his family, "when the world is so greatly in need of action as it is today."[44] Less than a month later, in another letter to his parents, he thrust aside any idea of becoming a minister. "The opportunities down here are simply wonderful. I could never settle down to a pastorate in the States unless the Lord made it tremendously clear that He wanted me there." "And," he confidently concluded, "I don't anticipate that He will."[45] Once Townsend sunk his teeth into something that he wished to accomplish, there was little anyone could do or say to dissuade him of the course of action he had settled on, especially if he was certain that it was God's design for him to carry it out.

Townsend Joins the Central American Mission

Taking notice of his desire to remain in Guatemala, and impressed with his record as an itinerant missionary, both CAM and the Presbyterian mission extended invitations. He had sufficiently impressed the Presbyterian mission-aries that the Presbyterian board of directors was prepared to overlook his lack of academic qualifications.[46] Also in the Presbyterians' favor was the fact that Townsend was smitten by one of their young missionaries, Elvira Malmstrom, and she fulfilled his longings by accepting his marriage proposal.[47] Joining the Presbyterian mission would, however, have entailed leaving Cakchiquel territory, something Townsend was not inclined to do. He later reminisced that after he had explored briefly the Presbyterian territory, "I felt as though I were leaving my home country."[48] So he hitched his fortunes to CAM, and Cameron and Elvira were accepted by the CAM board and married in July 1919 in Guatemala.[49]

44. Cameron Townsend to "Home Folks," April 24, 1918, TA 601.

45. Cameron Townsend to "Home Folks," May 17, 1918, TA 599.

46. Cameron Townsend to Judge D. H. Scott, CAM treasurer, November 15, 1920, TA 656; Cameron Townsend, Hefley interview, "Remembering Experiences in Guatemala 1917–1919," c. 1970, TA 43641.

47. Cameron and Elvira's marriage was beset with difficulties. Elvira suffered from both psychological and physical maladies, and the effects of these disabilities were exacerbated by Cameron's unpredictable and unsettled nature. William Svelmoe's *A New Vision for Missions: William Cameron Townsend, the Wycliffe Bible Translators, and the Culture of Early Evangelical Faith Missions, 1896–1945* (Tuscaloosa: University of Alabama Press, 2008) examines in detail the Townsends' sometimes difficult marriage.

48. Cameron Townsend, Hefley interview, c. 1970, TA 43628.

49. *Central American Bulletin*, July 1919, CAA; Report of Acceptance of W. Cameron Townsend and Elvira Malmstrom by CAM, July 1919, TA 44996.

CAM was founded in 1890 by Cyrus Ingerson Scofield, a Congregational minister best known for his editorship of the *Scofield Reference Bible*.[50] CAM was therefore quite naturally of a premillennial dispensationalist persuasion, and it was fundamentalist in character.[51] The mission could also be counted on to keep its distance from anything resembling the Social Gospel. Moreover, as with almost all faith missions, CAM advertised that it went to "God in prayer for all wants," would "solicit no gifts," and "take no collections."[52] In 1918, when funds were in desperately short supply, Scofield was tempted to send out a circular requesting financial aid. He later expressed his misgivings, admitting that "I had a little feeling in the back of my mind all the time that my proposal was after all a sort of begging, and we never do that, but look wholly to the Lord."[53] The faith basis of CAM placed a rather narrow set of limitations on how it could present its financial needs to the Christian public. The roots of CAM's attitude toward money, as with all faith missions, can be traced back to 1824 when Church of Scotland minster Edward Irving preached against the businesslike mission structures of his day. If the apostles of the New Testament sallied forth in faith without assured means of support, Irving argued, so too should modern-day missionaries. What Irving preached, the well-known missionary and orphanage founder George Müller popularized by not publicizing his financial needs.[54] Following the pattern articulated by Irving and modeled by Müller, the CAM council saw to it that the mission hewed closely to the faith mission ideal, but it was policy that Townsend struggled to follow.

Townsend completed his transition from mainline denominationalism to independent evangelicalism in January 1920 by severing his membership at the Clearwater Presbyterian Church and joining the independent Church of the Open Door (COD) in Los Angeles.[55] COD was a major fundamentalist base on the West Coast that was also behind the founding of BIOLA. Townsend's marriage to Elvira also linked him to the Moody Memorial Church in Chicago, since she was a member there as well as a personal friend of Moody's well-known pastor, Henry A. (Harry) Ironside. In less than a year, Townsend

50. *Central American Bulletin* 1, no. 1 (November 14, 1891): 1, CAA.

51. Dorothy Martin, *100 . . . and Counting: The Story of the CAM's First Century* (Dallas: CAM International, 1990), 36.

52. *Central American Bulletin* 1, no. 1 (November 14, 1891): 2, CAA.

53. Scofield to Scott, February 2, 1918, CAA.

54. David W. Bebbington, *The Dominance of Evangelicalism: The Age of Spurgeon and Moody* (Downers Grove: InterVarsity, 2005), 185–88.

55. Register of the Clearwater Presbyterian Church (copy), Clearwater, CA, pp. 114–15, TA 42056; Cameron Townsend to Church of the Open Door, letter read at the fiftieth anniversary service, September 12, 1965, TA 22361.

had established relationships with two prominent fundamentalist churches and become a member of a fundamentalist faith mission. It would be a mistake, though, to conclude that he had suddenly changed his stripes and become a fundamentalist. For example, although the *Scofield Reference Bible* was his main source of theological insight after college, when asked in later years if he agreed with Scofield's dispensationalism, Townsend said, "I don't know. I think he is a little bit extreme maybe on the matter of everything being divided up in dispensations."[56] During a heated intramural debate in CAM over modes of baptism in the mid-1920s, Townsend came out in favor of pouring. He nevertheless allowed that "not until we get to heaven can we know who was right." Therefore he thought it best "to go forward without dissension."[57] He was throughout his life at a bit of a loss (or at least he feigned such) when questioned closely about his theological beliefs. Queried in 1970 on whether or not he held to the doctrine of election, the best he could do was to say, "Well, I've not gotten into these fine points—I really don't know."[58] Perhaps the best summary of his lifelong outlook on such matters comes from a 1968 chapel talk during which he recollected his move into conservative evangelicalism. "I come from a fundamentalist background," he told a gathering of Wycliffe missionaries, "but I don't believe that to be saved, you have to go into a lot of detail."[59] Although his doctrinal views were generally of a conservative nature, Townsend was never narrow mindedly doctrinaire.

As a maverick out of step with the ways of fundamentalism, Townsend was destined to chart his own course, and in so doing he created new paths down which others would follow. His choice of fellow travelers was nonetheless fortuitous, for by taking up with the independents rather than the denominationalists, he sided with the eventual winners in America's competitive religious marketplace.[60] In fact, he would become one of a number of notable innovators who refashioned fundamentalism along progressive lines, thereby revitalizing evangelicalism and ensuring that it would remain a dynamic force throughout the second half of the twentieth century.

Townsend served with CAM from 1919 to 1933, but, as will become evident, he was too ambitious and too creative to have long remained within the confines of a traditional faith mission. While it is true that he was imbued with an evangelistic passion for taking the gospel into virgin territory, this impulse to

56. Cameron Townsend, Hefley interview, "Devotional and Doctrinal Stand," June 25, 1970, p. 1, TA 43653.

57. Cameron Townsend, "Water Baptism and the Biblical Mode," c. 1924, TA 1008.

58. Cameron Townsend, Hefley interview, "Devotional and Doctrinal Stand," p. 1, TA 43653.

59. Cameron Townsend, "Overcome Evil with Good," 1968, p. 4, TA 50001.

60. These events are discussed in chapter 5.

pioneer was bound up with a powerful desire for freedom of action away from the constraints and tedium of settled work. In a number of ways, the mind of Cameron Townsend presents nothing less than a study in paradoxical contrasts. Although he was a college dropout with anti-intellectual tendencies, he would nonetheless become a Bible translator, educator, and founder of a linguistic school for missionaries. Although possessed of an utterly pragmatic disposition, he yet retained the sentiments of a starry-eyed visionary. As a young missionary, Townsend elected to associate with fundamentalists, but his choice of company did little to dampen qualities more in keeping with those of a liberal persuasion. In the years before World War II, when many fundamentalists distanced themselves from the Social Gospel and from sociopolitical Progressivism, Townsend's outlook was a compound of these very elements. An examination of Townsend's particular approach to missions during his tenure with CAM reveals that many of the distinctive features that would define WBT-SIL were developed during his sometimes uneasy relationship with a classical faith mission. Therefore, rather than taking a chronological approach to Townsend's career with CAM, the next several sections will examine various factors and themes that were most significant in ultimately shaping Townsend's own mission.

Townsend's Progressive Vision for the Indians

Townsend had already decided to devote the largest share of his efforts to the Cakchiquels before he joined CAM. What he had in mind was nothing less than the subversion of the reigning social hierarchy that maintained the Indian in a subservient relationship to the *ladino*. Indeed, he had concluded by mid-1918 that the *ladinos*, "degenerated by generations of immorality," lacked the Indian's innate "moral fibre."[61] To his way of thinking, the Indian was naturally endowed with qualities that only needed revitalization. "Although real ambition generally lies latent and undetectable beneath the miserable mien of the average descendant of the formerly great Mayan race," the real tragedy, Townsend opined, was that "so little is done to quicken it and so very, very much to drown it in hopelessness."[62] Therefore, to gain for the Indians social justice and freedom from repression, he reckoned that it was necessary to break the stranglehold of social control held by *ladinos* and Catholic priests. He aimed to obtain this goal by initiating an indigenous language ministry, by undertaking educational

---

61. Cameron Townsend to "Home Folks," July 19, 1918, p. 5, TA 583.
62. Cameron Townsend, "The Language Project," n.d., p. 1, TA 946120.

efforts, and by developing independent indigenous congregations. Reaching peoples isolated by language and geography with the gospel while at the same time reversing centuries of social injustice was an ambitious plan, to say the least, but Townsend was an unusually ambitious young man. Even at this early point, mid-1918, he was dreaming of an Indian school, one he grandly hoped, if successful, could perhaps "become a blessing to the Indians of all C. America."[63]

In CAM, as with faith missions in general, education was considered less important than evangelization. This inclination to downplay education was exacerbated during the early part of the twentieth century when the "Great Reversal" was making itself felt in conservative evangelicalism. In keeping with its faith mission ethos and outlook on education, CAM directed most of its limited funds toward evangelistic efforts. When the discussion turned to the idea of establishing a Bible school at an August 1921 CAM council meeting, it was quickly dismissed.[64] If Townsend expected to see the full flowering of his ideas, he himself would need to marshal the necessary funds. This proved to be something at which he excelled. Townsend, a prolific contributor to the *Central American Bulletin*, in the summer of 1920 published a special insert for the periodical detailing his efforts among the Cakchiquel, which already included a children's boarding school and an adult evening school.[65] Not satisfied with the limited scope of CAM's donor list, he requested that the special bulletin be sent to numerous additional individuals and churches.[66] These publicity efforts produced the desired effect. Elvira was sufficiently embarrassed by the flood tide of donations received for their special projects to remark in a February 1921 letter to CAM treasurer Judge D. H. Scott that "we feel a little bad about having so much funds on hand for workers."[67] While his fellow missioners struggled financially, Townsend, by regularly priming the pump with his promotional efforts, generated ample cash flows for projects from numerous sources, such as his former Sunday school teacher Louise Heim, who donated the sizable sum of $5,100 in the early 1920s for a clinic and a boarding house.[68] Townsend's flair

63. Cameron Townsend to "Home Folks," July 19, 1918, p. 9, TA 583.

64. Scott to Bishop, August 27, 1921, CAA.

65. Cameron Townsend to Scott, July 27, 1920, p. 2, TA 675; Scott to Cameron Townsend, August 7, 1920, p. 1, TA 674.

66. Cameron Townsend to Scott, October 18, 1920, p. 4, TA 661; Elvira Townsend to Scott, September 1, 1920, p. 2, TA 669.

67. Elvira Townsend to Scott, February 14, 1921, TA 798.

68. Cameron Townsend, "A Training Center for Young Indian Leaders," n.d., TA 946095; Cameron Townsend, "The Louise Heim Clinic," n.d., TA 946096; Cameron Townsend to Lewis Sperry Chafer, president, CAM, October 22, 1923, TA 952; Paul Townsend, interview by Ethel Wallis, 1987, p. 48, TA 43778.

for garnering financial support would later prove to be an important factor in the expansion of his own mission.

"What a splendid Christian the Indian makes!" Townsend exclaimed in a 1920 *Central American Bulletin* article.[69] His jubilation was quickly tempered when it was realized that placing Indian converts in *ladino* congregations and under *ladino* leadership inevitably led to their falling away. The Townsends queried some Indian converts on the matter, and Elvira reported to CAM home secretary Judge Scott what they had discovered. "They all gave as the reason for not continuing that they would not attend services with the ladinos, for they were only laughed at by the ladinos [and] furthermore they felt they did not have [a] place there."[70] Townsend empathized with the Indians, and some of them began to look to him as their leader. Rather than use his stature to encourage them to remain under *ladino* leadership, he instead pointed them toward independence. Arguing that "he who pays, commands," he wanted them to have complete control over their church affairs.[71] The impoverished Indian congregations resisted his proposal, preferring instead to continue relying financially on CAM. Not until 1931, owing mainly to a growing nationalistic and anti-American sentiment in late-1920s Guatemala, did the Indian church leaders finally opt for full self-support.[72] Townsend, a fervent champion of indigenous ecclesiastical independence, set a pace for change that even the Indians found overly ambitious.

Determined to realize his hopes for an indigenous pastorate, Townsend launched a first-of-its-kind school in Guatemala to prepare indigenous preachers. He began by training Cakchiquel evangelists on an informal basis in 1921. The following year, in March 1922, he formally established the Indian Workers' Training School of Central America in Panajachel, Guatemala. The name was later changed to the Robinson Bible Institute (RBI) in honor of Townsend's recently deceased friend and fellow missionary Robert Robinson. The school, located in Panajachel because of its central location, allowed other missions to send students, and in its early years counted Indian students from among the Cakchiquels, Mams, Quichés, and Zutugils.[73] The establishment of RBI was an

---

69. Cameron Townsend, "The Guatemalan Indian and the San Antonio Mission," *Central American Bulletin*, no. 112 (September 15, 1920): 4, CAA.

70. Elvira Townsend to Scott, October 1, 1920, p. 6, TA 666.

71. Cameron Townsend, "The Development of the Indigenous Church," n.d., TA 946112.

72. Cameron Townsend, "Congregations Now Self-Supporting," n.d., TA 946114.

73. Cameron Townsend, *Central American Bulletin* 119 (November 1921): 19, TA 944955; Cameron Townsend, "The Robinson Bible Institute," n.d., pp. 2–3, TA 650; Cameron Townsend, "The Robinson Bible Institute," n.d., TA 946098; Cameron Townsend, "Preparation of Indian Workers," n.d., TA 946091.

enduring effort; the school eventually became the Guatemala Bible Institute in the late 1960s.[74] After his Bible translation efforts, RBI was the second of Townsend's two major accomplishments during his tenure with CAM.

Unburdened by deep attachment to the cardinal points of the faith mission approach, Townsend gave free rein to his idealistic impulses and outsized imagination. Moreover, having never been catechized into the fundamentalist movement, he was able to pursue social and educational goals fearlessly. Headstrong and all but blind to limitation, he crafted his own progressive program for the social uplift and religious conversion of Guatemala's indigenous peoples.

Bible Translation

In 1920 the Townsends were the only Protestant missionaries in Guatemala devoted primarily to Indian work, but not the only ones interested or engaged in reaching Guatemala's indigenous peoples.[75] Before Townsend took up work with CAM, there were a few small Indian congregations tucked away here and there in Guatemala, and CAM's Lucas Lemus occasionally engaged in indigenous evangelization.[76] In addition, CAM's own Benjamin and Louise Treichler, who joined in 1917, dreamed of evangelizing the Indians, but their aspirations were dashed by personal problems and language-learning difficulties.[77] Serving with the Presbyterian board in the Quiché territory were a frustrated Paul and Dora Burgess, who harbored ambitions for engaging in Indian work but were largely stymied by the typical missionary's crushing workload and the Presbyterian mission board's emphasis on Spanish ministry. "We envy you and your opportunity to do some real language study," Paul Burgess remarked to Townsend in 1920.[78] Burgess was a far more likely candidate for a Bible translator than was the minimally educated Townsend. The erudite Burgess had studied in Europe, was a seminary graduate, and possessed an earned doctorate. He eventually mastered seven languages, and was therefore as comfortable discussing philosophy in German as he was preaching in Spanish, according

74. Martin, *100 . . . and Counting*, 150.

75. Cameron Townsend, "The Guatemalan Indian and the San Antonio Mission Station," 1919, p. 4, TA 46144.

76. Bishop to Mr. and Mrs. McBath, Washington, DC, June 8, 1921, CAA.

77. Anna Marie Dahlquist, *Trailblazers for Translators: The Chichicastenango Twelve* (Pasadena, CA: William Carey Library, 1995), 16, 73; Cameron Townsend, "Mr. and Mrs. Treichler," typed note, n.d., TA 946086.

78. Dahlquist, *Trailblazers for Translators*, 15.

to his biographer.[79] While the Burgesses would eventually complete a Quiché translation of the New Testament, in 1920 it was the college dropout Cameron Townsend and his wife Elvira who were able to report progress in deciphering the complicated grammatical structure of Cakchiquel.

As Townsend took up the task of translating the New Testament into Cakchiquel in early 1921, his fellow missionaries were opposed to what they saw as a time-consuming and inessential task.[80] In 1908, CAM's Albert Bishop observed that "the Indians of Guatemala cannot read their own language; they have no literature in their own tongue, [and] schools in their own language are prohibited by the government." Both missionaries and the home council generally shared Bishop's sentiment that, since there "are Indians who read and speak Spanish," it was through "that language that the tribes must be evangelized, if evangelized effectively."[81] CAM's unofficial yet unmistakable policy accepted the prevailing inequalities of race, culture, and class, and this status quo was something the young Townsend was bent on changing. Because he sometimes treated his antagonists roughly, he found it much more difficult to convince his critics that his course of action merited consideration. Spanish-only ministry, he indelicately suggested to an opponent in 1927, might be "good for old missionaries or lazy ones who don't want to go to the effort of learning a new language."[82] In due course, he concluded that it must be "Satan [who] had blinded most missionaries in a greater or lesser degree of the need" for indigenous language work.[83] At least as troublesome as his remonstrative colleagues was the problem of fitting translation in among a multitude of other chores. In 1923, Townsend was placed in charge of all missionary work in the towns of San Antonio and Panajachel.[84] Illness, supervising national pastors, and a long list of other responsibilities threatened daily to impede progress on Bible translation.[85] These experiences convinced Townsend that Bible translation would remain, even under the best of circumstances, a sideline for CAM missionaries unless they could be convinced of its merits and then offered ample time for a long and tedious process.

At some point during his struggle to decipher the complexities of Cakchiquel, Townsend came across a grammar published in 1884 by an American

79. Anna Marie Dahlquist, *Burgess of Guatemala* (Langley, BC: Cedar Books, 1985).

80. Cameron Townsend to Scott, May 15, 1921, TA 771; Paul Townsend, "Paul Townsend's Memories of His Early Life," n.d., p. 11, TA 43776.

81. Albert E. Bishop, *Central American Bulletin* 14, no. 4 (1908): 5–6, CAA.

82. Cameron Townsend to Mr. Dunlop, December 22, 1927, TA 1245.

83. Cameron Townsend, "The Language Project."

84. Chafer to Cameron Townsend, May 2, 1923, TA 997.

85. Cameron Townsend to Howard B. Dinwiddie, May 7, 1921, TA 775; Cameron Townsend, Hefley interview, c. 1970, TA 43652; Elvira Townsend to Scott, January 11, 1921, TA 802.

archaeologist, Daniel G. Brinton.[86] Townsend later expressed his relief over not having discovered this work sooner, for he might have followed Brinton's flawed example by forcing the complex Cakchiquel verbal morphology into a Latin grammatical paradigm.[87] Townsend did analyze the language in a way vaguely analogous to what American structural linguists were attempting at the time, but it is likely that some timely advice set him on this course.[88] Townsend's popular biographers maintain that in 1919 an American archaeologist named "Dr. Gates" advised him to work out the grammatical structure of Cakchiquel on its own terms, cautioning against forcing the grammar into a Latin-based formula. These biographers also assert that this Dr. Gates introduced Townsend to the work of University of Chicago linguist Edward Sapir, a leading figure in the then emerging school of American structural linguistics.[89] On the other hand, Townsend's scholarly biographer makes no mention of any such encounter.[90] Although incontrovertible proof is lacking, there is credible evidence that Townsend chanced to meet William E. Gates, an American autodidact linguist, archaeologist, and collector of Mayan manuscripts dating from the Spanish conquest era. A biographical sketch of Gates, lodged in the L. Tom Perry Special Collections at Brigham Young University, places him in Guatemala, not in 1919, but rather between March and August 1921, the same year in which he was appointed honorary research associate of the Carnegie Institution of Washington, DC.[91] In a June 1921 letter, Townsend mentions meeting an "American scientist" and discussing matters related to the Mayan Indians, although he provided no further details.[92] In all likelihood, this "scientist" was Gates, who must have mentioned Sapir and opened the young missionary translator's eyes to the possibility of analyzing Cakchiquel from a more-or-less structural point of view. Lending further credence to a meeting of the two men is the fact that Townsend sent his completed grammar for Sapir's inspection in 1927, and in 1930 he appeared in

86. Kenneth L. Pike, "Foreword," *Mayan Studies I*, no. 5, ed. Benjamin Elson (1960): 3–7, TA 942957.

87. Cameron Townsend, "The Cakchiquel New Testament," n.d., TA 946100.

88. Cameron Townsend, "Cakchiquel Grammar," 1926, TA 42961; Cameron Townsend, "The Substantive Verb and Pronominal Ideas in Cakchiquel and Nahuatl," c. mid-1920s, TA 942962; Kenneth L. Pike, "Foreword," 3–7.

89. James C. Hefley and Marti Hefley, *Uncle Cam* (Huntington Beach, CA: Wycliffe Bible Translators, 1974), 47; Hugh Steven, *Wycliffe in the Making: The Memoirs of W. Cameron Townsend, 1920–1933* (Wheaton, IL: Harold Shaw, 1995), 14, 206.

90. Svelmoe, *A New Vision for Missions*.

91. MSS 279, Biography of William E. Gates, 20th and 21st Century Western and Mormon Americana, L. Tom Perry Special Collections, Harold B. Lee Library, Brigham Young University.

92. Cameron Townsend to Dinwiddie, June 20, 1921, p. 1, TA 757.

person to consult with Sapir.[93] It is plausible, then, that Gates and Townsend, both of whom were moving around the country at the time, crossed paths somewhere in Guatemala in June 1921. If this fortuitous encounter had never occurred, then Townsend might never have linked missionary Bible translation to the emerging discipline of structural linguistics, a move that would eventually have far-reaching effects not only on the development of SIL but also on the development of indigenous languages and the advancement of Bible translation theory in the mid-twentieth century.[94]

One of the most striking aspects of Townsend's approach to translation was his insistence that any indigenous translation of the Scriptures should be printed in parallel-columned Spanish and mother-tongue diglot form, for the express purpose of aiding the Indians in making the transition from indigenous-language literacy to Spanish literacy.[95] Townsend was innovatively linking Bible translation to bilingual education. On this point he was at least two decades ahead of his time. Not until the mid-1940s would bilingual education begin to achieve some measure of acceptance in Guatemala, and not until 1953 would the United Nations Educational, Scientific and Cultural Organization (UNESCO) conclude that bilingual education was preferable to monolingual education.[96] His concept apparently proved viable. In 1932 he reported that Cakchiquels taught to read in their mother tongue were subsequently able to utilize "the [New] Testament as a text book in their efforts to learn Spanish."[97] From these experiences Townsend concluded that bilingual education was potentially superior to the oft-failed attempts at Spanish monolingual education.

Translating the Cakchiquel New Testament was a momentous experience for Townsend and for the future development of his own mission. By whatever means, he had come to appreciate the value of linguistics for the missionary translator. Here was the kernel of an idea that resulted in the formation of Camp Wycliffe in 1933 to train missionary translators.[98] It is true that by later standards his grammar would prove to be of inferior quality. When Kenneth Pike

93. James Hefley, "Note on Edward Sapir," c. 1970, TA 43535; Eric M. North to Cameron Townsend, February 21, 1930, TA 1603; Sapir to Cameron Townsend, March 17, 1930, TA 1597; Cameron Townsend to North, American Bible Society, February 19, 1930, TA 901540.

94. The implications of Townsend's linking SIL with the discipline of structural linguistics are examined in chapters 2 and 3.

95. Dahlquist, *Trailblazers for Translators*, appendix A: "Minutes of the Chichicastenango Conference," 139.

96. Virginia Garrard-Burnett, *Protestantism in Guatemala: Living in the New Jerusalem* (Austin: University of Texas Press, 1998), 80–82; UNESCO, "The Use of Vernacular Languages in Education," *Monographs on Fundamental Education* 8 (Paris: UNESCO, 1953).

97. Cameron Townsend to Karl D. Hummel, March 9, 1932, p. 2, TA 1696.

98. The development of Camp Wycliffe is detailed in chapter 2.

examined Townsend's grammar from a professional linguist's point of view, he remarked that "it didn't look so hot." "It was," Pike added, "an amateurish job of somebody new to linguistics."[99] Yet these defects would in the long run prove insignificant, for it was ideas that lay behind these projects that would one day give birth to a strikingly novel variety of evangelical mission.

The Keswick Connection

The Keswick movement, also referred to as the Victorious Life Testimony, was an offshoot of Wesleyan Holiness and John Wesley's concept of "Christian perfection." The American glass manufacturer Robert Pearsall Smith and his wife Hannah were two of the foremost purveyors of this renewed emphasis on the Holy Spirit and a life of surrender in the late nineteenth century.[100] Influenced by strains of Romanticism, the movement accented religious experience rather than reasoned theological discourse or doctrinal deliberations.[101] One commentator said, "I never gave Smith credit for much intelligence. It was his heart, not his head, which attracted me."[102] Shirley Nelson sought to express the essence of Keswick in her novel *The Last Year of the War*, which is set at a fictitious Bible school during World War II. At one point Nelson has the fundamentalist professor Dr. Peckham holding forth in chapel on the "victorious life." Peckham challenged students "to be courageous, serene in the face of adversity, powerful in soul-winning, steady and unmovable in faith, free from the tyranny of self, flesh crucified." All this striving was to be miraculously accomplished "with sunshiny faces."[103] The potent spirituality of this movement was an important factor in creating a socioreligious milieu that encouraged performances of religious athleticism, where young people relentlessly subjected themselves to an almost endless round of witnessing, tract distribution, Bible study, and attending and leading church services and prayer meetings, all the while maintaining a submissive attitude and personal spiritual purity.

The emphases of Keswick were also valued by faith mission leaders. Charles Hurlburt, the general director of the Africa Inland Mission, insisted in 1917 that

99. Kenneth L. Pike, Hefley interview, c. 1970, p. 7, TA 43472.

100. J. C. Pollock, *The Keswick Story: The Authorized History of the Keswick Convention* (Chicago: Moody Press, 1964), 11–15.

101. Bebbington, *Dominance of Evangelicalism*, 184, 207–10; David W. Bebbington, *Evangelicalism in Modern Britain: A History from the 1730s to the 1980s* (New York: Routledge, 2002), 167–71.

102. Quoted in Pollock, *The Keswick Story*, 14.

103. Shirley Nelson, *The Last Year of the War*, rev. ed. (Wheaton, IL: Northcote Books, [1979] 1989), 197.

publicizing the task of worldwide evangelization at Bible conferences and in Bible schools should be coupled "with such teachings of the victorious life and complete surrender as might be needful to secure desirable candidates for the mission field."[104] In other words, the Victorious Life movement was expected to produce energetic but also compliant missionary recruits to the burgeoning faith mission movement.

In the fall of 1920, Howard B. Dinwiddie, the secretary of American Keswick, made his way to Guatemala City to hold a Victorious Life Conference for the missionaries. Townsend and Burgess shared with Dinwiddie their passion for reaching the Indians of Central America, and won for themselves an avid spokesman.[105] In December, Dinwiddie cabled another Keswick enthusiast, Leonard Livingstone (L. L.) Legters, inviting him to join them for a hastily planned Indian conference in Guatemala. Legters was a Presbyterian minister and former Dutch Reformed missionary to the Comanche and Apache Indians in Oklahoma. He also held the distinction of having conducted the burial ceremony of the legendary Apache chief Geronimo.[106] Already passionate about Indian missions, he needed little coaxing to join the conference.[107] The Townsends, Burgesses, and Treichlers, together with Legters, Dinwiddie, and a few other interested missionaries, gathered at Chichicastenango, Guatemala, in January 1921 to discuss what they saw as the pressing need for a specifically indigenous ministry. First, they agreed that the Indians should be trained to evangelize their own people. Second, it was decided that mother-tongue Bible translation was not a secondary or optional task but rather an absolute necessity. Toward this end the gathered ensemble unanimously passed a motion directing Townsend and Burgess to form a Bible translation committee.[108] By advocating indigenous language evangelization and mother-tongue Bible translation, the Chichicastenango group struck a pose that was at odds with prevailing missionary attitudes and practice among Protestant missions in Guatemala.

104. Quoted in Edwin L. Frizen Jr., *75 Years of IFMA, 1917–1992: The Nondenominational Missions Movement* (Wheaton, IL: Interdenominational Foreign Mission Association, 1992), 105.

105. Herbert Toms to Scott, January 29, 1921, CAA; Cameron Townsend, *Central American Bulletin*, March 15, 1921, 12, CAA; Elvira Townsend to Scott, December 7, 1920, TA 653.

106. Angie Debo, *Geronimo: The Man, His Time, His Place* (Norman: University of Oklahoma Press, 1976), 442; "Geronimo, Apache Warchief, Dead," *Native American* (Phoenix) 10, no. 7 (February, 20 1909): 70; Cameron Townsend to Dr. Henry Beets, president, *Reformed Press Digest*, November 5, 1943, p. 2, TA 903465; Cameron Townsend, Hefley interview, c. 1970, TA 43539.

107. Lawrence Dame, *Maya Mission* (Garden City, NY: Doubleday, 1968), 8–16; Cameron Townsend, "Dinwiddie and Legters," n.d., TA 946088; Cameron Townsend, "The Early Years of Wycliffe," 1949, rev. 1980, pp. 1–2, TA 42636.

108. Dahlquist, *Trailblazers for Translators*, appendix A, part 1, "Minutes of the Chichicastenango Conference," 139–49; Toms to Scott, January 29, 1921, CAA.

Fearing that their goals would never come to fruition through the efforts of existing missionary organizations, the group established a new mission, the Latin American Indian Mission (LAIM).[109] While it was expected that LAIM would fulfill its objectives "by contribution to and in cooperation with other agencies," the Chichicastenango group nonetheless opened the door to bypassing existing missions when they resolved that LAIM could engage in "direct activity to give the Gospel to the Indians of Latin America."[110] Forming an entirely new mission was tantamount to a palace coup, and it aroused the suspicion of several CAM council members.[111] When Townsend became aware of the growing hostility, he rather impertinently, especially for a newcomer on the scene, wrote Judge Scott, admonishing that "I trust the Council may be guided very definitely by the Lord in their attitude toward this matter. If taken up wisely, I think that great good can come of it, but if not, it is apt to result in misunderstandings."[112] Townsend's presumptuous attitude was hardly in keeping with Victorious Life submissiveness that faith mission leaders expected of their missionaries, and it was demonstrative of his headstrong nature that would eventuate in his breaking free from the restraints imposed by faith mission tradition.

There was a palpable air of distress throughout the summer of 1921 among members of the CAM council over Dinwiddie and Legters's Keswick connections. Typical of the prevailing apprehension was R. D. Smith's March 1921 report, in which he related that a fellow council member "was disturbed" after learning that Dinwiddie was "connected with . . . the men that lead the Victorious Life Conferences."[113] Another council member hoped that Dinwiddie and Legters "might be delivered from the extremes" of the Victorious Life teaching.[114] Exacerbating the council's angst was the fact that Dinwiddie and Legters did not, as Judge Scott put it, know "anything about a faith mission." Scott went on to point out that "Mr. Dinwiddie is a good beggar, but since we are only to beg from God, I do not see how we can use him."[115] Back in the United States, Dinwiddie and Legters were engaged in an all-out deputation operation that paid little heed to faith mission protocol. Legters, possessed of a hyperkinetic personality, was especially given to exaggeration. Chastised for public statements that implied that CAM had never engaged in any Indian work at all be-

---

109. Dahlquist, *Trailblazers for Translators*, 27.
110. Dahlquist, *Trailblazers for Translators*, 141.
111. R. D. Smith to Cameron Townsend, February 19, 1921, CAA.
112. Cameron Townsend to Scott, May 9, 1921, CAA.
113. Smith to Scott, March 10, 1921, CAA.
114. Luther Rees to Bishop, August 5, 1921, CAA.
115. Scott to Bishop, September 3, 1921, CAA.

fore the formation of LAIM, Legters nonetheless persisted in his claims. Bishop grumbled in July 1921 that Legters's "blunder [has] become . . . permanent propaganda."[116] The restrained old-school publicity methods of CAM were being turned upside down by these two impulsive and passionate men. "It is a case of enthusiasm ungoverned, untempered, by careful and thoughtful investigation," Bishop lashed out that same July.[117] Legters was deaf to reproach and Dinwiddie simply hoped that God would give the council "the mind and harmony of the Holy Spirit and lead [it] to the conclusions that shall bring forth the unfolding and the fulness of His plan for His ministry."[118] Filled with a sense of divine purpose, derived in no small part from a Keswick perfectionist-induced self-confidence in being Spirit-led, Dinwiddie and Legters had little patience with the niceties of the faith mission approach to public relations, and they were not about to let such restrictions impede their efforts.

At nearly the same time that Dinwiddie was convening a conference in Philadelphia to establish a home council for LAIM in October 1921, he and Legters were founding yet another organization, the Pioneer Mission Agency (PMA). Established on October 26, 1921, the PMA was largely an American Keswick affair. In addition to Victorious Life chairman J. Harvey Borton, Charles G. Trumbull and Howard Banks, both of the widely read *Sunday School Times* and exponents of Keswick theology, were appointed to the PMA board of directors.[119] The PMA eschewed directing missionaries on the field and focused exclusively on fund-raising and recruiting missionaries to unreached indigenous peoples.[120] Why the founders chose to launch another mission is unclear. Certainly the cold water thrown on their LAIM venture, not to mention CAM's wariness, must have played a part in their decision. By forming their own organization, Dinwiddie and Legters conveniently dispensed with the interagency polemics that threatened to undermine their ambitions; it also permitted them to exercise their style of animated public relations that other faith mission leaders found objectionable.

The PMA remained something of an irritant in the eyes of CAM conservatives. In 1929, CAM general secretary Karl D. Hummel complained to Townsend that Legters "overstates things" and "exaggerates."[121] But Townsend had concluded that Legters's enthusiasm was more a help than a hindrance, especially when making the case for Indian work before American audiences.

116. Bishop to Dinwiddie, July 9, 1921, CAA.
117. Bishop to Mr. and Mrs. McBath, June 8, 1921, CAA.
118. Dinwiddie to Scott, July 14, 1921, CAA.
119. Dinwiddie to Rees, October 15, 1921, CAA.
120. Dahlquist, *Trailblazers for Translators*, 66–71.
121. Hummel to Cameron Townsend, September 26, 1929, p. 2, TA 1453.

"His vision," Townsend later recalled, "was marvelous and we needed his help so I cultivated his friendship."[122] Although Dinwiddie died in December 1925, the Townsend-Legters friendship continued until the latter's death in 1941. Therefore, when Townsend eventually decided to part ways with CAM, he had a ready-made base of support in the PMA and the likeminded L. L. Legters.

Historians have stressed the connections between the Keswick movement and faith missions. For example, Joel Carpenter wrote in 1990 that "Keswick holiness teaching was thoroughly integrated into the fundamentalist network of Bible schools, summer conferences, and faith missions."[123] George Marsden has also conveyed the idea that Keswick teaching and fundamentalism were of a piece, save for the reproaches of the Warfieldians at Princeton.[124] The case of the Dinwiddie-Legters-Townsend triumvirate and the more staid CAM suggests that this assumption should perhaps be challenged. From the evidence offered here, it would appear that not all fundamentalists or faith missioners looked with favor on Keswick teaching, especially when it took the form of a self-confident dynamism that threatened the conventional patterns of discreet fund-raising and surrender to leadership expected by most faith missions. Dinwiddie, Legters, and Townsend parted with faith missions' traditional diffidence toward publicity and making appeals for missionary funds, and they innovatively turned the expected compliance of Keswick spirituality into a nonconformist self-confidence that engendered bold and independent action.

Politics and Diplomacy

The political atmosphere in late-1920s Guatemala became increasingly nationalistic and anti-American. In February 1931, Jorge Ubico assumed power as Guatemala's president. Essentially a dictator, Ubico pursued nationalistic policies and the centralization of government power. Beginning in 1932, he promulgated laws restricting Protestant missions by limiting their numbers and insisting upon government certification for any missionaries wishing to enter the country. A 1932 communist-inspired rebellion in neighboring El Salvador, which included indigenous elements among the insurgents, increased Ubico's wariness of Guatemala's Indian population and the missionaries who

122. Cameron Townsend, Hefley interview, c. 1970, p. 2, TA 43539.
123. Joel A. Carpenter, "Propagating the Faith Once Delivered: The Fundamentalist Missionary Enterprise, 1920–1945," in *Earthen Vessels: American Evangelicals and Foreign Missions, 1880–1980,* ed. Joel A. Carpenter and Wilbert R. Shenk (Grand Rapids: Eerdmans, 1990), 119.
124. Marsden, *Fundamentalism and American Culture,* 93–101.

resided among them.[125] Paul Burgess, a member of the Socialist Party in his younger days and now in intimate contact with the Quichés, came under particular suspicion. Burgess published a popular Quiché almanac of farming hints, witticisms, and Bible quotations. While the almanac's contents were typically innocuous, Burgess aroused the ire of the Ubico regime when he penned a somewhat critical editorial, in which he declared that the "government can err" and added that although it had a responsibility to "maintain justice, it practices injustice." Burgess was briefly jailed and thereafter forced to submit further editorials for government perusal or cease publication altogether.[126] By the early 1930s missionaries in Guatemala no longer occupied their former privileged position, and if they complained publicly, they could be arrested or see their activities curtailed.

In light of these events, the fact that the May 21, 1931, issue of the Guatemalan newspaper *El Libero Progresisto* ran a front-page article and photograph of Townsend presenting a copy of the Cakchiquel New Testament to President Ubico requires explanation.[127] Working through the president's chief of staff and the minister of education, Townsend secured an engagement with Ubico for himself, Trinidad Bac (one of his Cakchiquel cotranslators), and R. R. Gregory of the American Bible Society. With keen foresight he arranged for a photographer to be present. He had also incurred the extra expense of preparing a specially bound copy of the New Testament in anticipation of this auspicious occasion.[128] It can only be surmised why Ubico consented to Townsend's request or why he reportedly uttered during the half-hour assembly that "this book marks a great forward movement in our civilization."[129] Perhaps the most plausible explanation is that Ubico viewed the event as an opportunity to gain favor with the country's Mayan peoples as part of his overall nationalistic program for solidifying his grip on the country's fragmented population. It probably helped that Townsend pointed out the diglot's potential for drawing the indigenous population into the Spanish-speaking culture. What for the president likely amounted to mere rhetorical flourishes aimed at drumming up indigenous support was, for Townsend, simply the first of many instances where he catapulted himself into the public eye and in the process ingeniously

125. Adams, *Crucifixion by Power*, 174–77; Garrard-Burnett, *Protestantism in Guatemala*, 71–73.

126. Dahlquist, *Burgess of Guatemala*, 37, 122, 125–30.

127. "El Nuevo Testamento fue Traducido al Cacchiquel," *El Libero Progresisto* 2828 (May 21, 1931): 1, TA 45065.

128. Cameron Townsend, "President of Guatemala Receives First Copy," n.d., TA 946105; Cameron Townsend to "Home Folks," May 21, 1931, TA 1661.

129. R. R. Gregory, "Guatemala Receives the Cakchiquel New Testament," *Bible Society Record* 76, no. 8 (August 1931): 1, TA 45063.

garnered visible support from ruling elites, who may or may not have shared his social and religious goals.

By the time Townsend completed the Cakchiquel New Testament translation in 1929, his perspectives on religious and missionary matters were already well formed. The main points of his outlook can easily be summarized. First, unlike many fundamentalists of the period, he was not overly concerned with doctrinal punctilios. In fact, Townsend was more broadly evangelical in religious character than narrowly fundamentalist. Second, he pioneered efforts to reach indigenous peoples isolated by language and held a high regard for indigenous education and its benefits. Third, he had a pragmatic willingness to part with faith mission proprieties when it suited his purposes. Fourth, he insisted that Bible translation was central, not peripheral, to any missionary effort. Fifth, he understood, presciently, that the emerging discipline of descriptive linguistics had much to offer Bible translators in analyzing unwritten languages. And sixth, he used a diplomatic approach to government officials, seeking to win their favor rather than eschewing secular entanglements. Townsend soon carried this rather progressive missiology into Mexico, where he would have ample opportunity to practice his unique approach to missions.

WBT and SIL in the Making

By the late 1920s, Townsend's fertile mind was breeding schemes for missionary action of such magnitude as to make his departure from CAM a foregone conclusion. "I am convinced," he wrote Legters in April 1930, "that God is leading me to a spectacular undertaking" in South America. What he had in mind was using airplanes to reach isolated jungle areas of the Amazon Basin with the gospel. How would an "Air Crusade to the Wild Tribes sound?" he speculated.[130] The impetus for this extraordinary idea was twofold. Legters had returned from an exploration trip to Brazil in 1926 with photographs of some Xingu Indians, which sparked in Townsend a yearning " "to leave the work among the Cakchiquel Indians and go to Amazonia to pioneer with some tribe there."[131] That same year he chanced to meet US Army Major Herbert A. Dargue during the aviator's 1926 Pan-American Goodwill flight that circumnavigated South America. Awestruck by the mobility of Dargue's aircraft, he seized on the idea of using airplanes to reach isolated tribes in the Amazonian basin.[132] Having readily fused these two ideas in his

---

130. Cameron Townsend to Legters, April 24, 1930, TA 1529.
131. Cameron Townsend, "Wycliffe Lives Again," c. 1948, p. 6, TA 42642.
132. Dargue to Cameron Townsend, April 11, 1929, TA 1415; Dargue to Cameron Townsend,

mind, he just as effortlessly overlooked the complexities involved. For example, where would he obtain the money for this enormously expensive undertaking? Unshackling himself from any pretense of faith mission restraint, he proposed that "if this project is put before the public extensively and also in a striking way 500,000 Christians can be secured to send a dollar apiece."[133] That aircraft travel was still at an early stage of development, not to mention that America was feeling the first tremors of the Great Depression, bothered Townsend not in the least. "Maybe it is only a visionary idea," he admitted to CAM's Karl Hummel, "but I just can't help having them."[134] An "air crusade to the wild tribes" was, quite naturally, far beyond anything the cautious CAM council could even begin to imagine, and the council members struggled in vain to channel Townsend's enormous energy into more commonplace undertakings.

Townsend's foray into Mexico began while he was still involved in the Cakchiquel literacy campaign. In 1931 he chanced to meet Moisés Sáenz, a Mexican educator, diplomat, and politician who was visiting Guatemala to study the "Indian problem." Sáenz was impressed with Townsend's social and literacy work, and he suggested that this social reform-minded missionary establish a similar program among the Aztec Indians near Mexico City. Sáenz later repeated the invitation in writing and said such an endeavor would have the backing of Mexico's revolutionary leaders.[135] With visions of airplanes and "wild tribes" dancing in his head, Townsend was not immediately drawn to the idea of entering Mexico. Legters, seeing providence at work in the Sáenz encounter, urged him to consider the opening.[136] Townsend was finally convinced to settle on Mexico after Legters agreed to help him with another of his innovative ideas—a first-of-its-kind linguistic school to train potential missionary Bible translators in the rudiments of descriptive linguistics. The South American plan was shelved while the two men focused on gaining a foothold for Bible translators in Mexico and launching Camp Wycliffe, the name given to the linguistic summer camp in honor of the English translator John Wycliffe.[137]

January 4, 1930, TA 1615; Cameron Townsend, "An Airplane Crusade to the Unevangelized Jungle-Lands of Latin America," August 1930, TA 41806.

133. Cameron Townsend to Legters, April 24, 1930, TA 1529.

134. Cameron Townsend to Hummel, July 24, 1928, p. 2, TA 1389.

135. Cameron Townsend to Legters, November 11, 1931, TA 1630; Cameron Townsend, "Mexico's Gift Airplane 'Amauta Moisés Sáenz' Continues to Serve Peru's Amazonian People," 1969, TA 42690; Cameron Townsend, Hefley interview, note, re: Meeting with Moisés Sáenz in Guatemala, c. 1970, TA 43657.

136. Legters to Cameron Townsend, January 21, 1932, TA 1706.

137. Cameron Townsend to Dr. Henry Beets, president, *Reformed Press Digest*, November 5, 1943, p. 4, TA 903465.

The Sáenz invitation notwithstanding, Mexico appeared to be an unlikely destination for launching a new missionary endeavor in the early 1930s. The Mexican Revolution of 1910 had set political liberals against religion, and the country was effectively closed to new missions. The revolutionary 1917 constitution forbade religious processions, prohibited clergy from wearing priestly garb in public, barred the Catholic Church from owning property, and proscribed its involvement in education. President Plutarco Elías Calles, an avowed atheist who had assumed power in 1924, fulminated against the Roman Catholic Church, inciting the Cristero rebellion of the late 1920s that pitted the government against Catholic guerrillas. The bloody confrontation saw priests hanged and churches burned.[138] Mexico's revolutionary leaders and intellectuals considered religion an impediment to progress. Thus the drive to reconstruct education along secular lines was part of a larger attempt to supplant religious "superstition" with "rationality" in pursuit of modernization. Revolutionary Mexico of the early 1930s, by suppressing religion in an all-out effort to catapult the nation into modernity, seemed to offer little opportunity for establishing a new missionary venture or a program of Christian-based education.

If Mexico's revolutionary ideology posed an obstacle to Townsend's designs, the ideology of *indigenismo* worked in his favor. *Indigenismo* was an early twentieth-century elite reformulation of the centuries-old "Indian problem" that assumed a paternalistic attitude toward the uplift and integration of indigenous peoples into the nation-state. In a turn away from the social Darwinism of the nineteenth century, *indigenistas* constructed an integrative nationalistic ideology that attempted neither to erase nor to reify Indian ethnicity. Instead, Latin American intellectuals, such as the Mexican anthropologist and educator Manual Gamio—who is generally considered the father of *indigenismo*—developed a body of thought that conceptualized Indian integration as contributing to a cultural synthesis that combined the best of indigenous and Spanish qualities into a unique form of nationalism.[139] "In the great forge of America," Gamio wrote in 1916, "on the giant anvil of the Andes, virile races of bronze and iron struggled for centuries." The time had come, he proclaimed, for Mexico's leaders "to take up the hammer and gird themselves with blacksmith's apron, so that they may make rise from the miraculous anvil a new nation

---

138. Michael C. Meyer and William L. Sherman, *The Course of Mexican History*, 3rd ed. (New York: Oxford University Press, 1987), 542–45, 587–90; Alan Riding, *Distant Neighbors: A Portrait of the Mexicans* (New York: Vintage Books, 1986), 71–72.

139. Alan Knight, "Racism, Revolution, and *Indigenismo*: Mexico, 1910–1940," in *The Idea of Race in Latin America, 1870–1940*, ed. Richard Graham (Austin: University of Texas Press, 1990), 71–98.

of blended bronze and iron."[140] *Indigenismo* was inherently contradictory in that it at once sought Indian integration but without the loss of indigenous characteristics. *Indigenistas*, as one commentator remarked, "walk a tightrope between the 'colonialist' ideal of preserving the Indian through isolation and special protection, and imposed assimilation."[141] The project was an entirely top-down and paternalistic one. According to Gamio, the Indian population of Mexico was a "poor and suffering race," and he pontificated that "you will not awaken spontaneously. It will be necessary for friendly hearts to work for your redemption."[142] The ideology of *indigenismo*, with its designs for elevating and educating indigenous peoples and putting them on the path to citizenship, had much in common with Townsend's ambitions to raise the Indians out of the mire of social inequality. As will be seen, he shaped his venture to fit the intellectual contours of *indigenismo*, which was at its zenith in the 1930s, and he thereby gained a foothold in Mexico for SIL.

By the time Townsend seriously considered entering Mexico in 1933, Sáenz was no longer in a government post, and was therefore not in a position to facilitate his entry into the country. Knowing full well too that the prevailing intellectual climate in Mexico prohibited any kind of standard missionary strategy, Townsend conceived a novel approach that he laid out in a letter of introduction to the Mexican authorities. Shrewdly avoiding the term "missionary," he introduced Legters as a "lecturer, explorer and humanitarian" and himself as an "ethnologist and educator." He did not conceal his religious intentions when proposing what he referred to as the "Mexican Society of Indigenous Translations." This new organization, he promised, would carry out a dual program to "conserve for science a grammar and dictionary of each indigenous language" while also undertaking to "translate the New Testament in each language and publish it in bilingual edition." He took pains to demonstrate that his efforts were in keeping with those of Mexico's liberal educators. For example, aware that rural teachers were expected to model exemplary behavior among their charges, he emphasized that "no one will be used who would function as a bad moral example when living and working among the indigenous people." Announcing his readiness to place his organization at the disposal of the state, an unheard-of idea among faith missions, he offered that "your employees will try to inculcate notions against alcoholism and other bad habits that brutalize the Indians." He also explained that his organization would cooperate in the

---

140. Manuel Gamio, *Forjando Patria* (Mexico: Editorial Porrúa, 1960), quoted in Knight, "Racism, Revolution, and *Indigenismo*," 85.

141. Mörner, "Historical Research on Race Relations," 199.

142. Gamio, *Forjando Patria*, quoted in Knight, "Racism, Revolution, and *Indigenismo*," 77.

state's efforts to integrate the indigenous peoples into the nation. "We believe," Townsend wrote, "that the indigenous races will contribute in a great way to the enlargement of each nation where they live once they learn the native [national] language and are set on the right track in the national culture."[143] What Townsend spelled out was a two-pronged religious and scientific agenda that was calibrated to align with Mexico's revolutionary aims and the concepts of *indigenismo*.

Townsend and Legters crossed the border into Mexico on November 11, 1933.[144] Four days before their departure, Townsend resigned from CAM so that he could legitimately claim that he was not a missionary.[145] "Having to be so careful makes me feel rather like a spy," he confided, "but I'd be even that in order to get the Message to those poor Indian tribes."[146] Never deeply wedded to his missionary identity, Townsend simply dropped it in favor of referring to himself as an "educator."

Legters, chafing at the restrictions on preaching, returned to the United States after a few weeks, leaving Townsend to his own devices. His venturesome colleague was hardly at a loss in Mexico, and soon fell into the company of Frank Tannenbaum, a left-leaning American writer.[147] Tannenbaum was a Progressive activist who wrote on education, prison reform, and labor issues. Imprisoned in his early twenties for leading anarchic demonstrations in New York City, he later came under suspicion by the Federal Bureau of Investigation for associating with a "red cohort" of leftist intellectuals in Mexico.[148] The two men struck up a friendship, and Tannenbaum provided his new acquaintance with a note of introduction to Mexico's director of rural education, Rafael Ramírez, thus paving the way for Townsend to tour the country inspecting its educational system.[149]

Over a two-month period Townsend traveled over five thousand miles visiting schools and meeting with Mexican educators, businessmen, clergy, and military officials.[150] Upon his return to the United States in February 1934, he

143. Cameron Townsend to Al. C. Lic. José M. Soto, official mayor, Secretaría Gobernación, October 6, 1933, TA 2077 (translation by Svelmoe, *New Vision for Missions*, 241–42).

144. Cameron Townsend to Mr. and Mrs. Lewis Fall, November 11, 1933, TA 1729.

145. Cameron Townsend to executive council, CAM, November 7, 1933, TA 1733.

146. Cameron Townsend to William G. Nyman Sr. and Etta Nyman, April 8, 1934, TA 50920.

147. Cameron Townsend to Elvira Townsend, December 10, 1933, TA 1718; December 13, 1933, p. 2, TA 1717; December 20, 1933, p. 3, TA 1716.

148. Charles A. Hale, "Frank Tannenbaum and the Mexican Revolution," *Hispanic American Historical Review* 75, no. 2 (May 1995): 215–46.

149. Cameron Townsend to Elvira Townsend, December 20, 1933, p. 2, TA 1716.

150. Cameron Townsend, "Record, Part of Mexican Trip," December 21, 1933, to February 12,

published a number of articles lavishing with praise Mexico's educational system and the nation's efforts to educate the Indians and rural inhabitants.[151] He admitted in a 1935 piece that, while he was at first "prejudiced against the educational authorities" for their antireligious stance and purely rationalist aims, he had come to understand that "religion has played the traitor" in Mexico by its collaboration with "exploitation, political injustices, foreign imperialism, ignorance, superstition and even immorality." What was needed, Townsend contended in what was a direct attack on Roman Catholicism in Mexico, was not organized religion but rather "personal pious faith" and the Bible as "an antidote to fanaticism" and a "textbook of right living." In effect, he reasoned that the Bible would bring about the very results Mexico's revolutionary leaders and educators were laboring toward. He lauded the salutary benefits that accrued from literacy and reading of the Bible, arguing that "peasants formerly lacking in a desire for knowledge," after learning to read the Bible, "delve into its truths" and subsequently give up drinking, pay off their debts, and find their "standard of living" inevitably rising. "If educators find this transformation going on in its early stages before it has been cristalized [*sic*] in ecclesiastical molds," he concluded, "they can guide it so as to greatly aid them in their program of social uplift."[152] Townsend sought to secure his credentials as an exponent of the educational ideals of the Mexican Revolution while at the same time contending that the Bible in the hands of the peasantry functioned not only as a moralizing influence but also as a stimulus to social progress.

Mexican educators were hindered in attaining their objectives by the sheer variety of indigenous languages and a dearth of linguistic expertise. Nathaniel Weyl, an American economist and a sympathetic, firsthand observer of 1930s Mexico, noted in 1939 that "one of Mexico's greatest problems is the scarcity of capable technicians loyal to the revolutionary program of the Government."[153] Over the summers of 1934 and 1935 Townsend trained a handful of young missionary-linguists in Arkansas who could, if permanent access to Mexico

---

1934, TA 1892; Cameron Townsend to Josephus Daniels, US ambassador to Mexico, December 18, 1935, TA 1911.

151. W. C. Townsend, "Blazing a New Trail in Education South of the Border," 1934, TA 42603; W. Cameron Townsend, "The Guardians of the Mexican Revolution," c. mid-1934, TA 42602; W. Cameron Townsend, "Mexico's Astounding Program of Rural Education," 1934, TA 42604; W. Cameron Townsend, "Mexico's Program of Rural Education," *School and Society* 39, no. 1018 (June 1934): 848–51, TA 901866.

152. W. Cameron Townsend, "Is Religion Doomed in the Land of Cuautemoc?," 1935, p. 8, TA 42599.

153. Nathaniel Weyl and Sylvia Weyl, *The Reconquest of Mexico: The Years of Lázaro Cárdenas* (New York: Oxford University Press, 1939), 328.

was secured, help to alleviate this dearth of "technicians."[154] In August 1935 Townsend and one of his top linguistic students from Camp Wycliffe, Kenneth Pike, appeared at the Seventh Inter-American Scientific Conference in Mexico City. When Ramírez encountered Townsend, he enthusiastically welcomed him back to Mexico. Most importantly, he introduced the pair to Mariano Silva y Aceves, the director of the Mexican Institute of Linguistic Research, which had been established in 1933. Townsend regaled Aceves with his experiments with bilingual education in Guatemala and spoke of his vision for linguistic analysis, literacy, and Bible translation. Aceves was apparently impressed, and thus invited Townsend and his students to cooperate with the institute. While the conference was still in session, Pike was placed at Aceves's disposal as a linguistic "consultant," and the two worked together briefly collecting data in Mexico City from bilingual informants. The following year Aceves arranged for some of Townsend's budding linguists to become official researchers attached to the National University.[155] Also in 1936, at Townsend's urging, a linguistic conference was arranged in Mexico, where papers, mainly by his cadre of recently trained amateur linguists, were presented. Townsend expected that this event would help to establish the "thoroughly scientific" credentials of his embryonic organization in the eyes of Mexican scholars.[156] The door to Mexico was suddenly pried open and the welcome mat rolled out for him to begin implementing what he referred to in a report to the PMA as a "three point program of Bible translation, cooperation with the University in scientific linguistic research, and cooperation with the government in its welfare program."[157] Townsend had convinced Mexican officials and educators that his nascent organization could make real contributions, both scientifically and socially, to Mexico's ongoing revolution.

What had happened between 1933 and August 1935 that led to this state of affairs? In the first place, Townsend's laudatory articles published in the *Dallas News* and *School and Society* had convinced Ramírez and Secretary of Education Narciso Bassols that he would in fact shape his venture to fit the Mexican context.[158] In the second place, recently elected president Lázaro Cárdenas dis-

154. The establishment of Camp Wycliffe by Townsend in 1934 to train young missionary recruits in the rudiments of descriptive linguistics is discussed in chapter 2.

155. Kenneth L. Pike, Hefley interview, c. 1970, pp. 17–18, TA 43472; Cameron Townsend to PMA, September 8, 1937, p. 3, TA 2102; Cameron Townsend et al., *The Wycliffe Sapphire* (Huntington Beach, CA: Wycliffe Bible Translators, 1991), 55–56.

156. Quoted in Cameron Townsend to Hummel, February 12, 1937, TA 2158; Cameron Townsend to PMA, September 8, 1938, TA 2102; Cameron Townsend, "Memorandum para el C. Secretario de Educacion Publica," December 24, 1941, TA 2697.

157. Cameron Townsend to PMA, September 8, 1937, p. 4, TA 2102.

158. Ramírez to Cameron Townsend, March 15, 1934, TA 1886.

missed his cabinet. The new cabinet, installed in June 1935, had a much more moderate position on the role of religion in Mexican society than the extreme anticlericalism of the Calles era.[159] At the very same moment that Townsend's publicity efforts were dispelling skepticism over his intentions, the Mexican political winds were shifting in a more favorable direction to religion.

In late 1933 and early 1934, when Townsend was reconnoitering Mexico's education system, the country's next president was also perambulating around the country. Had Cárdenas chanced to meet Townsend, they would have discovered that they held much in common. Cárdenas, elected president on July 1, 1934, was a *mestizo* of Tarascan Indian heritage. He brought with him to the presidency a genuine heartfelt concern for Mexico's peasants and Indians, something he had already demonstrated during his governorship of Michoacán.[160] By tirelessly campaigning in far-flung rural areas and patiently lending an ear to peasants as they voiced endless complaints, he created for himself tremendous popular support, which allowed for his 1935 break with his political patron Calles. Perhaps the simplest way to characterize the president's outlook is to quote a rural working-class Mexican, who upon meeting Cárdenas said: "We are progressive men, Mr. General. We do not drink alcohol, because we repudiate vice and want to feed our families better, and because it gives us pleasure to see our wives with new clothes and shoes."[161] Cárdenas, like Townsend, was an exhibit in progressive idealism; therefore, encounters such as this one would certainly have brought a smile to the president's face, for this was precisely the aftereffect he expected from his version of Mexico's revolution.

Unlike his predecessor, Cárdenas saw no advantage in striking a bellicose attitude toward the church. His government, Cárdenas promised, would "not repeat the mistakes committed by previous administrations in considering the religious question the preeminent problem." "It is not the government's job," he emphasized, "to promote antireligious campaigns."[162] A moderate position on Roman Catholicism was no indication that Cárdenas had turned his back on the revolutionary drive toward modernity, socialism, and rationalism. Within months of his taking office, article 3 of the constitution was amended to the effect that "education imparted by the State shall be socialist and in addition to excluding all religious doctrines, shall combat fanaticism and prejudice."[163] On this point it would seem that Cárdenas and Townsend would have intractable

159. Weyl and Weyl, *The Reconquest of Mexico*, 162–64.

160. Meyer and Sherman, *Course of Mexican History*, 596–98; Riding, *Distant Neighbors*, 75.

161. Weyl and Weyl, *The Reconquest of Mexico*, 160.

162. Enrique Krauze, *Mexico: Biography of Power; A History of Modern Mexico, 1810–1996* (New York: HarperCollins, 1977), 459–60.

163. Krauze, *Mexico*, 433.

differences. Yet, Townsend was already advancing notions that the Bible could serve revolutionary ends as "an antidote to fanaticism" and a "textbook of right living." What Townsend was proposing was nothing less than a nonsectarian faith shorn of ecclesiasticism, where the Bible, freed from religious intermediaries, would serve as a moralizing and liberalizing force rather than as a tool of oppression and class interests. By Townsend's lights, religion was not Mexico's problem. Once it was torn from the grasp of Roman Catholic ecclesiastical power, Christianity, he argued, could both liberate and enlighten.

Consider just how radical Townsend's ideas were. The antagonism between conservative evangelicalism and the Social Gospel reached its peak in the 1920s and 1930s. Down to the early part of the twentieth century, North American evangelicals promoted both soul saving and social uplift. As the Social Gospelers began to place ever greater stress on social reform at the expense of individual conversion, conservative evangelicals reacted by emphasizing conversion and backing away from social concerns. The effects of this polarization were not confined to religious issues. Since sociopolitical Progressivism and the Social Gospel were deeply intertwined, conservative evangelicals also became suspicious of the early twentieth-century Progressive movement. Anything therefore that resembled socialism or communism tended to repulse fundamentalists. It is quite startling therefore to find Townsend not only associating his nascent mission with revolutionary Mexico but also championing the ideas of the revolutionary movement itself. Townsend was clearly on the leading edge of what would become known as the new evangelicalism in the 1940s; and even when some evangelicals began to address the importance of social issues, few were willing to go quite as far as the founder of WBT-SIL. The unconventional nature of what Townsend was doing in the 1930s should not be underestimated, for his perspective was far ahead of other evangelicals, and it would come to define the very nature of the mission he created.

Townsend understood that the best way to prove the validity of his intentions was to put them into action. He settled in the impoverished rural village of Tetelcingo, Morelos, where he initiated a multifaceted social, scientific, and religious program that set the pattern for WBT-SIL projects to come. Whether intentional or not, with ironic symbolism he parked his camper-trailer between the town's school and the local Catholic church. On the one side his stratagem was designed to supplant Roman Catholicism with a nonsectarian form of evangelicalism, while on the other side he was making an effort to fulfill revolutionary educational objectives. Townsend detailed the outlines of his program in a letter to the US ambassador to Mexico, Josephus Daniels, with whom he developed a long and lasting friendship.[164] He listed no fewer than nineteen separate projects, including whitewashing the insides of houses, planting five hundred trees, introducing dairy cows, and building an irrigation system. On the linguistic front he developed an Aztec (Nahuatl) reading primer, and made plans to launch a Bible translation project. On the whole, Townsend's religious goals were rather modest by most missionary standards. He certainly kept up a steady stream of personal evangelism behind the flurry of other activities that furthered the essential goals of the Mexican Revolution, but in his own words he was "determined not to engage in the propagation of sects but rather to give the simple Bible to people."[165] The casual observer happening upon Tetelcingo in 1935 or 1936 would have seen little indication that a missionary was in town; rather, one would have observed what looked like a rural community service project carried out under the direction of Cárdenas's government.

The most important eyewitness to Townsend's ambitious program of social uplift was President Cárdenas himself. The president's interest was aroused by reading reports from Ambassador Daniels about this intrepid American missionary's activities. Cárdenas paid an unexpected visit to the Townsends on January 20, 1936.[166] An enduring lifelong relationship between the two men ensued. "If before having the pleasure of knowing you, I loved and admired the revolutionary work of Mexico," Townsend wrote to Cárdenas after the president's stopover, "now, upon knowing its highest representative personally I feel more intimately identified with her and more resolved and determined in service."[167] Cárdenas was equally affable in his response. "I wish to congratulate you upon the noble service which you are accomplishing among the Indian towns in connection with your research studies," he wrote in March. Townsend had promised to bring a contingent of young American volunteers to develop the same kinds of projects throughout Mexico. Thus the president added that "I earnestly desire that you may be able to carry out your project of bringing a brigade of university trained young people to engage themselves in the same service as that which you are accomplishing, and to that end, my Administration would give you every aid which might be necessary."[168] Now that Townsend had won the president's admiration, his burgeoning field orga-

164. Josephus Daniels, *Shirt-Sleeve Diplomat: Ambassador to Mexico, 1933–1942* (Chapel Hill: University of North Carolina Press, 1947), 167–68.

165. Cameron Townsend to Daniels, December 18, 1935, TA 1911.

166. Elvira Townsend, *Moody Church News*, June 1936, TA 1983.

167. Cameron Townsend to Cárdenas, January 20, 1936, Archivo General de la Nación, Mexico, Fondo Lázaro Cárdenas, 710.1/1598, quoted in Svelmoe, *New Vision for Missions*, 270.

168. Cárdenas to Cameron Townsend, March 28, 1936, TA 2046 (translation by Calvin Hibbard).

nization, which he was beginning to call the Summer Institute of Linguistics (SIL), had not only gained unfettered access to Mexico but also had the full weight of the government behind its activities.

Perhaps the best way to summarize Cárdenas's assessment of SIL's contribution to Mexico is simply to quote at length from a 1937 letter he sent to Townsend.

> Being convinced of the value of the work which you and your group of North American teachers have been carrying on among the Indian peoples of this country, I extend to you the appreciation of the Government over which I preside, hoping you may continue cooperating with us with the same enthusiasm for the we[l]fare of the Indian races, in which you will have the realisation of having contributed your unselfish endeavor in behalf of these underprivileged classes, being rewarded for the discomforts and hardships which you must encounter frequently in your noble mission, by satisfaction of seeing the people bettered as a result of the great service which you are all rendering.[169]

Townsend and Cárdenas were united in a progressive vision for Mexico's Indians. This shared goal formed the basis for each to realize his separate religious and political aims.

Townsend's relationship with Cárdenas opened the way for him to channel his young Camp Wycliffe graduates into Mexico, where they engaged in language and community development projects coupled with Bible translation. However, Townsend's missionary-linguists did not preach, baptize converts, or found churches under SIL's control.[170] Thus, rather than entering Mexico as a classical faith mission, SIL was conformed by Townsend to Mexico's sociopolitical context. In this pragmatic adaptation to circumstance lie the roots of the WBT-SIL dual organization. Operating abroad under the banner of the Summer Institute of Linguistics conferred upon Townsend's mission the requisite scientific aura required for partnering with governments along secular lines. But with its quasi-secular status, SIL was not very well suited to the task of relating to the organization's evangelical constituency in North America. It was therefore necessary to form a second but parallel organization for the purposes of generating publicity, recruiting personnel, and carrying out essential

---

169. Cárdenas to Cameron Townsend, June 15, 1937, TA 2182 (translation by Calvin Hibbard).

170. Kenneth L. Pike, "Our Own Tongue Wherein We Were Born," *Bible Translator* 10, no. 2 (1959): 15; Cameron Townsend, "Notes on Spiritual Work," April 26, 1948, TA 42641; Cameron Townsend, "Early Years of Wycliffe," pp. 34–36, TA 42636.

administrative functions. From 1934 to 1941, the PMA mostly supplied these services. In 1941 the number of missionary-translators in Mexico rose to nearly one hundred, thus exceeding the administrative capacity of PMA's Philadelphia office.[171] Wycliffe Bible Translators was formed in 1942 to take up the tasks of publicity, recruiting, constituent relations, and forwarding of funds to SIL. In 1942, both WBT and SIL were officially incorporated as separate organizations, but with an overlapping membership, identical leadership, and parallel boards of directors, of which a majority were WBT-SIL insiders.[172] In effect, the two organizations were simply one mission with a twofold character.

The problem of gaining access to Mexico was solved, but this radical new approach to missions created at least four challenges. The first lay in the fact that Townsend was presenting SIL to Mexican authorities as a truly scientific organization and its missionaries as scientists and professional linguists. As the discipline of descriptive linguistics developed apace over the next couple of decades, to refer to SIL as "scientific" would demand far greater commitment to scholarship and research than Townsend had reckoned. In the not too distant future, deploying summer-school-trained amateur linguists, some even lacking college degrees, was not going to impress Mexican academics. In the second place, Bible translation would prove to be far more complex and time consuming than WBT-SIL's founder had assumed. Moreover, the Bible translation strategy itself rested on a strongly held belief that the translated Scriptures were the linchpin in a missionary program that would result in self-replicating and self-governing indigenous churches, and this concept would eventually be challenged from within SIL itself. Hence, establishing a foothold in Mexico and launching a summer linguistics course would prove rather simple by comparison to the actual enormity of the task of translating an ancient Greek text into unwritten indigenous languages. In the third place, after the contours of SIL were shaped to the Mexican context, its viability in places where anticlericalism was less pronounced and the Roman Catholic Church enjoyed greater respect was in question. Was this then a one-off project, or could it be repeated? Fourth, the mission strategy that Townsend developed was almost certain to perplex and annoy conservative evangelicals and fundamentalists in North America, on whom the mission depended for recruits and funds. Asking fundamentalist recruits to drop their missionary identity to work for a revolutionary socialist government did not appear to be a plan designed for success. This was espe-

171. PMA letter to North American constituents on the formation of WBT, July 10, 1942, TA 41526.

172. SIL Articles of Incorporation, August 12, 1942, WSA; WBT Articles of Incorporation, August 13, 1942, TA 41523.

cially true at a time when the fundamentalist-modernist controversies were still reverberating. Moreover, pressing for donations for this novel undertaking, the task given to SIL's sister organization in the United States, the Wycliffe Bible Translators, was fraught with difficulties. Each of these factors as it relates to the expansion and success of the WBT-SIL combination is explored in turn in the following four chapters.

Cameron Townsend pragmatically adapted his missionary program to prevailing sociopolitical contexts in both Guatemala and Mexico, while yet never giving up his overarching religious goals. Struck by the social injustice and inequality that he observed during his first months in Guatemala, he remained committed to the social uplift of Latin America's indigenous peoples. Along the way he framed readership of the Bible in the indigenous language as the key to evangelizing the hearts and reforming the minds of these peoples. His natural capacity for creative destruction—the breaking down of existing patterns of missionary practice to achieve superordinate aims—set him apart from many of his Central American Mission colleagues. When Townsend fell into the company of Howard Dinwiddie and L. L. Legters in 1921, his fate was all but sealed. These dynamic men, inspired with the outsized confidence that their brand of Keswick theology could engender, refashioned traditional patterns of evangelical missionary activity to fit their own vision. Paying little heed to the antithesis between the Social Gospelers and the fundamentalists, Townsend and his colleagues charted a middle course. He then carried this opportunistic approach into Mexico, winning for himself and SIL not only a respected place in a revolutionary and anticlerical Mexico but also the accolades of one of its most revered presidents, Lázaro Cárdenas. In the 1920s and early 1930s, Townsend dared to challenge social, religious, and missionary patterns that had come to be accepted as conventional wisdom, and in doing so he began carving out an entirely new approach to Christian missions that formed the basis for the development of the Summer Institute of Linguistics and the Wycliffe Bible Translators.

CHAPTER 2

The Linguistic Approach

Faith missions were founded to win souls, not to cultivate missionary scholarship. Camp Wycliffe, established in 1934 as the original training arm of the Summer Institute of Linguistics, was therefore conceived in a missionary intellectual milieu that did not give prominence to the life of the mind. Although it was designed for training missionary candidates in linguistics, Camp Wycliffe was structured along pragmatic lines in keeping with the spirit of fundamentalist Bible school endeavors. The fact that it was launched as a rustic summer camp, rather than a full-fledged academic institution, emphasizes this point. Such humble beginnings did not dampen Cameron Townsend's enthusiasm, for he tended to view his fledgling projects through spectacles that magnified their import to an almost preposterous degree. Thus, in typical fashion, he grandiosely billed graduates of his school as "linguists" upon completion of their short course of study. The camp's founder was certainly given to hyperbole, but, as was often the case, his extraordinary claims had an uncanny way of becoming reality. One of the most important steps he took was linking his enterprise with the emerging discipline of American structural linguistics. When he subsequently attracted two exceptionally gifted students, and then sent them off for doctoral studies in linguistics at the University of Michigan, Townsend set his organization upon a course that would carry it far beyond what even he could imagine. In the main, SIL's coming of age as a first-rank institute of applied linguistics is the tale of how a group of faith missionaries overcame the legacy of fundamentalist anti-intellectualism to create a bastion of scholarly accomplishment.

The Anti-Intellectual Tendencies of Fundamentalism

The way in which fundamentalists mounted their defense of the faith had the unfortunate effect of blunting the life of the mind, and this in turn had deleterious effects on many fundamentalist institutions of higher learning. In their polemics with modernists, fundamentalists often took tactical refuge in dogma rather than strategically developing the intellectual resources necessary to meet their foes on an equal footing. As the historian Joel Carpenter fittingly put it, fundamentalists waged battle with "discredited intellectual equipment."[1] Having lost their bid for control of the centers of power within mainline Protestantism, separatist fundamentalists, from the 1930s on, developed their own institutions, many of which neglected academic rigor in favor of simple piety and evangelistic activism. It became fashionable within fundamentalist circles to style oneself in opposition to ivory-towered intellectuals by striking a reactionary and populist pose. A case in point is Lewis Sperry Chafer, founder of Dallas Theological Seminary, who argued that a lack of formal theological education was for him an asset. In 1947, Chafer boasted that "the very fact that I did not study a prescribed course of study in theology made it possible for me to approach the subject with an unprejudiced mind and to be concerned only with what the Bible actually teaches."[2] A heavy emphasis on evangelism over erudition was another impulse fueling anti-intellectualist sentiments. Honoring the demands of donors and acting upon his own proclivities, the newly installed president of Wheaton College, V. Raymond Edman, dismissed the evangelical philosopher Gordon Clark in 1943. Following his departure, Clark's requisite and demanding courses on the history of philosophy and Christian apologetics were dropped in favor of courses on Bible memorization and evangelism.[3] Edman's move reflected a larger pattern prevailing at the college in the mid-twentieth century. In a 1994 doctoral dissertation, Michael Hamilton concluded that Wheaton probably had the most stringent academic acceptance criteria among Christian colleges at midcentury, and therefore could boast of a student body representing the cream of the crop of young evangelicals. On the other side of the coin, Hamilton uncovered evidence of Wheaton's trustees—fearing the loss of spiritual vigor if the faculty became too intellectually orientated—insisting that students should not so much be challenged to engage in critical thinking as fed a steady

1. Joel A. Carpenter, "From Fundamentalism to the New Evangelical Coalition," in *Evangelicalism and Modern America*, ed. George Marsden (Grand Rapids: Eerdmans, 1984), 4.

2. Quoted in C. F. Lincoln, "Biographical Sketch of the Author," in Lewis Sperry Chafer, *Systematic Theology*, 8 vols. (Dallas: Dallas Seminary Press, 1947), 8:5–6, further quoted in Mark A. Noll, *The Scandal of the Evangelical Mind* (Grand Rapids: Eerdmans, 1994), 128.

3. Carl F. H. Henry, *Confessions of a Theologian: An Autobiography* (Waco: Word, 1986), 66–67.

diet of fundamentalist doctrine coupled with evangelistic activism. The result obtained by this ethos, Hamilton pointed out, was an odd situation where a good many students were quite possibly more academically capable than were a number of their professors.[4] The populist reaction to theological liberalism and the accent on activism within fundamentalism produced nothing less than an intellectual rout from which later evangelicals struggled to recover. Thus, by the 1930s, fundamentalists were for the most part served by a host of Bible institutes and Bible schools, many of which were not of the academic caliber of Catholic universities and mainline Protestant seminaries, let alone America's better secular universities.

The decline of academic achievement and scholarly output within the fundamentalist subculture was a major impulse behind the formation of Fuller Seminary in 1947. The well-known pastor of Boston's Park Street Church, Harold J. Ockenga, who possessed a PhD in philosophy from the University of Pittsburgh, was the seminary's first president. Financial backing for the venture came from the popular radio evangelist Charles Fuller. Perhaps more than any other scholar attracted to the seminary, it was Carl F. H. Henry who symbolized the mind-set of the Fuller neo-evangelicals. In his *Remaking the Modern Mind* (1946), Henry went so far as to predict the collapse of Western civilization if evangelical Protestants failed to shore up the rotting pillars of the Judeo-Christian intellectual tradition. To accomplish their objectives, Fuller's neo-evangelical scholars felt it necessary to distance themselves from the militant and separatist tendencies of the more strident fundamentalists. Toward this end Henry delivered a polemic against what he saw as an ingrown and bellicose fundamentalism in his *Uneasy Conscience of Modern Fundamentalism* (1947).[5] Henry was not alone in his assessment of the fundamentalist movement. In 1959, the Fuller Seminary professor and neo-evangelical scholar Edward J. Carnell disparaged fundamentalism as "orthodoxy gone cultic."[6] The founders and faculty of Fuller had high hopes that the seminary would be the rampart from which a reformation of evangelical theology could be launched and, if providence favored, evangelicalism restored to its former preeminence in American culture.

The Fuller project was a perilous venture, and it initially foundered before regaining its equilibrium as an unapologetic neo-evangelical institution. In the

4. Michael S. Hamilton, "The Fundamentalist Harvard: Wheaton College and the Continuing Vitality of American Evangelicalism, 1919–1965" (PhD diss., University of Notre Dame, 1994), 105–15, 129–79.

5. Carl F. H. Henry, *Remaking the Modern Mind* (Grand Rapids: Eerdmans, 1946); Carl F. H. Henry, *The Uneasy Conscience of Modern Fundamentalism* (Grand Rapids: Eerdmans, 1947).

6. Edward J. Carnell, *The Case for Orthodox Theology* (Philadelphia: Westminster, 1959), 113.

late 1950s and early 1960s, the seminary experienced recurring convulsions when it was perceived by some fundamentalist leaders outside the seminary and by traditionalists on the faculty that the progressives were softening their position on scriptural inerrancy, discarding evidentialist apologetics, and straying from premillennial eschatology. The strains produced by these debates, coupled with the failure to achieve the status some of the faculty sought in the larger world of theological scholarship, proved costly. Wracked by dissension, the faculty split, with the traditionalists departing. Within the progressive group, two faculty experienced mental collapse. In the words of his biographer, George Eldon Ladd's alcoholism eventually led to "a process of emotional, physical, and spiritual disintegration."[7] Carnell died of an overdose.[8] Publicity surrounding the theological debates within the seminary also had adverse consequences for Charles Fuller's radio ministry, as one fundamentalist donor after another dropped his financial support.[9] As the case of Fuller Seminary clearly demonstrates, attempts by evangelical scholars to chart a viable path toward engagement with mainline Protestantism and to reconstruct evangelical theology and apologetics were not free from potentially debilitating effects.

The majority of fundamentalists were far more interested in evangelism than cultivating erudition. Reflection and scholarship were often considered of little help, and perhaps even a hindrance, to the practical aims of many fundamentalists. Arguably, the fundamentalism of the 1930s and 1940s would seem therefore to be poor soil for a project like Camp Wycliffe to become more than a summer training camp in the tradition of the Bible school movement. Townsend, however, broke more than a few rules in the fundamentalist playbook, thereby setting off a chain reaction that would transform Camp Wycliffe into a world-class institute of applied linguistics.

Kenneth L. Pike and Eugene A. Nida

Kenneth L. Pike and Eugene A. Nida were Townsend's two most outstanding students and the two figures largely responsible for establishing SIL's academic foundation. Pike and Nida first appeared at Camp Wycliffe in 1935 and 1936, respectively. For prospective faith missionaries of that period, they possessed

7. John D'Elia, *A Place at the Table: George Eldon Ladd and the Rehabilitation of Evangelical Scholarship* (New York: Oxford University Press, 2008), 149.

8. Rudolph Nelson, *The Making and Unmaking of an Evangelical Mind: The Case of Edward Carnell* (New York: Cambridge University Press, 1987), 117–21.

9. George M. Marsden, *Reforming Fundamentalism: Fuller Seminary and the New Evangelicalism* (Grand Rapids: Eerdmans, 1987), 220–28.

above-average academic qualifications, and both quickly demonstrated an outstanding aptitude for linguistic analysis. Had Townsend not stumbled upon these two precocious young men and, most importantly, had he not encouraged them to pursue advanced studies at the University of Michigan's Linguistic Institute in the early years of their missionary careers, it is doubtful whether SIL would ever have become a respected academic institution. This was especially true of Pike, for his contributions to SIL's development would overshadow those of his colleague, since Nida resigned in 1953.[10] With these two budding scholars joining his venture, Townsend was on the cusp of opening up entirely new vistas for young fundamentalists with an urge to use their minds in missionary service.

Kenneth Pike came of age in an evangelical home and attended a Congregational church in Woodstock, Connecticut, with his family.[11] In a number of ways, Pike was an unlikely missionary candidate, and his career as a missionary nearly ended before it began. In 1928, at the age of eighteen, he promised God that if his gravely-ill father recovered he would go into the ministry. Keeping his vow, he applied to the China Inland Mission (CIM) in December 1932, one semester before his 1933 graduation from the fundamentalist Gordon College of Theology and Missions in Boston. His future with CIM ended summarily when he was rejected during the mission's orientation process because, as Pike put it, they were "afraid that my nervous hulk would crack."[12] Veteran CIM missionaries were sure that this skinny and anxious youngster would never survive on the mission field. During his language examinations, it was also noted that he struggled excessively with the pronunciation of Mandarin Chinese. Dejected but still eager for Christian service, Pike returned to Gordon College for a graduate course in Greek, and it was during his second sojourn there that he learned of Camp Wycliffe.[13] The next summer the inhibited young man hitchhiked to Arkansas for the 1935 session, reasoning that the fifteen-hundred-mile trip would provide opportunities for "social training."[14] When the gruff-mannered L. L. Legters laid eyes on the rail-thin Pike perched in a tree, he purportedly grumbled to himself, "Oh Lord, why didn't you send us something decent?"[15]

---

10. Nida's resignation is covered in chapter 4.

11. Eunice V. Pike, *Ken Pike: Scholar and Christian* (Dallas: Summer Institute of Linguistics, 1981), 7.

12. Kenneth L. Pike, Hefley interview, c. 1970, p. 1, TA 43472.

13. Eunice V. Pike, *Ken Pike*, 7–13; Kenneth L. Pike to Cameron Townsend, May 2, 1935, TA 1946; Kenneth L. Pike to Sam Fisk, May 28, 1935, TA 1942.

14. Kenneth L. Pike to Calvin Hibbard, "Re: Your Question regarding Sam Fisk," December 19, 1986, TA 39527.

15. Kenneth L. Pike, Hefley interview, c. 1970, p. 5, TA 43472.

Townsend thought otherwise. Not for the last time would WBT-SIL's founder show contempt for judging missionary candidates by prevailing faith mission standards that emphasized physical hardiness, psychological steadiness, and spiritual ardor.

Eugene Nida was raised in an Oklahoma City Methodist church where he later professed to have had "the most meaningful experience of my life." On back-to-back Sundays, two visiting evangelists preached on the thirteenth chapter of Revelation from opposite perspectives. The perplexed youth urged his father to assess these contradictory interpretations of the Bible. Nida recounted his father saying that "in life it is even more important to be able to doubt than to believe, because too many people love the unbelievable."[16] He seems to have taken this lesson to heart, for it was his willingness to challenge conventional patterns of thought that would later prove invaluable to his theoretical insights on Bible translation. In 1936 he graduated *summa cum laude* from the University of California at Los Angeles (UCLA), where he majored in Greek and minored in foreign languages and the sciences.[17] At Camp Wycliffe it was immediately apparent that Nida was head and shoulders above his fellow classmates, and, although only a student, Townsend placed him on the teaching staff before the 1936 session had concluded.[18] It was not long before his genius for linguistics was again on display. Soon after he arrived in Mexico to take up translation work among the indigenous Tarahumara, he began to recognize subtle dialectal differences in the language area and he also produced a rather sophisticated morphological analysis. These linguistic insights were outstanding accomplishments after such a brief contact with the language.[19] The young Eugene Nida exhibited the qualities of a natural-born scholar, and he could presumably look forward to a successful career as a missionary linguist and Bible translator.

Unfortunately, Nida's physical constitution was not on par with his mental powers, and as a result he failed spectacularly as a pioneering missionary. Once in Mexico, his rapid progress in analyzing the Tarahumara language was matched by an almost equally swift decline in the state of his health. On December 6, 1936, the weary young man wrote to Townsend requesting leave to have a broken tooth treated in Chihuahua City, and he gloomily remarked that "this

16. Eugene A. Nida, *Fascinated by Languages* (Philadelphia: John Benjamins, 2003), 1.

17. Eugene A. Nida, "My Pilgrimage in Mission," *International Bulletin of Missionary Research* 12, no. 2 (April 1988): 62–65.

18. Philip C. Stine, *Let the Word Be Written: The Lasting Influence of Eugene A. Nida* (Atlanta: Society of Biblical Literature, 2004), 27–28.

19. Nida to Cameron Townsend, October 22, 1936, TA 2017; November 5, 1936, TA 2012; November 13, 1936, TA 2010; Nida to Cameron Townsend, November 25, 1936, TA 2004.

is surely one hard place to work."[20] His next letter, of December 19, arrived not from Mexico but from Garden City, California, where Nida reported that he was "getting repaired." Much to Townsend's dismay, Nida had perfunctorily packed up, left Mexico, and returned to his parents' home. A medical examination revealed that he was suffering from the symptoms of altitude sickness, as well as from a number of other undisclosed ailments.[21] Nida returned to Mexico and joined up with Pike in early 1937, but within a few short weeks he abandoned his colleague and returned to California; his days as a field translator were finished.

Yet it was evident to Townsend that Nida's bodily weakness was more than compensated for by his outstanding cerebral abilities. Therefore, when it became obvious that he would not be returning to Mexico, Townsend, although disappointed, determined that this young man's formidable intellect would not be lost to the cause of Bible translation. He arranged for Nida to work with the American Bible Society (ABS) on a part-time basis, and for him to pursue doctoral studies while continuing to teach each summer at Camp Wycliffe. The actual implementation of this partnership was not consummated until Nida completed his doctoral studies in linguistics and anthropology at the University of Michigan in 1943. Between 1937 and 1953, Nida continued to serve WBT-SIL in public relations work, teaching at Camp Wycliffe, and consulting on Bible translation projects. In addition, he served on the organization's board of directors from 1942 to 1953.[22] Rather than dismissing Nida as simply another regrettable missionary casualty, Townsend salvaged the young man's missionary career, and in doing so rescued for Bible translation what would become one of its foremost scholars, for it was Nida's destiny to revolutionize Bible translation theory.

Kenneth Pike is perhaps the most outstanding example of the type of fundamentalist candidate that Camp Wycliffe and SIL attracted and then afforded the opportunity to grow academically and intellectually. "I was a fire-eater," he recalled in a 1970s interview, "and unless the Holy Spirit tames me I am still a Son of Thunder that bungles, boggles and blows everything and stamps on everybody without mercy." In the same interview, he related that "[J. Gresham] Machen was right down my line," adding that had he not entered missionary work, he might have become like the ardent fundamentalist "Carl McIntire[,] slamming home to try to do something for God."[23] These very qualities were on

---

20. Nida to Cameron Townsend, December 6, 1936, TA 1999.

21. Nida to Cameron Townsend, December 19 1936, TA 1997.

22. Cameron Townsend to Kenneth L. Pike, April 7, 1937, TA 2153; Nida to PMA, August 19, 1937, TA 2230; Cameron Townsend to Eric M. North, secretary, ABS, September 15, 1937, TA 2094; Nida, "My Pilgrimage in Mission," 62–65; North to Nida, December 6, 1943, TA 3794.

23. Kenneth L. Pike, Hefley interview, c. 1970, p. 6, TA 43472.

display in a long and telling 1937 letter to Townsend, in which he pilloried Nida for his digressions into pure scientific research that, in his opinion, "made not a hoop nor holler of difference . . . in translation." Pike also took umbrage at his colleague's lack of pioneering missionary fortitude, speculating that he was a hypochondriac manifesting unspiritual fears of death. The "territory of the devil staked a claim," Pike thundered, "and has left a boy in bondage." Like himself, Nida should be "ready to meet the Lord to-morrow . . . with [his] boots on." By way of conclusion, he insisted that Nida should "forget his health, and come to live or die, sink or swim," and that he must "forget his science and get to translation."[24] In the mid-1930s, Pike's mind housed a mixed bag of scholarly potential, anti-intellectualism, and missionary ardor. As will become evident, Pike was more or less characteristic of the candidates attracted to Camp Wycliffe in the 1930s and 1940s, since many of them bore the marks of fundamentalism with its undertow of anti-intellectualism and passionate missionary idealism.

If future Bible translators arrived at the summer school with practical training uppermost in their minds, sooner or later a good number of them found the academic atmosphere of Camp Wycliffe intellectually stimulating. Pike once again is an excellent example. Even as he was berating Nida, he was beginning to experience a scholarly awakening. Pike later recalled that he found the study of phonetics "extremely exciting."[25] His earlier failure to master the subtle differences of Chinese pronunciation set the stage for an electrifying moment of illumination when he discovered during classes on phonetics that it was not so mysterious after all. There was a method for accurately reproducing the seemingly impossible jumble of sounds. At the end of the 1935 summer session of Camp Wycliffe, he traveled to Mexico, where he began an analysis of the Mixteco language in both Mexico City and the state of Oaxaca. Returning to Mexico in 1936, he settled in the village of San Miguel el Grande, where he carried out his Bible translation project. By 1937, he was exhausting his meager financial resources acquiring "every book on phonetics" that was available through a Mexico City bookstore.[26] Pike could also be found reading the eminent linguist Leonard Bloomfield's recently published *Language* (1933), after Nida had recommended it to him. This work was quickly becoming recognized as the period's definitive work on descriptive linguistics. Pike remarked to his sister Eunice in April of 1937 that his reading of that "plaguey Bloomfield" was slowing his analysis of Mixtec. Although he had read parts of *Language* four times without

24. Kenneth L. Pike to Cameron Townsend, March 29, 1937, pp. 5–10, PSC.

25. Kenneth L. Pike, Hefley interview, c. 1970, p. 14, TA 43472.

26. Kenneth L. Pike, "An Autobiographical Note on Phonetics," in *Towards a History of Phonetics*, ed. David Abercrombie, R. E. Asher, and Eugénie J. A. Henderson (Edinburgh: Edinburgh University Press, 1981), 182.

being able to comprehend it fully, he still thought of it as a "lovely companion."[27] Attending Camp Wycliffe and this first foray into field linguistics proved to be intellectually transformative experiences for the young Kenneth Pike.

Intending to make the most of Pike's abilities, Townsend urged him to write a book on phonetics in the fall of 1936. Pike later recalled that he was "aghast" at the proposition, since he considered himself to possess a "near-zero background" in linguistics.[28] Only after a broken leg left him immobilized in Mexico did he decide to make the best of the situation by working on the manuscript. Townsend sent a draft of the work to Edward Sapir, who offered an optimistic appraisal and suggested that this promising student pursue advanced studies at the University of Michigan's Linguistic Institute. Townsend readily agreed to the proposal. In the spring of 1937, Pike made his way to Michigan, where he experienced his first foray into the world of postgraduate scholarship, and, as he later put it, "I never recovered."[29] At the University of Michigan he pursued doctoral studies each summer under the supervision of Charles Fries, who was both the director of the Linguistic Institute and a professor at the university, and in the fall of 1941 he successfully defended his dissertation on phonetics.[30] Pike's academic achievement and intellectual awakening should not be underestimated. He had accomplished what few conservative evangelicals at the time could have imagined was possible within the confines of a faith mission, and he charted the way for many who followed in his footsteps in the coming decades in SIL.

Completing his doctorate and establishing a foothold in academia were only the beginnings of Pike's university career. In 1942 he was appointed part-time research associate in the English Language Institute at the University of Michigan, and for the academic year of 1945–1946 he was awarded a postdoctoral fellowship. Then, in 1948, he received an associate professorship, serving one semester each year at the university with the rest of his time dedicated to SIL work. In 1955 he was promoted to a full professorship at Michigan on the same rotational basis. Pike's long tenure with the University of Michigan stood him and SIL in good stead, for it ensured his ongoing intellectual development while also helping to bolster SIL's academic credibility.

Pike's career in secular academia was marked by some rare achievements for an evangelical. In the first place, as is discussed at length below, Pike became

27. Kenneth L. Pike to Eunice Pike, April 12, 1937, p. 2, PSC.

28. Kenneth L. Pike, Hefley interview, c. 1970, p. 1, TA 43473.

29. Kenneth L. Pike, "Autobiographical Note," 182.

30. Kenneth L. Pike, "A Reconstruction of Phonetic Theory" (PhD diss., University of Michigan, 1941), later published as *Phonetics: A Critical Analysis of Phonetic Theory and a Technic for the Practical Description of Sounds* (Ann Arbor: University of Michigan, 1943).

a leading figure within American structural linguistics, and his "tagmemic" theory was an original and daring contribution to the discipline of linguistics. A measure of his scholarly status was his election as president of the Linguistic Society of America in 1961, taking up a position that had been filled by such luminaries as Bloomfield and Sapir. In 1974 he was awarded a named professorship, the Charles C. Fries Professorship in Linguistics at the University of Michigan, which he held until his retirement in 1979, and he served as director of the English Language Institute at the University of Michigan from 1975 to 1977. Pike also collected a string of honorary doctorates along the way. In 1973 the University of Chicago bestowed on him this mark of distinction, and he was awarded the Docteur Honoris Causa, L'Université René Descartes, at the Sorbonne, Paris, in 1978.[31] This synopsis could be lengthened considerably, but even this abbreviated account is ample evidence that Pike lived up to his own ideals and proved that evangelicals could pursue productive academic relationships outside the confines of their religious subculture.

Pike's journey from a failed CIM candidate to an accomplished linguistic scholar illustrates the sort of intellectual transformation that Townsend's approach to Bible translation unwittingly set in motion. That Townsend had the foresight to salvage Pike's and Nida's careers, and then encourage them to develop their minds in the service of Bible translation, is remarkable within the context of faith missions. At a time when the prospects for academic excellence and intellectual striving were few within the subculture of conservative evangelicalism, SIL was opening up opportunities for scholarly achievement. The radical nature of the venture did not, however, always develop smoothly. As had Pike, many recruits came to WBT-SIL bearing the marks of fundamentalism and missionary idealism. Thus they would sometimes experience deep doubts and considerable inner tension as Camp Wycliffe and SIL became more academically orientated and even somewhat secularized. Likewise, Townsend was at times apprehensive with where Pike and Nida wished to take his nascent organization. Yet, by advancing these men's scholarly careers, Townsend had already let the proverbial genie out of the bottle, for they pursued a course of action that was to challenge the prevailing fundamentalist proclivity to shun scholarship in favor of heartfelt evangelistic action.

31. Thomas N. Headland, "A Tribute to the Life of Kenneth L. Pike: A Perspective from One of His Students," in *Language and Life: Essays in Memory of Kenneth L. Pike*, ed. Mary Ruth Wise, Thomas N. Headland, and Ruth M. Brend (Arlington: University of Texas at Arlington and SIL International, 2003), 11–12; Eunice V. Pike, *Ken Pike*, 181–82.

Heart and Mind?—the Struggle for Balance

Flush with scholarly passion and youthful enthusiasm, Kenneth Pike and Eugene Nida pressed their notions of academic rigor at the 1937 session of Camp Wycliffe. This first attempt to boost the camp's academic standing swiftly met with a backlash from the student body. On September 14, Townsend informed his wife Elvira that Nida had given a "rather hard exam" resulting in "plenty of indignation at the table this noon."[32] The situation continued to deteriorate. A few days later he reported that two students had "decided to quit and several had decided not to recommend the camp to their friends."[33] Townsend wrote Legters that "over half the students were so discouraged they did not know what to do." This impending disaster was partly the result of Nida's instituting a grading system based on college standards, rather than on the less rigorous Bible school standards most of the students were accustomed to. When Pike and Nida criticized students who did not "have the proper background to enable them to keep up," it only served to fan the flames of hostility.[34] To quell the agitation, Townsend delivered two devotionals and arranged for two convocations so that students could air their grievances. He also convinced these two up-and-coming scholars to cool their academic ardor, thus staving off disaster, but this reverse did not dampen Pike and Nida's ambitions to raise the academic qualifications of applicants.[35]

If academic standards were set too high, then Townsend's vision of deploying hundreds of missionary-translators would grind to a halt. He therefore argued against moves to upgrade the educational requirements of Camp Wycliffe applicants. During the 1937 crisis, Townsend remarked to Legters that "I feel that it is very important in the future for all of us to take the stand that the men and women whom God sends here should be helped, whether we feel that they are properly gifted or not."[36] Two years later, the debate over student qualifications remained unsettled, and Townsend again weighed in. "Personally, I would rather accept five failures," he declared to an SIL translator in January 1939, "than accept the responsibility of denying God's Word to a single tribe on account of standards which God has laughed at and utterly disregarded time and again."[37] Townsend believed the evidence was on his side, and he pointed to a number of minimally educated SIL missionaries who were apparently en-

32. Cameron Townsend to Elvira Townsend, September 14, 1937, TA 2095.
33. Cameron Townsend to Elvira Townsend, September 18, 1937, TA 2092.
34. Cameron Townsend to Legters, September 20, 1937, TA 2089.
35. Cameron Townsend to Elvira Townsend, September 18, 1937, TA 2092.
36. Cameron Townsend to Legters, September 20, 1937, TA 2089.
37. Cameron Townsend to Max Lathrop, January 27, 1939, p. 4, TA 2478.

joying success in their Bible translation projects.[38] The issue of education prerequisites was finally resolved by permitting applicants possessing a minimum of a high school diploma and some Bible school credits to attend courses, while insisting upon adequate academic performance during summer studies to gain acceptance by SIL as a missionary-translator.[39]

Townsend worried too that SIL might lose its missionary focus if the organization was taken too far down the scholarly path. "I am happy over my 50 years diploma-less missionary effort," he wrote in a 1967 essay. Taking his own experience as an example, he argued that it was better to delay college education in order to obtain some practical missionary experience. By pursuing a degree before beginning one's missionary career, Townsend warned, "You run the risk of losing your missionary vision and never going."[40] In keeping with this perspective, he even refused honorary doctorates from Wheaton College and the Bible Institute of Los Angeles.[41] Townsend was not opposed to advanced education; in fact, he championed the idea, but only so long as garnering credentials did not slow the output of translated New Testaments or cause candidates to lose their missionary zeal.

With something of a *modus vivendi* between Townsend and his two wunderkinder providing a middle path between laxity and rigor, Camp Wycliffe proved itself a roaring success. By 1940 concerns over low attendance were replaced by worries over how to house an enlarged student body.[42] To accommodate the growing number of students, the 1940 session was moved to facilities on the campus of John Brown University in Siloam Springs, Arkansas. Camp Wycliffe had enrolled 174 students since its inception in 1934. With 32 of these students having returned for one or more sessions, a total of 142 individuals—78 women and 64 men—had received linguistic training at Camp Wycliffe by 1941.[43] The large number of women testifies to the willingness of faith missions to mobilize and deploy single women under the banner of urgency, and it demonstrates that women were drawn to missions knowing that it afforded them greater opportunities for equal service with men than they would have in many conservative churches in North

38. Cameron Townsend to Lathrop, January 27, 1939, pp. 3–4, TA 2478.

39. Nyman to Georgia May Loper, October 17, 1945, p. 2, TA 4113.

40. Cameron Townsend, "How Much Education Do You Need?," 1967, pp. 2–3, TA 42696.

41. Sam H. Sutherland, dean, BIOLA, to Cameron Townsend, June 16, 1952, TA 7588; Cameron Townsend to V. Raymond Edman, president, Wheaton College, June 2, 1952, TA 50888; Cameron Townsend to Sutherland, June 30, 1952, TA 43591.

42. Legters to Cameron Townsend, April 4, 1940, pp. 1–2, TA 2657.

43. "Detailed Analysis of Information regarding Students of Camp Wycliffe," 1941, TA 43046.

America.[44] Townsend's vision of nonsectarian service was patently evident in the diverse denominational makeup of the students attending the first eight years of Camp Wycliffe. Presbyterians topped the list with 40 students, followed by Baptists with 32. The Christian and Missionary Alliance was a distant third, represented by 9 students. Completing the list were Methodists, Bible Presbyterians, Assemblies of God, Disciples of Christ, Mennonites, United Presbyterians, Church of the Brethren, Plymouth Brethren, Congregationalists, Swedish Covenant, United Brethren, Southern Presbyterians, Four-Square Gospel, Mission Covenant, and Friends. Nida was sufficiently impressed with the Presbyterian students, who came from a denominational tradition of academic achievement, to single them out by remarking that they were "well trained and well qualified." However, only a minority of the Presbyterian students joined SIL, since most of them were already commissioned to serve with the Presbyterian Board, USA. The geographic spread was of equal breadth, with 59 from the East Coast, 43 from the Midwest, 40 from the West Coast, and 23 from the South.[45] The rapid growth and wide attraction of Camp Wycliffe suggest that a wide variety of mission boards were eager to upgrade their candidates' linguistic skills. Townsend's move to sell science in the service of faith was timely, for he was helping to create a trend while at the same time riding it to success.

Pike and Nida had eased off on their demands at Camp Wycliffe, but they still managed to keep the pressure on translators serving in Mexico.[46] Thus, students who took up service with SIL were expected to make regular contributions to the discipline of linguistics. Pike and Nida were not alone in stressing academic output. Richard Pittman, a Methodist of scholarly demeanor who took over Townsend's work in Tetelcingo during the late 1940s, and then later became the Mexico director of SIL, was another.[47] Pittman, like Pike, recognized from his experience in Mexico that for SIL to maintain its integrity in the eyes of Mexican officials and educators it would have to produce more than translated Bibles. "Prepare to publish," Pittman challenged his colleagues in 1942. "By that," he specified, "I am not thinking primarily of our Scripture publications, but scientific publications." Pittman did not think it "too high a standard" to expect each translator to produce during the course of a Bible

44. Dana L. Robert, *American Women in Mission: A Social History of Their Thought and Practice* (Macon, GA: Mercer University Press, 1996), 200–205, 253–54.

45. "Detailed Analysis of Information," TA 43046; Nida to Cameron Townsend, July 10, 1943, TA 3564; Nida to WCT, February 11, 1944, TA 3843.

46. The establishment of SIL in Mexico is detailed in chapter 1.

47. Robert Pittman (son of Richard S. Pittman), email to author, subject: early life of Richard Pittman, July 3, 2011.

translation project a "creditable, if not exhaustive, grammar, dictionary, [and a] book of texts."[48] Later that same year at the WBT-SIL founding conference, in keeping with SIL's claim to be fielding qualified linguists, delegates voted to make it obligatory for translators to submit a "linguistic or ethnological article in form for publication" at least once every six months.[49] This was an ambitious goal, and in hindsight it proved impossible to achieve, since scholarly pursuits had to compete with most SIL translators' preferred activity of Bible translation. Yet, by setting the bar high, SIL demonstrated that it intended to live up to its billing as a scientific institution.

Two other transformational events in 1942 helped to propel Camp Wycliffe and SIL in a more scholarly direction. First, Townsend turned the presidency of SIL over to Pike, thus giving Pike full charge of SIL's academic activities. Second, Camp Wycliffe broke decidedly with its backwater roots by partnering with the University of Oklahoma at Norman. This latter move significantly enhanced the organization's academic credibility, but it was not realized without complications. Pike and Nida's encounter with student unrest in 1937 was not their last. So long as Camp Wycliffe continued in its rustic Arkansas setting, it remained insulated from the wider arena of university learning save for the influence of the more scholastically minded faculty such as Pike, Nida, and Pittman. Once Camp Wycliffe formally engaged with a secular university, fundamentalist tendencies among faculty and students, such as separatism and anti-intellectualism, were put to the test.

In the early 1940s, Della Brunstetter, a French-language instructor at the University of Oklahoma, attended Camp Wycliffe. It was her hope that the missionary-linguists there could help her to untangle the complexities of Cherokee phonology and to unlock the secrets of the language's intricate tonal system. Brunstetter was impressed with Camp Wycliffe, and she initiated a campaign to have the summer school transferred to the University of Oklahoma. Nida commenced what proved to be successful negotiations, and the camp was moved to Norman for the 1942 session.[50] With its keen interest in American Indian languages, the faculty of the university's Department of Modern Languages unanimously approved the partnership.[51] R. T. House, a professor at the

48. Richard S. Pittman to Mexico branch of SIL, February 18, 1942, TA 903353.

49. "Summary of the Minutes of the Annual Meeting of the Summer Institute of Linguistics, 1942," September 5–18, 1942, p. 1, TA 40250.

50. "Memo of Discussion between Pike and Nida," February 21–28, 1942, TA 43039; Cameron Townsend, Hefley interview, re: "Invitation to the Campus of U. of Oklahoma," c. 1970, TA 42966.

51. Gustavo Mueller to Brunstetter, October 5, 1941, UOA, record group 3, Presidential Papers, Joseph A. Brandt, box 7, folder Linguistic Institute; Fritz Frauchinger to Joseph A. Brandt, October 8, 1941, UOA, record group 3, Presidential Papers, Joseph A. Brandt, box 7, folder Linguistic

university, captured the prevailing sentiment of the faculty when he declared that the "Institute [SIL] is in the charge of men who rank with the best equipped anywhere, and are developing instructional methods of remarkable effectiveness."[52] An examination of the institute's 1941 prospectus illustrates in part why the university faculty was keen to join hands with SIL. The curriculum was much improved over that of the mid-1930s, and it now sported an expanded number of courses exhibiting greater sophistication, including second-year seminars for advanced students and a course in anthropology. These improvements were a direct result of Pike's and Nida's graduate studies and university relationships, for the courses were designed along the same lines as those offered at the University of Michigan's Linguistic Institute. In fact, what was on offer at Camp Wycliffe was perhaps even more extensive than what was presented at Michigan. Not only was Camp Wycliffe's course of study longer by 50 percent (twelve rather than eight weeks), but it also combined theory with practice. The more theoretical "General Linguistics" course was rounded out with "Field Problems" and "Translation Problems" practicums. This ensured that students could actually apply what they learned in a real-life setting.[53] By the time of the university partnership, the camp's curriculum was demanding and thorough enough to gain accreditation by the university.[54] In Mexico the state made common cause with SIL; at the University of Oklahoma, another secular institution was affiliating with SIL for the quality of service it could provide.[55]

Judged by faith mission standards, where educational attainment was not typically counted as a major factor in a candidate's qualification, the academic credentials of many students arriving at Camp Wycliffe were above average.[56]

Institute; R. T. House to Board of Regents, October 9, 1941, UOA, record group 3, Presidential Papers, Joseph A. Brandt, box 7, folder Linguistic Institute; Ellsworth Collings to Joseph A. Brandt, October 13, 1941, UOA, record group 3, Presidential Papers, Joseph A. Brandt, box 7, folder Linguistic Institute; Joseph A. Brandt to Board of Regents, October 14, 1941, UOA, record group 3, Presidential Papers, Joseph A. Brandt, box 7, folder Linguistic Institute.

52. R. T. House, "Memo," October 9, 1941, UOA, record group 3, Presidential Papers, Joseph A. Brandt, box 7, folder Linguistic Institute.

53. Course Brochure and Syllabus: "*The Summer Institute of Linguistics*—Camp Wycliffe, June 12 to September 4, 1941," Sulphur Springs, Arkansas (1941), 7–8, TA 42582; Cameron Townsend to J. K. M. Kimber, September 3, 1941, TA 2733.

54. Brunstetter to Brandt, "Faculty Report," December 16, 1941, UOA, record group 3, Presidential Papers, Joseph A. Brandt, box 7, folder Linguistic Institute.

55. SIL's work in Mexico is examined in chapter 1.

56. Joel A. Carpenter, "Propagating the Faith Once Delivered," in *Earthen Vessels: American Evangelicals and Foreign Missions, 1880–1980*, ed. Joel A. Carpenter and Wilbert R. Shenk (Grand Rapids: Eerdmans, 1990), 102–4; Klaus Fiedler, *The Story of Faith Missions: From Hudson Taylor to Present Day Africa* (Irvine, CA: Regnum, 1994), 396–97.

Analysis of the 142 students who had attended Camp Wycliffe between 1934 and 1941 reveals that 85 had completed a bachelor's degree, 25 had a seminary degree, and 9 had arrived with graduate degrees. Not surprisingly, 91 possessed some Bible school training, with 55 having graduated from a Bible college course of two to four years.[57] These statistics are quite remarkable when compared to the whole of the American population: in 1940, only about one in four had graduated from high school and a mere one in twenty had completed college.[58] Camp Wycliffe was drawing students who might have otherwise entered middle-class, white-collar careers in business and education had they not chosen Christian missions as a vocation. The quality of students coming to Camp Wycliffe allowed for Pike and Nida gradually to advance their designs for upgrading the quality of instruction. Thus, by the mid-1940s, the camp had garnered something of a reputation for its demanding coursework. SIL missionary-translator Betty Adams recalled that she was considering Camp Wycliffe in 1946, but was concerned because some recent camp alumni at Bible Institute of Los Angeles "had brought such gory tales back to school about Camp Wycliffe and its stiff curriculum that I never really wanted to go, though I felt that I should." Only at the urging of a Wycliffe board member did Adams finally apply.[59] Camp Wycliffe was in the vanguard of a movement to deploy better-educated evangelical missionaries, a movement that would eventuate in the establishment of institutions such as Fuller's School of World Mission and Ralph Winter's US Center for World Mission.

The partnership with the university enhanced SIL's academic credibility, but the move also incited fears that the school was in danger of sliding down the all-too-familiar slippery slope toward liberalism. Recent religious history worked against the University of Oklahoma and SIL alliance, since Camp Wycliffe drew many of its students from fundamentalist and conservative evangelical backgrounds. By the mid-1940s, Camp Wycliffe was serving over thirty mission boards and denominations, many of them quite conservative, such as the Africa Inland Mission, the China Inland Mission, the Sudan Interior Mission, the Christian and Missionary Alliance, the South American Indian Mission, and the Conservative Baptist Foreign Mission Society.[60] Marking off boundaries

57. "Detailed Analysis of Information," p. 2, TA 43046.

58. Richard Polenberg, *One Nation Indivisible: Class, Race, and Ethnicity in the United States Since 1938* (New York: Viking, 1980), 20.

59. Quoted in Ethel Emily Wallis, *Lengthened Cords: How Dawson Trotman—Founder of the Navigators—Also Helped Extend the World-Wide Outreach of the Wycliffe Bible Translators* (Glendale, CA: Wycliffe Bible Translators, 1958), 98.

60. "Detailed Analysis of Information," p. 5, TA 43046; Howard Van Dyck, staff secretary, Christian and Missionary Alliance, to Nyman, December 29, 1948, TA 5087; Benjamin F. Elson

against religious liberalism and modernism came naturally to many of these faith missions. Separatist tendencies therefore functioned as an impediment to SIL's taking a more moderate stance. For students from other faith missions, and even a good number of the camp's SIL faculty, to lay aside their ingrained penchant for separation from perceived apostasy meant breaking with the fundamentalist conviction that they should never bend to the winds of liberalism.

World War II interrupted the tie-up with the University of Oklahoma, and events that transpired during the interlude serve as a context for better understanding the conflict that lay just over the horizon. In late 1942 the US military essentially took over the university campus as part of the overall war effort to train army and navy personnel.[61] Forced to relocate temporarily, SIL accepted an offer from the Northern Baptist Home Mission Board for the use of its Bacone College campus.[62] The move to Bacone for the 1943 and 1944 sessions was accompanied by an outpouring of missionary idealism and evangelistic fervor. Taking note of the mood, Nida informed the Pioneer Mission Agency that the camp was enjoying a "fine spiritual atmosphere." Indeed, students quickly set about organizing "spontaneous prayer groups for Africa, the heart of Asia, South America and Mexico." Dormitory prayer meetings sprang up on a daily basis. Visits by mission leaders from several mission boards added to the ferment. Nida also reported that on weekends the students preached in local churches and that "many have been saved" through their efforts.[63] With Camp Wycliffe's move to Bacone, it was exhibiting what Joel Carpenter has referred to as a "potent combination of Keswick piety and missionary idealism, brought together in the hothouse environment of the Bible schools, [which] made North American fundamentalism a leading recruiter of twentieth-century missionaries."[64] When the camp's classes were relocated to the University of Oklahoma in 1945, the staff and students would come to lament the loss of spiritual intensity.

By the time the 1947 session commenced, there was no denying the adverse effects that the cooperative relationship with the university was having on the school's spiritual vitality. In the first place, the Camp Wycliffe name, with its

---

and Adelle Elson to "Friends," October 1947, TA 4946; Kenneth L. Pike to Cameron Townsend, August 20, 1947, TA 4837; Kenneth L. Pike to Raymond Buker, Conservative Baptist Foreign Mission Society, May 5, 1948, TA 5659; Richard S. Pittman to Cameron Townsend, August 8, 1946, TA 4450; August 12, 1946, TA 4448.

61. Nida to Cameron Townsend, February 11, 1943, TA 3604; Nida to PMA, August 23, 1943, p. 1, TA 43032.

62. Nida to Cameron Townsend, March 26, 1943, p. 1, TA 3593.

63. Nida to PMA, August 23, 1943, TA 43032.

64. Joel A. Carpenter, *Revive Us Again: The Reawakening of American Fundamentalism* (New York: Oxford University Press, 1997), 83.

specifically religious connotation, was dropped and thereafter the school was referred to as the Summer Institute of Linguistics at Norman. In the second place, Pike and Nida, the school's codirectors, argued that SIL was "officially non-religious"; therefore, dropping prayer before class was in keeping with WBT-SIL's "basic policies and continuous attempts to distinguish between the academic character of the Summer Institute of Linguistics and the missionary program of the Wycliffe Bible Translators." By Pike and Nida's reasoning, SIL had departed from established principle in allowing prayer in class in the first place. Ending it was therefore not a novelty but rather a return to Townsend's basic operating principles. They concluded that "it seems wise to suspend the practice of prayer before classes in order that we can conform to the academic practices of the University." After the matter was discussed, the SIL faculty voted thirty-one to three to drop classroom prayer.[65] This majority decision suggests that the faculty was well on its way to accommodating the demands of associating closely with a secular university.

For students coming from faith mission boards, the abandonment of prayer before the start of each class was a most worrying omen. Indeed, a few students threatened to report this egregious lapse to their mission boards. There was yet another issue in play. Since several liberal Protestants and Roman Catholics had gained access to SIL courses through the university's admission process, apprehension over having to rub shoulders with liberals and Catholics was fast becoming another hot-button issue among the more conservative students. Attempts were made to shore up the school's spiritual foundations via daily dormitory devotions and noon chapel, but this failed to stem the rising tide of discontent.[66] These events culminated in a series of WBT-SIL conference sessions held at the end of July, where the future direction of SIL's summer school at Norman would be determined.

When WBT and SIL were incorporated in 1942, ultimate authority over the organization was democratically vested in its membership through the biennial conference. Therefore, since the WBT-SIL conference of delegates was the highest body of authority in the organization, decisions stemming from conference deliberations were binding on the board and general director.[67] The way the ad hoc SIL conference at Norman handled these issues would therefore largely determine the future of the organization. Fortunately a verbatim record was kept of the late-July conference proceedings, and this single-spaced, sixty-eight-

65. SIL minutes, June 14, 1947, pp. 1–2, WSA.

66. SIL corporate conference minutes, June 12, 1947, pp. 1–3, WSA.

67. Articles of Incorporation for WBT and SIL, 1942, TA 41523; George M. Cowan, *The Word That Kindles: People and Principles That Fueled a Worldwide Translation Movement* (Chappaqua, NY: Christian Herald Books, 1979), 235.

page transcript provides an extraordinarily comprehensive window into this seminal event in the organization's history, and Kenneth Pike's incomparable role in its outcome.

Few postwar conservative evangelicals were entirely free of fundamentalist tendencies, and therefore militancy and separatism could easily surface if they felt threatened. The SIL faculty members were not immune to this variety of reactionary impulse. As the 1947 session advanced, it became obvious that the teaching staff were increasingly uneasy with the SIL and University of Oklahoma relationship. The shift in sentiment was startling. Whereas thirty-one of the faculty at the beginning of the 1947 session had voted to end classroom prayer and had made little fuss over the admittance of nonevangelicals, now, less than a month later, twenty-three of them wanted to deny liberals and Roman Catholics admission to SIL courses, and perhaps even to see SIL terminate its connection with the university.[68] This sudden reactionary turn threatened to undermine Pike and Nida's long-standing efforts to garner academic legitimacy for SIL.

Just how deep-seated the fears and antagonisms were among some SIL staff can be seen in faculty members' expression of apprehension over having to mix with and teach nonevangelicals. With a number of liberals and Roman Catholic priests attending SIL at Norman that year, it was suggested by some faculty that SIL was casting its linguistic pearls before the proverbial swine. Ambrose McMahon, a translator working in Mexico, worried that after receiving SIL's linguistic training, liberal missionaries or Catholic priests might return to the field and "beat SIL to the job." For McMahon, it was a travesty that "sticking with the University leaves us open to give the course to people who are our enemies and who fight us."[69] Donald Sinclair, another SIL translator, pushed this principle even further. He argued that SIL should not even disseminate its scholarly works publicly.[70] The earlier advance in a progressive direction was rapidly coming unraveled by reactions to the perceived dangers emanating from cooperation with liberal Protestants and Catholics.

The issue of separation was also bound up with the question of whether or not the university relationship was essential to buttressing SIL's academic credibility. SIL had leaned heavily on its academic credentials in Mexico and utilized its university connections to open the door to Peru.[71] Indeed, Pike had recently gained a foothold for SIL in Peru by leveraging the prestige of his University of

68. Minutes of July, 26, 1947, WSA.

69. Ambrose McMahon, quoted in minutes of July 26, 1947, p. 5, WSA.

70. Donald Sinclair, quoted in minutes of July 26, 1947, p. 24, WSA.

71. The linguistic aspect of SIL's contribution in Mexico is discussed in chapter 1, and SIL's work in Peru in chapter 4.

Michigan connections and his scholarly publications.[72] These facts notwithstanding, unmistakable echoes of fundamentalist anti-intellectualism surfaced during the debates over just what constituted adequate academic standing or whether it was even necessary. SIL had brought some of its finest missionary-translators to serve as faculty at Norman, but they were not necessarily as enamored with linguistic research as were Pike and Nida. SIL translator Joyce Jenkins almost certainly voiced the practical-minded sentiment of other faculty members when she remarked that "we are technicians." She wanted to know if there was "any reason to feel that we might not stand on our own two feet as a technical institution."[73] Translator Ethel Wallis also called into question the use of scholarship as a strategy by pointing out that three missionaries had recently gained entry to Mexico without any academic credentials at all, thus presumably establishing the fact that "academic prestige is not necessary."[74] The average SIL missionary-translator, although likely more academically inclined than his or her typical faith mission counterpart, was usually more interested in linguistics as a practical tool than as an intellectual pursuit. For them linguistics was merely the handmaiden of Bible translation, whereas for a much smaller minority, such as Pike, Nida, and Pittman, linguistic research and scholarship were the *sine qua non* of SIL's strategy. The conundrum faced by the camp's directors was how to mediate between the seemingly incongruent realities of faith missionary pragmatism and the necessity of maintaining SIL's academic standing.

Deeply committed to the university relationship, Pike was not about to back down without a fight. He struck hard; it was almost as if he wanted to embarrass his colleagues for their lack of scholarly enthusiasm. The young Kenneth Pike was certainly capable of delivering such a broadside. In his mature years, he expressed chagrin that he was not more like the kindly and thoughtful Edward Sapir. "I often wished I had a gentle personality like his," he wrote in the early 1980s.[75] Warming to his task, Pike lamented that the only SIL linguist who had the capacity for independent research was William Wonderly, a rising academic star in SIL who was pursuing his doctorate at the University of Michigan.[76] As for the rest of the SIL translators, it was commendable that a few members had managed to produce a few articles on phonemics, but this did not, he charged, do away with the deplorable fact that no grammars had yet been published.[77]

72. Kenneth L. Pike, "General Report on South American Trip," February 21, 1944, TA 3875.

73. Joyce Jenkins, quoted in minutes of July 26, 1947, p. 12, WSA.

74. Ethel Wallis, quoted in minutes of July 26, 1947, p. 9, WSA.

75. Kenneth L. Pike, with Hugh Steven, *Pike's Perspectives: An Anthology of Thought, Insight, and Moral Purpose* (Langley, BC: Credo Publishing, 1989), 14.

76. Kenneth L. Pike, minutes of July 26, 1947, p. 13, WSA; Stine, *Let the Words Be Written*, 77.

77. Kenneth L. Pike, quoted in minutes of July 26, 1947, p. 11, WSA.

"As long as we tell anybody that we are scientists," Pike lectured his faculty, "in my opinion it is absolutely essential that we do not be liars. We claim that we are scientists, we must be scientists."[78] Pike was not about to equivocate on the point that if SIL professed to be scientific, it was therefore obligated to fulfill the requirements of that declaration according to the standards set by the wider world of academia.

A poignant moment during the evening's session afforded Pike the opportunity to link SIL's strategic purpose with the winning of souls. This interlude proved particularly powerful in stirring the affections of the faculty. According to the detailed notes, it must have been late in the evening when J. Dedrick, a faculty member not affiliated with the dissenting group, wondered aloud whether it was proper for SIL to distance itself from the scholars who, although perhaps not Christians, had nonetheless extended a helping hand to the organization and some of its members over the years. "What kind of debt do we owe the unregenerates?" asked Dedrick. "We have taken so much from [Leonard] Bloomfield and the rest of them [professional linguists]. Does that have any bearing on the unregenerate here [at SIL Norman]?"[79] "Yes," Pike affirmed, "we owe them a debt." "One of the saddest things about Wycliffe . . . ," he said, before pausing abruptly in midsentence. After a moment's hesitation, he continued, "I hate to think of Sapir sizzling in hell." He then began to weep. Still sobbing, he lamented that "the only thing we can do to repay them is get them to heaven, and I don't know how to do it."[80] "Praise God, you've got a better opportunity to do it than anybody else because of your linguistic field," offered Howard McKaughan, one of the dissenters.[81] This sentimental moment temporarily broke the tension. Although Pike's emotional reaction did not end the debate, it made a deep impression on the gathered assembly.

Pike's wife Evelyn was one of the last to speak before a midnight vote was taken. Her words seemed to sum up the necessity of staying the course at the university and keeping up the academic side of the work. She rightly pointed to a rising tide of nationalism around the world, and warned the group that "these foreign people aren't going to accept our religion." "The only basis on which we can bring them the Lord Jesus Christ," she added, "is to avail ourselves of the linguistic approach."[82] The lengthy discussions had brought the group full circle; whatever enthusiasm they had for separation had largely dissipated by this point of the evening.

78. Kenneth L. Pike, quoted in minutes of July 26, 1947, p. 15, WSA.
79. J. Dedrick, quoted in minutes of July 26, 1947, p. 19, WSA.
80. Kenneth L. Pike, quoted in minutes of July 26, 1947, pp. 19–20, WSA.
81. Howard McKaughan, quoted in minutes of July 26, 1947, p. 20, WSA.
82. Evelyn Pike, quoted in minutes of July 26, 1947, p. 25, WSA.

The ebb and flow of the Saturday, July 26, conference held the potential for a volatile and fissiparous outcome. Evangelicals of the fundamentalist persuasion were certainly imbued with qualities that could make for ugly endings. However, much like a good revival meeting, this meeting also depended on the dynamics of the moment. The evening had, in characteristic fashion, opened with prayer, but the solemn and reflective tone was short-lived. Mutually opposed positions were staked out and defended at length, followed by Pike's strident jeremiad against the separatists. Then came that portentous moment that saw the melting of the hearts, and, after the manner of congregants duly penitent after a well-delivered sermon, the faculty was humbled for the equivalent of an "altar call." Just after midnight on Sunday, July 27, a weary faculty voted twenty-five to seven in favor of admitting Catholics and liberals to SIL classes, so long as no fewer than five board members approved. The resolution to separate from the University of Oklahoma was defeated twenty-five to six.[83] In the end, a majority of the dissenters decided to stay the course at the university, while relying upon the board of directors to act as a check on the unorthodox (enrollment through the university was unaffected by this decision). By choosing to remain within the university system, the SIL staff demonstrated that an overwhelming majority of its members were willing, if somewhat unenthusiastically perhaps, to swear off any full-fledged separatism.

In the wake of the 1947 turmoil, SIL continued to make academic progress; this is reflected in the growing number of SIL missionary-linguists who earned doctorates in linguistics: no fewer than fourteen by 1959.[84] Kenneth Pike once recalled feeling "academically alone" in SIL of the mid-1950s; by 1959 he had plenty of company.[85]

Progress was also visible in academic publishing. In fact, even within the dissenting group of 1947, no fewer than eight went on to make scholarly contributions to the discipline of linguistics, including Ethel Wallis, who also became a prolific writer of popular books on Wycliffe.[86] In 1949, Kenneth Pike reported that articles being produced by SIL missionary-linguists "do not call for shame." "They are good," he added approvingly.[87] The University of Okla-

83. Minutes of July 26, 1947, p. 39, WSA.

84. Frank E. Robbins, "Training in Linguistics," in *The Summer Institute of Linguistics: Its Works and Contributions*, ed. Ruth M. Brend and Kenneth L. Pike (The Hague: Mouton, 1977), 59–60; Gary Simons, "Early Ph.D.s Report," on file at the office of SIL's chief research officer.

85. Kenneth L. Pike, with Hugh Steven, *Pike's Perspectives*, 168.

86. The eight are Benjamin F. Elson, Harold Key, Mary R. Key, Howard W. Law, Cornelia Mak, Howard McKaughan, Velma B. Pickett, and Ethel Wallis; see *Bibliography of the Summer Institute of Linguistics* (Dallas: Summer Institute of Linguistics, 1992).

87. Kenneth L. Pike, "Report of the General Director's Appointee on Linguistic Matters," SIL board of directors meeting, minutes, appendix I, September 12–18, 1949, p. 1, WSA.

homa took note of this trend in the quality of SIL's academic output. In 1949 the university president, George L. Cross, informed Pike that SIL was "making such fine contributions to knowledge" that the faculty requested that the institute's scholarly publications "byline" the university affiliation.[88] Moreover, at both the 1948 and 1949 annual Linguistic Society of America conferences, approximately a fifth of the twenty to twenty-five papers presented were read by SIL members.[89] This level of academic production was a phenomenal feat among North American evangelicals. By way of comparison, professor and theologian Edward J. Carnell complained to Fuller Seminary president Harold J. Ockenga in 1953 that the school's faculty had not "published as much as one article in a scholarly journal" since its founding in 1947.[90] (The slow start at Fuller is no indication of its ultimate scholarly production, for its faculty eventually produced its share of publications in both quantity and quality.) SIL's scholarly output increased apace over the ensuing decades. In the hundreds of new translation projects that were embarked upon, each SIL team was required to produce an analysis of the language in which it was working, which included a detailed description of the language's phonological system and grammatical structure. In addition to a translated New Testament, teams often produced a bilingual dictionary. Added to these publications were hundreds, and then thousands, of indigenous-language primers and other mother-tongue reading materials.[91] By 1984, SIL sported an impressive 9,876 articles and books in its academic bibliography. The faculty at SIL Norman in 1947, by choosing to set aside their fundamentalist habits of mind, kept SIL from becoming merely a technical or vocational-type school.

SIL also excelled in the area of women's contribution to scholarship; they outpaced by a wide margin the number of women involved in mainstream American linguistics. A recent study by Margaret Thomas, a linguist at Boston College, is instructive.[92] "Early to mid twentieth-century American linguistics," Thomas noted in 2008, "was rather unreceptive to scholarship by women." She found that only three non-SIL female linguists, Alice Vanderbilt Morris (1874–1955), Gladys Amanda Reichard (1893–1955), and E. Adelaide Hahn (1893–1967),

---

88. Cross to Kenneth L. Pike, October 1, 1949, UOA, record group 3, Presidential Papers, George L. Cross, box 66, folder Linguistic Institute.

89. Kenneth L. Pike, "Report of the General Director's Appointee," p. 2, WSA.

90. Carnell to Ockenga, September 15, 1954, quoted in Marsden, *Reforming Fundamentalism*, 142.

91. Brend and Pike, *The Summer Institute of Linguistics*.

92. I am indebted to SIL linguist and chief research officer Gary Simons for bringing Thomas's chapter in a 2008 compilation of papers from the Eleventh International Conference on the History of the Language Sciences to my attention.

participated in American professional linguistics and made scholarly contributions to the discipline in the middle part of the last century.[93] When Thomas
examined SIL's scholarly output, she discovered that the 880 articles produced
by the organization's women missionary-linguists between 1944 and 1970 constituted 38 percent of the organization's total output for the period. These articles appeared not only in in-house publications but also in refereed journals
such as *Language, International Journal of American Linguistics,* and *American
Anthropologist.* "SIL women," Thomas appositely noted, "worked alongside men
on a relatively even footing in the profession of missionary linguistics." "This
fact," she added, "seemed to be taken for granted, so that differential treatment
of the two genders is remarkably absent in the execution of SIL's core linguistic-
religious endeavors."[94] In the mid-1930s, Legters and Townsend had tried to
limit Camp Wycliffe and pioneering field service to single men and married
couples, but by 1938 these efforts crumbled under pressure from two very determined young single women. Florence Hansen and Eunice Pike (Kenneth Pike's
sister) turned the table on the general director by arguing that God had called
them, and they therefore had both the right and the obligation to learn and to
serve alongside men and married couples.[95] Although women would not find
their way into the upper echelon of organizational leadership in the period covered by the present study, they were accorded equal rank with men in scholarly
linguistic pursuits as well as in remote pioneering missionary-translation work
from near the beginning of the organization's existence.

As a percentage of its total membership, the number of doctorates in SIL
was not impressive. A mere 4.2 percent of SIL members possessed an earned
PhD in 1981.[96] By way of example, 94 percent of the faculty members at As-
bury Theological Seminary, Fuller Seminary, Gordon-Conwell Theological
Seminary, and Trinity Evangelical Divinity School combined, in the early
1980s, possessed earned doctorates. In actual numbers, however, SIL was
leading the way with 188 doctorates over against a total of 34 in the above-

93. Margaret Thomas, "Gender and the Language Scholarship of the Summer Institute of Linguistics in the Context of Mid Twentieth Century American Linguistics," in *History of Linguistics
2008: Selected Papers from the 11th International Conference on the History of the Language Sciences,*
ed. Gerda Hassler (Philadelphia: John Benjamins, 2011), 389.

94. Thomas, "Gender and the Language Scholarship," 394.

95. Hummel to Legters, December 21, 1934, TA 43067; Cameron Townsend, "Camp Wycliffe
Activities Camp during Past Year," 1936, p. 4, TA 43067; Cameron Townsend to PMA, September
8, 1938, p. 7, TA 2102; Wycliffe, third session bulletin, 1936, TA 43067.

96. "The Five Principles," progress report, a special edition of *In Other Words* 8, no. 4 (Summer
1982): 18, GIAL; Hyatt Moore, "Editorial: PhD's and Fools," *In Other Words* 8, no. 5 (September
1982): 3, on file at GIAL, Dallas. (N.B. Kenneth L. Pike counted 125 members with earned doctorates at this point: *Pike's Perspectives,* 122.)

named schools.[97] When Kenneth Pike retired from his post as president of SIL in 1979, he could take some measure of pride in SIL's academic credentials, since the record spoke for itself.

Tagmemics: Pike's Theory of Language

In the early part of the twentieth century, linguistic scholarship in North America transitioned away from nineteenth-century conceptualizations of language influenced by social Darwinism and Romanticism, which saw language as "embodying the soul of a race," and toward synchronic structural description that promised a more scientifically rigorous approach to linguistics.[98] Leonard Bloomfield and Edward Sapir were two of the most prominent linguists of the American "school" of structural linguistics, but they held differing views on the scope of the discipline. Bloomfield and his students focused primarily on describing the autonomous structure, or "linguistic forms," of individual languages apart from reference to meaning or the mentalist aspects of human volition.[99] As the writers of one historiographical essay put it, post-Bloomfieldian linguistics from the 1930s to the 1950s was marked by "rigor of method as against speculative interpretation; the facts of science as against popular misconception and entrenched intellectual prejudice."[100] Linguists working in the Bloomfieldian tradition also maintained that various levels of language, specifically phonology (sounds) and morphology (prefixes, infixes, and suffixes), should be analyzed separately. Along with the maxim against mixing of levels, structural linguistics excluded from its purview grammar, since it would naturally entail questions of meaning. Linguists in the Bloomfieldian tradition, convinced of the scientific objectivity of their procedures, primarily focused their efforts on describing the phonological and morphological patterns of human speech in isolation from the social or mental worlds of the speakers of the language under consideration.[101]

---

97. Mark A. Noll, *Between Faith and Criticism: Evangelicals, Scholarship, and the Bible in America* (San Francisco: Harper and Row, 1986), 126.

98. Geoffrey Sampson, *Schools of Linguistics* (Stanford: Stanford University Press, 1980), 60.

99. John E. Joseph, "Trends in Twentieth-Century Linguistics: An Overview," in *A Concise History of the Language Sciences: From the Sumerians to the Cognitivists*, ed. E. F. K. Koerner and R. E. Asher (New York: Pergamon Press, 1995), 221–25; Sampson, *Schools of Linguistics*, 74–76.

100. Dell Hymes and John Fought, eds., *American Structuralism* (The Hague: Mouton, 1981), 103.

101. Erik C. Fudge, "Post-Bloomfieldian Phonology," in Koerner and Asher, *A Concise History of the Language Sciences*, 306–11.

Although Sapir and Bloomfield followed much the same methodology in the analysis of linguistic data, Sapir and his students, especially Benjamin Lee Whorf, maintained an interest in the connection between language and the mind and the role of language in shaping culture. The Sapir-Whorf hypothesis, as their theory became known, claimed that language determines perception. "We dissect nature along lines laid down by our native languages," Whorf asserted in 1940. He explained further: "The categories and types that we isolate from the world of phenomena we do not find there because they stare every observer in the face; on the contrary, the world is presented in a kaleidoscopic flux of impressions which has to be organized by our minds—and this means largely by the linguistic systems in our minds."[102] Sapir and Whorf passed from the scene in 1939 and 1941, respectively, and in the two decades following their deaths little research was directed at substantiating or invalidating the Sapir-Whorf hypothesis.[103] Hence the more narrowly defined approach to linguistics pursued by the Bloomfieldians overshadowed that of Sapir and his students from the early 1940s to the late 1950s, and, as a result, most mid-twentieth-century North American linguists were more inclined to emphasize structural description of unwritten languages than to theorize in the manner of Sapir and Whorf.[104]

The structural approach to the study of unwritten indigenous languages was well suited to Townsend's hopes for training missionary translators, since it offered them useful heuristic techniques for cracking the mysteries of complex indigenous languages. Moreover, Townsend found the applied methodology attractive because, at least in his mind, it was more practical than theoretical. What Townsend never anticipated was that Pike and Nida were both destined to depart from the Bloomfieldian mainstream, and in the process both men made important theoretical contributions to the discipline of linguistics and to translation theory.

In a 1947 article, Pike signaled his break with the Bloomfieldians by arguing that a complete phonological analysis of a language was impossible without reference to grammar. Contrary to the customary proscription against mixing levels in analysis, Pike stipulated that it was crucial to investigate how the various levels of the linguistic hierarchy interacted, since there were always inexplicable anomalies that could not be resolved without reference to adjacent levels.

102. Benjamin L. Whorf, "Science and Linguistics," *Technology Review* 42, no. 6 (1940): 229–31, 247–48, reprinted in Whorf, *Language, Thought, and Reality: Selected Writings of Benjamin Lee Whorf*, ed. John B. Carroll (Cambridge, MA: MIT Press, 1956), 213.

103. Whorf, *Language, Thought, and Reality*, 21, 29.

104. John G. Fought, "American Structuralism," in Koerner and Asher, *A Concise History of the Language Sciences*, 304–5.

Therefore, whereas the post-Bloomfieldians chose to postpone indefinitely such irregularities, Pike instead sought to solve intractable phonemic problems by the mixing of levels, even if the result was a more complex and perhaps less elegant analysis.[105] Few post-Bloomfieldian linguists were convinced to extend the range of phonemic analysis in the wake of Pike's groundbreaking article, for it threatened a theoretical paradigm to which they were fully committed. The only immediate reward for his scholarly independence was to have his innovations labeled the "Pikean heresy."[106] Undaunted, Pike maintained his course. This first break with convention was only the beginning of where he was ultimately destined to go on the theoretical front.

In 1954, Pike issued the first volume of what would become his three-volume magnum opus, *Language in Relation to a Unified Theory of the Structure of Human Behavior*, in which he articulated his "tagmemic" theory of structural linguistics.[107] Recounting the historical development of tagmemics in 1976, Pike said that by early 1948 he had become bored with the study of phonology and therefore turned his attention to grammar.[108] The magnitude of the task he set for himself was astounding. He aspired to account for "the total productive possibilities within [a] language" by way of a "mechanical discovery procedure," and this in a fashion that did not divorce meaning from structural analysis. Pike soon realized that his quest for a systematic method on such a grand scale was unrealistic, but the wide-ranging nature of his theoretical outlook remained productive.[109] With its wider view of linguistics, tagmemics naturally encouraged increasingly higher levels of analysis above the sentence, and this broader outlook eventuated in some of SIL's top scholars making significant contributions to discourse analysis.[110] Moreover, by not setting strict boundaries on what was admissible in linguistic analysis, tagmemics proved quite useful for describing unwritten languages; eventually the structure of hundreds of languages worldwide was analyzed from a tagmemic perspective by SIL linguists.[111]

105. Kenneth L. Pike, "Grammatical Prerequisites to Phonemic Analysis," *Word* 3, no. 3 (December 1947): 155–72.

106. Fudge, "Post-Bloomfieldian Phonology," 312.

107. Kenneth L. Pike, *Language in Relation to a Unified Theory of the Structure of Human Behavior*, 2nd rev. ed. (The Hague: Mouton, 1967).

108. Kenneth L. Pike, "Toward the Development of Tagmemic Postulates," in *Tagmemics*, vol. 2: *Theoretical Discussion*, Trends in Linguistics 2, ed. Ruth M. Brend and Kenneth L. Pike (The Hague: Mouton, 1976), 94.

109. Kenneth L. Pike, "Toward the Development of Tagmemic Postulates," 94–97.

110. Discussed in chapter 3.

111. Bruce L. Edwards, "Pike's Tagmemics and Its Impact on Rhetoric and Composition Theory," in Wise, Headland, and Brend, *Language and Life*, 573–74; Kenneth L. Pike, "Our Own

As the title of Pike's most significant contribution to the discipline of linguistics indicated, tagmemics embodied much more than just linguistic theory. In an even more radical break from the Bloomfieldian tradition, Pike advanced the idea that language itself was a unit of culture, and, furthermore, he mounted the argument that nonverbal cultural behavior was unconsciously structured in much the same manner as was language. Tagmemic theory therefore drew a sharp distinction between a cultural insider's "emic" internal and socially acquired understanding of a cultural phenomenon and the observable outward "etic" appearances of that same phenomenon.[112] According to Pike, cultural insiders have accumulated knowledge that shapes the way they understand an event or action that outsiders lack. Just as the speakers of a language have subconscious control of the rules that govern the structure of their language, they have the same kind of internalized mastery of the structure of their culture. Thus, one always risks misinterpreting a wide range of observations until one comes to an "emic" understanding of cultural phenomena, since every individual is culturally conditioned to arrange various aspects of experience within specified preexisting patterns at a subconscious level. "All phenomena," Pike asserted, "all 'facts,' all 'things,' somehow reach him [the individual observer] only through perceptual and psychological filters, which affect his perception of the structuring of and relevance of the physical data he observes."[113] By the early to mid-1950s, Pike had clearly parted ways with the traditional fundamentalist commonsense variety of knowing in favor of a rather more Kantian epistemology that recognized the active part the mind played in one's perception of the external world. In this respect, tagmemics clearly owed a much greater debt to Sapir and Whorf than it did to Bloomfield, and Pike fittingly dedicated *Language* to the memory of Sapir.[114] In the decades since Pike first postulated a distinction between the "etic" and the "emic," scholars have employed the terms and the associated theory not only in ethnography but also in psychology, sociology, medicine, education, and the study of the phenomenology of religion, to name but a few disciplines.[115] Pike's etic-emic conceptual framework

---

Tongue Wherein We Were Born," *Bible Translator* 10, no. 2 (April 1959): 14; Sampson, *Schools of Linguistics*, 79–80.

112. Kenneth L. Pike, *Language*, 37–39.

113. Kenneth L. Pike, *Language*, 658.

114. Kenneth L. Pike, *Language*, 3.

115. Ward H. Goodenough, "Anthropology in the 20th Century and Beyond," *American Anthropologist*, n.s., 104, no. 2 (June 2002): 434–35; Thomas N. Headland, "Introduction: A Dialogue between Kenneth L. Pike and Marvin Harris on Emics and Etics," in *Emics and Etics: The Insider/ Outsider Debate*, ed. Thomas N. Headland, Kenneth L. Pike, and Marvin Harris (Newberry Park, CA: Sage Publications, 1990), 16–24; Russell T. McCutcheon, "Etic and Emic Standpoints for the

is perhaps his most significant and durable contribution to the wider academic world.[116]

Pike's excursion into the nonfundamentalist intellectual world of secular academia encouraged him to accept some measure of philosophical idealism and cultural relativism, which in turn allowed him to explore dimensions of language and social behavior that would likely have been impossible had he remained within a strictly fundamentalist intellectual milieu. In *Language* he staked out his position by declaring that "In my epistemology I assume that there is some type of ultimate truth, including an ultimate way of looking at the structure of physical reality. The truth, in my view, would be the emic perception experienced by God, who in turn could focus upon the emic perception of individual men as a component of the total reality available to His observation."[117] Pike emphasized that this perfect comprehension of reality was reserved for God alone. Since God's "views on such matters are not available to us," he asserted, it "leaves us always with the empirical possibility of a plurality of equally-true—or equally-false—observations, coming from different standpoints and from different observers."[118] It would seem that Pike had wandered far afield from the conservative evangelical variety of epistemology that placed great confidence in the capacity of the human mind to grasp ultimate truth.

As an evangelical, however, absolute philosophical idealism or cultural relativism was not an option for Pike. Yet, if it was impossible for the human intellect to grasp absolute truth, what option was there for avoiding some form of epistemological skepticism? He eventually took refuge in the Enlightenment distinction between scientific theory and religious faith. "The choice of an epistemology," Pike concluded, was "a moral choice," and as a consequence he dropped his adherence to evidentialist apologetics in favor of presuppositionalism during the period in which he developed tagmemics.[119] Pike pursued science on the same rationalist terms as his non-Christian colleagues, but, by grounding his religious epistemology on fideism rather than on rationalism, he

---

Description of Behavior," in *The Insider/Outsider Problem in the Study of Religion: A Reader*, ed. Russell T. McCutcheon (New York: Cassell, 1999), 28–36.

116. Philip C. Stine claims, in *Let the Words Be Written*, that it was Nida who introduced Pike to the concepts of etic and emic; however, Stine provides no evidence for his assertion (96–97). It is true that Nida introduced Pike to the notion of a "phoneme" and pointed him to Bloomfield's 1933 *Language*, but I found no evidence while researching the present volume to invalidate Pike's claim that he not only coined the terms but also defined them with respect to ethnography.

117. Kenneth L. Pike, *Language*, 658–59.

118. Kenneth L. Pike, *Language*, 659.

119. Kenneth L. Pike, *With Heart and Mind: A Personal Synthesis of Scholarship and Devotion*, 2nd ed. (Duncanville, TX: Adult Learning Systems, [1962] 1996), 75–78.

was freed from the potentially debilitating effects of having his scientific work clash with his evangelical faith.

The dichotomization of faith and science remained a permanent feature of Pike's mind, and an examination of his scholarly corpus indicates that he by and large approached linguistics from a naturalistic point of view.[120] It was only in his devotional works or, for example, in articles published in the evangelical *Journal of the American Scientific Affiliation* that one finds discussion of his Christian commitment at any length.[121] It was Pike's inclination to respect the post-Enlightenment distinction between scientific facts and religious values.[122] This division was, on the whole, respected in SIL's linguistic scholarship. It is therefore rather striking to find SIL linguist Robert Longacre—who perhaps ranked second to Pike in erudition and academic output—developing a theistic philosophy of language. Longacre explained in the preface to his *Anatomy of Speech Notions* (1976) that the volume "treats the dream of universal grammar."[123] The far-reaching nature of the book offered the ideal occasion to invoke God as the creator of human language. Although the chapter in which Longacre set forth his philosophy of language was only eighteen pages long, he nonetheless presented a well-developed argument that language was not an accident of evolution but was created by God. For reasons that remain unclear, when Longacre revised *An Anatomy of Speech Notions* as *The Grammar of Discourse* in 1983, this entire chapter was dropped, and God was not to be found in the index at all.[124] From the wealth of knowledge on language and linguistics in SIL, this sole chapter in one volume represents a singular burst of theological insight into the nature and meaning of human language from a specifically theistic perspective.[125]

120. Joan Spanne and Mary Ruth Wise, "The Writings of Kenneth L. Pike: A Bibliography," in Wise, Headland, and Brend, *Language and Life*, 57–75.

121. Kenneth L. Pike, *Stir, Change, Create: Poems and Essays in Contemporary Mood for Concerned Students* (Huntington Beach, CA: Wycliffe Bible Translators, 1967); Kenneth L. Pike, "Christianity and Culture: III. Biblical Absolutes and Certain Cultural Relativisms," *Journal of the American Scientific Affiliation* 31, no. 3 (September 1979): 139–45; Kenneth L. Pike, *With Heart and Mind*.

122. It could be argued that Pike did in fact reflect on the methods of scientific inquiry in his 1962 *With Heart and Mind*; however, this small volume was not intended as scholarly literature but was written to encourage his students and to shed some light on his own personal approach to science and faith.

123. Robert E. Longacre, *An Anatomy of Speech Notions* (Lisse, Netherlands: Peter de Ridder Publications, 1976), 5.

124. Robert E. Longacre, *The Grammar of Discourse* (New York: Plenum Publishing, 1983).

125. I am indebted to SIL's Karl Franklin for pointing out the appearance of Robert Longacre's philosophy of language in *An Anatomy of Speech Notions* and the deletion of this material in *The Grammar of Discourse*.

Unlike Fuller Seminary, where religious thought took center stage, the very character of SIL's scholarship was marked by a general tendency to maintain a distinction between science and religion.

Respect for Enlightenment categories was appropriate if not obligatory in SIL, but this by no means implied, at least in Pike's mind, that Christians should cede academic ground to secular scholars. He was provoked by his own successful career in academia into quarreling with evangelicals over the anti-intellectualist tendencies that remained a legacy of fundamentalism. "For the past generation or two," Pike wrote in his 1962 *With Heart and Mind: A Personal Synthesis of Scholarship and Devotion*, "the evangelical wing of the Christian church has viewed scholarship with suspicion. Reeling under attacks internally from higher criticism and externally from science, it has sometimes withdrawn into a defensive cyst formation in order to weather the storm." This was certainly not the Pike of the mid-1930s. In his estimation science for the sake of science had become not only an approved enterprise but also an obligation for evangelicals. Thus he urged evangelicals to undertake active designs for "making positive contributions to the world's knowledge." Lamenting the caliber of evangelical scholarship in many Christian colleges, he suggested not only that these schools should pray for "research workers to be appointed to their faculties," but also that they should "*pay*" for them.[126] As a scholar, Pike tirelessly pitted himself against the anti-intellectual legacy of fundamentalism, and SIL stood as a testament to his vision of evangelical scholarship.

SIL's coming of age is a chronicle of how Cameron Townsend's ambition to field better-trained missionary-translators not only was realized but also fortuitously stimulated a movement to revitalize missionary scholarship. Kenneth Pike and Eugene Nida deserve an outsized share of the credit for these accomplishments, especially considering that SIL's founder was sometimes a fly in the ointment of scholarly progress. Townsend, his occasional foot-dragging on academic matters notwithstanding, still deserves recognition for seeing the potential of these two missionary "failures." There too was the critical factor of Townsend's linking SIL to the discipline of American structural linguistics. This move not only shaped the academic character of SIL but also helped to ensure that the organization's research and scholarly production often met the prevailing academic standards at research universities. The tie-up with the University of Oklahoma was another key factor in ensuring SIL's academic character. Under Pike and Nida's leadership, then, SIL evolved along academic lines, becoming a respected institution of applied linguistics. For an organization with roots in fundamentalism to rise to the level of scholarly attainment

126. Kenneth L. Pike, *With Heart and Mind*, viii, 23, 26–27.

that SIL achieved is, perhaps, an accomplishment unmatched in North American evangelicalism. The case of SIL is certainly an outstanding demonstration of mid-twentieth-century evangelicals transcending their anti-intellectualist habit of mind to enjoy fruitful engagement with academia. The development of Camp Wycliffe and the Summer Institute of Linguistics represents nothing less than a revival of scholarship among evangelicals from the unlikely confines of a faith mission.

CHAPTER 3

Translating the Word

An overwhelming majority of WBT-SIL members considered Bible translation the paramount task of the organization. Conversion to Christianity was certainly the ultimate spiritual objective, but the completion of New Testament translations remained the most tangible goal. Occasionally the utility of linguistic scholarship was questioned, but never the idea that every person should have the Scriptures available in the language he or she knew best, and this objective remained, no matter how small the population of speakers of a language, or how geographically or culturally isolated. Indeed, the organization gave priority to small and neglected indigenous peoples. It is rather striking then to find that while SIL excelled in linguistics, the organization was slow to advance in translation theory and practice. The road to better translations of the Scriptures proved to be somewhat rocky at times. Likewise, sustained scholarly reflection on Bible translation as a specific missionary strategy was not carried out with the same force and rigor as was linguistic scholarship. These two important subjects will occupy a significant portion of the present chapter.

Although translation occupied a privileged place in WBT-SIL, it is one of the most difficult aspects of the organization to analyze and narrate adequately. Not only were individual translation teams—typically a married couple or two women—different from one another due to personality, experience, and translating ability, the countries and regions in which SIL undertook translation also differed widely due to cultural, religious, and political factors, among others. The model developed in Latin America under the direction of Cameron Townsend, which focused on projects situated among remote tribal peoples and operating under government contracts, was not always well suited to other parts of the world. In Africa, for example, governments were typically less inclined to partner with SIL and pressed the organization to work with universities and in some cases churches. In Africa, too, the language groups tended to be much larger than, for example, in the Amazon Basin.[1] On the other hand, translation projects in places such as Papua New Guinea, where hundreds of small indigenous peoples lived in geographically isolated areas, had much in common with those of Latin America. With that said, the Latin American model was one Townsend championed throughout his life, and it more or less provided the initial template for most other parts of the world. Therefore, Latin America receives greater attention in the present chapter than other regions.

The Bible translation strategy of WBT-SIL was unique not only in faith mission circles but also among all modern-era Christian missions from the late eighteenth century down to the mid-twentieth century. A 1943 statement of the organization's principles of expansion enumerated three objectives: "(1) A portion at least of the Word of God translated for the tribe. (2) That a group of people be taught to read the Word of God. (3) That a nucleus of believers be raised up instructed in the Word with a reasonable assurance that they will be able to proceed with effective expansion of the work and spread of the Word of God."[2] Of these three aims, a translation of the New Testament was foremost. "We have considered it important," Kenneth Pike wrote in 1959, "if we were to accomplish the main purpose for which we feel called of God—translation of the Scriptures into tribal languages—our energies needed to be concentrated on the one specific task, that of getting the Word of God to people in their own language."[3] As Townsend had stipulated in Mexico, SIL's missionary-translators were not permitted to preach, baptize converts, or establish churches under SIL's control. These typical missionary functions were left to the local believers or other Christian missions. In an address to faculty and students at the 1960 session of SIL's linguistics courses in Norman, Oklahoma, Townsend defended this minimalist strategy. "One of the criticisms that is brought against us is that we win converts, translate the Bible for them, and then go on. . . . But we say that is our plan and that is the program, so people say[,] 'Oh, you leave those believers orphans.'" Townsend rebutted this assertion. "Do you know," he opined, "my experience has been He [the Holy Spirit] does the job better when missionaries don't stay around too long so that the people get to leaning on the missionary."[4] A translated New Testament, a few literate readers, and a

---

1. John Bendor-Samuel, interview by author, February 21, 2006, Nairobi, Kenya.

2. "Statement on Principles of Expansion," September 15, 1943, WSA.

3. Kenneth L. Pike, "Our Own Tongue Wherein We Were Born," *Bible Translator* 10, no. 2 (1959): 15.

4. Cameron Townsend, "Pioneering and Linguistics and God's Almighty Power" (chapel talk, Norman, Oklahoma, July 1960), 3, TA 50222.

handful of believers were considered sufficient to deem a translation project essentially complete. There were departures from this policy, depending on the individual SIL branch in question, but once translators achieved the minimal objectives, they generally moved on to another translation project or, as was most often the case, into administration. During his 1960 chapel talk, Townsend emphasized the pioneering imperative with an allusion to Revelation 7:9: "'To every language,' Those are marching orders."[5] If nothing else, WBT-SIL rarely if ever wavered from this ideal.

Also reinforcing the narrow focus on indigenous languages was Townsend's insistence that newly deployed translators learn the tribal language before studying Spanish, or any particular nation's language of wider communication. "If you have lived with your tribe for six months and yet use more Spanish in conversation with bi-lingual Indians than you use the Indian language," he instructed SIL translators in 1941, "there is something wrong with your approach."[6] Townsend also feared that if translators mastered Spanish first, they might come to depend on it as a crutch and never master the indigenous idiom. The major thrust of Camp Wycliffe, as discussed in the previous chapter, was not to teach majority languages such as Spanish, but to equip WBT-SIL missionary-translators with the necessary linguistic knowledge required to analyze, learn, and alphabetize indigenous languages in preparation for producing a New Testament translation. Although statistics are not available, the extant record suggests that a large majority of the organization's translators did learn the indigenous language, and a good many eventually turned out a translated New Testament.

As Townsend's frequent calls to pioneer echoed down through the years, a steady stream of translators set out to work in remote locations among isolated indigenous peoples. In his letters and oratory, the founder frequently referenced Romans 15:20, where the apostle Paul wrote, "It has always been my ambition to preach the gospel where Christ was not known, so that I would not be building on someone else's foundation."[7] By singling out linguistically isolated indigenous peoples as their chief concern, SIL missionary-translators were drawn into cultural contexts that imposed significant physical and psychological stress upon even the hardiest individuals. This was particularly the case in places such as Latin America and Papua New Guinea.

After a second session of Camp Wycliffe in 1939, a young and single Herman Aschmann from Port Arthur, New York, found himself among the Highland

5. Cameron Townsend, "Pioneering and Linguistics," 6.

6. Cameron Townsend to "Fellow Workers," March 5, 1941, p. 2, TA 2820.

7. Cameron Townsend, "Pioneering and Linguistics," 2.

Totonacs of southeastern Mexico. Eager to establish himself in the ideal location for learning the Totonac language, Aschmann was directed by a mule driver to consider San Felipe Tecpatlan. Arriving in a downpour after a two-day journey by mule, he found himself in the town's single store, where he spent his first night sleeping on the floor. Awakened by the commotion of the store owner beating his wife, Aschmann later recalled that he "felt so hopeless and wondered what was coming next." The next morning he met the town's "president," who was far from welcoming. Informed that the only available lodging was one of the town's two jail cells, Aschmann accepted the unusual living arrangement. Virtually ignored by the town's people, he found it difficult to obtain food, and he despaired of ever learning the language, which would only be possible by conversing with speakers of the unwritten Totonac language. Aschmann recorded in his journal that after "four miserable months," he contracted malaria. With no one to provide medical assistance, he progressively deteriorated to the point of fearing death. Not until a mule driver happened through San Felipe was he able to ride out and find a doctor. Eager for a more favorable situation, he returned to the town of Zapottitlán on the advice of a young Totonac man, who promised that his mother would welcome Aschmann. If he had been ignored before, he now found himself with plenty of company, living in a one-room house, in which he slept in the only bed with three boys arranged on the floor around him, while the single mother of the family and her two daughters slept in a lean-to kitchen.[8] Aschmann's early experience as an aspiring missionary-translator mirrors that of many others who had to overcome less-than-welcoming initial contact and difficult living situations.

SIL's missionary-translators frequently endured a near complete loss of personal space. SIL's Mildred Larson found that the luxury of privacy was all but nonexistent when living among the Aguaruna of Peru in the early 1950s. She was forewarned by veteran translators that when living in the village she would "feel like an animal in the zoo." "But that wasn't the half of it!" Larson exclaimed in her autobiography. "Our observers were in the cage . . . with us! They inspected us from head to foot, felt us all over, and then inspected everything in the cage with us. Our half open, thatched roof house didn't help; it was like being on a stage on which we were the continual entertainment." The loss of privacy could prove exhausting, and Larson admitted that she "began to resent the people I had come to serve." "It was," she confessed, "an awful feeling."[9] The

---

8. Hugh Steven, *Translating Christ: The Memoirs of Herman Peter Aschmann, Wycliffe Bible Translator* (Pasadena, CA: William Carey Library, 2011), 52, 56–57.

9. Mildred Larson and Lois Dodds, *Treasure in Clay Pots: An Amazon People on the Wheel of Change* (Dallas: Person to Person Books, 1985), 21–23.

cultural stress translators endured notwithstanding, a sizable majority of SIL's missionary-translators persevered and became acclimated to what were, at least for most Westerners, claustrophobic social settings.

At least as difficult as the cross-cultural strains were the countless linguistic challenges confronting translators. Many indigenous languages possessed a structure unlike any that SIL translators had previously studied. This astonishing range of linguistic variation presented them with many unexpected difficulties. The problem could be something as deceptively simple as differences in vowel length that changed the meaning of a word, a phenomenon that, to an outsider, would remain almost undetectable. Tone languages were some of the most difficult to analyze. SIL translators encountered languages marked by as many as five different tones, and therefore a single phonetic word shape could have a variety of meanings based on the pitch superimposed on the vowels. Grammar too could prove extraordinarily complex. Translators regularly encountered linguistic structures that exhibited no resemblance whatsoever to western European languages. Learning and analyzing unwritten indigenous languages was an enormously demanding assignment.

With the eventual translation of the New Testament dependent on mastering the local language, SIL translators tended to measure their performance in their first few years by accomplishments on the linguistic front. Since a preponderance of translators possessed only average linguistic abilities, many struggled in the early phase of their missionary careers to cope with the bewildering complexity of the task before them. In 1941, SIL translator Evelyn Woodward reported that her Indian language informant had "ask[ed] the Lord Jesus to come into her heart." Yet, winning a convert seems to have paled before the lack of advancement in linguistic analysis. Woodward continued her narrative, stating that "this leads me to a report of my progress on the language. I returned to the United States with a deep sense of failure in this particular. . . . As it is, I still feel like a misfit and a complete novice at the work of furreting [*sic*] out an unwritten language."[10] Woodward's sentiments were hardly unique, for her lament was echoed time and again over the decades by other struggling translators. Likewise, Bible translation itself was rife with complications. The honest assessment of David Watters is apropos. "By the time we finished the New Testament," Watters related in his 2011 autobiographical account of his SIL career in the 1970s, "our early work appeared so terribly crude compared to our later work that we didn't even try to revise it. We threw it out and started over. All our efforts for the first four or five years had

---

10. Woodward to PMA, August 16, 1941, p. 1, TA 903055.

been no more than practice."[11] The task to which SIL missionary-translators set themselves was exceedingly arduous; in fact, it would ultimately prove far more complex than was realized in the first several decades of SIL's existence.

All SIL translators were entirely dependent upon the willingness of at least one indigenous person to help them acquire the language and to assist them with the translation process. In 1947, Eugene Nida penned a culturally sensitive article praising the virtues of indigenous cotranslators. "The translation helper may be a blind Navaho," Nida wrote, "as Geronimo Martin is; but he may have that same genius for shedding light on obscure idioms and revealing the truth to his fellow speakers of this difficult language." Of another, Nida remarked, "Or the translator may be a former guitar singer in the village saloons, as was Angel Merecias; but this brilliant man has become a translator of hymns and renders difficult passages into his own Mixteco language with a profound insight."[12] On the other hand, at times SIL translators unconsciously overlooked the obvious and missed identifying talent. Herman Aschmann related in a 2006 interview that he worked with a young Totonac Indian cotranslator named Manuel Arenas in the 1940s. Arenas was more precocious than Aschmann initially realized, and he honestly and regretfully acknowledged his failure to notice the young man's talent (Arenas eventually pursued education in the United States and Germany, and mastered several European languages).[13] "My problem was I underestimated the brain capacity of an Indian, awful fatal thing." Why had this occurred? Aschmann explained: "Well, they're Indians, they don't have an education . . . that's where I failed, and I think that's something that all translators are prone to do."[14] During the course of his next two translation projects, Aschmann changed tactics and had the indigenous cotranslators work semi-independently producing the initial drafts.[15] This too was the approach taken by Pike with his Mixteco translation in the 1940s, during which Angel Merecias produced the first drafts of the translation.[16] The indigenous participants in SIL's Bible translation projects, without whose help the entire linguistic and translation process would have ground to a halt, were an integral part of whatever success SIL enjoyed on the translation front.

11. David E. Watters, *At the Foot of the Snows: A Journey of Faith and Words among the Kham-Speaking People of Nepal* (Seattle: Engage Faith Press, 2011), 172.

12. Eugene A. Nida, "The Indispensables," *Bible Society Record* 92, no. 3 (March 1947): 1, TA 44259.

13. Hugh Steven, *Manuel* (Old Tappan, NJ: Revell, 1970); Hugh Steven, *Manuel: The Continuing Story* (Langley, BC: Credo Publishing, 1987).

14. Herman Aschmann, interview by author, July 20, 2006, Dallas, Texas.

15. "Tontonac Testament," *Translation*, Fall 1962, 4–6; Steven, *Translating Christ*, 141–43.

16. Evelyn Pike, interview by author, July 19, 2006, Dallas, Texas.

The WBT-SIL missionary strategy placed great confidence in the potential for the Scriptures in the mother tongue. "You just give them the Word and God will do the rest," exclaimed SIL translator Vivian (Forsberg) Van Wynen during an interview for this study.[17] In an article outlining WBT-SIL's missionary program in 1959, Kenneth Pike declared that the "*Scriptures are a means of evangelization*—not just a means of strengthening the church. Hence the Scriptures are exceedingly useful in going ahead of the place where the church exists."[18] Pike also explained that SIL believed a full-orbed missionary strategy was unnecessary. "Members of a culture need to be able to get much of their spiritual sustenance directly from the Scriptures rather than indirectly through someone else."[19] It was considered an article of faith that the New Testament in the indigenous language would do the heavy lifting otherwise supplied by traditional missionary activity. The potency with which this outlook was held sometimes blinded organizational leaders and translators when the facts suggested that the entire process of Bible translation and its reception might be more complex than they had assumed. It is therefore fitting at this point to examine developments in translation theory and practice, as well as the various debates and issues related to the translation as mission strategy, in WBT-SIL from the 1940s down to the early 1980s.

Translation Theory and the Inerrancy Debate

Most mid-twentieth-century fundamentalists and conservative evangelicals were of a literalist cast of mind, which insisted upon an intimate correlation between the structure of biblical texts and truth. Put another way, literal interpretations of Scripture, literal translations of the Bible, and notions of truth were all closely interrelated. This outlook led the fundamentalist editor of the *Sword of the Lord*, John R. Rice, in 1953 to praise the literal American Standard Bible's "holy reverence for the actual wording of the original manuscripts."[20] Likewise, not a few SIL translators were more interested in the structure of a particular text than in how that structure facilitated or inhibited the transfer of meaning in translation. Whether a translator's source text was the King James Bible, a Greek text, or some other version of the Bible, he or she was prone to reproduce the

17. Vivian (Forsberg) Van Wynan, interview by author, September 7, 2007, Dallas, Texas.
18. Kenneth L. Pike, "Our Own Tongue," 4.
19. Kenneth L. Pike, "Our Own Tongue," 3.
20. John R. Rice, "God's Own Translation of Isaiah 7:14 Says Virgin," *Sword of the Lord*, September 25, 1953, 11, quoted in Peter J. Thuesen, *In Discordance with the Scriptures: American Protestant Battles over Translating the Bible* (New York: Oxford University Press, 1999), 112.

source text's structure in the target language. Cameron Townsend's Cakchiquel translation is a fitting example. Townsend maintained that his translation was "idiomatic," but in the late 1960s the Guatemala branch of SIL initiated a project to revise it.[21] One of the revisers observed that it was, contrary to Townsend's vigorous protestations, "very literal."[22] Overly literal translations of the Bible posed the very real danger that the "message" (meaning) would, in a manner of speaking, get lost in the translation. Eventually these difficult-to-read translations became widely and uncharitably referred to as "wooden translations."[23]

In the late 1940s and early 1950s, Eugene Nida and his younger protégé William Wonderly became interested in translation theory, or what was sometimes referred to as communication theory. More specifically, the two men began investigating why the meaning of biblical texts was all too often obscured by the process of translation. What they began to discover was that overly literal or "wooden" translations played a significant part in the failure to communicate meaning, and they set out to rectify this problem.

"Nida has made the one greatest contribution to Bible translation of recent times," Kenneth Pike declared to the WBT-SIL board in 1948, adding that his colleague had "taken over literal wor[d] for word translation and . . . smashed it."[24] There was certainly a good measure of hyperbole in Pike's remark, but Nida was quick to identify the problem of overly literal translations from his earliest days in SIL. Drawing on his experience in working with SIL translators and helping them with the countless difficulties that translation invoked, Nida eventually developed what he referred to as "dynamic equivalence." Hints of where Nida was heading on the theoretical front were visible in his 1947 work entitled *Bible Translating*, in which he urged translators away from literalism and slavishness to the form of the source text, while yet cautioning against excessive paraphrasing. He directed translators to aim for the "closest 'natural' equivalent to the statement of the [source] text." What Nida sought was a middle path between "awkward literalness on the one hand and unjustified interpretations on the other." The key concept that he introduced was the "translation of ideas."[25]

21. David Oltrogge to Beekman, October 22, 1969, TA 27018; Cameron Townsend, Hefley interview, June 23, 1970, p. 1, TA 43642.

22. Martha (King) Diebler, interview by author, June 14, 2006, Waxhaw, North Carolina.

23. Richard Blight, interview by author, July 2, 2009, Dallas, Texas; Ellis Diebler, interview by author, June 14, 2006, Waxhaw, North Carolina; Nida to Harold Key, March 5, 1954, MBA; Robert Longacre, interview by author, June 29, 2010, Dallas, Texas.

24. Kenneth L. Pike, "Report of the General Director's Appointee on Linguistic Matters," SIL board of directors meeting, minutes, appendix I, September 12–18, 1949, p. 8, WSA.

25. Eugene A. Nida, *Bible Translating: An Analysis of Principles and Procedures, with Special Reference to Aboriginal Languages* (New York: American Bible Society, 1947), 12–13.

This notion was not fully developed in *Bible Translating*, but here was the germ of an idea that Nida would in due course develop into his theory of dynamic equivalence.

Nida's innovative approach to Bible translation practice and theory was spurred by a strong desire to see that the meaning of the translated Scriptures was adequately conveyed to the reader. Dissatisfied with the Bloomfieldians' tendency to neglect meaning in their pursuit of strictly rule-based structural linguistic descriptions, Nida, as did Pike, took a more wide-ranging approach that insisted on reference to meaning in linguistic analysis.[26] Nida's approach was also at odds with literal biblicism. In 1947, he wrote that "words are merely vehicles for ideas. They are symbols, and as such they usually have no special significance over and above the actual objects which they symbolize."[27] Few fundamentalists would have followed Nida in allowing for such contextual conditioning and semiotic functionalism; rather, they would have insisted on a stronger if not immutable relationship between a specific word and its referent. Not only were Nida's attempts in the late 1940s and 1950s to treat meaning in his linguistic analysis a departure from the practices of the Bloomfieldians, but his moves also served notice that he was parting ways with the literal biblicism common in conservative evangelical circles.

In 1959, Nida introduced the notion that the readers' response to a biblical text should determine the adequacy of a translation; that is, readers of the translated text should respond to it in essentially the same fashion as the readers of the original source text responded.[28] Thus the quality of a translation hinged not so much on translating key words exactly the same way in every instance, or the literalistic mapping of equivalent structures, but rather on whether or not the reader was able to decode and understand the message conveyed in the translation.[29] This approach to translation in part drew its inspiration from Nida's engagement with neo-orthodoxy. Nida explicitly noted his debt to a Barthian position in his 1964 book *Toward a Science of Translating*. "One must recognize," he wrote, "that neo-orthodox theology has given a new perspective on the doctrine of divine inspiration. For the most part, it conceives of inspiration primarily in terms of the response of the receptor, and places less emphasis on what happened to the source at the time of writing." "Such a concept of inspiration means, however," Nida went on to explain, "that attention is inevitably shifted away from the details of wording in the original to the means

26. Chapter 2 discusses these linguistic issues at length.

27. Nida, *Bible Translating*, 12

28. Eugene A. Nida, "Principles of Translation as Exemplified by Bible Translating," in *On Translation*, ed. Reuben A. Brower (Cambridge, MA: Harvard University Press, 1959), 11–31.

29. Eugene A. Nida, *Fascinated by Languages* (Philadelphia: John Benjamins, 2003), 76.

by which the same message can be effectively communicated to present-day readers." On the other side of the coin, he argued that translators "who espouse the traditional, orthodox view of inspiration . . . often tend to favor quite close, literal renderings as the best way of preserving the inspiration of the writer by the Holy Spirit."[30] However, there were limits on just how far Nida was willing to go in reformulating the text. For example, he was not willing to reformulate figures of speech. Nida was not advocating paraphrastic Bible translations; dynamic equivalence was more about linguistic structure and a preservation of meaning across languages than outright paraphrasing of the text into the indigenous idiom. With that said, it remains that by driving a wedge between the text and its message Nida was assailing the idea that straightforward literalness functioned to preserve truth.

Dynamic equivalence was a revolutionary approach to Bible translation that steered translators away from too closely adhering to the linguistic forms of the source texts while urging them instead to recast source texts into the natural-occurring linguistic forms of the receptor languages. In its various permutations, Nida's concept of dynamic equivalence was destined to become the accepted translation theory among a majority of missionary translators by the 1970s. His work also had significant consequences for evangelicalism in the English-speaking world, since dynamic equivalence to varying degrees also formed the theoretical basis for most modern vernacular English translations.[31] By linking SIL to the discipline of American structural linguistics and then salvaging Nida's translation career, Townsend set in motion a chain of events that not only led to innovations on the missionary front but also influenced Bible translation and readership around the world. But, for SIL, that is only part of the story.

SIL translator William Wonderly made his own explorations into what he referred to as "communication theory." This line of inquiry also led him to question the doctrine of inerrancy. In the July 1952 and January 1953 issues of the American Bible Society's journal, the *Bible Translator*, Wonderly published a two-part article on "information-correspondence" in which he discussed the difficulties of translating a biblical text when the structure of the source language differed significantly from that of the receptor language. These differences in structure posed a number of problems for the translator, because "certain items of information . . . [that] are obligatory" in the source language "are either

30. Eugene A. Nida, *Toward a Science of Translating* (Leiden: Brill, 1964), 27.

31. D. A. Carson, "The Limits of Dynamic Equivalence in Bible Translation," *Notes on Translation* 121 (1987): 1–14, on file at GIAL; William A. Smalley, "Language and Culture in the Development of Bible Society Translation Theory and Practice," *International Bulletin of Missionary Research* 19, no. 2 (April 1995): 64–67.

absent or can be translated only by rather awkward circumlocution" in the receptor language. This addition or subtraction of information, even when held to a minimum, Wonderly maintained, could lead to "ambiguities not present in the [original] Greek" text of the New Testament. As such, "divine revelation" only reaches the reader of translated Scripture "in a form that has been modified." Wonderly therefore argued that a translator could not "claim nor expect divine inspiration for his version in the sense we claim it for the original texts."[32] Responding to a May 1955 letter from the SIL Mexico branch executive committee that all but accused him of heresy, Wonderly retorted that "if freedom from all manner of error is an absolutely essential feature of inspiration, it would seem that when inerrancy disappears as a result of translating we are left with a message that is no longer essentially inspired." As Wonderly understood it, a translation was merely "the best substitute that we can produce for a divinely inspired message."[33] While it was generally agreed that translations were not inspired in the same sense as the original autographs of Scripture, these were dangerous words to utter in conservative evangelical circles in the 1950s, since belief in inerrancy marked the boundary between the more progressive evangelicals on one side and the conservative evangelicals and fundamentalists on the other.[34]

At the time Wonderly began airing his views, WBT-SIL's stance on inspiration was broadly evangelical in character. Applicants in the 1930s and early 1940s were required only to grant "the full inspiration of the Scriptures."[35] With the official incorporation of WBT and SIL in 1942, this point was elaborated only slightly by requiring members to concur with the "divine inspiration and consequent authority of the whole canonical Scriptures."[36] Until the ferment surrounding Wonderly's views began to stoke fears, biblical inspiration was not a matter of much concern. However, as will be seen, the controversy surrounding his perspective led some conservative members to press for a narrower definition of the doctrine of inspiration. Indeed, demands were made that WBT-SIL members ascribe to inerrancy, a doctrine insisting that there were no errors of any kind in the original autographs of the Scriptures.

---

32. William Wonderly, "Information-Correspondence and the Translation of Ephesians into Zoque," part I, *Bible Translator* 3 (July 1952): 138–42, and "Information-Correspondence and the Translation of Ephesians into Zoque," part II, *Bible Translator* 4 (January 1953): 14–21.

33. Wonderly to WBT-SIL board of directors, June 8, 1955, p. 5, TA 11793.

34. George M. Marsden, *Reforming Fundamentalism: Fuller Seminary and the New Evangelicalism* (Grand Rapids: Eerdmans, 1987), 224–28.

35. "Application Blank for Entrance to Camp Wycliffe," 1940, 1, TA 43057.

36. "Corporate By-Laws of Wycliffe Bible Translators," September 15, 1942, 7, TA 41523.

Under a pall of suspicion in May 1955, Wonderly's future in SIL looked dim.[37] Despite the atmosphere of mistrust, Pike unflinchingly stood by his colleague, expecting him not only to carry on teaching at SIL but also to share his theoretical insights with students. "By all means," Pike assured Wonderly, "you should continue to use communication theory in your classes." When Townsend read the letter, he fumed, and in the margin of his carbon copy he scribbled a large "NO!," accompanied by an arrow pointing directly to the word "theory."[38] Still bristling, he followed up with a censorious letter to Pike. "Surely," he implored, "that theory isn't essential to good translating. Then, why wreck us over it?" "Theorizing," he vented, "is extremely dangerous." "What our students need," Townsend lectured, "are *practical aid[s]* to Bible translating."[39] Townsend was clearly upset, and he feared that Pike and Wonderly were acting dangerously by toying with theoretical matters, especially ones that touched on inspiration. With that said, he did begrudgingly allow that linguistic research might entail some theoretical matters, but that there was no place for it in the classroom. "There is," Townsend wrote the board of directors, "plenty to be said on Bible translation of a purely practical nature to occupy all the classroom time available."[40] This was not the only occasion where the general director balked at what he thought was legitimately beyond the bare technical necessities for turning out adequate translations. In the early 1960s, one of SIL's top linguists was developing original approaches to the study of discourse, but Townsend refused to release him for a short period from his translation work in order to disseminate his theoretical concepts at SIL's summer school, for it would slow the Bible translation project.[41] Townsend never appreciated fully the implications of pursuing a truly scholarly approach, whether in linguistics or translation; nor did he ever understand completely what constituted the scientific enterprise. In his mind science was mainly a matter of acquiring technical competence and then applying it to a specific task. In a word, Pike and Wonderly needed to get back to the basics.

After learning that at least two unnamed but "influential and valuable" WBT-SIL members were threatening to leave the organization if he were allowed to remain, Wonderly finally resigned over the inerrancy issue in August

37. Leal to Wonderly, June 23, 1955, TA 11784; Kenneth L. Pike to Wonderly, May 30, 1955, TA 11340; Cameron Townsend to WBT-SIL board of directors, June 1, 1955, TA 11343.

38. Kenneth L. Pike to Wonderly, Townsend's carbon copy, May 30, 1955, TA 11340.

39. Cameron Townsend to Kenneth L. Pike and Evelyn Pike, June 15, 1955, TA 11335.

40. Cameron Townsend to WBT-SIL board of directors, June 1, 1955, TA 11343.

41. Beekman to James Loriot (alternatively, Lauriault), September 11, 1962, TA 21182.

1955, and he subsequently joined Nida at the American Bible Society.[42] Wonderly's departure would prove to be a not insignificant loss to SIL.

Wonderly's position on inspiration had been a source of apprehension for several years before his departure. In an attempt to block his ideas from spreading, a few of WBT-SIL's more conservative members initiated a movement in 1951 to narrow the organization's doctrinal position on inspiration. Exceptionally concerned was one of SIL's foremost up-and-coming scholars, Robert Longacre, who later recalled that he was terribly upset over Wonderly's playing "fast and loose with inerrancy."[43] Longacre and fellow SIL member Otis Leal led a campaign to have the 1951 WBT-SIL conference replace the organization's moderate "inspiration" statement with a stricter one that insisted on "inerrancy." Both men were educationally equipped to launch a fight on inerrancy. Longacre and Leal had graduated in the mid-1940s from Faith Theological Seminary and Westminster Seminary, respectively. In the 1940s and 1950s, these two seminaries, along with Dallas Theological Seminary, constituted a trio of unapologetically fundamentalist institutions of higher learning where academic standards remained a notch above those of most other independent Bible schools.[44] Longacre and Leal successfully convinced the 1951 conference to append a "declaratory statement" to the organization's 1942 doctrinal statement that read: "We affirm that the doctrine of Divine inspiration of the Scriptures includes their being free from all manner of error in the original manuscripts." Every candidate joining after 1951 was required to agree with this amended version of the doctrinal statement, and had to do so "without mental reservations and in full faith."[45] At the next biennial conference in 1953, conformity to this qualifying statement was required of the entire membership.[46] WBT-SIL's position on the doctrine of Scripture had narrowed considerably by 1953, reflecting a more fundamentalist position.

Despite the controversy surrounding the Wonderly affair and the conference action on the doctrine of inspiration, not everyone in WBT-SIL in this period was a committed exponent of absolute inerrancy. Therefore the revised

42. Wonderly to WBT board of directors, August 5, 1955, TA 11773; September 15, 1955, TA 11768. (N.B. It is very likely that the two men in question were Otis Leal and Robert Longacre, since they were the leaders of the movement to narrow WBT-SIL's doctrine of inspiration to bring it into alignment with the inerrancy view.)

43. Robert Longacre, interview by author, June 29, 2010, Dallas, Texas.

44. Joel A. Carpenter, *Revive Us Again: The Reawakening of American Fundamentalism* (New York: Oxford University Press, 1997), 22; Marsden, *Reforming Fundamentalism*, 24.

45. Robert Longacre, interview by author, June 29, 2010, Dallas, Texas; WBT conference minutes, September 13, 1951, WSA.

46. "Letter to Members," Pucallpa, Peru, February 1, 1954, TA 41409.

statement on inerrancy did not sit well with more moderate-minded members, such as the young Frank Robbins, who would one day rise to the presidency of SIL. Robbins, recalling the events surrounding Wonderly's departure, indicated that both he and his wife "were very much for Bill." Although they were Baptists at the time of Wonderly's resignation, "We believed [then] . . . more or less what our [current] Presbyterian Church says, 'the Bible is trustworthy' . . . , God got his message across, but that doesn't mean that every little scientific detail is correct."[47] As the agitation mounted between the two camps, Pike thought that the organization "was in for a rough time unless the Lord lets us find a quiet solution for agreement."[48] Apparently the parties to the debate found the Lord's favor. Only a month after Wonderly resigned, the 1955 Wycliffe conference once again amended the doctrinal statement. Conference delegates did affirm that the concept of "the divine inspiration and consequent authority" of the Bible "implies Scriptural inerrancy." However, while this statement would seem to lock WBT-SIL into an unequivocal position on inerrancy, the conference specified three different, and somewhat inconsistent, qualifying interpretations. Candidates and members could choose the one that best represented their view. The first and third qualifying statements were essentially inerrantist. The second choice was somewhat less constricting, allowing one to "affirm that the doctrine of divine inspiration of the Scriptures includes their complete truthfulness."[49] This somewhat ambiguous compromise reflected an effort to find some middle ground that would satisfy a majority of WBT-SIL's members. Thus the 1955 statement on inerrancy allowed some breadth of opinion while still maintaining a broadly evangelical position on the doctrine of inspiration.

The upshot of the 1955 compromise was that the WBT-SIL membership continued to exhibit a remarkable variety of opinions on the subject of inspiration. Responses in interviews to questions about the doctrine of inspiration during their WBT-SIL careers ranged from that of Glen Stairs, a 1948 Bob Jones University graduate, who averred that "inerrancy is absolute," to that of John Alsop, a 1956 Fuller Seminary graduate, who offered that he "avoided discussions about inerrancy" and simply believed in the "full reliability" of Scriptures.[50] Within WBT-SIL, where a variety of views prevailed, members kept peace by generally eschewing debate on such matters. Alsop's comment, that he had avoided discussion on inerrancy, was typical after the mid-1950s,

47. Frank Robbins, interview by author, September 2, 2008, Dallas, Texas.

48. Kenneth L. Pike to Cameron Townsend, June 20, 1955, TA 11337.

49. WBT, corporation meeting minutes, September 15, 1955, p. 14, WSA.

50. Glen Stairs, interview by author, June 29, 2009, Dallas, Texas; John Alsop, interview by author, September 4, 2008, Dallas, Texas.

and it became something of an unspoken rule in the organization that one did not discuss doctrinal matters, especially inerrancy, openly. As Robert Longacre trenchantly put it in an interview, inerrancy was treated in the manner of the US military's "don't ask, don't tell" policy.[51] The fractious nature of inerrancy was dodged in WBT-SIL by sweeping the matter under the rug.

After the controversy of the 1950s, the closest WBT-SIL came to elaborating a detailed position on inspiration occurred in 1966. Otis Leal, looking for some measure by which to judge candidates' views on inspiration, requested Kenneth Pike's opinion on the subject. In the main, Pike believed "the Bible is not to be treated as a textbook of science, but as teaching faith and practice in the Christian life." In fact, Pike feared that a "rigid legalistic view could lead to great distress of mind." Therefore, it was his judgment that "we should be as concerned about over-rigidity in a legalistic but non-realistic view of the nature of Biblical language, as we are in a liberalistic view." Pike's understanding of the subject at this point was remarkably similar to that of Wonderly in the 1950s. This was especially evident when he qualified that "Jesus Spoke Human Language, and within human language spoke truth."[52] This was certainly no argument for absolute inerrancy, but rather was an appeal for toleration within limits on the matter when evaluating new recruits on their doctrinal beliefs.

Another measure of the breadth of opinion on Scripture was the favorable attitude among some SIL translators toward the Revised Standard Version of the Bible (RSV). The release of the complete RSV in September 1952 met with considerable consternation within conservative evangelicalism. More than anything else, it was the RSV translators' choice to render the Hebrew word *almah* in Isaiah 7:14 as "young woman" rather than "virgin" that caused distress.[53] The RSV was particularly anathematized by fundamentalists, especially those of the more militant variety, such as Carl McIntire.[54] The Reverend Martin Luther Hux, a Southern Baptist minister in Wake Forest, North Carolina, gained nationwide notoriety when he burned a page torn from an RSV Bible in November 1952.[55] While Hux was making headlines and McIntire was railing against the new translation, the RSV was showing up on SIL translators' desks. Turner Blount, translator of the Navajo New Testament, was "convinced that it was the best version," and he planned to use the RSV text as the basis for his diglot translation. He worried, however, that the conservative backlash would cripple his desire to use "the most accurate and readable translation for the

---

51. Robert Longacre, interview by author, June 29, 2010, Dallas, Texas.
52. Kenneth L. Pike to Leal, "Topic: Inspiration," August 15, 1966, TA 24502.
53. Thuesen, *In Discordance with the Scriptures*, 124.
54. Thuesen, *In Discordance with the Scriptures*, 101–2, 106–8, 112–13.
55. Thuesen, *In Discordance with the Scriptures*, 93–95.

Navajos."[56] Kenneth Pike expressed his approbation of the RSV, saying he was "impressed with its integrity" and its "scholarship." "I am personally convinced," Pike asserted, "that no combination of conservative scholars with whom I am personally acquainted was in a position to do as fine a job as that which has been done by these liberals."[57] The reception of the RSV in SIL suggests that whatever undercurrent of fundamentalist conservatism existed within the organization regarding the Scriptures, it was far removed from the style of militant reaction that was cropping up elsewhere.

The Beekman Revolution and the Bible Translation Strategy

When Eugene Nida and William Wonderly resigned in 1953 and 1955, respectively, they took with them to the American Bible Society much of the emphasis on translation theory that existed in SIL at the time. Yet, interest in translation theory did not forever lie dormant in SIL; it was resuscitated under the direction of SIL translator John Beekman in the 1960s. Throughout the late 1940s and 1950s, Beekman struggled to render the New Testament into the Chol language of southern Mexico, and his natural sensitivity to cross-cultural communication barriers caused him to worry over how to ensure a readable translation. As Beekman put the finishing touches on his Chol translation in the late 1950s, he undertook to advance SIL's work in Central America, where he became aware that many missionary-translators were struggling to produce idiomatic translations. It was his ambition to eliminate overly literal translations by implementing a more or less dynamic equivalence approach to translation, but one that reflected a distinctively SIL approach to translation theory. He also noted that every translation team was wading through essentially the same thick pile of commentaries and lexicons in an attempt to root out bits of information that would guide their work. It was from these observations that Beekman arrived at his vision for a reconstructed approach to translation.

Beekman took a four-pronged approach to realize these goals. In the first place, he sought to train and equip SIL's best translators to become consultants on par with those of the American Bible Society, such as Nida and Wonderly. Second, he initiated an effort to provide translators with commentary compilations and back translations. Commentary compilations keyed to verses would reduce redundancy, as translators would no longer have to mine commentaries for the needed data. Coupled with the commentaries, back translations into

---

56. Blount to Cameron Townsend, October 12, 1952, TA 8178.
57. Kenneth L. Pike to Nyman, January 7, 1953, p. 1, TA 8663.

English of the most outstanding translations already completed were supplied to translation teams, allowing them to observe how others had solved problems such as translating metaphors. In the third place, Beekman developed an ongoing program of translation workshops where translators received advanced training and consultant help away from the rigors and isolation of the village. Fourth, he launched *Notes on Translation*, an in-house journal for disseminating and sharing scholarly developments in translation theory and practice.[58] Beekman's solution was nothing if not comprehensive, and that he carried out this program while suffering from a malfunctioning aortic valve, for which he received an experimental plastic valve that was audible to bystanders, gained him fame as the "man with the noisy heart" in Wycliffe. Thus there is little wonder that he was twice immortalized, once by Wycliffe writer Hugh Steven and on another occasion by Wycliffe's chief outside chronicler, James C. Hefley. It cannot be denied that Beekman deserved these accolades, since by the mid-1960s he had revolutionized SIL's approach to translation.[59]

Although having earned only a master of arts degree, Beekman was nonetheless a gifted linguist. Most importantly, he possessed the ability to relate his ideas in a less intellectually intimidating framework than the erudite Nida, and he was therefore the ideal person to reintroduce the concept of dynamic equivalence into SIL.[60] "The clear implication from the differences in languages," Beekman wrote in 1965, "is that any message to be communicated from one language to another should be conveyed in the linguistic form of the receptor language." "Only thus," he emphasized, "can meaning be preserved."[61] Beekman convincingly argued that overly literal translations, when they failed to communicate, actually impaired inspiration.[62] With Beekman leading the way, interest in translation theory was revived in SIL, and the results were rapidly integrated into the translation process. By 1966 he was able to report that "our translators have moved away from any traces of extreme or recurring literalism

---

58. Doris Bartholomew, interview by author, August 4, 2009, Catalina, Arizona; Richard Blight, interview by author, July 2, 2009, Dallas, Texas; John Beekman to SIL branches, August 23, 1965, TA 22669; Beekman to SIL directors, August 24, 1965, TA 22666; John Lind, interview by author, July 27, 2009, Wilcox, Arizona; Eugene Minor, interview by author, September 10, 2008, Dallas, Texas; Bruce R. Moore, "Translation Theory," in *The Summer Institute of Linguistics: Its Works and Contributions*, ed. Ruth M. Brend and Kenneth L. Pike (The Hague: Mouton, 1977), 148.

59. James C. Hefley, *Peril by Choice: The Story of John and Elaine Beekman, Wycliffe Bible Translators in Mexico* (Grand Rapids: Zondervan, 1968); Hugh Steven, *The Man with the Noisy Heart: The John Beekman Story* (Chicago: Moody Press, 1979).

60. Watters to Cameron Townsend, April 15, 1959, p. 2, TA 17170.

61. John Beekman, "Idiomatic versus Literal Translations," *Notes on Translation* 18 (November 1965): 9, on file at GIAL.

62. Beekman, "Idiomatic versus Literal Translations," 8–12.

as of several years ago."[63] SIL missionary-translators were, in Beekman's words, no longer turning out "blunt swords."[64]

John Beekman did not simply follow Nida's approach to translation; he too was an innovator. In addition to recasting the structure of the source text into the linguistic forms of the receptor language—one of the most basic principles of dynamic equivalence—Beekman also encouraged translators to reformulate difficult-to-understand aspects of the source text in the idiom of the receptor language. By way of example, one SIL translator in the mid-1960s rendered the phrase "washed the feet of the brethren" in 1 Timothy 5:10 as "it was no trouble for them to help the brethren," since the indigenous readers would not understand the meaning behind foot washing. In another place, to avoid confusing readers who were apparently unfamiliar with the significance of gold, the same translator reworded "gold ring" in James 2:2 as "fancy ring."[65] The essence of this problem was later restated by a translator in a 1975 issue of *Notes on Translation* entitled "The Gospel of Mark: Good News or Confusion?" "In certain tribal situations," wrote SIL's Peter K. E. Kingston, "the receptor culture is so radically different from that of the Gospel [of Mark], that there is considerable danger of the message being lost in a confusing welter of new cultural information."[66] To solve this problem, SIL translators were encouraged to produce what were referred to as "idiomatic" or "meaning-based" translations. This method not only deployed the structural conventions of the receptor language after the manner of dynamic equivalence, but also rendered implicit information explicit, reworked figures of speech into comprehensible local idiom, and generally clarified passages that would otherwise have mystified readers who were uninitiated in biblical knowledge, and all this without resorting to extensive footnotes.

The American Bible Society (ABS) published a majority of SIL's translations. Therefore, when SIL's New Testament translations became, in varying degrees, more paraphrastic in the mid to late 1960s, ABS began expressing misgivings about these moves beyond what it saw as the limits of good dynamic equivalence translation theory and practice. Of one SIL translation he inspected in early 1968, Eugene Nida remarked that it was "good Christian literature but not a translation."[67] Later that same year, Nida complained to Beekman that SIL was "departing further and further from the norms which the Bible Societies

63. John Beekman, "Translation Report to the 1966 Mexico Branch Conference," 1, TA 40292.

64. John Beekman and John Callow, *Translating the Word of God, with Scripture and Topical Indexes* (Grand Rapids: Zondervan, 1974), 349.

65. Wonderly to Beekman, June 12, 1968, MBA.

66. Peter K. E. Kingston, "The Gospel of Mark: Good News or Confusion?," *Notes on Translation* 57 (September 1975): 22, on file at GIAL.

67. Quoted in Beekman to Elson, February 5, 1968, MBA.

have found to be essential for accurate, faithful translation."[68] At the heart of this debate between SIL and ABS were differing perspectives on the role of the Scriptures in missions and church life. Whereas SIL maintained that the Bible was the cornerstone of its missionary strategy, ABS insisted that the Scriptures were the possession of the church. Put another way, the Bible Society believed the church interpreted the text, whereas SIL argued that the Bible, if appropriately translated into the local idiom, was essentially self-interpreting. The implications of these differing views for Bible translation theory and practice were substantial. The essence of the debate is clearly seen in an argument that occurred when Nida was consulting on an SIL translation of the Gospel of Mark. In Mark 9 the metaphor "you are the salt of the earth" was rendered by the SIL translator as "salted with fire." Nida objected to this rephrasing. He insisted that if the metaphor would not be understood, then it could be footnoted, but certainly not reconfigured, since that would entail crossing the boundary into paraphrasing.[69] According to SIL, a monolingual reader with no prior biblical knowledge should be able to access the meaning of Scripture without ecclesiastical intermediaries, and it was therefore necessary to produce translations that were as free as possible from obscure or difficult readings without recourse to numerous footnotes.

Another area of disagreement between SIL and ABS was the publication of New Testaments in cases where the use of Scriptures was in doubt. The Bible Society wanted assurance that the translated Scriptures would be used by an existing church; SIL was content to leave matters in the hands of a few literate believers. This was a long-running debate between SIL and ABS stretching back to 1950, when the Bible Society refused to print Kenneth Pike's Mixteco New Testament translation because its Committee on Versions was unwilling to incur the cost of publication until it had sufficient assurance that a "self-sustaining" church was in place.[70] It was the policy of ABS, in language communities where the number of speakers was few or the Christian community small, to "publish only if the translator, [or] his church or mission agrees to purchase at Agency cost price all copies remaining in the Society's inventory four years after publication date."[71] As for SIL, it had never allowed the population of the language group or the number of believers to influence its production of a

68. Nida to Beekman, October 4, 1968, MBA.

69. Beekman to "Williams," selected excerpts relevant to ABS relation with WBT, December 16, 1968, MBA.

70. Quote from Eric M. North to Cameron Townsend, December 12, 1950, p. 1, TA 6498; Elson to SIL "Colleagues," November 1, 1966, MBA; North to Kenneth L. Pike, December 12, 1950, PSC; Kenneth L. Pike, "Our Own Tongue," 15.

71. "Publication Policy for Foreign Language Translations," ABS to SIL, August 6, 1956, MBA.

translated New Testament. "If we say that a small tribe is not worth the effort, the lives, and the investment necessary to reach them," Pike wrote in 1959, "then in our view we have denied the gospel since we have denied the worth of the individual."[72] The merits of either argument aside, SIL could never be faulted for considering even the smallest or remotest of peoples unworthy of its efforts.

By the late 1960s, the relationship between ABS and SIL was in tatters.[73] In Beekman's words, for SIL to cooperate with and have the Bible Society publish its translations entailed nothing less than becoming a "submissive satellite" of the ABS.[74] In response to the Bible Society's criticism, the WBT-SIL board of directors encouraged SIL branches around the world to seek other publishers for its New Testament translations.[75]

In the late 1970s, SIL translator T. Wayne Dye released the initial results of a study in which he concluded that there were "dozens of languages where vernacular New Testaments remain[ed] essentially unread." "In a good many places," Dye asserted, "spiritual results of a lifetime of work were very small, at least up to the present time."[76] This piece of research seemed to indicate that the Bible Society's concerns over readership of translations were well founded. Dye went on to argue that it was imperative for translators to train church leaders in the application of translated Scriptures to the lives of their church members. During the course of his research, Dye found that "new converts did not simply pick up Bibles, study them and come to understand and apply them to their lives. In most cases," he continued, "the translators were the key people who showed the beginning new church how to apply the Scriptures."[77] Moreover, he discredited the idea that the Bible alone was an instrument of Christian conversion. "My data indicate that in Mexico less than one convert in a thousand became a believer by reading the Bible alone. In the Philippines I found that none did."[78] In summary, Dye concluded that "all of my data went against the idea that the churches would have been better off left completely alone."[79] To those who insisted on following the classical SIL approach to translation, these were troubling words.

---

72. Kenneth L. Pike, "Our Own Tongue," 6

73. By the 1990s, the relations were much improved. At the time of this writing, the relationship between SIL and ABS is functioning harmoniously, as is the broader relationship between SIL and the Bible societies under the umbrella of the United Bible Societies.

74. Beekman to SIL branch directors, December 21, 1968, MBA.

75. Beekman to SIL branch directors, December 21, 1968, MBA.

76. T. Wayne Dye, *The Bible Translation Strategy* (n.p.: n.p., 1980), 261.

77. Dye, *The Bible Translation Strategy*, 191.

78. Dye, *The Bible Translation Strategy*, 201.

79. Dye, *The Bible Translation Strategy*, 241.

The impulse for Dye's research project actually originated outside of SIL. Donald McGavran, at Fuller Seminary's School of World Mission and the Institute of Church Growth, was a vocal and influential proponent of applying social science research to missionary activity as a means for uncovering the factors that stimulated or impeded church growth.[80] McGavran insisted in his 1955 work, entitled *The Bridges of God: A Study in the Strategy of Missions*, that "what is called for is an extended series of factual studies of the effectiveness of missions, the growth of churches, and the ways in which people become Christian," and he continued to ring the clarion for church growth studies over the next twenty-five years.[81] This style of technical missiology cut against the grain of missionary thinking, where results were generally considered to be mostly dependent on the ineffable movements of the Holy Spirit. For McGavran, it was possible to discover the patterns by which the Holy Spirit worked, and he therefore maintained that missionaries should not blindly follow traditional practices but should put their strategies to the test through rigorous social science research.

McGavran, an acquaintance of SIL's executive director Benjamin Elson, goaded the somewhat reluctant Elson into carrying out research on the organization's translation projects. He did this by convincing the leadership of Trinity United Presbyterian Church in Santa Ana, California, a significant sponsor of the WBT-SIL cause, to fund research aimed at discovering the factors behind both effective and ineffective Bible translation projects. Finding himself backed into a corner, Elson chose Dye, who held an MA in anthropology from the University of Michigan, to conduct the study. Beginning in 1974 and continuing over the next several years, Dye researched in Mexico and the Philippines as part of a doctoral program at Fuller's School of World Mission.[82]

Dye's findings were not well received in some quarters. SIL's Mexico branch, the oldest and probably the one most steeped in tradition, was strongly opposed.[83] SIL's chief linguist was disturbed by what he read. In a November 1979 response to Dye, Kenneth Pike wrote that "you might wish to consider the following to see if it would lead you to the change of a sentence here and there." What followed was a strenuous six-page exercise in chopping away at the very foundations of Dye's research.[84] Dye had wanted to dedicate the published

80. Donald A. McGavran, *The Bridges of God: A Study in the Strategy of Missions* (London: World Dominion Press, [1955] 1957); Marsden, *Reforming Fundamentalism*, 237–44; Donald A. McGavran, *Understanding Church Growth*, 3rd ed. (Grand Rapids: Eerdmans, [1970] 1990).

81. McGavran, *The Bridges of God*, 153.

82. T. Wayne Dye, interview by author, July 22, 2014, Dallas, Texas.

83. T. Wayne Dye, interview by author, July 22, 2014, Dallas, Texas.

84. Kenneth L. Pike to Dye, November 15, 1979, PSC. (I am grateful to SIL's Vurnell Cobbey for bringing this letter and the one that follows to my attention.)

dissertation to SIL's top academic figure, but after receipt of this sharply critical assessment, he informed Pike that "I will not embarrass you by dedicating the book to you." "Maybe," Dye added, "there will be another more neutral topic someday."[85] Although SIL published the dissertation in book form in 1980, no publisher was listed. In the foreword, Beekman distanced SIL somewhat from the volume. "Publication," he wrote, "does not imply an endorsement by the SIL organization." "Rather," he qualified, "it indicates a desire that they [the results] should be made available to stimulate further discussion and research on an important topic."[86] Coming from SIL's top translation consultant and theorist, Beekman's circumspect disclaimer, not to mention SIL's refusal to list the organization as publisher, reveals the depth of dissension that Dye's research caused some of his colleagues.

SIL was not unaware that its translation-as-mission strategy could potentially miscarry. As early as 1938, Pike seemed to comprehend the importance of developing a sufficiently trained cadre of local Christian leaders to ensure readership of the translated Scriptures. Training indigenous church leaders from the earliest stages of a translation project was critically important, he argued, "for men are not raised up and given full spiritual growth in a day." He even suggested that if insufficient results were visible upon completion of a New Testament, then the translator should remain in place to guarantee the development of a church, "or else the Testament may never be of value to the tribe."[87] Pike's advice was not entirely disregarded, but the bar for a successful translation project remained low—a minimum of a few literate readers and believers. Better results were hoped for but not required for translators to move on to other efforts, especially in administration and leadership. Pike's worries came home to roost in the very situation in which he had translated the New Testament. Visiting the Mixtecs in the early 1970s, he found little to show for his efforts.[88] Pike was not alone; WBT-SIL's founder made the same discovery. In 1963, Townsend frankly admitted that his Cakchiquel New Testament had "never been used a great deal in the pulpits of the native churches." "Had I continued among the Cakchiquels," he added, "it would have been introduced with great advantage into the public life of the church but as you know, God had other things for me to do."[89] Taken together, the practice of pressing translators into other areas of service upon the completion of a New Testament, a prevail-

85. Dye to Kenneth L. Pike, January 1980, PSC.

86. Dye, *The Bible Translation Strategy*, 10.

87. Kenneth L. Pike to Cameron Townsend, March 31, 1938, pp. 2–3, TA 2357.

88. Kenneth L. Pike, with Hugh Steven, *Pike's Perspectives: An Anthology of Thought, Insight, and Moral Purpose* (Langley, BC: Credo Publishing 1989), 61–62.

89. Cameron Townsend, "Views of Vernacular Scriptures," February 1, 1963, TA 21396.

ing sense of urgency, and the belief in the power of the Scriptures to function in the absence of missionaries overrode concerns about the future use of translated Scriptures in the wake of SIL's departure from a language community.

All this is not to say that WBT-SIL never enjoyed widespread readership of its translated New Testaments or the development of a sizable number of Christian converts as a result of its efforts. When the historian Todd Hartch examined the work of SIL in Mexico, he found cases of both success and failure. Renowned for completing three New Testaments, the team of Marianna Slocum and Florence Gerdel, translator and nurse, respectively, was destined to triumph over initial resistance of the Tzeltals of Chiapas, Mexico. Although carrying official letters from the ministry of education, Slocum and temporary coworker Ethel Wallis were rebuffed by the Tzeltals in the town of Bachajón in the early 1940s. Finding the welcome mat rolled out by the Tzeltals in Corralito, Slocum and Gerdel worked side by side translating and offering medical services. By the time the Tzeltal New Testament was published in 1956, the Corralito church that had come into existence under their tutelage was itself sending out missionaries, who founded an additional twelve churches, with the total number of Protestant converts in the thousands.[90] In 1941, SIL translators Kenneth and Martha Hilton took up work among the widely dispersed Tarahumaras, where Eugene Nida had failed after only a few months.[91] Persevering over an extended period that was marked by hardships both physical and psychological, the Hiltons published the Tarahumara New Testament in 1972. Yet there was little to show for all their labors. They could count only one convert, their indigenous cotranslator, and only a handful of individuals had learned to read.[92] These two cases represent the poles between outstanding success and near abject failure of WBT-SIL's translation strategy. The hundreds of other translation projects carried out by SIL fell somewhere between them, and it was this wide variation in results that Dye addressed in his study.

If there was stiff resistance in some quarters to Dye's study, in others the publication of *The Bible Translation Strategy* in 1980 marked something of a turning point. In 1985 a revised and expanded edition of Dye's book appeared. In the new edition, he detailed some important changes taking place in SIL's approach to translation projects that had occurred since the mid to late 1970s. Greater attention was being given to shaping translation projects to fit the specific sociocultural contexts in which they were situated. Moreover, translators were given help in "program planning" and taught principles of Scripture ap-

90. Todd Hartch, *Missionaries of the State: The Summer Institute of Linguistics, State Formation, and Indigenous Mexico, 1935–1985* (Tuscaloosa: University of Alabama Press, 2006), 95–100.

91. Nida's inability to withstand the physical and psychological strains of living among the Tarahumaras is recounted in chapter 2.

92. Hartch, *Missionaries of the State*, 100–104.

plication in "Scripture-in-Use workshops." As well, a new in-house journal, *Notes on Scripture Use*, was launched. "The current focus on Scripture in Use," Dye wrote, "comes from a recognition that the principal contribution of Bible translation to the church is the local language Scriptures, which God can use to build up His church."[93] Not all these developments were directly attributable to Dye's research, but his work gave credence to those translators who were orientated toward a more comprehensive approach to the Bible translation strategy. By the mid-1980s, the "Bible alone" concept was eroding in at least some SIL branches, and an increasing number of translators were moving closer to the Bible translation strategy long advocated by Eugene Nida.

There were, however, no winners or losers in the translation theory and practice debate. Down to at least the 1990s, SIL and the Bible Society generally followed the meaning-based and dynamic equivalence approaches, respectively. Both methods were destined to come in for criticism from various perspectives, and from within and without both organizations.[94] Furthermore, over the past couple of decades, as WBT and SIL began to translate more often where existing churches were present, the trend slowly began to shift back toward a somewhat more literal style of translation. These multifaceted translation theory debates, which remain alive down to the present day, are beyond the bounds of the present study. What can be said is that both SIL and the Bible Society were working on the theoretical frontiers of textual translation, and both organizations were making genuine efforts to produce both accurate and comprehensible Scripture translations. The means to this end remained challenging, and translation difficulties abounded on every side. Each new language encountered threatened to throw old verities into question. One veteran SIL translator, "always a bit smug" about how well she had handled the translation of metaphors into Toboli, was later brought up short when her methods proved inadequate during a late 1970s translation workshop in which she was teaching. "Where just the moment before there had been one very new and frustrated translator and one very wise and experienced consultant, there were now two frustrated translators."[95] There

---

93. T. Wayne Dye, *The Bible Translation Strategy*, rev. ed. (Dallas: Wycliffe Bible Translators, 1985), 273.

94. Carson, "Limits of Dynamic Equivalence," 1–14; Ernst-August Gutt, *Translation and Relevance: Cognition and Context* (Oxford: Basil Blackwell, 1991); Ernst-August Gutt, *Relevance Theory: A Guide to Successful Communication in Translation* (Dallas: SIL International, 1992); Stephen Pattemore, "Framing Nida: The Relevance of Translation Theory in the United Bible Societies," in *A History of Bible Translation*, ed. Philip A. Noss (Rome: Edizioni Di Storia E Letteratura [American Bible Society], 2007), 217–63.

95. Vivian Forsberg, "Understanding Metaphors," *Notes on Translation* 68 (March 1978): 30, on file at GIAL.

had been and always would be a multitude of complex and interrelated factors that could undermine the Bible translation effort, such as the capability of the translators, the readability of the translation, the prevailing level of literacy, the sociocultural context, bilingualism or multilingualism, and other mission efforts, to name but a few.

The one area in which SIL indubitably led that way was the study of discourse. Beginning in the late 1950s—and displaying scant regard for the Bloomfieldian notion that the sentence was the upper limit of proper linguistic analysis after the fashion of Pike's tagmemics—several SIL linguists began to carry out pioneering work on the study of discourse.[96] In 1958, SIL's James Loriot produced a groundbreaking study of Shipibo paragraph structure from a tagmemic perspective. Loriot's detailed analysis revealed the underlying structural conventions that governed paragraph-level discourse in this indigenous language spoken in Peru.[97] Robert Longacre, another leading scholar of discourse analysis, spent the greater part of his long SIL career producing innovative approaches to elucidating the structural aspects of various genres of literature, including Old Testament texts.[98] That Longacre was both an outstanding scholar and an ardent exponent of inerrancy indicates that these traits are not mutually exclusive. In fact, during an interview for this study, he pointed to his high view of Scripture as a primary impulse behind his ambition to lay bare the discourse features of biblical texts.[99] Joseph E. Grimes's *Thread of Discourse*, published in 1975, was another significant contribution by an SIL scholar to this burgeoning discipline.[100] An expanding body of scholarship by other SIL linguists, including John Beekman, Sarah Gudschinsky, Eugene Loos, Velma B. Pickett, Viola G. Waterhouse, and Mary Ruth Wise, to name but a few of the most noteworthy, conclusively demonstrated that connected discourse was not merely sentences or clauses strung together, but rather, various genres of dis-

96. Pike's tagmemic theory of language and structural linguistics is covered at length in chapter 2.

97. James Loriot, "Shipibo Paragraph Structure" (unpublished manuscript, 1958), later published as James Loriot and Barbra Hollenbach, "Shipibo Paragraph Structure," *Foundations of Language* 6 (1970): 43–66.

98. Robert E. Longacre, "String Constituent Analysis," *Language* 36, no. 1 (January–March 1960): 63–88; Robert E. Longacre, "Some Fundamental Insights of Tagmemics," *Language* 41, no. 1 (February 1965): 65–76; Robert E. Longacre, "Hierarchy in Language," in *Method and Theory in Linguistics*, ed. Paul L. Garvin (The Hague: Mouton, 1970), 173–95; Robert E. Longacre, *Discourse, Paragraph, and Sentence Structure in Selected Philippine Languages* (Santa Ana, CA: Summer Institute of Linguistics, 1968); Robert E. Longacre, *An Anatomy of Speech Notions* (Lisse, Netherlands: Peter de Ridder, 1976).

99. Robert Longacre, interview by author, June 29, 2010, Dallas, Texas.

100. Joseph E. Grimes, *The Thread of Discourse* (The Hague: Mouton, 1975).

course were structured in recognizable forms that carried semantic weight at a level above the sentence.[101]

Advances in discourse studies, while significant in their own right, also provided some of the essential techniques required for producing better-quality meaning-based and dynamic-equivalence-style translations. Once it became better understood how units of language above the sentence were instrumental in conveying meaning within a language, it then followed that translation from one language to another required that Bible translators possess an understanding of the discourse features of both the target language and the original source text. In part by drawing upon the advances in discourse analysis, three SIL linguist-translators authored two important works on producing meaning-based translations. John Beekman and John Callow's 1974 *Translating the Word of God* was the first to appear.[102] This work was followed by Mildred Larson's *Meaning-Based Translation* in 1984.[103] Whereas much of Nida's writing on translation remained at theoretical and somewhat abstract levels, this body of translation scholarship developed by SIL from the 1960s advanced specific procedures for producing meaning-based translations, and these volumes, especially Larson's, came to be recognized as standard works on Bible translation.[104]

SIL's progress in Bible translation theory and practice notwithstanding, garnering credentials in linguistics, and to a lesser degree literacy and education, remained the ticket for making one's career in SIL into the 1980s. The focus on linguistics was also driven by the practical need to decipher unwritten languages in many Bible translation projects, and by the requirements of SIL's government contracts. Therefore a vast majority of the organization's scholars continued to undertake postgraduate studies in linguistics at secular universities, and they

101. John Beekman, "Propositions and Their Relations within a Discourse," *Notes on Translation* 37 (1970): 6–23, on file at GIAL; Joseph E. Grimes, "Positional Analysis," *Language* 43 (1967): 437–44; Sarah C. Gudschinsky, "Discourse Analysis of a Mazatec Text," *International Journal of American Linguistics* 25, no. 3 (July 1959): 139–46; Eugene E. Loos, "Capanahua Narration Structure," in *Studies in Literature and Language* 4 (supplement) (Austin: University of Texas, 1963), 697–742; Velma B. Pickett, "The Grammatical Hierarchy of Isthmus Zapotec" (PhD diss., University of Michigan, 1959); Viola G. Waterhouse, "The Grammatical Structure of Oaxaca Chontal" (PhD diss., University of Michigan, 1958); Mary Ruth Wise, "Identification of Participants in Discourse: A Study of Aspects of Form and Meaning in Nomatsiguenga" (PhD diss., University of Michigan, 1970).

102. Beekman and Callow, *Translating the Word of God, with Scripture and Topical Indexes.*

103. Mildred L. Larson, *Meaning-Based Translation: A Guide to Cross-Language Equivalence* (New York: University Press of America, 1984).

104. Peter Kirk, "Holy Communicative? Current Approaches to Bible Translation Worldwide," in *Translation and Religion: Holy Untranslatable*, ed. Lynne Long (Buffalo: Multilingual Matters, 2005), 91.

subsequently maintained relationships with nontheological professional organizations, such as the Linguistic Society of America and the American Anthropological Association.[105] Likewise, their professional scholarly output was overwhelmingly published in linguistic and anthropological journals, such as the *International Journal of American Linguistics, Language*, and *Anthropological Linguistics*.[106] Important contributions to Bible translation methodology notwithstanding, linguistic research remained SIL's scholarly hallmark.

The Christian missionary endeavor has always been marked by patterns of resistance and acceptance, and WBT-SIL's work is no exception to this rule. To one degree or another, though, the uneven results of the Bible translation strategy in SIL were perhaps self-inflicted. Wonderly's departure over the inerrancy controversy, following on the heels of Nida's resignation in 1953, almost certainly slowed developments in translation theory and practice for nearly a decade. As with the inerrancy controversy sparked by Wonderly's speculations, the Dye study proved a hard pill to swallow for some, since it not only submitted religious activity to sociological inquiry but also challenged the conviction that the Scriptures could carry their own freight. Although the organization was, over time, able to digest Dye's controversial findings and eventually put the information to good use, the initial resistance to the study likely had at least some deleterious effect on Scripture use. However, in-depth studies on the results of the Bible translation strategy, such as Dye's, are lacking. Therefore, a more thorough assessment remains out of reach due to a lack of evidence. It can only be hoped that this lacuna in the missiological literature will be rectified.

Yet, when the enormity of the Bible translation task with its multitudinous challenges and complexities is borne in mind, it must be acknowledged that WBT-SIL accomplished no mean feat in the realm of modern-era Christian missions by having turned out no fewer than 160 New Testament translations with hundreds more under way by 1982.[107] The quality of these translations certainly varied; after all, most of them were produced not by scholars but by ordinary missionary-translators. What is remarkable is that many of them were read and are still in use today by churches around the world. Perhaps more importantly, and this would only become evident in later decades, WBT-SIL played an important part in kindling a worldwide Bible translation movement.[108] SIL's heavy emphasis on linguistics, especially from a tagmemic perspective,

105. SIL's relationship to anthropology is covered in chapter 6.

106. *Bibliography of the Summer Institute of Linguistics* (Dallas: Summer Institute of Linguistics, 1992).

107. "The World of Wycliffe," progress report, special issue, *In Other Words* 8, no. 4 (Summer 1982): 1, on file at GIAL.

108. The evidence for this assertion is discussed in the epilogue.

paved the way for advances in discourse studies. In addition, the utility of linguistics for mastering languages was itself an important factor in better translations, since language competence is a fundamental factor in producing more readable New Testaments. By way of summary, it can be said with confidence that WBT-SIL was true to its founder's unequivocal belief that no matter how small the population of speakers of a language, how geographically remote they might be, and how insignificant they might be in the eyes of others, God valued them, and they were therefore deserving of the Scriptures in their language.

CHAPTER 4

Cameron Townsend and the Strategy of "Service to All"

Having parted with the limitations imposed by the traditional faith mission ethos in Mexico to pursue a multidimensional religious, scientific, and humanitarian approach to Christian missions, Cameron Townsend opportunistically pushed his organization even further along a radical course in Peru beginning in 1946. Although SIL was founded in Mexico, the SIL experiment in Peru was Townsend's flagship operation, and he was deeply involved in its development. In the words of former SIL executive director John Bendor-Samuel, the Peruvian venture was "Uncle Cam's pride and joy."[1] The excursion into Peru also came when Townsend was in his prime and at the peak of his influence; he therefore loomed large over the developments recounted in this chapter. As in Mexico, he insisted that SIL should cooperate with the Peruvian government and follow the linguistic approach, but these strategies were extended in ways that indelibly shaped the organization for decades to come. WBT-SIL's first executive director, Benjamin Elson, wrote in 1976 that "Uncle Cam's first operating principle is service to all."[2] Many aspects of the SIL approach to missions examined in this chapter are, in one way or another, a function of Townsend's insistence that SIL should serve everyone regardless of political persuasion, religious perspective, or social class. "If they would let me teach the Bible in Russia," Townsend wrote in 1939, "I would gladly abstain from censorship of their policies I did not like." "After all," he added, "who called us to pass judgment on our

---

1. John Bendor-Samuel, interview by author, February 21, 2006, Nairobi, Kenya.

2. Ben Elson, "Service to All," in Cameron Townsend et al., *The Wycliffe Sapphire* (Huntington Beach, CA: Wycliffe Bible Translators, 1991), 59, from an article that originally appeared in the September 1976 issue of SIL's *Intercom* magazine.

rulers?"[3] This was no idle boast, for he would one day prove himself true to his word in the USSR.[4] Townsend insisted that what had worked so magnificently in Mexico would succeed as well in Peru. "Many, many self-sacrificing young workers will be needed," Townsend wrote in 1945, on the eve of the Peruvian venture, "but only those should apply who are willing to become all things to all men that by all means they might save some."[5] This was a strategy that some new WBT-SIL missionaries would struggle to follow, but the policy of serving all was one that Townsend was utterly committed to pursuing.

In November 1953, Townsend was in Mexico celebrating the twentieth anniversary of his 1933 crossing into the country. To the gathered assembly of SIL Mexico branch members, he recollected the occasion when L. L. Legters returned from an exploratory trip to Brazil with some pictures of the Xingu Indians. "I couldn't forget those Indians," he reminisced, "and so I told the Lord at least by 1927 that I would be glad to pioneer again in a tribe down there."[6] Despite having shelved plans for South America to enter Mexico, Townsend often thought about those "fine stalwart fellows" who had "not a strip of clothing, but fine expressions on their faces, just anxious to have someone come and tell them about God and His love."[7] "Called through Pictures," as he retrospectively characterized the experience, produced a thirst for moving into South America that could only be satiated by action.[8]

The Townsend Factor

As Townsend set about establishing WBT-SIL in Peru, the dual-organization approach was on full display. WBT-SIL's 1948 "Principles and Practices" explicitly stated that the "Wycliffe Bible Translators, Inc. exists for one purpose: to obey Christ's command to 'go into all the world and preach the Gospel to every creature.'"[9] Wycliffe's publicity organ, *Translation* magazine, referred to

3. Cameron Townsend, "Answer to Critics of Our Policy of Cooperating with Governments and Scientific Organizations," November 29, 1939, p. 2, TA 2436.

4. Townsend's excursions in the USSR are discussed in chapter 6.

5. Cameron Townsend, "The Director's Column," *Translation*, Spring 1945, 1, TA 942655.

6. Cameron Townsend, "Cameron Townsend's 40th Anniversary Comments," October 30, 1957, p. 4, TA 12719.

7. Cameron Townsend, "God's Faithfulness and the Continuing Vision after Twenty Years," November 11, 1953, p. 1, TA 50237.

8. Cameron Townsend, "Wycliffe Lives Again," c. 1948, p. 6, TA 42642.

9. "Principles and Practices—Wycliffe Bible Translators in Cooperation with the Summer Institute of Linguistics," 1948, p. 2, TA 41458.

the organization as "basically a missionary enterprise" and "a faith missionary enterprise," and to its personnel as "Wycliffe missionaries."[10] One would
therefore assume that the organization's personnel were in fact missionaries.
Townsend argued to the contrary, that since the organization's members went
out as translators and linguists under the scientific and cultural SIL side of the
organization, they were not missionaries. "We are not now and never have been
a missionary organization," Townsend declared in 1943.[11] Yet, when speaking to
the Christian public in North America, as in a 1948 *Sunday School Times* article,
he referred to WBT-SIL personnel as "Wycliffe missionaries."[12] In a 1953 letter
to SIL members, he declared that "We may not boast about being missionaries,
but the opportunities we get through our double approach are priceless."[13] With
the founder muddying the waters, it comes as no surprise that the dual organization was the most misunderstood of WBT-SIL's strategies. In an interview
for this study, translator Dorothy Minor, who joined the organization in 1949,
wryly remarked that WBT-SIL members were "two-headed monsters."[14] During
the early 1950s, charter board member Eugene Nida became increasingly dis-
enchanted with what he saw as the semantic elasticity of the dual-organization
rhetoric. When Nida tendered his resignation in September 1953, he explained
that it was because he could no longer tolerate the "degree of misrepresentation"
that accompanied "the explanation of the SIL-WBT program." "In the same way
that splitting of personality is disastrous to effective living," Nida reasoned, "so
artificial differences between SIL and WBT contain the seeds of ultimate disrup-
tion and lack of integration." "All this strikes me," he concluded, "as based on the
principle that the 'ends justify the means.'"[15] When Kenneth Pike was pressed
to explain the dual setup, he replied that "SIL and WBT are for *accountability* to
two different audiences."[16] This was probably as close to the truth as any other
explanation, for WBT and SIL had differing constituencies, Christians at home
and governments abroad, respectively. Internally, however, the two organizations were often conflated, as anyone immersed in the corporate archives soon
realizes by noting the pervasive tendency of its leaders to carry out business as if
the two organizations were in fact a single entity. Indeed, the introduction of the

10. *Translation* 3, no. 2 (June 1950): 16; *Translation*, Spring–Summer 1957, 6.

11. Cameron Townsend to staff members of Camp Wycliffe, July 14, 1943, TA 3479.

12. Cameron Townsend, "Overcoming Barriers to Reach Bibleless Tribes," *Sunday School Times*, January 24, 1948, 67, TA 44391.

13. Cameron Townsend to an unnamed WBT-SIL member, c. September 1953, p. 1, TA 8824.

14. Dorothy Minor, interview by author, September 10, 2008, Dallas, Texas.

15. Nida to WBT board of directors, September 9, 1953, pp. 1–2, TA 9256.

16. Kenneth L. Pike, explanation of the dual organization to an unidentified inquiry, n.d., TA 42517.

1948 "Principles and Practices" explained that only Wycliffe would be referred to therein "to make for a more simple presentation of the overall principles and procedures of the two organizations."[17] As perplexing as it was, the dual nature of WBT-SIL permitted organizational leaders and members to emphasize either the religious or the scientific aspect as called for by the public with which they were engaging at the time.

Because Townsend presented SIL to governments first and foremost as a linguistic institution, rather than as a mission, he insisted that SIL members refrain as much as possible from emphasizing SIL's missionary character. Open evangelism was especially discouraged, and he cautioned his young recruits that while a missionary's "soul may burn within him with the desire to preach the Way of Salvation, . . . he will get much further if he lets his life talk more than his words."[18] When a translator in Peru violated the policy against open proselytization in the late 1940s, Townsend complained that he had come down with a case of "preacheritis."[19] If SIL was a scientific and cultural organization that had the government's interests in mind, it should seek to maintain an image congruent with the state's expectations. Fearing that SIL would appear as just another typical missionary outfit, Townsend once ordered that a regular meeting to sing Christian hymns in an SIL missionary's home should cease.[20] On another occasion, in 1954, some non-SIL evangelical missionaries lodging at an SIL guesthouse in Peru were abruptly put onto the street, where they "spent long hours on the sidewalks as a result." This was done to ensure that there would be little or no obvious evangelical atmosphere during a Peruvian government official's visit.[21] Townsend strove constantly to lessen the possibility that SIL would be mistaken for a conventional missionary enterprise. In fact, he was unwavering in his belief that outside North America, SIL would publicly reflect its scientific and humanitarian character more than its religious nature.

WBT-SIL's board of directors sometimes looked upon Townsend's innovative ideas with consternation, but the board generally failed to impede the implementation of the founder's plans. Townsend was therefore able to stamp the Peru branch with his unique brand of mission in large part because of a weak board of directors. Kenneth Pike once recalled that whenever the board sided against Townsend, he would use "his kind of end-run tactics to get his own way." "If there is a motion passed which goes his way," Pike elaborated, "he immediately acts on it fully. If the motion goes against him, he just walks

17. "Principles and Practices," p. 2, TA 41458.
18. Cameron Townsend, "Notes on Spiritual Work," April 26, 1948, pp. 2–3, TA 42641.
19. Cameron Townsend to "Dr. Friesen," May 13, 1948, p. 2, TA 5312.
20. Hefley interview notes, "Unique Policies of WCT," c. 1970, TA 43516.
21. Cameron Townsend to Leal, July 15, 1954, TA 10112.

around it any way he can."[22] He also frequently employed coercion when he felt strongly about an idea. As former Wycliffe president Bernard May put it, Townsend was a "power player."[23] Former SIL president Frank Robbins trenchantly recalled that "he twisted people's arms right out of their sockets."[24] It was quite natural, then, that Townsend evoked a full range of emotions from his contemporaries, ranging from exasperation to reverence, but, by dint of sheer stubbornness, he most generally had his way, despite resistance.

Another key to Townsend's success was a temperament that put him at ease with political leaders of the sort that most other faith mission leaders would have gone out of their way to avoid. A summary of an April 1945 meeting with the president of Venezuela, Rómulo Betancourt, who had just come to power in a military coup, demonstrates just how relaxed Townsend was in the company of Latin American heads of state. "The way of a reformer is hard," he recorded, so it was to be expected that the Presidente de la Junta Revolucionaria was "taking a well-earned vacation" after "overthrowing the government" of General Medina. Townsend noted that when Betancourt was in exile, he had learned "about the art of overthrowing dictators," and that some of his fellow revolutionaries had "attempted to blow the props out from under Gen. Gomez," a former president of Venezuela. The assassination attempt failed, and the bombers were jailed. After recounting these events, he boasted that he "ate dinner with one of the would-be bombers."[25] As he had already demonstrated in his personal relationship with Lázaro Cárdenas in Mexico, Townsend enjoyed the company of revolutionary figures who proclaimed democracy and social uplift, even if, as with Betancourt, their route to power subverted the democratic process.

Townsend's genius for forming friendships with an extraordinarily wide range of people extended to his Stateside relationships. In October 1944, he wrote to WBT-SIL secretary William Nyman Sr. from Scotty's Castle in Death Valley, California, where he was having a "very interesting [and] restful time." Scotty's Castle was not a likely vacation spot for furloughing missionaries. Walter E. Scott, better known as Death Valley Scotty, was, in the words of one of his biographers, an "ordinary one-blanket, jackass prospector."[26] Scott, a former

---

22. Kenneth L. Pike, quoted in Tom Moore, "Report to the Administration on Opposition" (unpublished report), October 1989, 55, Pittman Special Collection, Language and Culture Archives, file cabinet 1, drawer 2, folder Report to the Administration on Opposition.

23. Bernard May, interview by author, September 18, 2009, Waxhaw, North Carolina.

24. Frank Robbins, interview by author, September 2, 2008, Dallas, Texas.

25. Cameron Townsend, notes on visit with President Rómulo Betancourt, April 1945, TA 4005.

26. Stanley W. Paher, *Death Valley's Scotty's Castle: The Story behind the Scenery* (Las Vegas, NV: K. C. Publications, 1993), 48.

stunt rider in Buffalo Bill Cody's Wild West Show, found himself in dire financial straits in 1902, so he borrowed two gold nuggets, claimed he had discovered
them in Death Valley, and went looking for financers to back the development
of his fictitious gold deposit. Eventually "Scotty" lured the millionaire and co-
owner of the National Life Insurance Company of Chicago, Albert M. Johnson,
into underwriting the development of his nonexistent gold mine. When Johnson later discovered that the mine was fraudulent, he quixotically took the news
in stride and befriended the conniving Scott. Discovering that the Death Valley
climate suited his tenuous health, Johnson built a Spanish villa in the desert at
a cost of $1.4 million. Delighting in the mystery surrounding his cowboy col-
laborator, Johnson encouraged Scott to claim surreptitiously that it was he who
was building the "castle" (and paying for it in gold, of course), thereby adding
to the mystique surrounding Scott and the castle. Johnson relished his odd
friendship with Scott, and provided him with financial support until Johnson
died in 1948.[27] As for Townsend, he had somehow managed to stumble onto
Johnson as the insurance executive lay sick in a Mexico City hotel in January
1944.[28] Apparently, Johnson was in Mexico attempting to deposit gold there in
the wake of the Roosevelt administration's 1933 restriction on private ownership
of bullion.[29] Exploits to thwart government regulations aside, Johnson had a religious streak that, along with his fondness for eccentricity, rendered him highly
susceptible to Townsend's grandiose plans. The two men struck up a lasting
friendship, and Johnson became known thereafter as "Uncle Al" in Wycliffe
circles.[30] Townsend's association with Johnson is another classic example of
his uncommon capacity to make acquaintances and to attract supporters from
well outside the typical circle of faith mission donors.

Kenneth Pike once remarked of Townsend's disarming manner: he "was
very mild looking[,] like a lost farmer in the middle of the city. . . . He looks
helpless and makes you want to help him."[31] A 1964 photograph of Townsend
strolling the halls of a newly dedicated SIL facility in the company of Mexico's
president Adolfo López Mateos and a bevy of other government officials is
illustrative of Pike's point. SIL's Benjamin Elson and the government officials
are all stylishly decked out in well-fitted business suits and all sport nicely
trimmed executive-style haircuts. Townsend, walking alongside the president,
is wearing a wrinkled suit and an obviously worn shirt, and his tie is askew.
Adding to the effect, his hair is cropped well above his protruding ears, after

27. Paher, *Death Valley's Scotty's Castle*, 6–16.
28. Cameron Townsend to Nyman, January 20, 1944, TA 3721.
29. Cameron Townsend, interview by James and Marti Hefley, n.d., TA 43614.
30. Cameron Townsend to Nyman, March 5, 1945, TA 3954.
31. Kenneth L. Pike, Hefley interview, c. 1970, p. 5, TA 43472.

the fashion of a farm boy whose father had set a bowl on his head before taking the shears to him. His looks were beguiling, for this naïve exterior disguised a master of public relations and a skillful negotiator. Not a few business leaders or government bureaucrats, perhaps thinking they could easily dispense with this ungainly American, would subsequently find themselves doling out favors to this intrepid missionary diplomat.

Townsend was not shy about taking advantage of social occasions and forays into the halls of power to engage in personal evangelization. For instance, the US ambassador to Peru, Prentice Cooper, and his wife were present at the Townsend residence when it came time to read the devotional *Daily Light*, something of a *de rigueur* exercise for conservative evangelicals at the time. Townsend's wife later remarked that "we hope the Coopers went away thinking of spiritual things."[32] He was able to engage routinely in evangelization without offense because he was more patient and subtle than many evangelicals. Indeed, in a 1958 letter to corporate secretary Nyman, he put it thus:

> As a boy I hunted squirrels. If a greenhorn went hunting with me, I always warn[ed] him to keep still and above all not to shoot until we got close enough to the game. I reserve that right today when I engage in hunting for men. If you ever go hunting with me among the ruling classes of Lima, I'm quite likely to say, "Will, please don't open your mouth until I let you know that we're ready." Sooner or later we always get to testify for our Lord, but we must be willing to take time to stalk the game.[33]

Townsend had developed his own personal brand of evangelism, and it was a strategy that did not put Latin American cultural elites on the defensive, as would have more direct methods. Moreover, Townsend's evangelistic efforts ensured that nearly everyone who ever rubbed shoulders with him knew that he was a sincere Christian.

Townsend was the guest of honor at a 1961 banquet hosted by Mexican elites to celebrate SIL's work among the indigenous peoples of Latin America. Attending were ambassadors from Bolivia, Brazil, and the Philippines, along with representatives from the United States, Canada, Venezuela, Guatemala, Honduras, Peru, and Colombia. Speaking on behalf of the Mexican committee, the poet, politician, judge, and former mayor of the state of Sonora, F. Arellano Belloc, aptly framed the twofold nature of Townsend's mind that gave rise to the policy of service to all and the dual-organization strategy. Belloc began by

32. Elaine (Mielke) Townsend to Robert Cole, September 8, 1946, TA 4285.
33. Cameron Townsend to Nyman, March 27, 1958, TA 16292.

professing that "Mr. Townsend is one of these mystics in whom two tendencies meet." The first of these, Belloc asserted, was "the salvation of souls"; the second was one that "applies positive good in our civilization, so that not only souls but also bodies may be freed from the horrors of sorrow, sickness, po[v]erty, exploitation and premature death."[34] Townsend was more than a missionary with a passion for Bible translation. He was also a committed humanitarian, whose missionary organization was fittingly described in a 1964 letter of recommendation for a public service award as a "Peace Corps with wings and a soul."[35] As this chapter unfolds, the aptness of this characterization of WBT-SIL will become palpably evident.

The Post–World War II Peruvian Context

Peru's civilian political institutions were particularly weak throughout much of the first three-quarters of the twentieth century. The country was in effect ruled by an elite oligarchy that consolidated its power around an export economy based on foreign capital (originating mainly from the United States) and natural resources exportation. By and large, traditional laissez-faire capitalism prevailed and the state was relegated to combating inflation, controlling labor, and encouraging foreign investment. Challenges were levied from the political left and by labor against the dominant class. The most significant expression of discontent with the ruling class and US domination of the economy was the appearance of the American Popular Revolutionary Alliance (APRA) in 1931. The *Apristas*, as members of the APRA were called, were unable to consolidate power before World War II due to the entrenched power of the conservative Right and because Peru's illiterate peasants and Indians were prevented from voting by laws stipulating a literacy test. Its efforts thwarted, the APRA radicalized in the difficult depression years of the early 1930s, which led to violence. The Peruvian congress called on the armed forces to assume power in 1933 to quell the unrest. The country returned to civilian control after democratic elections in 1939. A 1948 coup once again returned Peru to military control under an army general, Manuel A. Odría. Civilian rule resumed from 1956 to 1968, save for a short interregnum in 1962–1963 when the armed forces intervened to prevent the APRA candidate, Víctor Raúl Haya de la Torre, from assuming power.[36] During SIL's

---

34. "Missionary Statesman Honored," WBT-SIL press release, January 1961, TA 20699.

35. Nomination of WBT-SIL for the Lane Bryant Award, 1964, TA 42248.

36. Daniel Masterson, *The History of Peru* (Westport, CT: Greenwood Press, 2009), 95–102, 112–18, 141–46, 159–61.

first twenty-five years in Peru, the military was a dominant force in the nation's political affairs.

Of particular importance for the future of SIL in Peru was the distinctive intellectual outlook of the armed forces on Peruvian development. The influence of French military thought on colonial affairs helped shape the thinking of Peru's military officers from as early as 1896 when, under the leadership of a French colonel, Paul Clément, the Peruvian army was reorganized and modernized. French colonial ideology was mediated through the education of the general staff at, for example, the newly established Escuela Superior de Guerra (1904), where concepts such as the penetration and control of the country's remote interior, the army's role in carrying out a civilizing mission, and the function of education in national development were all inculcated from the turn of the century until about 1940. The upshot of four decades of French training and the accompanying professionalization of the officer corps was that the army came to consider itself the most capable instrument of state modernization in Peru.[37] An influential essay written by Peruvian Lieutenant Colonel Manuel Morla Concha in 1933 is a testament to the French influence. Morla viewed the army as a nation-building tool that could form the "vegetating masses" into an industrious citizenry, and he argued that the army was ideally suited to effect the incorporation of Peru's indigenous peoples into the state and to undertake their education, while still allowing them to preserve their "positive attributes." He also called for the settlement of the frontier by building roads, constructing railroads, and establishing air routes, and envisaged trained "legions" leading a charge to "forge nationhood" under the army's tutelage.[38] Morla was proposing nothing less than a modernizing project along the lines of French colonial projects in Africa and Asia. Writing in 1964, the army general and leading military intellectual Edgardo Mercado Jarrín argued that the military was the ideal agent to modernize the state, since French training and guidance had "facilitated the formation of a nucleus of officers with modern attitudes, new expertise, revolutionary spirit, social consciousness, and inclined to maintain peace and order."[39]

37. Daniel M. Masterson, *Militarism and Politics in Latin America* (New York: Greenwood Press, 1991), 12–20; Frederick M. Nunn, "Professional Militarism in Twentieth-Century Peru: Historical and Theoretical Background to the Golpe de Estado of 1968," *Hispanic American Historical Review* 59, no. 3 (August 1979): 391–417.

38. Manuel Morla Concha, "Función social del ejército en la organización de la nacionalidad," *Revista militar del Perú*, October 1933, 843–72, quoted in Nunn, "Professional Militarism in Twentieth-Century Peru," 400.

39. Edgardo Mercado Jarrín, "El ejército de hoy y su proyección en nuestra sociedad en período de transición, 1940–1965," *Revista militar del Perú*, November–December 1964, 9, quoted in Nunn, "Professional Militarism in Twentieth-Century Peru," 394.

Institutionalized over the course of several decades, this French-inspired colonial ideology was a primary impulse behind the military coup in 1968, in that it was sparked by frustration over the civilian government's inability to resolve internal conflicts and to modernize the state effectively.[40] At the time of SIL's arrival in Peru, the Peruvian military leadership was confident that the armed forces were ideally suited to effect the nation's transition to modernity.

Within a few short months of Minister of Education Enrique Laroza's signing of the Peru-SIL agreement in June 1945, he was succeeded by the historian, journalist, politician, and ethnologist Luis Valcárcel Vizcarra. Valcárcel was especially influential in mediating both the ideology of the Mexican revolution and the intellectual currents of *indigenismo* in Peru.[41] Like Manuel Gamio in Mexico, Valcárcel contended that his country was fashioned from two irreconcilable populations.[42] On one side were the indigenous peoples of Inca descent, and on the other were those of Spanish ancestry. He argued in 1927 that the answer to this perceived problem was not to be found in the triumph of the dominant Spanish culture over the indigenous Incas, but rather in "a return to our Inca roots." Inca "culture will come down again from the Andes," he rhapsodized, and it "will reappear in a dazzling form, haloed by its eternal values."[43] Valcárcel used his stature and influence in government circles to inaugurate an institute for the study of Peru's indigenous peoples, the Instituto Indigenista Peruano, of which he became director in 1946. He was not alone in the immediate post–World War II period in his research aims and ambitions for rehabilitating Inca cultural values. Among a number of other projects was a cooperative research program between Peru and Cornell University. The twin goals of this project were "to conduct a form of experimental research on modernization processes" and "to help this community [Peru's indigenous peoples] to change from a position of relative dependence and submission . . . to a position of relative independence and freedom in the framework of Peruvian national life."[44] Townsend and SIL happened upon the Peruvian scene at the very moment when social anthropology and indigenous

40. Jane S. Jaquette, "The Peruvian Experiment in Retrospect," *World Politics* 39, no. 2 (January 1987): 281–82.

41. Jorge Coronado, *The Andes Imagined: Indigenismo, Society, and Modernity* (Pittsburgh: University of Pittsburgh Press, 2009), 150–55; Jorge P. Osterling and Héctor Martínez, "Notes for a History of Peruvian Social Anthropology, 1940–1980," *Current Anthropology* 24, no. 3 (June 1983): 343–44.

42. Manuel Gamio and *indigenismo* are discussed in chapter 1.

43. Luis E. Valcárcel, *Tempestad en los Andes* (Lima: Universo, [1927] 1972), 23–25, quoted in Osterling and Martínez, "Notes," 346.

44. Quoted in Osterling and Martínez, "Notes," 349.

concerns were becoming institutionalized under the direction of intellectuals such as Valcárcel.

Whereas the military leadership and the *indigenistas* shared conceptual ground with SIL, the Roman Catholic hierarchy in Peru would prove a determined enemy of the organization in the 1950s. The Catholic Church in Peru generally resisted the liberal strains of modernity. For example, in the 1930s a number of clergy in the upper echelons of Peruvian Catholicism became infatuated with fascism, since it complemented Roman Catholic ideas of authoritarianism, hierarchical society, and corporatism. This obsession with fascism was no small part of the church's efforts to reassert its place in society.[45] A singular indicator of the influence of Catholicism in Peru at midcentury was in evidence when the newly elected Peruvian president, Manuel Prado, in 1945 terminated all Protestant proselytizing among the nation's indigenous peoples, since, in his words, "The Constitution protects the Catholic religion."[46] In the years leading up to World War II and in the decade that followed it, the Catholic hierarchy in Peru attempted to erect and maintain a bulwark against Protestantism, and the state itself seemingly offered its support in this effort.

At that time in Peru, the most powerful political institution, the army, and the nation's *indigenistas* and educational elites shared a number of overlapping goals with SIL. It was natural then that SIL would form alliances with these institutions. It was also quite logical for the Roman Catholic hierarchy to feel threatened by SIL's advance into the frontier zones. The fact that the Catholics had reason to protest SIL's presence in the first place raises an important question: Why, with Prado's cancellation of Protestant work in 1945, was SIL welcomed in the first place? And how, after securing access to Peru, did SIL manage to survive a concerted effort by the Roman Catholic hierarchy to eject the organization? To answer these questions, we explore one of the most fascinating chapters in the twentieth-century evangelical missionary movement.

The Founder in Transition

The mid-1940s marked the beginning of a new chapter in life for Cameron Townsend. On Christmas Eve 1944 his wife Elvira suddenly died of a stroke in his arms.[47] A subdued but undaunted Townsend remained purposeful in his

---

45. Fredrick B. Pike, "Church and State in Peru and Chile Since 1840: A Study in Contrasts," *American Historical Review* 73, no. 1 (October 1967): 42–47.

46. John J. Considine, *New Horizons in Latin America* (New York: Dodd, Mead, 1958), 254.

47. "Elvira Malmstrom Townsend Called Home," funeral announcement by WBT, December

vision. "If I have been devoted to my Lord's service in the past," he declared at Elvira's funeral, "by his grace my devotion shall be a passion from now on."[48] Townsend was a man of his word, as the next four decades would prove. Indeed, the very next day he wrote to SIL Mexico director Richard Pittman briefly remarking on the previous day's funeral. He then rather abruptly informed Pittman that this "note will have to be about business." Should he plan to come to Mexico? What about the program to publicize Wycliffe that he was planning with the famous radio evangelist Charles Fuller?[49] Above all else, Peru was beckoning, and Townsend, still in his prime at forty-eight, was straining at the leash to pioneer once again.

A close reading of Townsend's correspondence from early 1946 intimates that he had taken more than a passing interest in Miss Elaine Mielke, a WBT-SIL missionary twenty-five years his junior. Several times she is singled out for special notice in Townsend's correspondence. He had particular praise for her successful literacy campaign in Mexico, where she was then serving with SIL.[50] In a letter to his niece, Evelyn Pike (Kenneth Pike's wife), Townsend confided that he had fallen for Elaine but was determined that "my head shall steer my heart."[51] Apparently his head said yes, and they were married on April 4, 1946, at the home of Lázaro Cárdenas, with the former president standing as Townsend's best man and Mrs. Amalia Cárdenas acting as Elaine's matron of honor.[52] After a brief honeymoon the couple embarked for Peru.[53] Where Elvira had struggled with her husband's impulsive nature and unsettled ways, Elaine seems to have taken these characteristics in stride, providing Cameron the ideal mate as he carried out his visionary plan for making the Bible available to thousands of language groups around the world.[54]

26, 1944, p. 2, TA 3731; Cameron Townsend to Pittman, December 24, 1944, TA 3733; Cameron Townsend to Mrs. Harvey J. Borton, secretary, PMA, telegram, December 26, 1944, TA 3732.

48. Cameron Townsend, "Statement of Purpose Made at Elvira's Funeral," December 28, 1944, p. 1, TA 3731.

49. Cameron Townsend to Pittman, December 29, 1944, TA 3730.

50. Cameron Townsend to A. M. Johnson, April 11, 1945, TA 4020; Cameron Townsend to Lathrop, April 11, 1945, TA 4019; Cameron Townsend to "supporters," April 20, 1945, TA 4015.

51. Cameron Townsend to Evelyn Pike, June 14, 1945, TA 3994.

52. "Wedding of Elaine Mielke and Cameron Townsend at the Summer Home of General and Mrs. Lázaro Cárdenas," reported by Mrs. Reimer, 1946, TA 42032; Cameron Townsend to "friends and relatives," April 11, 1946, TA 4346.

53. Cameron Townsend to Nyman, April 12, 1946, TA 4203.

54. Townsend's first marriage was beset with difficulties. Elvira suffered from both psychological and physical maladies, the effects of which were exacerbated by his unpredictable and unsettled nature. William Lawrence Svelmoe, *A New Vision for Missions: William Cameron Townsend, the*

The Establishment of SIL in Peru

SIL's invitation to Peru came as a direct result of its linguistic research and educational work in Mexico. In 1943 the American Bible Society requested Kenneth Pike's assistance in developing a common script for the various Quechua dialects spoken in the Peruvian Andes. While in Lima, in January 1944, Pike gave a series of lectures on phonetics to high school teachers of English at the request of Peru's minister of public education, Enrique Laroza. While there, he also described SIL's work in Mexico to Laroza. The minister recognized the value of the services SIL potentially offered in his nation's struggle to incorporate its indigenous peoples into the state, and he therefore invited SIL to take up work similar to what had been done in Mexico.[55] "No doubt," wrote Laroza to Townsend in June 1944, "the research work that the institute intends to perform in my country will constitute a most important contribution to remedying the multiple problems which we are engaged in solving."[56] Upon receipt of this letter, Townsend embarked on an exploratory survey of Peru, during which he secured an official agreement for SIL's services. At a time when Protestant missionaries were encountering barriers to access, Peru extended an invitation to SIL based upon the merits of its scientific and educational credentials.

The June 25, 1945, agreement with the Peruvian Ministry of Public Education offers a classic example of Townsend's unorthodox approach to missions and SIL's participation in state modernization. The first cluster of objectives mainly concerned academic matters. Along this line the agreement called for a "thorough study of each language" and a "comparative study of the native languages, both among themselves and in relation to other languages of the world." In addition, SIL agreed to produce in-depth anthropological studies, the chief end of which was to record and preserve for posterity the "Indian tribal" way of life. The second emphasis of the agreement was on practical service. SIL personnel were required to act as interpreters, offer "linguistic courses for groups of rural school-teachers," prepare reading primers, and engage in the "fostering of sports, civic duties, and cooperative services," along with "the uprooting of vice by all means possible." In keeping with SIL's linguistic emphasis, the agreement called for "the translation into the native tongues of laws, sanitary advice, handbooks dealing with agriculture, . . . as well as books

---

Wycliffe Bible Translators, and the Culture of Early Evangelical Faith Missions, 1896–1945 (Tuscaloosa: University of Alabama Press, 2008), examines in detail the tribulation of this marriage.

55. Kenneth L. Pike, "General Report on South American Trip," February 21, 1944, TA 3875.

56. Laroza to WCT, June 24, 1944, TA 3822, translation by author.

of great moral and patriotic value." SIL was to undertake this two-pronged program largely at its own expense, save for the training of rural teachers, for which SIL would receive remuneration. For its part in the arrangement, the Peruvian government was to render various services to SIL. The Department of Immigration was to eliminate the head tax on SIL personnel; the Ministry of the Interior was to secure for SIL the use of government land; the Ministry of Aeronautics was to issue permits for SIL to import and acquire in-country aircraft and to operate them; and the Ministry of Government and Ministry of Police were likewise to permit the use of radio and communications equipment. In addition, SIL received duty-free import status and fully equipped offices in the Ministry of Public Education building in Lima.[57] Other missions could only dream of such cooperation and governmental aid. As in Mexico, SIL was once again making common cause with a Latin American state in its efforts of social uplift and goals for the incorporation of the nation's indigenous peoples into the political and economic structures of the state.

In securing this agreement, Townsend seemed to have left out one important topic: not once did it explicitly mention Bible translation. Buried in the detailed four-page agreement was the point that SIL would translate "books of great moral . . . value." This bit of semantic ingenuity was an oblique reference to Bible translation, and such tactics eventually resulted in accusations that WBT-SIL was acting deceitfully.[58] Clearly, the relationship between the secular requirements of the agreement and the allowance for spiritual work was oddly out of proportion when WBT-SIL's primary goal of Bible translation is taken into consideration. If the agreement were strictly adhered to in its general outline, it would be very difficult for SIL to accomplish its Bible translation goals. In fact, the main thrust of agreement was on linguistic and anthropological research and the integration of the indigenous inhabitants of Peru into the national life of the country. Conversely, there was only the barest hint of spiritual or missionary work, and no mention of Wycliffe Bible Translators. In Mexico, Townsend had cast Bible translation in terms of liberating the Indians from avarice and superstition and as a means for weakening the influence of Roman Catholicism. In this agreement, it looks as if Townsend concealed SIL's Bible translation intentions in the minutiae of bureaucratic language. Statements in the press at the time the agreement was signed tend to suggest that this was the case. For example, two prominent Peruvian newspapers made no mention of Bible translation or religious activities when publicizing the arrival of SIL's first

57. "Agreement between the Ministry of Public Education of Peru and Mr. William Townsend, General Director of the Summer Institute of Linguistics," June 25, 1945, TA 40628.

58. Aspects of this issue are discussed below and also in chapter 6.

contingent of missionary-linguists in June 1946.[59] Townsend had succeeded in crafting an agreement that effectively subsumed Bible translation under a comprehensive program of cultural, social, and scientific service.

While it is true that Townsend downplayed the Bible translation angle, and that he reinterpreted it in less than strictly religious terms as a book of morals that carried patriotic overtones, he did not practice outright deception when negotiating the agreement. He later reported that he had verbally informed Peruvian officials of SIL's spiritual aims, but purposely avoided mention of Bible translation in the contract so as not to give the Roman Catholic hierarchy reason to mount an attack.[60] SIL's religious intentions did not long remain a secret. A September 13, 1946, *Peruvian Times* article on SIL's nascent operations in the Amazonian jungle briefly noted that SIL was translating "selections from the Bible." Nevertheless, as with the agreement itself, the *Peruvian Times* article implied that such endeavors were rather limited in comparison with the larger scientific and cultural work of SIL.[61] Townsend had not deceived Peruvian government officials, but he had couched his Bible translation ambitions in minimalist terms.

Townsend employed his diplomatic skills in Peru to establish an extraordinarily wide-ranging circle of relationships. An examination of his correspondence during the summer of 1946 is revealing. His letters refer to almost daily meetings with dignitaries of one variety or another. This never-ending stream of diplomats, ministers, educators, and members of the intelligentsia that Townsend encountered ranged from Peruvian radical political theorist and politician Víctor Raúl Haya de la Torre to American Admiral William "Bull" Halsey Jr., both of whom he met at the home of Prentice Cooper, the American ambassador to Peru, who was a frequent guest of the Townsends.[62] By mid-October 1946, the Townsends had personally entertained over fifty public figures at their Peruvian residence, four of whom were cabinet-level ministers.[63] Once he established rapport with those who could help him in furthering his objectives, Townsend set about weaving those friendships into

---

59. "Ha Llegado una Misión Cultural y Científica de Estados Unidos," *La Croncia*, April 27, 1946, TA 45569; "Llegada de une Misión Científica y Cultural Norteamericana," *El Comercio*, April 27, 1946, TA 45568.

60. Cameron Townsend to "Dr. Friesen," May 13, 1948, TA 5312.

61. "The Summer Institute of Linguistics: Indian Languages of the Jungle," *Peruvian Times*, September 13, 1946, TA 45565.

62. Robert G. Schneider to Nyman, August 5, 1946, TA 4570; Cameron Townsend to Nyman, June 11, 1946, TA 4192.

63. Cameron Townsend to Johnson, October 6, 1946, TA 4268; Cameron Townsend to Amos Baker, October 12, 1946, TA 4265.

a web of mutually reinforcing connections. In November of 1946 he mailed to University of Oklahoma president George Cross some newspaper clippings in which Minister of Education Valcárcel had mentioned the University of Oklahoma when extolling the merits of SIL's program. In a letter accompanying the clippings, Townsend suggested that Cross should reciprocate by sending a letter of gratitude to Valcárcel, and he requested additional copies.[64] Cross complied, and as a result Townsend obtained a handful of letters useful for impressing lower-level ministerial bureaucrats.[65] By the late 1940s, Townsend was probably as well connected in Peru as many diplomats, and certainly more so than any North American evangelical missionary.

SIL's Peruvian literacy program carried out in cooperation with the Peruvian government is a classic example of the organization's efforts to fulfill the scientific and educational requirements of its contract with the Department of Education. At the time the bilingual education project was initiated in 1952, Peru was again under military rule, following the seizure of power by General Manuel Odría in 1948.[66] The minister of education, Colonel Juan Mendoza Rodriguez, was instrumental in setting up this experimental program in bilingual education, which was calibrated to facilitate the integration of Peru's indigenous peoples into the social, economic, and political structures of the nation-state.[67] Toward this end, Supreme Resolution 909, authorizing the program, decreed that "students will be trained for productive work and taught the basic cultural norms of Western civilization necessary for participating in national life [and] the concept of citizenship."[68] In a 1981 review of the project, SIL's Mildred L. Larson found that by the display of flags, a recitation of the national anthem, and the keeping of national holidays the program's schools exuded an "atmosphere of patriotism" and encouraged "loyalty to Peru."[69] Another project reviewer, SIL's Mary Ruth Wise, observed that "through the bilingual school system thousands have become literate in both their native language and in Spanish, and have learned of the extent of their native land and of the existence and func-

64. Cameron Townsend to Cross, November 7, 1946, TA 904259.

65. Cross to Cameron Townsend, November 18, 1946, TA 4394; Cross to Valcárcel, November 18, 1946, TA 4509.

66. Masterson, *The History of Peru*, 145.

67. Rodríguez to SIL, February 9, 1951, TA 7159; Juan Mendoza Rodríguez, "Curso de Capacitación para Nativos Alfabetizados de la Selva," November 28, 1952, TA 8232.

68. Resolution Authorizing Bilingual Education in the Peruvian Jungle: Supreme Resolution No. 909, Lima, Peru (November 28, 1952), reprinted in *Bilingual Education: An Experience in Peruvian Amazonia*, ed. Mildred L. Larson and Patricia M. Davis (Washington, DC: Center for Applied Linguistics, 1981), 393.

69. Mildred L. Larson, "The Role of Vernacular versus Prestige Languages in Primary Education," in Larson and Davis, *Bilingual Education*, 29.

tioning of its government."[70] In all, by the time Peru assumed full operational control of the program in 1975, 210 communities were affected, 320 teachers were prepared, and 12,000 pupils were trained.[71] WBT-SIL wanted literate readers for its translated Scriptures and wished to maintain its access to Peru; to gain these objectives, it pragmatically aligned itself with the nation-making and state-modernization goals of Peruvian educators and Peru's military leadership, and thereby fulfilled the requirements of its government contract.

Struggling to Adapt to the Dual-Organization and Government Approach

As the founder took SIL into Peru, his trailblazing missiology was on full display. This was particularly evident in the degree to which SIL engaged in the Peruvian government's project of state modernization. It was also apparent in Townsend's insistence that his mission would serve everyone regardless of political persuasion, religious creed, or social status. It was clear too that he had little patience with any narrow focus on salvation at the expense of social concern. The "Bible," he insisted in 1945, "tells us of a better age to come, [but] it also tells us how to better this age."[72] Townsend placed SIL at the service of all, regardless of their political or religious affiliation, to achieve the twin goals of the salvation of souls for eternity and the embodiment of the progressive ideal in the present world, and in doing so he advanced his project of creating an entirely new type of evangelical missionary organization. This transformation was not effected without growing pains. As was the case the previous year at SIL's school at the University of Oklahoma at Norman, the mostly young and inexperienced members of the newly established Peru branch of SIL in 1948 reacted in a sudden outburst to the unsettling effects of serving the government and of keeping their religiosity under wraps.[73]

A 1948 letter written by SIL missionary-translator Sylvester Dirks, a Canadian Mennonite and the chairman of the SIL Peru branch executive committee, reveals the psychological strain that adapting to the dual organization and to government cooperation could have on Townsend's fledgling missionaries. Looking around at his fellow Peru branch colleagues, Dirks believed that he

70. Mildred L. Larson, Olive A. Shell, and Mary Ruth Wise, "Overview of the Program of Bilingual Education in the Peruvian Jungle," in Larson and Davis, *Bilingual Education*, 37.

71. Larson, Shell, and Wise, "Overview," 38.

72. Cameron Townsend, "The Director's Column," *Translation*, Spring 1945, 10, TA 942655.

73. SIL's school at the University of Oklahoma at Norman, and the near fatal reaction to SIL campus and academic policies in 1947, is discussed in detail in chapter 2.

detected a dark "under-current" resulting from the "chameleonic veneer characteristic of our organization." Called to share the "burning message" of the gospel, Dirks lamented that WBT-SIL missionaries found themselves instead constrained to "speak at length about the purely scientific aspect" of SIL's work in an attempt to "convince people that we are not missionaries." We are "dogs that do not bark," he groused. He worried what supporters at home would think if they discovered this state of affairs. "I venture to say," he speculated, "that 95% of our support would be cut off to-morrow." Dirks also accused the organization of failing to present candidates with the full picture before departing for service abroad. "We were never told," he charged, that discussing Wycliffe was "taboo." He also decried the informal rule instructing SIL members "not to attend evangelical services too frequently." As Dirks wound down his litany of grievances, he struck a rueful tone, confessing that he had given testimony in church, held Bible studies, and played gospel records despite such prohibitions. In closing he avowed that he was not alone, for other SIL missionaries were experiencing "similar difficulties." Dirks wondered if SIL could perhaps change its contract with the government. "Many of us," he reported, "more or less feel a need of that."[74] While the overwrought Dirks undoubtedly exaggerated at points in this letter, his assessment of the group's sentiment was not far from the mark, as would soon become evident. Once again, as it had at Camp Wycliffe in 1947, the cognitive dissonance between these young missionaries' ingrained understanding of missions and Townsend's unique approach was creating more than a little anxiety.[75]

The stress of adapting to SIL's strategy came to a head during the March 1948 Peru branch conference. Townsend, who was at the time immersed in his ambitious attempt to set up an aviation program (discussed below) and producing WBT-SIL's first publicity film, sent his protégé and Mexico branch director Richard Pittman in to quell the impending revolt.[76] Unfortunately for the historian, stenographic reports of the conference sessions were never typed and the originals were apparently lost. Furthermore, the only surviving attender was unable to recall details of the event.[77] What can be gleaned from the extant record is that SIL members in Peru were afflicted by qualms similar to those troubling Dirks. They therefore pressed for greater openness with the government that Bible translation was SIL's primary goal and registered the opinion that SIL members should not attend diplomatic functions

74. Dirks to Cameron Townsend, January 25, 1948, TA 5564.

75. The crisis of 1947 at Camp Wycliffe is discussed in chapter 2.

76. Cameron Townsend to Pittman, February 23, 1948, TA 5168.

77. Gloria (Grey) Wroughton, interview by author, June 20, 2008, Dallas, Texas; "Report of the Peru Branch of Summer Institute of Linguistics," March 22–31, 1948, p. 4, TA 40599.

where movies were shown and liquor was served (as was presently the case). They also requested that restrictions on attendance at evangelistic services should be eased. The only point where the group remained divided was over whether or not the dual structure should be done away with by reconstituting the organization under one name.[78] The overall thrust of the Peruvian branch members' protest was an attempt to shift SIL into the more familiar orbit of a faith mission.

These matters were discussed at considerable length and then put to a vote, and it appears that the very act of voting on these issues had a cathartic effect on the Peru branch members. Pittman reported that in the wake of the intensity surrounding the discussion and voting, "an immediate and overwhelming sense of relief" came over the group. He also sensed that the voting had acted as a "safety valve," letting off "the pent up steam of many months." Having aired their frustrations and expressed their fears, the members now felt a "humble willingness to admit possible immaturity and error in voting."[79] Similar to the previous summer's Camp Wycliffe group, the SIL missionaries in Peru seemed to be gripped by a sudden spasm of guilt after having rebelled. This transient paroxysm left in its wake contriteness and a willingness to suppress their apprehensions. Therefore they swallowed their grievances out of respect for "Uncle Cam," who, they acknowledged by a unanimous vote (with a single abstention), was "the man whom the Lord has chosen to direct the work of SIL in Peru and that it is our desire that he continue as our director for the next three years at least."[80] Veteran WBT-SIL missionaries time and again recounted in interviews that they often exceeded their own expectations of themselves because Townsend's leadership inspired them to do so. The sentiments expressed are perhaps best summed up by Lois Hesse, who joined WBT-SIL in 1955. She said of Townsend, that "we had faith in him as well as in the Lord."[81] Once again, out of respect for Townsend's leadership and under the deft guidance of another one of his lieutenants, WBT-SIL missionaries struggled successfully to overcome their deep-rooted understanding of Christian mission based on the traditional missionary ideology.

Of course, not everyone in WBT-SIL was able to make the necessary adjustments to work within what was a unique organizational culture. Sylvester Dirks and his wife Mattie ultimately resigned in October 1948 over

78. SIL Peru branch, conference minutes, April 1, 1948, TA 40595.

79. Richard S. Pittman, "Report of Conference of Peru Branch of Summer Institute of Linguistics at Ahuaytia, Loretto, Peru," March 22–31, 1948, Pittman Special Collection, file cabinet 1, drawer 4, folder Peru 1945–1953.

80. SIL Peru branch, conference minutes, April 1, 1948, TA 40595.

81. Lois Jean Hesse, interview by author, August 29, 2008, Dallas, Texas.

their inability to come to terms with the dual-organization strategy.[82] Eugene Nida, as noted above, also found that he could not continue under the dual-organization structure and all it entailed. Pittman worried in the wake of the Peru conference that, the affirmative vote aside, SIL's advance in Peru might grind to a halt if new workers did not receive adequate "indoctrination in Mr. Townsend's method and principles."[83] The extant record suggests that very few members left WBT-SIL over the unusual WBT-SIL policies. This was likely attributable in part to the fact that, as Pittman suggested, new recruits were thereafter more thoroughly instructed in the particulars of the WBT-SIL strategy before departing for their assignments.[84] While there remained confusion and disagreement over the exact nature of the dual-organization setup, the orientation of new candidates seems to have mostly weeded out conscientious objectors before they departed for missionary service with SIL.

The cadre of young missionaries who joined WBT-SIL in the mid to late 1940s struggled when confronted with the full ramifications of Townsend's approach. For many of them his innovations transgressed the boundaries of their inherited fundamentalist values. Therefore they remained apprehensive until coming to the realization that they could flout ingrained ideological boundaries without necessarily undermining their faith. Once they made this discovery, many quickly acclimatized to this new approach. Indeed, they were often eager for a freer environment. A typical example is Nancy Lanier, who joined WBT-SIL in 1952 after attending the austere fundamentalist Bible Institute of Los Angeles (BIOLA). Lanier admitted in an interview that she never "fit in very well with the BIOLA context." "I was asked to leave the school because I got too many demerits," she forthrightly recalled, adding that BIOLA "was a little strict I guess for me. I think I fit in better at Wycliffe."[85] The organizational culture that was developing in the 1940s and 1950s in WBT-SIL paralleled that of the wider evangelical subculture in North America, where progressive evangelicals were distancing themselves from their fundamentalist past.[86] What set WBT-SIL apart from this broader evangelical movement was the organization's willingness under Townsend's influence to break nearly every rule in the fun-

82. Sylvester and Mattie Dirks to Cameron Townsend, October 23, 1948, TA 5421; Watters to Nyman, October 27, 1948, TA 5104.

83. Pittman to Cowan, June 21, 1948, Pittman Special Collection, file cabinet 1, drawer 4, folder Peru 1945–1953.

84. SIL board of directors meeting, minutes, April 12, 1948, WSA; Cameron Townsend, general director's report, September 1951, p. 4, TA 6860.

85. Nancy Lanier, interview by author, July 31, 2009, Catalina, Arizona.

86. Discussed briefly in chapter 1 and more extensively in chapter 5.

damentalist playbook, and this becomes exceedingly evident when examining the development of SIL's aviation program.

Jungle Aviation and International Goodwill

Cameron Townsend never gave up on his vision of an "air crusade to the wild tribes."[87] As he set about establishing SIL in Peru, he seized the opportunity to realize this ambition, in part because reaching the indigenous peoples inhabiting the remote jungles of Peru's nearly impenetrable Amazonian basin was perfectly suited to the use of aircraft. Journeys that would take weeks or even months by pack animal or canoe could be reduced to mere hours by airplane travel. Moreover, as World War II came to an end, surplus aircraft appeared on the market, and these airplanes were much improved over those available in the early 1930s when Townsend first fantasized over using them in missionary work. That the time was ripe for such a venture was recognized by several former military aviators. US Navy pilots James Truxton and James Buyers formed the Christian Aviators' Missionary Fellowship (CAMF) in 1944 for the express purpose of offering evangelical missions aviation services.[88] The CAMF's first customer was the Mexico branch of SIL, with the renowned—at least in evangelical missionary circles—Elizabeth (Betty) Greene doing the flying. Greene had earned her wings serving with the Women's Air Force Service Pilots during World War II.[89] Therefore, SIL's aviation requirements were well cared for by experienced pilots working within a specialized organization along the very lines that Townsend had envisaged twenty years earlier.[90]

Townsend, however, chafed at having to rely on the Missionary Aviation Fellowship (MAF) for SIL's aviation needs. Thus, whereas close cooperation between SIL and MAF was called for to establish an effective jungle aviation program, he instead waged a protracted campaign to wrest from MAF control over the aviation operations that it was conducting in Peru on SIL's behalf. The primary impulse behind this desire for personal control was his ambition

---

87. Townsend's early ideas for missionary aviation are discussed in chapter 1.

88. The CAMF was renamed the Missionary Aviation Fellowship (MAF) in 1946.

89. Dietrich G. Buss and Arthur F. Glasser, *Giving Wings to the Gospel: The Remarkable Story of Mission Aviation Fellowship* (Grand Rapids: Baker, 1995), 13–28; Betty Greene, *Flying High: The Amazing Story of Betty Greene and the Early Years of Mission Aviation Fellowship* (Camp Hill, PA: Christian Publications, 2002), 1–6.

90. The name was again changed in 1971 to Mission Aviation Fellowship in order to dispense with the term "missionary," as a concession to growing nationalistic and anti-Western sentiment (Buss and Glasser, *Giving Wings to the Gospel*, 27).

for a more expensive and far-reaching operation than MAF could ever begin to imagine. "We simply must not skimp on this tremendous undertaking," Townsend insisted when the MAF persisted in its plan for a minimal, one-aircraft operation in Peru.[91] That his technical knowledge was inferior to that possessed by MAF personnel mattered not in the least to him either; he simply wanted to call the shots on all matters related to SIL's advance in Peru. The MAF was responsible for the safety of aircraft under its operational control. It was therefore naturally determined to draw upon the collective expertise of its professional cadre of pilots and mechanics. MAF's secretary-treasurer, Charles Mellis, therefore informed Townsend in 1947 that "we have found by experience that no major decisions in missionary aviation should ever be made by any *one* person."[92] Also standing in Townsend's way was the fact that the WBT-SIL board was perfectly satisfied to have MAF fulfill SIL's aviation needs. What ensued from 1946 on was a contest of wills over who was going to determine the scope and nature of the aviation program supporting SIL's expansion into Peru and beyond.

Becoming impatient with MAF's delay in repairing and transporting a Waco airplane from Mexico for service in Peru, Townsend impulsively leapt at the opportunity in June 1946 to obtain a Grumman J-2 amphibian airplane, or "Duck," as it was commonly described, that the US naval mission in Peru was selling as war surplus.[93] Townsend excitedly wrote to WBT-SIL secretary William Nyman that the aircraft could likely be had for between $2,500 and $5,000. He also noted that the navy had assured him that the Duck was recently "reconditioned" and had seen little use since. Bursting with excitement, Townsend exclaimed to Wycliffe's financial supporters in North America that the Duck could be had for less than 5 percent of its $80,000 original cost.[94] When the WBT-SIL board asked MAF's Mellis for advice on the Grumman, he cautioned Townsend to spend no more than $2,500.[95] Aware that he was overreaching with the intended purchase, Townsend confessed to Betty Greene "that it seems like presumption for us to talk about $4,000, when we don't have enough money to buy a good drink of gasoline for it, . . . [but] it seems so providential that I believe that the Lord intends to give us the plane."[96] A lack of funds was no impediment at all to

91. Cameron Townsend to Charles J. Mellis Jr., November 30, 1946, TA 4237.

92. Mellis to Cameron Townsend, January 25, 1947, p. 2, TA 4919.

93. Cameron Townsend to Robert Cole, June 14, 1946, TA 4328; Cameron Townsend to Mabel Smart, June 15, 1946, TA 4324; Cameron Townsend to Truxton, June 22, 1946, BGA, MAF collection 136, box 60, folder 34.

94. Cameron Townsend to "supporters," July 9, 1946, TA 4316.

95. WBT board of directors meeting, minutes, June 22, 1946, TA 41499.

96. Cameron Townsend to Greene, June 19, 1946, TA 4323.

Townsend, for he had once again concluded that something was preordained, and it was therefore all but impossible to dissuade him from the course of action he had set upon.

Townsend bargained with the navy, pleaded with donors, and prayed for the needed $4,000. His connections at home paid off. A businessman and associate of Charles Fuller sent $3,000, Clarence Erickson of the Chicago Gospel Tabernacle donated $700, and MAF magnanimously supplied the remaining $300.[97] The navy was less obliging, setting the final price at $4,500, thus leaving Townsend $500 short.[98] This proved to be less of a problem than an opportunity for SIL's enterprising general director, who embarked on a public relations campaign that redounded to good effect in short order. He reported to a supporter in June 1946 that "as fellow missionaries hear what the Peruvian Government is doing for us, they simply marvel and so do the officials at the American Embassy."[99] He was not embellishing the truth. Peru's ministries of education and health agreed to partner with SIL in the use and maintenance of the Duck, thus substantially cutting subsequent operational costs. In the second place, Ambassador Cooper agreed to Townsend's suggestion that he "intervene" on SIL's behalf to obtain a reduction of the navy's stated price—and the navy lowered the price to $3,000.[100] After all was said and done, the reduced price proved fortunate, for when Betty Greene inspected it she discovered that it was actually in rather poor condition. Under Greene's direction, the Duck was grounded for a complete inspection and overhaul. On a more positive note, it was hinted that the US government might supply a new engine, since the navy had apparently been less than forthright about the plane's condition when selling it. (With a buyer like Townsend in hot pursuit, it is little wonder that the navy did not dwell on any deficiencies.) So, once again, Townsend leaned on Ambassador Cooper for his aid in obtaining a new engine, and the American embassy obliged by paying for the transport of the replacement engine.[101] Townsend's willingness to ignore church-state boundaries in serving governments was paying handsome dividends, but it was also leading SIL ever further along a path that would prove to have some rather pronounced effects on the organization.

The MAF was the ideal organization to serve SIL's aviation needs. After all, it was founded and administered by experienced pilots and mechanics, whereas

---

97. Nyman to Pittman, June 22, 1946, TA 4592; Herbert Rankin to Cameron Townsend, July 13, 1946, TA 4458; Cameron Townsend to Rankin, July 15, 1946, TA 4312.

98. Cameron Townsend to Kenneth L. Pike, June 28, 1946, TA 4321.

99. Cameron Townsend to Smart, June 15, 1946, TA 4324.

100. Cameron Townsend to Nyman, July 9, 1946, TA 4187.

101. Cameron Townsend to Nyman, August 21, 1946, 1, TA 4183; Greene to Nyman, October 11, 1946, TA 4540.

SIL's expertise was in linguistics. Indeed, that Townsend had naïvely purchased an aircraft that, unbeknownst to him, required a complete overhaul suggests that his aeronautical knowledge left much to be desired. All this mattered little to Townsend, who had plans for nothing less than an expansive jungle airline, complete with large aircraft and a short-wave radio communications system. The MAF's modest operational goal, by contrast, was to provide safe and reliable missionary transport at the lowest possible cost. Theirs was a fairly straight-forward approach to missionary aviation, where aircraft were simply tools for efficient transportation.[102] This moderate outlook showed itself also in MAF's tendency to economize by limiting the number of aircraft deployed as well as minimizing the number of personnel engaged in any single field of operation. In November 1946, Townsend took MAF's secretary-treasurer, Charles Mellis, to task over this very point, insisting that a single-pilot operation was inadequate for "the Herculean task that confronts this epochmaking project from the aero-nautical standpoint." He concluded his letter to Mellis by suggesting that only a "lack of vision" on MAF's part would stymie his proposal for a multiaircraft and multipilot aviation operation.[103] In a five-page rebuttal, Mellis let it be known that the MAF could agree with "practically none" of Townsend's "*aero-nautical* reasons" for having additional pilots in Peru, and, in so many words, he suggested that Townsend should stick to Bible translation and let the MAF handle the technical details of flying and maintaining aircraft.[104] Put concisely, Townsend and the MAF leadership held fundamentally different conceptions over what constituted an adequate missionary aviation program.

In June of 1947, Townsend expressed his misgivings about "turning over our 'lifeline' . . . to an extraneous organization."[105] This backhanded slap at MAF was not his first. Another came by way of an event that Townsend hoped would lend weight to his argument for a break with MAF. On February 25, 1947, Cameron, Elaine, and their firstborn daughter Grace barely managed to wedge themselves into the backseat of a commercial Piper Super Cruiser in Mexico when the pilot hurriedly began his takeoff. The heavily loaded plane struggled for altitude, and the pilot's attempt to avoid some trees resulted in an emergency landing. The infant escaped unharmed, but Cameron's leg was broken and Elaine suffered a dislocated ankle. The pilot sustained life-threatening injuries.[106] Townsend later claimed that the first thought that leapt into his mind while lying be-

102. Buss and Glasser, *Giving Wings to the Gospel*, 26, 59–66.

103. Cameron Townsend to Mellis, November 30, 1946, TA 4237.

104. Mellis to Cameron Townsend, December 18, 1946, TA 4375.

105. Cameron Townsend to Nyman, June 20, 1947, TA 4654.

106. Cameron Townsend to Robert G. Schneider and Pittman, February 25, 1947, TA 4758; Cameron Townsend to "home folks," March 3, 1947, TA 4752.

side the wrecked craft was that "God is going to use this accident to arouse greater interest in providing *adequate* aviation for our young pioneers."[107] This was no exaggeration, for he halted the rescue operation and insisted upon the injured being photographed beside the wrecked craft before being moved.[108] Furthermore, within hours of the incident, he penned a letter declaring that "we are really thankful for the accident for it shows conclusively that for such an important project as the one in which we are engaged it is necessary to have the best aircraft and pilots possible."[109] That the MAF had nothing to do with the calamity, and was already supplying safe aviation services, was apparently beside the point. The ever imaginative Townsend was attempting to turn this close brush with death into a publicity event that would provide him with the justification and the funds needed for the ambitious aviation program that he was itching to launch.

If anything, the accident lent weight to the WBT-SIL board's belief that MAF was the key to a safe and reliable aviation service. In the year following the mishap, the entire of board of directors, which at this time included inside directors Kenneth Pike, Eugene Nida, Richard Pittman, William Nyman Sr., and volunteer Wycliffe deputation secretary Earl Wyman and outside directors Dawson Trotman, founder of the Navigators, and California businessman E. S. Goodner, remained steadfast in their resolve to avoid any breach with the MAF.[110] In April 1948, Pike more or less summed up the board's sentiment in a telegram in which he declared that he "strongly support[ed]" MAF's recommendations and "absolutely oppose[d] rupture with the M.A.F."[111] The MAF argued against SIL forming another aviation organization, since it would compete for funds and add to the public's confusion over an already growing profusion of mission organizations.[112] The most the WBT-SIL board was willing to do to assuage Townsend was to form a Jungle Aviation and Radio Service (JAARS) "committee" that was mainly constituted as a fund-raising instrument in North America.[113] Neither the MAF nor the WBT-SIL board of directors was inclined to allow Townsend to take control of the Peruvian aviation operation.

107. Cameron Townsend, "The Airplane Crash," February 25, 1947, p. 3, TA 4757.

108. Dale Kietzman, Hefley interview, c. 1970, TA 43675.

109. *Steam from the Kettle*, extra edition, Summer Institute of Linguistics, Mexico City, March 4, 1947, p. 1, TA 4999.

110. Goodner to Cameron Townsend, April 13, 1948, TA 5545.

111. Kenneth L. Pike to WBT-SIL board of directors, April 12, 1948, TA 5079.

112. Mellis to WBT board of directors, January 24, 1948, BGA, MAF collection 136, box 60, file 30.

113. Cameron Townsend to Donald Kennedy, March 23, 1948, TA 5341; Cameron Townsend to Grady Parrot, March 25, 1948, TA 5340; Cameron Townsend to Schneider, March 3, 1948, TA 5348.

Townsend was making a futile effort to relax while vacationing in April 1948 at the home of former president Cárdenas in Pátzcuaro, Mexico. Still fuming over what he saw as the board's intransigence, he decided to pull out all the stops and make a stand on the MAF issue. On April 27 he threw down the gauntlet in a letter to board member Kenneth Pike, informing him that "I cannot return to Peru unless I have full charge of the aviation program."[114] The same day he repeated his ultimatum in a lengthy letter to MAF president Jim Truxton, announcing that he could no longer accept the "double leadership" situation, nor could he continue to tolerate MAF's "shoe string" economizing— if "extravagance" was called for, so be it, he insisted.[115] Truxton and Townsend met for what proved to be an unsuccessful meeting on May 8, in the wake of which Townsend repeated his refusal to return to Peru without full control of the aviation program.[116] Relating details of this encounter to WBT-SIL board member E. S. Goodner, Townsend complained of what he saw as MAF's belligerent unwillingness to follow his prescriptions for a large-scale air operation. Casting himself in the role of aviation expert, Townsend went so far as to claim that Truxton's and Mellis's "aeronautical grasp [was] far from perfect." He closed his letter to Goodner with an ultimatum: if the board of directors sided against him, he was "perfectly willing to withdraw from leadership in Peru and serve Wycliffe" elsewhere.[117] Left with the choice of wrecking the organization or supporting the founder, the board capitulated. A sense of unease over Townsend's ability to oversee the technical aspects of the program remained despite the decision. Pittman pleaded with Townsend in June 1948 to the effect that "I hope very earnestly that you will seek and use to the fullest extent possible their [MAF] advice in all technical matters." Pittman also worried over the potential publicity ramifications: "I also strongly hope that there may be no occasion . . . to cast an unfavorable light on MAF."[118] To Townsend's credit, the concerns expressed by Pittman never materialized. In May 1948 the limited JAARS committee became a full-fledged aviation and radio subsidiary organization of SIL under the general director's control.[119] Townsend obtained his wish—the opportunity to assemble, as he put it, an "airline of the magnitude that we need."[120]

114. Cameron Townsend to Kenneth L. Pike, April 27, 1948, TA 5325.

115. Cameron Townsend to Truxton, April 27, 1948, p. 2, TA 5321.

116. Cameron Townsend to Nyman, May 8, 1948, TA 5146.

117. Cameron Townsend to Goodner, May 11, 1948, p. 2, TA 5316.

118. Pittman to Cameron Townsend, June 2, 1948, Pittman Special Collection, file cabinet 2, drawer 2, folder Townsend-Pittman Correspondence, 1942–1949.

119. WBT board of directors meeting, minutes, May 21, 1948, WSA; Pittman to Cameron Townsend, June 2, 1948, TA 5514; WBT board of directors meeting, minutes, June 19, 1948, TA 941472.

120. Cameron Townsend to Goodner, May 11, 1948, p. 3, TA 5316.

In a 1954 booklet describing the institute's work, the assistant director of the SIL Peru branch, Harold Goodall, explained to readers that "because of the extreme isolation of these Indian tribes and the utter absence of any efficient transportation and communication, the Institute has been forced to establish its own airline and communications."[121] The founder had obviously managed to effect a historical reconstruction of the events of 1948 to reflect his perspective. He had done more than create a bit of organization myth over the past six years, for JAARS was now serving translation and literacy projects among twenty indigenous peoples located throughout central and eastern Peru.[122] By the mid-1950s, SIL's JAARS operation had at its disposal two small single-engine Aeroncas, a powerful 650-horsepower Nordyne "Norseman" float plane, and a twin-engine Consolidated PBY Catalina capable of international flights.[123] By the end of 1956, flying and servicing these craft were a twenty-six-man crew of pilots and mechanics.[124] The organization's airplanes were not idle. Townsend reported in October 1954 that over the previous six months JAARS aircraft had flown an astonishing 483,583 passenger miles. In addition, radio communication equipment connected each of SIL's jungle locations with its headquarters at Yarina Cocha, located on the banks of the Ucayali River near Pucallpa. Perhaps most intriguing of all, Townsend reported a "clear profit" of $1,230.[125]

To examine the factors that permitted the JAARS missionary aviation operation to generate a profit is to take yet another journey into the extraordinarily imaginative mind of WBT-SIL's founder. In the first place, the JAARS program deepened the relationship between SIL and the Peruvian military government. With the ministries of education and health taking a half interest in the Grumman Duck, it was quite natural for the Peruvian air force, the Fuerza Aérea del Perú (FAP), to take a hand in its overhaul.[126] This initial cooperation between SIL and the FAP expanded as the JAARS operation grew, and in 1953 SIL obtained an agreement with the FAP to operate as an official airline carrying passengers, cargo, and mail along routes determined by the military.[127] It had not taken Peru's military leaders long to seize upon the utility of SIL's aircraft. Vast areas of the Amazonian basin remained largely inaccessible until such time as the government could deploy an adequate fleet of aircraft. Eager to extend political control over the nation's nearly impenetrable geography of lofty

---

121. "The Work of the Summer Institute of Linguistics in Peru," June 1954, p. 10, TA 940661.
122. Hibbard to Kenneth L. Pike, July 19, 1953, TA 8884.
123. "Work of the Summer Institute of Linguistics," p. 10, TA 940661.
124. Lester Bancroft to Cameron Townsend, December 27, 1956, TA 12157.
125. Cameron Townsend to "members of WBT-SIL," October 16, 1954, p. 5, TA 9946.
126. Cameron Townsend to Mellis, October 4, 1947, TA 4772.
127. "Convenio de Cooperacion" between SIL and FAP, April 30, 1953, TA 43268.

mountains and dense jungle, and spurred by a desire to develop the country's inaccessible natural resources, the Peruvian military was keen to see SIL expand its services. The FAP therefore offered all the assistance it could to SIL, including supplying it with free fuel and oil for its aircraft.[128] SIL proved itself a valuable ally of the armed forces by, for example, carrying military personnel and transporting prisoners to the penal colony at Sepa.[129] JAARS pilots also flew in support of the US Four Point Program, which was a technical assistance program inaugurated in January 1949 by the Truman administration as a deterrent against communism in developing nations.[130] In 1956, SIL's aviation operation was placed under the authority of the Peruvian army's Transportes Aereos Militares.[131] Regularly renewed, SIL's contract with the army remained in effect until 1983.[132] By pursuing the mantra of "service to all" with respect to aviation, SIL's JAARS effectively became an adjunct of the Peruvian military in the mid-1950s.

Townsend remarked to the WBT-SIL board in 1953 that he had long wished to make SIL "seem indispensable . . . to the Government." "I knew that if people got to look upon us as indispensable it would be practically impossible for anybody who opposed us to cause us trouble." He had certainly accomplished that aim. In fact, he reported to the board that "it is just a little embarrassing to Peruvians for us to have an air service that goes where the Peruvian Air Force doesn't go, and has won a better reputation for safety, etc."[133] Townsend was convinced that good public relations were the key to mollifying any incipient resentment, and he therefore labored to diminish the possibility that SIL would manifest, as he once put it, that "old attitude of gringo imperialists."[134]

128. Cameron Townsend to Henry C. Crowell, October 16, 1954, p. 3, TA 909977; Cameron Townsend to "members of WBT-SIL," October 16, 1954, p. 3, TA 9946.

129. Manuel Basulto, director of the Sepa Penal Colony, to Cameron Townsend, January 12, 1957, TA 13121; Cecil Hawkins, interview by author, July 10, 2009, Dallas, Texas; Cameron Townsend to Basulto, May 11, 1954, TA 10195.

130. Thomas G. Patterson, J. Garry Clifford, and Kenneth J. Hagan, *American Foreign Relations: A History Since 1895*, vol. 2, 4th ed. (Lexington, MA: Heath, 1995), 295; Cameron Townsend to "members of WBT-SIL," October 16, 1954, p. 5, TA 9946.

131. Montgomery to Lynn Bollinger, Helio Aircraft Corporation, August 25, 1956, TA 12526; Schneider to Cameron Townsend, January 18, 1957, TA 13602; Cameron Townsend to Admiral Roque A. Saldias, Presidente del Consejo de Ministros y Ministro de Hacienda, June 6, 1956, TA 12033; Cameron Townsend to Joe Qualm, January 27, 1959, TA 16880.

132. Gerald K. Elder and Calvin Hibbard, "Background on the SIL Cooperative Program with Peruvian Military," September 1983, TA 41068; Eugene Loos, interview by author, June 25, 2009, Dallas, Texas; Lester Bancroft, interview by author, September 17, 2009, Waxhaw, North Carolina.

133. Cameron Townsend to WBT-SIL board of directors, March 20, 1953, p. 1, TA 9027.

134. Cameron Townsend, "The Vital Role of Courtesy in Missionary Endeavor," SIL Oklahoma lecture no. 173, c. 1945, p. 2, TA 50076.

One way of accomplishing this was to involve Latin American elites in his projects. Sometime in mid-1950 Townsend was offered, at a cost of $15,000, a Catalina PBY "flying boat" by a southern California aircraft dealer.[135] With a 104-foot wingspan and a 2,500-mile range, it was both enormous and complex by missionary aviation standards. This suited Townsend's purposes perfectly. While in Mexico in November 1950, he convinced his longtime acquaintance and Mexico's minister of finance, Ramón Beteta, to form a committee of Mexican dignitaries to obtain the Catalina, christen it the *Moisés Sáenz* after the educator who invited Townsend to Mexico, and then donate it to Peru for use in SIL's program as a gesture of international goodwill.[136] Mexico's president Miguel Alemán Valdés authorized $10,000 for the Catalina purchase. A committee comprised of, among others, Manuel Gamio, the director of the Inter-American Indian Institute; Gual Vidal, the minister of education and a wealthy industrialist; and Moisés Sáenz's brother, Aarón Sáenz, collectively contributed the remaining $5,000.[137] The presidents of both nations, along with a host of notable personages, attended the christening ceremonies in Mexico and in Peru, respectively, winning for SIL a public relations coup in both countries.[138] Townsend understood intuitively that aircraft (especially large ones) were not simply a means of transportation but were also symbols of prestige and could therefore be deployed as instruments of statecraft and public relations.

The *Moisés Sáenz* was not Townsend's only venture in international relations. He routinely coupled his faith with diplomacy. Not infrequently this came in the form of a rebuke of the United States for not living up to its professed ideals in international affairs. When Mexico's president Lázaro Cárdenas nationalized American oil companies' assets in 1938, Townsend toured several southern US states attempting to influence public opinion in Mexico's favor.[139] He followed up with a book entitled *The Truth about Mexico's Oil*, wherein he charged that "the history of the oil industry in the United States is full of pages stained black."[140] Franklin D. Roosevelt received a complimentary letter from

135. Nyman to Cameron Townsend, November 30, 1950, TA 6277.

136. Cameron Townsend to Nyman, November 27, 1950, TA 6312.

137. Cameron Townsend to Nyman, December 1, 1950, TA 6311; Cameron Townsend, "Memorandum," April 1951, TA 907238.

138. Hibbard to Schneider, April 6, 1951, TA 6950; Schneider to Cameron Townsend, April 7, 1951, TA 7119; Cameron Townsend to "supporters," April 12, 1951, TA 6947.

139. William L. Svelmoe, "W. Cameron Townsend as Lázaro Cárdenas's 'Man in America,'" in *The Foreign Missionary Enterprise at Home: Explorations in North American Cultural History*, ed. Daniel H. Bays and Grant Wacker (Tuscaloosa: University of Alabama Press, 2003), 171–90.

140. W. Cameron Townsend, *The Truth about Mexico's Oil* (Los Angeles: Inter-American Fellowship, 1940), 1.

Townsend in 1940 praising his Good Neighbor policy, but, as with several presidents to follow, he was treated to another in 1943 lamenting America's failure to embody that policy fully.[141] Townsend also concerned himself with relations among Latin American states. In 1956 he petitioned Billy Graham to "sponsor a Peace Boat on the Napo River to foster better relationships between Ecuador and Peru."[142] Examples of Townsend's designs for encouraging better relations between nations could easily be multiplied, since peaceful international relations and gestures of international goodwill were fundamental components of his approach to missions.

Beginning in 1956, Townsend combined his passion for diplomacy and aviation to create yet another strikingly innovative project. In late 1955, Townsend cast his eyes upon a revolutionary short-takeoff-and-landing aircraft, the Helio Courier, which had recently arrived on the market.[143] Mesmerized by the remarkable short-field performance and superior low-stall speed of the Helio Courier, Townsend lost interest in all other airplanes. The fact that the Helio was triple the cost of the more pedestrian Pipers, Aeroncas, and Cessnas did not dampen his enthusiasm, and he placed a verbal order with the company's president, Lynn Bollinger, for six Helios at a cost of $22,000 each.[144] In typical fashion, he had no board authorization and no money to pay for the acquisitions. He therefore entreated with his wife Elaine to pray for funds, but all this proved too much for his usually accommodating wife, and she refused to trouble God for more than one plane at a time.[145] Townsend was convinced, however, that he was to have all six. Writing to JAARS pilot Merrill Piper in October 1955, he declared, "I have tried to dodge the issue for a long time, but at last the Lord cornered me and I've promised Him to trust Him from now on for what His work really needs rather than [settle] for the second rate stuff we can afford."[146] It would seem that Townsend, who liked to exercise his enormous faith by "putting God on the spot," was now audaciously claiming that God had turned the tables and put him on the spot.[147]

Making his case for the acquisition of the Helios in a November 21, 1955, letter, Townsend confessed that the "expense is great, but our God is greater," and

141. Cameron Townsend to Roosevelt, September 16, 1940, TA 2591; April 14, 1943, TA 3495.

142. Cameron Townsend, "Possible Ways in Which Dr. Graham Can Help Wycliffe," June 21, 1956, TA 12022.

143. Merrill Piper, Hefley interview, "Aviation Program," c. 1970, TA 43702.

144. Bernard May, interview by author, September 18, 2009, Waxhaw, North Carolina; Cameron Townsend to Lawrence Routh, November 19, 1955, TA 11293.

145. Hefley interview note, c. 1970, p. 2, TA 43513.

146. Cameron Townsend to Piper, October 14, 1955, p. 3, TA 11308.

147. Cameron Townsend, quoted in Kenneth L. Pike, Hefley interview, c. 1970, p. 2, TA 43474.

therefore to settle for second best would amount to a "lack of faith." Although "the flesh flinched at the thought," he warned the board that he intended to seek "non-evangelical assistance" to purchase the Helios. By and large, it was considered taboo in faith mission circles to seek funding for God's work from outside the evangelical camp. SIL had accepted secular funds in Latin America, but the organization had never done so in North America, where some of its evangelical constituency might be offended. Townsend therefore attempted to craft a loophole to maneuver around this impediment. He planned to rally local businesses and community groups in cities across the United States to raise funds for the Helios as part of an international goodwill effort. These aircraft would then be donated to various countries under the sponsorship of SIL as a gesture of inter-American cooperation. To "strengthen the Good Neighbor feeling even more," Townsend suggested, the planes should be referred to as the "Inter-American Friendship Fleet." He also insisted that the donor city's or state's name be painted on the cowling of each aircraft. He explained that this approach essentially solved the problem of secular funding, since the aircraft would be donated by American cities to the respective countries for which they were bound. Hence secular funds would not be directly linked to spiritual work. This assessment conveniently overlooked the fact that SIL's subsidiary, JAARS, would fly and maintain the donated aircraft.[148] The old faith-mission wall of separation between unsullied Christian monies and tainted secular mammon crumbled under Townsend's unrelenting drive to enlarge WBT-SIL's donor base as a means to expand the organization's operations.

The WBT-SIL board rightly read Townsend's November 21 letter for exactly what it was: nothing less than another ultimatum. And the board once again conceded with only a single caveat, and one not likely to be obeyed, that he was not to engage directly in "solicitation" on SIL's behalf.[149] The lone dissenter was the fiscally and religiously conservative BIOLA professor John Hubbard, who wrote Townsend after the board's decision to complain that the entire project smacked of "fanfare," something he felt should have no part "in connection with the Lord's work."[150] Townsend was handed permission for an aggressive expansion of the SIL-JAARS aviation program that now included creative financing and international goodwill components.

Over the next twenty-six years, twelve Helio Couriers and ten other aircraft of various types were donated to eight different countries under the auspices of

---

148. Cameron Townsend to WBT-SIL board of directors, November 21, 1955, TA 11291.

149. SIL board of directors meeting, minutes, November 26, 1955, WSA.

150. Hubbard to Cameron Townsend, December 1, 1955, TA 12183; Cameron Townsend to WBT-SIL board of directors, November 21, 1955, TA 11291.

what became known as the International Goodwill project, when it expanded beyond Latin America.[151] For the christening of each airplane, SIL sought out local and national dignitaries to make speeches and to sign letters to the recipient country's leaders. To create advance interest, SIL sent press releases and pictures of its far-flung operations to local newspapers, and then sent invitations to prominent community leaders to attend each ceremony. SIL was able to attract significant political and religious personalities to these events, such as Chicago mayor Richard J. Daley, Vice President Richard M. Nixon, evangelist Billy Graham, and former president Harry S. Truman.[152] In June 1958, SIL's Richard Pittman, now the architect of the organization's advance into Asia, sat down to assess the results of the Seattle project, in which a Helio Courier was donated to the Philippine government. Pittman's report describes some of the significant results that would accrue from the International Goodwill project. In addition to an airplane being supplied for SIL's use, the University of Washington, prompted by the events surrounding the ceremony in Seattle, invited SIL to offer linguistics courses at its campus along the same lines as those at the University of Oklahoma. The project also brought SIL two significant donors, the Pew Foundation of Sun Oil Company and the lumber magnate C. Davis Weyerhaeuser, both of whom were major donors to evangelical causes. Several Seattle churches also began to support WBT-SIL. Pittman related that the project resulted in the strengthening of relationships with US officials and agencies, such as Vice President Nixon, the undersecretary for Far Eastern affairs, several unnamed congressmen and senators, and the United States Information Agency. In the Philippines, SIL extended its range of associations to an even greater extent, including the president, the secretary of defense, a presidential aide, an ambassador, and several high-level military men.[153] Each time SIL successfully completed a Good Will project, it secured for the organization an increasingly longer list of friends in high places and well-heeled donors.

As the Helio program expanded, Townsend enterprisingly situated himself between the Peruvian army and the Helio Corporation, which saw Peru as a lucrative market. For each aircraft sold on Helio's behalf, SIL earned a sizable commission

151. Hugh Steven, *Yours to Finish the Task: The Memoirs of W. Cameron Townsend, 1947–1982* (Huntington Beach, CA: Wycliffe Bible Translators, 2004), 271–72.

152. Bollinger to Cameron Townsend, November 16, 1955, TA 11295; "Chicago Sending Plane to Ecuador," *Chicago Daily News*, December 17, 1955, TA 44099; "Gift of Plane to Peru," *Peruvian Times*, September 28, 1956, 10, TA 45694; Cameron Townsend to Donald H. Burns, November 13, 1955, TA 11296; Cameron Townsend to Crowell, June 11, 1956, TA 12038; Cameron Townsend to Watters, June 11, 1956, TA 12037; Cameron Townsend to Schneider, July 30, 1956, TA 12008; Cameron Townsend to Truman, January 22, 1958, TA 14840.

153. Pittman to Nyman, June 25, 1958, TA 15964.

in the form of credits toward the purchase of additional airplanes.[154] The Helio Aircraft Corporation had secured the services of a middleman, but he was no match for Townsend, whose connections with the Peruvian army and air force were unmatched, and whose sales techniques sometimes verged on subterfuge.[155] At one point Townsend boldly elbowed his way into a meeting of Peru's general staff in what could plausibly be construed as an attempt to outmaneuver the middleman and secure a sales contract.[156] Eventually Townsend triumphed over his competitor, largely because he was producing the sales. Indeed, between the International Goodwill airplane project and sales to the Peruvian government, SIL became Helio Courier's top customer cum sales representative in the late 1950s.[157]

Such questionable tactics were not confined to the founder. In 1961, SIL Brazil director Dale Kietzman expressed his frustration that the government of Brazil was not "buying" its International Goodwill program, mainly because government officials suspected that SIL was merely attempting to "use the prestige of the President of Brazil as a gimmick for raising money in the states." Kietzman and his administrative team devised a solution, one that would presumably allay suspicion that SIL was the central player in the project. First, the SIL Brazil team intended to ghostwrite cables, which would be sent by the Friendship Fleet committees in Philadelphia, Pennsylvania, and Greensboro, North Carolina, to the president of Brazil. A second set of ghostwritten cables would then be crafted, which the two Stateside committees would send to the SIL Brazil branch, requesting Kietzman to pay a call on the government to check and see if the president's cables had arrived. This latter set of cables, Kietzman said, would provide the "ostensible reason for a visit to the presidential palace." It was presumed that this somewhat conspiratorial plan would result in a conference with the president. "We will," Kietzman disclosed, "be prepared with a complete 'dossier' for him to examine on the subject."[158] It is unclear if this scheme was ever executed. However, it is obvious that SIL was wandering far afield from traditional faith mission methods and engaging in practices that would certainly offend the sensibilities of many less-daring evangelical missionaries.[159]

---

154. Cameron Townsend to Nyman and Watters, February 27, 1957, TA 12638; Cameron Townsend to Watters, March 29, 1957, TA 13022.

155. Cameron Townsend to Bollinger, February 23, 1957, p. 1, TA 13045; March 2, 1957, p. 1, TA 13036; Cameron Townsend to G. A. Alvarado, export manager, Helio Aircraft Company, May 23, 1957, TA 12889.

156. Cameron Townsend to Bollinger, February 28, 1957, TA 13038.

157. Bollinger to William Retts, May 1, 1957, p. 1, TA 13450.

158. Kietzman to Cameron Townsend, April 10, 1961, TA 20272.

159. The reception of SIL's atypical strategies among North American evangelicals is examined in chapter 5.

By essentially becoming an airline, JAARS was able to develop a much more diverse and far larger customer base than would have been possible had it remained solely a missionary carrier. In 1966, for example, nearly 50 percent of all JAARS flying was for other missions, oil companies, the military, and other commercial traffic.[160] This affair was no small undertaking. By 1970 the JAARS aircraft fleet was flying in the vicinity of 2.5 million passenger miles per year.[161] SIL missionaries also benefited from subsidized rates, allowing them greater freedom of movement than would have otherwise been possible.[162] By operating as both an adjunct to the military and a commercial enterprise, the JAARS subsidiary of SIL was financially able to deploy the number and types of aircraft of which Townsend had always dreamed.

Townsend's conflict with the leadership of Missionary Aviation Fellowship (MAF) is another graphic illustration of his thoroughgoing break with traditional approaches to missions. Just as he had bristled at the strictures imposed by the Central American Mission, he had little patience with the conventional practices of MAF. Even though MAF was innovative in bringing aviation into the mainstream of missionary activity, its leaders felt little or no compulsion to offer more than the most basic aviation services to missionaries. They were content simply to replace the canoe and the burro with the airplane. In Townsend's imaginative approach, aircraft could perform functions beyond their practical use, by also fulfilling diplomatic and public relation roles. While Bible translation remained a central concern of SIL, the dual-organization strategy offered ample opportunity for the founder to pursue his own version of the good neighbor policy. The dual organization also allowed for the Peruvian state and SIL, with their shared goals, to coalesce into a partnership of convenience. This, of course, made for strange bedfellows, and not without effects on SIL, which was taking on characteristics of what would later be designated as a nongovernmental organization (NGO), as opposed to remaining a traditional faith mission. The purely missional aspects certainly remained, in that Bible translation and low-key evangelization were carried out, but they coexisted with what might be referred to as secularizing forces that led SIL down some unexpected paths for an evangelical mission. One of the most significant outcomes of the policy of serving everyone was that SIL became so deeply embedded in the Peruvian state that it became indispensable, just as Townsend had long desired.

---

160. Omer Bondurant, "Aviation Report—Conference," 1967, p. 1, TA 41011.

161. Harold Goodall, Hefley interview, "Aviation Program," c. 1970, TA 943772.

162. Larry Montgomery, JAARS annual report (1955), p. 1, TA 11723.

The Catholic Hierarchy's Reaction to SIL

As SIL expanded its operations, especially the bilingual education program, it was gaining the confidence of the government on the one hand and provoking the ire of the Roman Catholic hierarchy on the other. One tactic used by the Roman Catholics to thwart SIL's efforts was the spreading of rumors among Peru's indigenous inhabitants. Perhaps the most original of these allegations claimed that SIL was abducting Indians and rendering them for fat as a way to supply grease for its airplanes. When an SIL missionary casually discarded a human skull, one she had previously discovered in an old Inca burial ground, this rumor took on a life of its own.[163] More potentially damaging on the national scene were recriminations published in Lima papers. The first major broadside, from which several followed, was launched publicly against SIL by Jesuit missionary José Martín Cuesta on February 28, 1953, in the pro-Catholic and conservative *El Comercio*, one of Peru's leading papers. Cuesta correctly perceived SIL as a Protestant threat to Catholicism, and incisively noted that SIL was "composed exclusively of evangelicals."[164] What Cuesta pointed out, but SIL was reluctant to admit, was that the organization was nonsectarian in whom it served but not in the composition of its membership or in its missiology. Townsend, and SIL with him, assumed that the simple gospel message and Bible distribution constituted a nonsectarian Christianity. In his own *El Comercio* article, Townsend stated that "[with] our non-sectarian nature, we are not responsible for the teaching of rituals and ecclesiastical systems of any nature." Of course, this minimalist evangelical gospel was in fact a sectarian gospel in the eyes of Catholics.[165] Cuesta therefore concluded that SIL was "an organ for propaganda and dissemination of evangelical Protestantism."[166] In August, *El Comercio* featured a second article, this one by a Franciscan, Fr. Buenaventure Leon de Uriarte, vicar apostolic of Ucayali, which was SIL's base of operations. Uriarte charged that the "grievous wolves" of SIL were carrying out "among the indigene savages . . . a work of protestant proselyting [*sic*] for the evangelical sect."[167] Both Cuesta and Uriarte claimed they were not inveighing against

163. Cecil Hawkins, interview by author, July 10, 2009, Dallas, Texas; Lois Jean Hesse, personal communication to author, September 25, 2008.

164. Rev. Fr. José Martín Cuesta, SJ, "Literacy Campaign in the Peruvian Jungle," *El Comercio*, February 28, 1953, 3, TA 40703, translation by Robert L. Russell.

165. Cameron Townsend, letter to the editor of *El Comercio*, August 18, 1953, 3, translation by Cal Hibbard, TA 40686.

166. Cuesta, "Literacy Campaign," 5, TA 40703.

167. Fr. Buenaventure L. de Uriarte, OFM, "The Summer Institute of Linguistics Is a Sectarian and Proselytist Institute," *El Comercio*, August 15, 1953, 1, TA 45594, translation unattributed.

SIL as individuals, but were speaking on behalf of all the "High Ecclesiastical Authorities," including the archbishop of Lima, Juan Gualberto Guevara. In the early 1950s, SIL was clearly perceived as a growing Protestant threat by the Catholic hierarchy.

Peru's Roman Catholic hierarchy underestimated Townsend's political acumen and, at the same time, committed several serious blunders in making their case before the public. Uriarte fumbled badly when he claimed that SIL missionary-linguists were "false scientists" operating deceitfully under "the pompous name of Summer Institute of Linguistics."[168] Townsend easily refuted this point by quoting from the July–September 1948 issue of the prestigious journal *Language*, wherein the Linguistic Society of America lavished praise on SIL by referring to the organization's "impressive series of publications" and stating that SIL was "one of the most promising developments in applied linguistics in the country."[169] Kenneth Pike and Eugene Nida's efforts to secure SIL's academic credentials were effective in blunting attempts to question SIL's capacity for making a real scientific contribution to the nations in which it served.

Second, the Catholic clergy attempted to create an aura of suspicion around the organization by labeling SIL a conspiracy. With SIL aircraft crisscrossing the Peruvian jungle and flying along the frontier borders of Brazil, Colombia, and Bolivia, Uriarte contended that "the Sovereignty and security of our Nation are at stake."[170] Cuesta, framing SIL as a Protestant intriguer, called on "Peruvian authorities . . . to investigate carefully the position of the members of the Summer Institute of Linguistics in light of these facts and to consider whether it is in keeping with the Constitution."[171] In making these accusations and calling for government investigation of SIL, the Catholic leadership in Peru aimed to damage the relationship between the government and SIL. This too proved to be a false step.

By the time Cuesta had made his public allegations in February 1953, SIL's relationship with General Manuel Odría's military regime was all but cemented. Less than a month after the appearance of the *El Comercio* article, SIL signed the cooperative agreement with the Peruvian air force. Hence the Odría military dictatorship was obviously well aware of SIL's aviation operations, since its aircraft were operating on behalf of the government. Likewise, the bilingual education program remained under the direction of Minister of Education Juan

168. Uriarte, "Summer Institute of Linguistics," 2.

169. *Language* 24, no. 3 (July–September 1948): 4, and quoted in Cameron Townsend to editor of *El Comercio*, August 18, 1953, 4, TA 40686.

170. Uriarte, "Summer Institute of Linguistics," 3, TA 45594.

171. Cuesta, "Literacy Campaign," 5, TA 40703.

Mendoza Rodriguez, who had recently been promoted to the rank of general.[172] While it is unclear from the available literature where the balance of Odría's allegiances lay between the Catholic hierarchy and SIL, the president's actions at the time clearly signaled that his regime was fully behind SIL. In June 1953 Odría met with Townsend personally, and placed his seal of approval on SIL's bilingual education program.[173] Then, in September, the Ministry of Education doubled the bilingual education program's budget, leaving little doubt that it was siding with SIL.[174] It was also in September that Peru's Ministry of External Relations, by authorization of the president, bestowed upon Townsend the Merit for Distinguished Service, a commendation that was awarded for service to Peru in the arts, sciences, or industry.[175] What the Catholic hierarchy touted as a possible conspiracy was in fact simply a partnership of convenience, and one that the Odría regime apparently considered of sufficient value to risk offending the Catholic hierarchy. It could also be suggested that the Peruvian regime's sanctioning SIL was part and parcel of its deepening relationship with the United States in the early 1950s. For example, a bilateral military assistance program was signed on February 22, 1952, between Peru and the United States, and the Eisenhower administration later decorated Odría for his staunch anticommunism.[176] In a cooperative and accommodating SIL, the military government had a valuable and loyal ally in its project of incorporating Peru's indigenous peoples into the state and extending its reach over the nation's rugged geography, and was therefore willing to brush off the Catholic hierarchy's protests.

The final nail in the coffin of Catholic opposition was SIL's service to priests and nuns in the jungle. Townsend had long admonished his colleagues to love their enemies. He therefore insisted that his pilots look for opportunities to serve Catholic missionaries, and he instructed JAARS pilots never to overfly a Catholic mission station without stopping to at least to drop off a newspaper or offer to pick up mail.[177] Ideally pilots would invite Catholic priests or nuns aboard SIL's aircraft, thereby relieving them of long and hazardous foot or canoe journeys. It would be naïve to assume that Townsend's motives for insisting on these practices were unadulterated. His pilots were expected to carry cam-

172. Jeffrey Klaiber, *The Catholic Church in Peru, 1821–1985: A Social History* (Washington, DC: Catholic University of America Press, 1992), 343.

173. Hibbard to Nyman, June 15, 1953, TA 8619.

174. Hibbard to Nyman, September 13, 1953, TA 8605.

175. Captioned photograph of Cameron Townsend with Merit for Distinguished Service, n.d., TA 44488; copy of certificate of Merit for Distinguished Service awarded to Cameron Townsend by the president of Peru, dated May 25, 1953, awarded September 1953, TA 43205.

176. Masterson, *Militarism*, 140.

177. Lester Bancroft, interview by author, September 17, 2009, Waxhaw, North Carolina.

eras for the express purpose of snapping photographs of Catholic missionaries boarding SIL airplanes.[178] Townsend himself occasionally boarded flights so that he could build relationships with these isolated Catholic missionaries, who truly welcomed the opportunity for stimulating conversation and news of the outside world. At other times he would simply invite them over to enjoy Elaine's homemade bread and pickles.[179] This policy of serving Catholics was an especially effective approach in Peru, where the local clergy mainly drew support from the community and where the Catholic hierarchy's authority and the pope's directives rarely penetrated to the local level.[180] Townsend resourcefully took advantage of this cleavage to win the support of the provincial clergy at the expense of the national and regional Catholic leadership. In addition, SIL shared its linguistic research with local priests working in the jungle. Grateful for the hospitality and services rendered, these Catholic missionaries often dropped Townsend a letter or note to express their gratitude. Townsend was thus able to quote from one of these letters in his *El Comercio* article; he chose a June 1953 letter from a Dominican missionary, Francísco Alvarez, who had expressed his appreciation for SIL's sharing "the results of the [linguistic] investigations" and thanked the organization for the "great service you did me when you flew me from Atalaya to Sepahua."[181] Townsend not only quoted from these letters to refute his adversaries' claims, but he was also known to carry these letters and photographs as he made his rounds of government offices, proffering them as examples of SIL's "service to all."[182] Therefore, even before the Catholic hierarchy mounted its attacks, Townsend had steadily built up SIL's defenses for the coming battle through a strategy of divide and conquer.

Townsend insisted that SIL should serve Catholics and that it should share its research with them, but he did not stop there. He also publicly lavished praise on his antagonists. "One of the heroes whom I admire the most," Townsend averred in his 1953 *El Comercio* article, "is the celebrated Fray Bartolomé de las Casas." Approbation of this nature was not limited to this sixteenth-century Dominican friar, since Townsend frequently praised Catholics in his public pronouncements and in his written discourse. In 1958, Kenneth Pike bared

178. Calvin Hibbard, interview by author, August 6, 2007, Waxhaw, North Carolina; Cameron Townsend, "Overcome Evil with Good," c. 1968, p. 2, TA 50001.

179. Elaine (Mielke) Townsend, Hefley interview, c. 1970, TA 43484.

180. Edward J. Williams, "The Emergence of the Secular Nation-State and Latin American Catholicism," *Comparative Politics* 5, no. 2 (January 1973): 264.

181. Alvarez to Cameron Townsend, June 23, 1953, TA 9308, also quoted in part in Cameron Townsend, letter to the editor of *El Comercio*, August 18, 1953, 5, TA 40686.

182. Calvin Hibbard, interview by author, August 6, 2007, Waxhaw, North Carolina; Cameron Townsend, "Overcome Evil with Good," TA 50001.

his soul to Townsend, recounting how he "reacted with violence inwardly" to these pro-Catholic proclamations. He confessed that "to read some of these letters which you have written to some of these people in South America about turns my stomach."[183] The ever pragmatic Townsend knew exactly what he was doing. His was a stratagem designed not only to disarm his enemies but also to keep them off balance. It would be a mistake to conclude that Townsend's tactics were entirely Machiavellian, since he genuinely enjoyed a number of Catholic friendships. A perfect example was his long and warm relationship with a Maryknoll priest, Father Joseph A. Grassi, who had attended classes at SIL in Norman, Oklahoma, in 1957.[184] It remains true, however, that there was a subversive angle to his designs with respect to the institution of Catholicism. For example, in a September 1953 letter to SIL members, he allowed that "we are accomplishing a tremendous amount to loosen that monster's grip" in Peru.[185] Townsend was a formidably astute political strategist, and his maneuvers did much to keep SIL's Catholic adversaries on the defensive.

By the mid-1950s, a growing progressive wing within Peruvian Catholicism, which was more in touch with the changing social realities, came to the fore. The 1955 succession of the conservative Cardinal Juan Gualberto by the more progressive Juan Landázuri Rickets as archbishop of Lima marks the inflection point where the militant and conservative wing of the church was surpassed by a more progressive and modern wing of Peruvian Catholicism. Over the next thirty-five years, Landázuri patiently but firmly pressed the Catholic Church in Peru to take up the question of social justice. Change in the church's outlook was visible in a 1958 pastoral letter from Peru's bishops in which they spoke of the need for Christians to work toward wide-ranging change of the prevailing social order, unlike in the past, where the church had limited its criticism to specific social injustices.[186] The central thrust of Landázuri's progressive program foreshadowed the reforms of the Second Vatican Council of the early 1960s, which undertook an ideological reorientation that moderated the church's authoritarian, paternal, and antiprogressive perspectives, and it also marked the point when the Vatican began to emphasize ecumenism.[187] After the Second

183. Kenneth L. Pike to Cameron Townsend, December 8, 1958, p. 2, TA 14277.

184. Grassi to Kenneth L. Pike, August 18, 1958, TA 15820; Grassi to Cameron Townsend, September 21, 1965, TA 22616; June 25, 1970, TA 27784; Cameron Townsend to Grassi, November 22, 1966, TA 23478.

185. Cameron Townsend to an unnamed WBT-SIL member, c. September 1953, p. 3, TA 8824.

186. Klaiber, *Catholic Church in Peru*, 24–26, 209–13, 245–46, 252–53, 256.

187. Catalina Romero, "The Peruvian Church: Change and Continuity," in *The Progressive Church in Latin America*, ed. Scott Mainwaring and Alexander Wilde (Notre Dame: University of Notre Dame Press, 1989), 253–75; Williams, "Emergence of the Secular Nation-State," 264–74.

Vatican Council, progressive Latin American Catholic bishops increasingly assumed a lead role in contributing to social justice within the framework of the modern nation-state, and the animus of the Catholic hierarchy toward SIL therefore slowly abated over the ensuing years.

By the mid-1970s, the attitude of the Catholic hierarchy toward SIL had come full circle. SIL Peru branch member Allan Shannon was a key figure in developing relationships with Catholic clergy in the 1970s. The combined effects of Vatican II and the Catholic charismatic renewal movement offered Shannon numerous opportunities to engage Catholic clergy on the individual, regional, national, and international levels. Shannon's efforts not only fostered better SIL and Catholic relations, but the relationships he established also won Catholic imprimatur of a number of New Testament projects.[188] Perhaps the most striking evidence of this shift of Catholic sentiment was Archbishop Landázuri's endorsement and backing of SIL in 1976.[189] SIL's most vociferous antagonist in Peru of the 1950s, the Catholic hierarchy, now professed its support for the organization.

There is no question that WBT-SIL was a Protestant evangelical organization, but by serving and befriending the Catholic missionaries in the jungles, by assiduously avoiding ecclesiastical forms and clerical functions, by dampening outward shows of religiosity, by discouraging SIL members from clustering around other evangelical missionaries, and by operating under the authority of government ministries, SIL presented a maddeningly difficult-to-hit target. Moreover, putting his antagonists on the defensive and securing SIL's place in Peru made a lasting impact upon Townsend's mind. "I believe," he wrote in September 1953, "our position is impregnable." This state of affairs imbued Townsend with a great deal of confidence in his particular approach. "I believe," he added, "that God has given us the principles on which we can go into every land on the face of the earth, Russia included."[190] From this point forward, Townsend was unyielding in his insistence that the patterns established in Mexico and Peru were inviolable.[191]

The methods Townsend developed in Mexico proved just as useful in Peru. SIL's linguistic expertise opened the door to Peru because it supplied a key ingredient in Peru's modernization project. The dual-organization approach and

188. Allan Shannon and Gerald K. Elder, "Reflections on the First Congress of Bishops," January 9, 1973, TA 41122; Shannon to SIL Peru branch director, April 8, 1974, TA 31157; November 17, 1975, TA 31965; Shannon to Elder, November 16, 1976, TA 33160.

189. Shannon to Cameron Townsend, October 11, 1976, TA 32806.

190. Cameron Townsend, transcript of a speech given at 1953 WBT-SIL corporate conference, p. 8, TA 42373.

191. The organization's development from the mid-1960s is detailed in chapter 6.

the development of JAARS facilitated SIL's becoming an extension of the Peruvian state. The dual approach also permitted Townsend to utilize SIL's quasi-secular status to pursue projects under the banner of international goodwill, something that would have been difficult or impossible for a typical faith mission. All this secured for SIL multiple benefits, such as friends in high places at home and abroad, not to mention wealthy donors. The strategy of "service to all" was clearly an important ingredient in securing for SIL a respected position in Peru, since it allowed for the fullest expression of the organization's progressive approach, and thus for SIL to engage effectively in the Peruvian project of state modernization. Ultimately the single most important factor for SIL's achievements in Peru was Townsend's extraordinary mind and personality. It was he who developed the basic principles guiding the organization, demolished perceived barriers, and led the charge into new territory both geographically and ideologically. Townsend's mantra of service to all formed the basis for success in otherwise difficult-to-access countries while, at the same time, it created a new kind of evangelical missionary organization, one that not only translated the Bible and sought to save souls but also endeavored to weaken the social and political influence of Catholicism, to make productive citizens of indigenous peoples, to strengthen the fabric of the modern nation-state, and to foster better relations between nations.

CHAPTER 5

On the Home Front

WBT-SIL's expansion abroad hinged on cultivating a dedicated North American constituency from which the organization could draw recruits and funds. As the organization developed its base of support, it was forced to contend with significant structural shifts occurring within evangelicalism. In the 1940s and 1950s, "progressive fundamentalists" parted ways with the separatist and militant "classical" form of fundamentalism that had taken shape in the 1920s and 1930s.[1] This project of reform opened up fissures within the fundamentalist coalition, and WBT-SIL was thrust into the conflict since it was situated astride one of the fault lines. From the early 1950s, WBT-SIL's innovative strategies began to trouble a growing number of fundamentalists at home in North America. As the criticism mounted, it became increasingly evident that the organization was transgressing the boundaries of both classical fundamentalism and the faith mission ethos. WBT-SIL's uneasy relationship with the conservative Interdenominational Foreign Mission Association in the late 1950s was the most significant symbol of changing perceptions of the organization among fundamentalists. Despite these controversies over its innovative strategies, WBT-SIL experienced uninterrupted growth in both personnel and finances. How did the organization enjoy such enduring success even as it came under fire from a number of outspoken fundamentalists?

A twofold approach is taken here toward answering this question. In the first place, WBT-SIL is considered within the context of the post–World War II reordering of conservative evangelicalism. Under fire from fundamentalists and

---

1. Joel A. Carpenter, *Revive Us Again: The Reawakening of American Fundamentalism* (New York: Oxford University Press, 1997), 233.

other faith missions, WBT-SIL was faced with the prospect of either changing its strategies or offending conservatives on the right. In the second place, the organization's success at home was contingent upon Wycliffe's ability to promote the rather unusual work of SIL to an evangelical public that was accustomed to traditional faith mission methods. An examination of these topics will demonstrate that WBT-SIL resourcefully met the challenges it faced at home in North America, and by doing so, took yet another step in altering the contours of the organization.

WBT-SIL and North American Fundamentalism

In the first decade and a half after its founding, WBT-SIL was believed to be a fundamentalist institution, albeit a somewhat unconventional one. This perception was reinforced by the Pioneer Mission Agency's administrative oversight of SIL and its sponsorship of Camp Wycliffe until 1941. Also, in the early years before moving to the University of Oklahoma, Camp Wycliffe's Bible school–like character reassured fundamentalists that, despite its focus on linguistics, it was a fellow traveler. For instance, Camp Wycliffe's brochure of 1936 served notice that "no modernists need apply."[2] Wycliffe's acceptance into the conservative and separatist Interdenominational Foreign Mission Association (IFMA) in 1949 also suggested to the faith mission community that WBT-SIL was a legitimate fundamentalist mission. Up to at least 1950, it was assumed that WBT-SIL was deserving of its place in the fundamentalist and faith mission coalitions.

To Cameron Townsend belongs an outsized share of credit for securing WBT-SIL's place in North American fundamentalism. During the organization's formative years of the 1930s and 1940s, he built up an impressive array of contacts among fundamentalist personalities and institutions. Townsend was a member of the Church of the Open Door in Los Angeles, a leading fundamentalist outpost on the West Coast, and his first wife, Elvira, maintained close ties to her home church, the Moody Memorial Church in Chicago, where the prominent fundamentalist teacher Harry Ironside led the congregation.[3] By 1930, Townsend was well enough acquainted with Charles Fuller to convince the radio evangelist to publicize his fanciful "air crusade to the wild tribes" on the radio.[4] Oswald J. Smith, the well-known pastor of the People's Church in

2. Camp Wycliffe brochure, 1936, TA 2073.

3. Elvira (Malmstrom) Townsend, "From Central America," *Moody Church News*, March 1923, TA 1002; Elvira (Malmstrom) Townsend, "A Letter from Mrs. Townsend," *Moody Church News*, January 1928, TA 1428.

4. Cameron Townsend to Hummel, November 1, 1930, p. 4, TA 1491.

Toronto, Canada, was another advocate and supporter of Wycliffe.[5] In 1945, when Youth for Christ (YFC) was still in its infancy, Townsend cemented a personal relationship with YFC's Torrey Johnson.[6] This short list could be lengthened considerably to include, among others, the YFC evangelist Jack Wyrtzen; the fundamentalist theologian and president of Dallas Theological Seminary, Lewis Sperry Chafer; editor of the *Sunday School Times* Charles G. Trumbull; and the popular Bible teacher Donald Grey Barnhouse. The list of Bible schools in which WBT-SIL regularly publicized its efforts and from which it drew recruits was just as extensive. Among these were some of the largest and best-known schools of the day, such as Moody Bible Institute, BIOLA, Columbia Bible College, Prairie Bible Institute, and Denver Bible College. These associations and relationships offer ample evidence that Townsend had, by the mid-1940s, established WBT-SIL as a creditable member of the North American fundamentalist network.

WBT-SIL's acceptance in fundamentalist circles was also enhanced by its following the traditional faith mission approach to individual missionary support. Whereas the mainline mission boards paid salaries to their missionaries from denominational coffers, Wycliffe missionaries had no such ready-made sources of income. They had to garner their own personal financial support, which, if the necessary funds were forthcoming, served as a seal of God's calling. Under the faith system, missionaries were not permitted to solicit funds. Thus potential donors had to be approached by indirect means that did not violate the principle of never asking for funds directly. For example, Kenneth Pike addressed this subject in a *Sunday School Times* lesson of May 1948 entitled "Living on Manna." Pike took the biblical story of God's providing manna for the Israelites during their forty-year desert sojourn as a metaphor for the faith principle. "The missionary who has no guarantee of income," Pike wrote, "may similarly find himself in a strange country with no way of supporting himself."[7] This short lecture aimed to reinforce the idea that a missionary walked by faith, depending on God alone to provide. By constant reminders of this tenet, churchgoers were conditioned to respond to the Lord's leading by fulfilling their part of the contract. Thus the missionary heroically stepped out "in faith," which in turn offered the church member at home the privilege of vicariously participating in the missionary venture and in the outworking of God's plan. This approach was a hallowed tenet of faith missions, where the refrain "full

---

5. Smith to Cameron Townsend, August 11, 1943, TA 3551.

6. Cameron Townsend to William G. Nyman Sr., March 21, 1945, TA 3952; March 26, 1945, TA 3949.

7. Kenneth L. Pike, "Living on Manna," *Sunday School Times*, May 16, 1948, 387, TA 44385.

information, no solicitation" was the order of the day; to ask directly for money not only was taboo but also was thought to usurp the work of the Holy Spirit.

"Turning Trials into Triumphs" was the title of Townsend's parting speech at the close of WBT-SIL's September 1959 biennial conference. He began his address by recounting the Old Testament story of the prophet Daniel. Townsend reminded his auditors of how Daniel served King Darius while remaining faithful to God, and of how jealous government officials plotted Daniel's demise. Townsend never tired of metaphorically casting WBT-SIL into this kind of biblical narrative, for it fitted perfectly with his triumphal vision of WBT-SIL conquering its enemies through unwavering faith in God. "Now as we scatter from this Conference," Townsend announced to his assembled colleagues, "I'm reminded of the words of our Lord when he said to the seventy, 'I send you forth as lambs among the wolves.'"[8] The "wolves" Townsend spoke of were not only Catholic antagonists abroad; they now included a growing number of conservative evangelicals at home. Disturbing news began to trickle back from Peru and Ecuador concerning SIL's peculiar activities from the early 1950s. Missionaries serving in proximity to SIL's operations were dismayed to discover that SIL workers attended diplomatic functions where liquor was served and avoided gatherings of other evangelical missionaries. Fellow missioners also noted that SIL members seemed to have a propensity for concealing their real identity, often referring to themselves as linguists rather than explicitly as missionaries.[9] This remained one of the most persistent complaints throughout the 1950s. Africa Inland Mission's Ralph T. Davis, while serving as president of IFMA, complained to Townsend in 1958 that "I have never been able to be convinced in my own heart that the primary purpose of you and Wycliffe, as such, was the spiritual purpose of your work rather than the scientific." "Are you fish or fowl?" Davis wanted to know.[10] Perhaps the most disturbing reproach along this line occurred inside the Moody Bible Institute, the premier fundamentalist missionary training school in North America. In the mid-1950s, Harold R. Cook, a Moody professor of missions and author of the widely used textbook *Missionary Life and Work*, was heard complaining of how WBT-SIL members referred to themselves as missionaries at home but apparently denied this when on the foreign field. Cook also spoke of the dual organization's "chameleon-like character" during class discussions.[11] The occasion when some non-SIL missionaries were turned out of SIL's guesthouse and left to pace the sidewalks of

8. Cameron Townsend, "Turning Trials into Triumphs," September 1959, 2, TA 50017.

9. Details of these events are discussed in chapter 4.

10. Davis to Cameron Townsend, November 3, 1958, pp. 1–2, TA 15024.

11. Cowan to Cameron Townsend, December 14, 1957, p. 2, TA 12660; quotation from John W. Newman to Robert William Wyatt, December 10, 1957, TA 13681.

Lima in 1954, for fear that they might not temporarily mask their evangelical missionary identity during a government official's visit, seemed to prove to opponents that SIL was less than forthright about its intentions.[12] This incident became something of a staple criticism that circulated for years after the original event had occurred. The organization's policies abroad in the 1950s were cause for mounting consternation at home, which threatened WBT-SIL's established position in the fundamentalist coalition.

Among the novel strategies instituted by Townsend, serving Roman Catholics may have been the most controversial. In mid-twentieth-century America, fundamentalists were not the only purveyors of anti-Catholicism. Mainline Protestants had their own fears, as exemplified by a series of anxious articles published in 1944 and 1945 by Harold Fey, the editor of *Christian Century*, entitled "Can Catholicism Win America?"[13] Indicative of a wider cultural anti-Catholicism was the publication of *American Freedom and Catholic Power* in 1949, by Paul Blanshard, assistant editor of the *Nation*, a widely read magazine of politics and culture. As the title suggested, Blanshard worried that Catholic power was a threat to American democracy and the nation's freedom.[14] Fellow missionaries were therefore naturally alarmed when they discovered WBT-SIL's pilots flying Catholic priests and nuns in the organization's aircraft. The use of aircraft to serve everyone was, in the words of Philip E. Howard Jr., the president and editor of the *Sunday School Times*, nothing less than "lending aid and comfort to the enemy."[15] When Donald Moffat, of the Association of Baptists for World Evangelism, heard that SIL was flying Catholics in 1953, he demanded an explanation of why WBT-SIL condescended to serving the "Romanists, who are . . . the instruments of Satan in every way." "If ever there was a counterfeit that springs from Hell," Moffat sermonized, "it is the Roman church."[16] In late 1957, C. Stacey Woods, the secretary general of the InterVarsity Christian Fellowship (IVCF), expressed his dismay over the attendance of Catholic priests at SIL Norman and SIL's Serving Catholics abroad. Woods admitted that "we must be 'as wise as serpents, as harmless as doves,'" but he also believed it was just as important "to have no fellowship with unfruitful works of darkness." He therefore informed Townsend that the IVCF was determined to stand by its policy of not collaborating with any organization that consorted with Roman Catholics.[17] This news was disturbing indeed, for the IVCF was an important

12. This episode is described in chapter 4.

13. Carpenter, *Revive Us Again*, 188.

14. Paul Blanshard, *American Freedom and Catholic Power* (Boston: Beacon, [1949] 1950).

15. Howard to Cameron Townsend, June 6, 1956, p. 2, TA 12289.

16. Moffat to Carolyn Orr, November 21, 1953, TA 9492.

17. Woods to Cameron Townsend, October 29, 1957, TA 12728.

source of WBT-SIL recruits. By choosing to serve Roman Catholics, WBT-SIL risked offending its entire North American constituency.

Even as Townsend was securing WBT-SIL's place within North American fundamentalism, he was flirting with the acceptable boundaries of the movement. With his innovative strategies in Mexico, which he further developed in South America from 1946, he often transgressed these boundaries. WBT-SIL's unusual policies remained largely hidden from view until events in Peru and Ecuador attracted attention in the early 1950s. Many fundamentalists considered WBT-SIL a kindred spirit. Thus, when it became known that the organization had embarked on a path that was, at many points, inimical to the fundamentalist tradition, it struck fear and loathing in the hearts of a number of WBT-SIL supporters. The revolts of 1947 and 1948, at Camp Wycliffe and in the Peru branch of SIL, respectively, were ample evidence of the unintended consequences of Townsend's innovations.[18] Although WBT-SIL wrapped itself in fundamentalist integuments, the organization was quite unlike the typical fundamentalist institution. In effect, the paradoxes of the dual organization were to blame for the growing unease among observers of WBT-SIL. At home Wycliffe, with its conservative doctrinal basis and faith mission stance, stressed born-again conversions through Bible translation; in academic circles and abroad SIL evinced a progressive social outlook and chose to serve non-evangelicals, Roman Catholics included. The fundamentalist image created in North America was partly an illusion. WBT-SIL, in all its parts combined, was more broadly evangelical than fundamentalist. As the organization's nature and strategies came to light over the course of the 1950s, WBT-SIL's place within the fundamentalist coalition became an increasingly uneasy one, and the most telling evidence of this apprehension was the organization's fitful relationship with IFMA in the late 1950s.

Progressive Fundamentalism and the IFMA Controversy

During the 1940s and 1950s, progressive fundamentalists made significant strides toward establishing a broad, but also rather loose, evangelical front shorn of the most unconstructive traits of classical fundamentalism. Beginning in the late 1930s, with bright hopes of igniting revival fires, progressive fundamentalists sallied forth to win America for Christ. While remaining committed to the doctrinal "fundamentals of the faith," they aimed to put a cheerful face

18. These transient upheavals over Townsend's methods are discussed in chapters 2 and 4, respectively.

on their religion. One of the most visible features of progressive fundamentalism was evangelical youth movements, such as InterVarsity Christian Fellowship; Youth for Christ, in which Billy Graham launched his evangelistic career;
Dawson Trotman's Navigators; and Percy Crawford's radio ministry, the Young
People's Church of the Air. Progressive fundamentalists also constructed new
institutional bases. The formation of the National Association of Evangelicals
(NAE) in 1942 was the paramount example of the new evangelical thrust to
establish a nationwide presence and to reengage American culture. This cadre
of younger fundamentalists combined their fathers' old-time religion with an
updated and fashionable approach to presenting the gospel.[19] By the mid to
late 1940s, progressive fundamentalists were well on the way to creating a viable alternative to the older separatist and militant fundamentalism that was a
product of the contentious 1920s and 1930s.

The progressive fundamentalist movement sparked heated controversy.
With the founding of the NAE, some militant fundamentalists sniffed apostasy. One of the most pugnacious was Carl McIntire, the leader of the newly
established militant and separatist American Council of Christian Churches,
who led the opposition against the NAE. McIntire was quick to charge the NAE
leadership with a failure to "fight the enemies of the Lord Jesus Christ" in the
Federal Council of Churches.[20] Anything less than full-throated opposition to
modernism and ecumenism quickly drew the wrath of those, such as McIntire,
who saw it as their calling to police the boundaries of fundamentalism. These
internecine quarrels heralded the coming rupture between classical fundamentalists and the post–World War II new evangelicals. Billy Graham's 1957 New
York Crusade, during which he cooperated with mainline Protestants, is generally considered the seminal event that finally drove a lasting wedge between
the classical fundamentalists and the progressive fundamentalists. As George
Marsden, the most recognized and widely quoted scholar of American fundamentalism, fittingly put it, "By the time of Graham's New York crusade . . . it
was all over for the classic fundamentalist coalition."[21] After about 1960, then,
in the wake of Graham's innovations and the emergence of the new evangelical
movement, the classical fundamentalist churches and institutions constituted
something of a separated subgroup within North American evangelicalism.

19. Carpenter, *Revive Us Again*; Garth M. Rosell, *The Surprising Work of God: Harold John
Ockenga, Billy Graham, and the Rebirth of Evangelicalism* (Grand Rapids: Baker Academic, 2008);
Bruce Shelley, "The Rise of Evangelical Youth Movements," *Fides et Historia* 18 (January 1986):
47–63.

20. Quoted in Carpenter, *Revive Us Again*, 151.

21. George M. Marsden, *Reforming Fundamentalism: Fuller Seminary and the New Evangelicalism* (Grand Rapids: Eerdmans, 1987), 165.

The expanding fissure in the fundamentalist coalition was mirrored in the faith mission community during the 1950s and early 1960s. This rift was perhaps most obvious in the Interdenominational Foreign Mission Association's (IFMA) refusal to cooperate with the NAE-sponsored Evangelical Foreign Missions Association (EFMA), after EFMA's founding in 1945.[22] That IFMA sided with the classical fundamentalists would prove significant for WBT-SIL, since it ultimately forced WBT-SIL to choose sides in the debate.

The impetus for the establishment of IFMA in 1917 came from four nondenominational faith missions, the Africa Inland Mission, the Central American Mission, the China Inland Mission, and the South Africa General Mission, when they were restricted from full participation in the Foreign Missions Conference of North America by the more powerful mainline denominational missions.[23] In the wake of the fundamentalist-modernist controversy, IFMA became something of an "accrediting association," and thus served to certify a mission's conservative credentials at a time when some denominational mission leaders seemed to be edging toward theological liberalism.[24] In 1946 IFMA once again left no doubt as to where it stood when its member missions voted unanimously to reject formal relations with EFMA. IFMA's refusal to collaborate with EFMA was based on its strict separatist stance and its wariness over EFMA's cooperation with mainline denominations.[25] (In 1963, driven by aspirations for hastening worldwide evangelism and prompted by desires for demonstrating evangelical solidarity over against ecumenism and liberalism, IFMA at last established a cooperative relationship with EFMA.)[26] IFMA missions' unwillingness to join hands with the progressive fundamentalists in EFMA signaled that there remained a rather sharp division within the faith mission community at midcentury.

Wycliffe applied to IFMA in 1948 at the urging of the Canadian pastor of the People's Church in Toronto, Oswald J. Smith, who saw it as a way for the young organization to secure accreditation among North American fundamentalists.[27] During the application process, IFMA raised only two concerns. One

22. Edwin L. Frizen Jr., *75 Years of IFMA, 1917–1992: The Nondenominational Missions Movement* (Wheaton, IL: Interdenominational Foreign Mission Association, 1992), 192–93.

23. J. Herbert Kane, *Faith, Mighty Faith: A Handbook of the International Foreign Mission Association* (New York: Interdenominational Foreign Mission Association, 1956), 8.

24. Kane, *Faith, Mighty Faith*, 11.

25. Frizen, *75 Years of IFMA*, 193.

26. Frizen, *75 Years of IFMA*, 256–70.

27. Nyman Sr. to Cameron Townsend, May 15, 1948, TA 5068; Smith to Nyman Sr., May 10, 1948, TA 5145; Smith to Cameron Townsend, June 28, 1948, TA 5489; Cameron Townsend to Nyman Sr., May 17, 1948, TA 5141; WBT board of directors meeting, minutes, April 16, 1949, WSA.

unnamed member mission secretary, apparently well informed of the organization's strategy, was concerned that SIL's standing as a scientific organization might be harmed if Wycliffe joined the religiously orientated IFMA. Another unnamed mission secretary expressed concern over the religious status of Wycliffe members, wanting to know whether they were "missionaries" or simply "translators and scientists."[28] As for Townsend, he was ambivalent about joining IFMA. He understood that his policies were potentially problematic, so he directed WBT-SIL secretary William Nyman Sr. to provide a detailed description of SIL's overall strategy to the association. He then ended his instructions to Nyman by remarking that "it might be better for us to withdraw our application."[29] As it turned out, the IFMA board was apparently satisfied with Wycliffe's explanations and conferred membership on March 17, 1949.[30] Townsend's apprehension was not misplaced, as WBT-SIL's relationship with IFMA would eventually prove.

Wycliffe's fortunes in IFMA dimmed considerably with the election of J. O. Percy of the Sudan Interior Mission and Ralph T. Davis of the Africa Inland Mission to the respective positions of general secretary and president of IFMA in 1956.[31] The installation of Percy intimated that IFMA's sympathies, at least for the next few years, would remain with the separatist-orientated classical fundamentalists rather than with the emerging new evangelicals. Percy's wariness of the new evangelicals was exemplified by his antipathy toward Billy Graham for his cooperative spirit.[32] As for Davis, although he was an early leader in the formation of NAE and more moderate than Percy, he remained cool toward WBT-SIL and continued to harbor doubts about the mission's dual strategy.[33] While both men denied any personal animosity toward Wycliffe, they leaned in the direction of WBT-SIL's critics and worked to ensure that IFMA remained within the confines of the classical fundamentalist coalition.[34]

28. A. B. Holm, secretary, IFMA, to WBT, December 6, 1948, TA 5037.

29. Cameron Townsend to Nyman Sr., February 5, 1949, TA 5818.

30. Nyman Sr. to A. B. Frost, April 5, 1949, BGA, Records of the IFMA, collection 352, box 6, folder 5; WBT board of directors meeting, minutes, April 16, 1949, WSA.

31. Philip Grossman to Cameron Townsend, November 19, 1956, TA 12200.

32. Percy to Cameron Townsend, July 22, 1957, BGA, Records of the IFMA, collection 352, box 8, folder 4; Cameron Townsend to Percy, May 4, 1957, TA 12926; October 2, 1957, BGA, Records of the IFMA, collection 352, box 10, folder 7.

33. Carpenter, *Revive Us Again*, 151–52, 276–77n34; Grossman to Cameron Townsend, November 5, 1958, pp. 2–3, TA 15020.

34. Davis to Cameron Townsend, November 3, 1958, TA 15024; Grossman to Cowan, November 24, 1959, TA 17410; Cameron Townsend to Kenneth L. Pike, November 10, 1958, TA 14410; Cameron Townsend to Davis, November 13, 1958, TA 15025; Watters to Blount, July 24, 1958, TA 15891; Frizen, *75 Years of IFMA*, 197–279.

The opening moves of the conflict between WBT and IFMA came from a familiar quarter. Although not a member of IFMA, the Association of Baptists for World Evangelism nonetheless felt compelled in February 1957 to lodge a number of charges against Wycliffe with the association, including complaints that SIL was transporting Catholics in its aircraft, that SIL members were attending diplomatic functions where wine and cocktails were served, and that SIL was making literacy materials and Bible portions available to Catholic missionaries. The group was also distressed over what it saw as a deception being carried out under the guise of the dual-organization structure.[35] Then, in June 1958, SIL offended the Gospel Missionary Union (GMU), a long-standing IFMA member mission, when an SIL pilot landed two Roman Catholic priests on a GMU airstrip in Ecuador.[36] Townsend made an already tense situation worse when he sent off a prickly letter to GMU's vice president, R. J. Reinmiller, declaring that he hoped SIL would one day have the opportunity to serve "Mohammedans, Buddists [*sic*], Atheists, Jews, and everyone."[37] In the aftermath of these incidents, the situation between Wycliffe and IFMA deteriorated.[38]

Wycliffe's northeast region home director, Philip Grossman, met with IFMA in late August 1958 to smooth ruffled feathers, but this encounter was doomed before it began because Townsend's 1953 *El Comercio* article, with its glowing praise of Roman Catholic missionaries, had mysteriously fallen into the hands of the IFMA general secretary.[39] (Grossman reported that it was forwarded to Percy by a "large Bible school.") Already incensed over Townsend's grating response to GMU, Percy was further agitated after reading the *El Comercio* article. In fact, he was sufficiently disturbed to demand that any future communiqués not come from Townsend but from the president of Wycliffe's board of directors.[40]

At the height of the IFMA controversy, Wycliffe received overtures from progressive fundamentalists and specifically from EFMA. In January 1958, Billy Graham professed to Townsend that "Wycliffe is increasingly on my heart." Graham went on to explain that "since we are planning a foreign department in our organization [the Billy Graham Evangelistic Association], I am asking our Board of Directors to give priority to Wycliffe Translators in their prayers and consideration. I want you to count me a part of the great Wycliffe family."[41] Although WBT-SIL's top leaders hoped to salvage the IFMA connection, they

35. Harold Key to Association of Baptists for World Evangelism, February 11, 1957, TA 14143.
36. R. J. Reinmiller to Cameron Townsend, June 6, 1958, TA 14710.
37. Cameron Townsend to Reinmiller, July 6, 1958, p. 2, TA 14681.
38. Percy to Blount, June 26, 1958, TA 15910.
39. Details of Townsend's *El Comercio* article are covered in chapter 4.
40. Grossman to WBT board of directors, August 28, 1958, p. 3, TA 15796.
41. Graham to Cameron Townsend, January 6, 1958, TA 15418.

were somewhat ambivalent as to where the organization belonged in the emerging evangelical landscape. Nevertheless, they were quick to take Graham up on his overture, and in 1958 installed him on the WBT-SIL board of directors, where he remained until 1964.[42] Graham's tenure on the board was largely that of a figurehead but, as SIL's Mexico branch director Benjamin Elson observed in late 1959, in what was a perceptive reading of the contemporary evangelical situation, Graham was, "to many people[,] much more of an accreditation than IFMA."[43] Indeed, securing Graham for the board in the midst of the IFMA controversy communicated to the evangelical world Wycliffe's position within the evolving religious landscape. The following year, in May 1959, Larry Love wrote from the Graham team office in North Carolina, reassuring Townsend that he had personally interrogated Harold J. Ockenga and the EFMA's executive secretary, Clyde Taylor, as well as a number of undisclosed "others," and they had all expressed unwavering support for Wycliffe.[44] Wycliffe's Dale Kietzman, who had extensive experience representing WBT-SIL in the United States, also confirmed what he saw as broad support coming from a wide spectrum of evangelicals.[45] WBT-SIL had not changed its stripes, but by placing Graham on the board of directors, it had taken an important step toward allying itself with the new evangelicalism, where the organization was obviously welcome.

The differing stances taken by Townsend and Wycliffe leaders (a number of whom sat on the board of directors) during the IFMA controversy gave Percy and Davis the impression that many of the leaders were not entirely in step with their founder. They therefore assumed it was possible to isolate Townsend, and thereby keep one of the association's largest and most influential member missions under the IFMA umbrella. What appeared as a rift between Townsend and the board was in fact something of a mirage. Internal debate was not only expected but also encouraged in WBT-SIL. In May 1947, the board reminded the membership that "in view of the many severe and delicate problems which we have to face[,] . . . we reaffirm the necessity of complete freedom of expressing opinions and judgments . . . within the organization."[46] It should also be recalled that when all was said and done, the membership and the board most often fell into step with Townsend.[47] For example, Elson recalled in a 1970s interview that

42. Philip Grossman, "Summary Report of West Coast Trip," May 1958, TA 16016; *Translation*, Spring 1964, 15.

43. Benjamin F. Elson, "Report of Impressions of the Meeting between IFMA and WBT," October 2, 1959, TA 17504.

44. Love to Cameron Townsend, May 18, 1959, TA 17119.

45. Kietzman to Cameron Townsend, July 27, 1959, TA 17046.

46. SIL board of directors meeting, minutes, May 18, 1947, WSA.

47. Cameron Townsend's extraordinary capacity to win over detractors is detailed in chapter 4.

"there hasn't been a major decision in Wycliffe without a person thinking, 'How will this affect Uncle Cam[?] How will he take it?' He's got weight. He counts for ten on the board."[48] Thus, while there were debates within the upper echelon of leaders, these clashes rarely if ever resulted in irreparable schisms. Unlike so many other fundamentalist and conservative evangelical enterprises, intramural quarrels in WBT-SIL were generally conducted without lasting fissiparous effects. It was quite natural, then, that Percy failed to realize that the board was unlikely to defy Townsend, at least publicly.

During an April 1959 visit to the SIL branch in Peru, Percy was dismayed to discover that not only was WBT-SIL's leadership committed to Townsend's strategies, but so too were most of the organization's members. Although thoroughly impressed by SIL's efficient operations and genuinely touched by Townsend's "deep spiritual concern," Percy nonetheless reported in a confidential memo to the IFMA board of directors that he could not abide SIL's policy of serving Catholics, nor its cooperation with the Peruvian government, nor its members' tendency to downplay their missionary status. These points constituted what Percy saw as a "lopsided program." He also contended that, even if Wycliffe withdrew from the association, such a move would not "answer the criticism of Dr. Bob Jones [Jr.] and others."[49] By legitimizing the criticism of this militant fundamentalist who had joined the fray against WBT-SIL in late 1958, Percy unambiguously indicated where IFMA's sympathies lay in the rift between the classical and progressive fundamentalists.[50] He was plainly urging Wycliffe to align with the nonprogressive wing of fundamentalism. Percy closed his letter to the IFMA board by suggesting that WBT-SIL members should come out decidedly as missionaries, that the organization should align itself unconditionally with other "fundamental missionary bodies," that it should refuse to serve nonevangelicals, and, lastly, that it should come clean with the general public about the true nature of the dual organization.[51] Needless to say, with this line drawn, there seemed to be little or no recourse but for Wycliffe to separate from IFMA.

At the WBT-SIL board's request, Kenneth Pike made one last attempt to win the confidence of critics in IFMA. In a series of working papers completed in September 1959, Pike took pains to explain WBT-SIL's policies in a reasoned

---

48. Benjamin F. Elson, Hefley interview, c. 1970, p. 21, TA 43768.

49. J. O. Percy, "Confidential Memo to Official Board," IFMA, May 4, 1959, BGA, Records of the IFMA, collection 352, box 10, folder 9.

50. Jones to Walter M. Montano, editor, *Christian Heritage*, December 6, 1958, TA 16819; Jones to Cameron Townsend, December 29, 1958, TA 16817; Cameron Townsend to Jones, December 12, 1958, TA 16822; Watters to John Whaley, Bob Jones University, December 4, 1958, TA 16823.

51. Percy, "Confidential Memo."

and winsome fashion.[52] The thrust of his apologetic evinced a progressive tone. The reader was led point by point to the realization that WBT-SIL was following a bold strategy of eschewing separatism for positive engagement as a means of furthering the gospel. This progressive sentiment was on full display in Pike's summary of WBT-SIL's threefold strategy, which combined "(1) a spiritual contribution worked out especially through our Bible translation activities; (2) scientific research and publication; and (3) cultural (e.g. educational, medical, and literacy) service." Perhaps the most pointed evidence that WBT-SIL had little in common with classical fundamentalism came in Pike's emphasis that the "*whole man*, we feel, must be affected by the Gospel—his spirit, intellect, and culture."[53] WBT-SIL was expressing much the same variety of sentiment on the foreign mission front as were the new evangelicals at home in America.

The position outlined by Pike was in keeping with a salient feature of the new evangelicalism that George Marsden has remarked upon. Marsden observed that the better-educated new evangelicals, such as Carl F. H. Henry and Harold J. Ockenga, "while remaining premillennialist in a general sense, abandoned the central dispensationalist preoccupation with reading the prophetic signs so as to indicate that the present was incontrovertibly the end time." According to Marsden, the new evangelicals were therefore more optimistic of the potential for "transforming culture to bring it more in conformity with God's law and will."[54] Contrasting views on the outworking of history between the two sides is an especially helpful characteristic to focus on when attempting to situate WBT-SIL in the shifting currents of midcentury evangelicalism. During the course of research for this study, an attempt was made to ascertain the level of adherence to premillennial dispensationalism that existed in WBT-SIL before the early 1980s. The archived materials offer little indication that this eschatological theory had much influence on WBT-SIL, save perhaps for Townsend, who was in the habit of declaring that the "Lord will return . . . when the last tribe is reached."[55] Yet it can be doubted that he was a committed dispensationalist. After all, as already noted, he thought C. I. Scofield was "a little bit extreme maybe on the matter of everything being divided up in dispensations."[56] Moreover, one could certainly not classify him as a pessimist when it came to social action. Therefore, his proclivity for this expression was probably more rhe-

---

52. Kenneth L. Pike, "IFMA Issue," Work Papers I–VI, WBT, September 1959, MBA.

53. Kenneth L. Pike, Work Paper VI.1, September 1959, MBA.

54. Marsden, *Reforming Fundamentalism*, 76.

55. Cameron Townsend to Howard Unser, February 21, 1967, TA 25088. (N.B. This is only one example among many.)

56. Cameron Townsend, Hefley interview, "Devotional and Doctrinal Stand," June 25, 1970, p. 2, TA 43653.

torical than indicative of adherence to classical dispensationalism. Interviews revealed that very few of the organization's missionaries ever possessed more than a rudimentary knowledge of dispensational theology. Furthermore, some members who carried dispensationalist ideas into the organization dropped them after a period of intense Bible study and translation. Eugene Loos, a Baptist who joined WBT-SIL in 1952, parted ways with dispensational eschatology after "examining the statements that came out of that camp with scriptures themselves."[57] Close scrutiny of the Scriptures during translation had the same effect on SIL missionary-translator Richard Blight. Soon after he joined WBT-SIL in 1951, he dropped his dispensationalist beliefs because, as he dryly put it, "I read the Bible."[58] Perhaps the most significant evidence of dispensationalism's status in WBT-SIL came in 1958 when Kenneth Pike's sister, Eunice Pike, published *Words Wanted*, a book intended for WBT-SIL home constituency in which she openly criticized dispensational thinking.[59] WBT-SIL was, from its founding, of a progressive cast of mind and never wedded to dispensationalism, and therefore, with respect to eschatological doctrine, it was situated on the new evangelical side of the developing fault line of the 1950s.

In October 1959, IFMA requested permission from Wycliffe for Pike's papers to be submitted for expert theological scrutiny. The choice of two leading fundamentalist academics, John F. Walvoord, the president of the Dallas Theological Seminary, and Charles J. Woodbridge, a former Fuller Seminary professor, attested to IFMA's conservative bias. Pike's response to IFMA's proposed reviewers is also instructive: he suggested that the review board also include Fuller Seminary progressives Paul Jewett and George Eldon Ladd.[60] This request demonstrated that Pike understood very well that WBT-SIL had more in common with the new evangelicals than with the classical fundamentalists, and that only by balancing the review board in this fashion would WBT-SIL gain an equitable hearing.

The review of Pike's papers never took place, mainly because of Townsend's protestations that there was little chance of convincing the "old line mission boards in the IFMA" of the wisdom of Wycliffe's position.[61] Townsend was doubtless correct, since the divide between the classical fundamentalists and the new evangelicals was sufficiently wide as to force WBT-SIL to choose sides. That reconciliation was impossible between Wycliffe and IFMA was in evidence

57. Eugene Loos, interview by author, June 25, 2009, Dallas, Texas.

58. Richard Blight, interview by author, July 2, 2009, Dallas, Texas.

59. Eunice V. Pike, *Words Wanted* (Huntington Beach, CA: Wycliffe Bible Translators, 1958), 176–84.

60. Cowan to Cameron Townsend et al., October 19, 1959, p. 1, TA 16987.

61. Cameron Townsend to WBT-SIL board of directors, October 22, 1959, TA 16377.

at a meeting between the disputing parties in Racine, Wisconsin, on October 2, 1959. Townsend was not in attendance, having become *persona non grata* in the eyes of IFMA leadership, but some of Wycliffe's top brass, including Benjamin Elson, George Cowan, Richard Pittman, Kenneth Pike, Harold Goodall, Turner Blount, and Philip Grossman, appeared to defend Wycliffe. Leaders from the Africa Inland Mission, the China Inland Mission, the Central American Mission, the Sudan Interior Mission, the Berean Mission, and the South Africa General Mission were present on behalf of IFMA. The Wycliffe team's strategy was to avert verbal combat and to present a united front, while making their case one last time. SIL's policy of serving Catholics and its cooperation with foreign governments remained the chief points of contention. The meeting was therefore mainly a rehash of long-standing issues, and it ultimately ended in a stalemate that brought no resolution to the crisis.[62] Rather than risk possible ejection from IFMA, Wycliffe opted to withdraw from the organization.[63] The long struggle to convince its critics in IFMA had come to an end.

As progressive evangelicals began embracing WBT-SIL, a number of rock-ribbed fundamentalists stepped up their criticism. An apt example was Robert T. "Fighting Bob" Ketcham, who was one of the founders of the separatist General Association of Regular Baptists (GARB), which was formed in 1932. While serving as GARB's national representative in 1960, Ketcham assailed WBT-SIL in the *Baptist Bulletin*. Ketcham confessed that Wycliffe operated the finest school available for training missionaries in the science of linguistics, but the organization's stance on serving Roman Catholics was simply too much for this separatist and militant fundamentalist to bear. With a number of GARB churches supporting Wycliffe missionaries, he felt that it was his duty to warn member churches exactly what they were endorsing when they backed a Wycliffe missionary.[64] Always one to turn events to his own advantage, Townsend clipped the Ketcham article and mailed it to at least one bishop in Peru as proof that SIL was paying a price to serve Catholics.[65] On the home front the article had less salutary benefits. Acting on the evidence of Ketcham's article, the fun-

62. Cowan to Pittman et al., October 8, 1959, TA 17499; Elson, "Report of Impressions," TA 17504; Lorin Griset, "Personal Report on the Racine Meeting with I.F.M.A. Board," October 7, 1959, TA 17501; Percy to Watters, December 10, 1959, BGA, Records of the IFMA, collection 352, box 16, folder 4; Pittman to Cameron Townsend, October 5, 1959, TA 17000; Watters to Cameron Townsend et al., October 23, 1959, TA 16982.

63. Cowan to "Member Missions of the I.F.M.A.," December 1, 1959, TA 17389.

64. Robert T. Ketcham, "Wycliffe Bible Translators and the Roman Catholic Church," typed copy of *Baptist Bulletin* article, n.d., TA 18950.

65. Cameron Townsend to Monseñor Gustavo Prevost, Obisipo Vicario Apostolico, Pucallpa, Peru, April 6, 1960, TA 18471.

damentalist Prairie Bible Institute in Alberta, Canada, stopped recommending Wycliffe to its graduates.[66] Apparently Prairie did more than halt recommendations. Wycliffe lost a potential candidate in 1965 after he attended classes at Prairie where, in the words of Wycliffe's candidate secretary Otis Leal, the student was "poisoned against Wycliffe."[67] After the early 1960s, the criticism directed at the organization came almost exclusively from within the militant and separatist wing of fundamentalism and, as the next chapter will show, from secular anthropologists.

If progressive fundamentalists were willing to accept, or at least overlook, most of WBT-SIL's unusual policies, there remained the stumbling block of anti-Catholicism, since few evangelicals, even after 1960, were prepared to lower their guard when it came to Roman Catholics. No evidence suggests that WBT-SIL was ever able to convince any other evangelical organization to cooperate with Roman Catholics. However, WBT-SIL managed to persuade at least two skeptics that its policy of service to all was legitimate. In October 1958, C. Stacey Woods wrote Townsend confessing that "God gives different commissions to different people, so that in the complex army of the Lord, different folks do different things." Woods acknowledged that "even in the Roman Catholic Church there are those who are truly born again and devoted to our Lord Jesus Christ."[68] Grady Parrot of MAF softened his anti-Catholicism in 1954, after MAF was confronted with the question of flying an extremely ill priest out of the jungle to a hospital. Parrot was struck by the need for a humane response to these kinds of situations, and soon after the rescue flight he informed Townsend of his change of heart, even though MAF did not change its position on not serving Catholics under normal circumstances.[69] The policy of lending aid to Catholics caused less difficulty for WBT-SIL than might have been expected because it was seldom mentioned by members or in the organization's publicity. According to one long-serving translator, revealing to churches and supporters that SIL served Catholics was done only with "discretion."[70] When queried about how they handled the Catholic issue in the United States, interviewees almost unanimously echoed the response of WBT-

66. Grossman to L. E. Maxwell, principal, Prairie Bible Institute, April 25, 1960, TA 19521; May 19, 1960, TA 19472; Grossman to Pat Cohan, September 19, 1960, TA 19315; Maxwell to Grossman, April 29, 1960, TA 19473; June 13, 1960, TA 19437.

67. Leal to WCT, August 23, 1965, TA 22670.

68. Woods to WCT, October 14, 1958, TA 15053.

69. Grady Parrot, quoted in Cameron Townsend to Key, January 18, 1954, TA 10359; James C. Truxton, vice-president, MAF, to Eldon Larsen, "Policy Discussion with Neill Hawkins," July 21, 1960, BGA, Records of the MAF, collection 136, box 62, folder 38.

70. Dorothy Minor, interview by author, September 10, 2008, Dallas, Texas.

SIL translator Glen Stairs, who said, "We didn't talk about it."[71] Some things were apparently better left unsaid, and this circumspection served WBT-SIL well, since there is little evidence that SIL's service to Catholics was cause for much criticism after about 1960.

Behind all the noisy polemics created by the fundamentalist leadership, there remained a large number of conservative evangelicals in the pews who did not join in the fray. In 1942, Harold J. Ockenga spoke of the "unvoiced multitudes," adducing that there were millions of conservative evangelicals outside the bastions of militant and separatist fundamentalism.[72] The theologian and former editor of *Christianity Today*, Carl F. H. Henry, concurred, and he once estimated that about 85 percent of the Northern Baptist Convention churches remained staunchly evangelical in the mid-1940s, even as they kept their distance from the militant and separatist fundamentalists.[73] Evidence of this broader evangelicalism was also on display when churches affiliated with the Federal Council of Churches by their denominational hierarchy, but not necessarily by their own choice, joined the NAE by way of a clause allowing them to do so individually.[74] All this is not to underestimate the very significant impact that fundamentalism had on the evangelical mind, however. The difficulties that Wycliffe recruits experienced in adjusting to Townsend's methods and the reactions by other conservative evangelicals to WBT-SIL attest to the widespread influence of fundamentalist tendencies. So too does Carl Henry's somewhat contradictory remark that "in the 1930s we were all fundamentalists."[75] The considerable effects of fundamentalism notwithstanding, it was the larger body of relatively more irenic evangelicals located across the religious spectrum who ultimately shaped the contours of post–World War II evangelicalism.

WBT-SIL's success in North America after about 1960 therefore rested more on its capacity to win the favor of this large body of moderate evangelicals and progressive fundamentalists than it did on convincing its most vocal critics on the far right. The way in which the Wycliffe side of the dual organization promoted the work of SIL to various North American audiences is the subject that will occupy the remainder of this chapter.

71. Glen Stairs, interview by author, June 29, 2009, Dallas, Texas.

72. Harold J. Ockenga, "The Unvoiced Multitudes," in *Evangelical Action! A Report of the Organization of the National Association of Evangelicals for United Action* (Boston, 1942), 35, quoted in Marsden, *Reforming Fundamentalism*, 49.

73. Carl F. H. Henry, *Confessions of a Theologian: An Autobiography* (Waco: Word, 1986), 110–11.

74. Louis Gasper, *The Fundamentalist Movement* (The Hague: Mouton, 1963), 27.

75. Quoted in Marsden, *Reforming Fundamentalism*, 10.

WBT-SIL Publicity in North America: Tradition and Innovation

Despite incurring more criticism from within the evangelical community than at any other period in its history, WBT-SIL continued to grow apace during the 1950s. In 1959, at the peak of the IFMA controversy, Wycliffe picked up 135 new recruits, the largest number in one year up to that time.[76] In December 1962, Townsend informed Billy Graham that WBT-SIL had recently become the largest North American evangelical mission with 1,325 missionaries, having surpassed Sudan Interior Mission, which counted 1,263.[77] The 1950s was marked by an astounding expansion of WBT-SIL. On a fiscal year basis, the organization expanded from 269 members and $307,000 in receipts in 1951 to 1,122 members and $2.2 million collected in 1961.[78] In addition, by the early 1960s, WBT-SIL was also becoming a more international organization, with Wycliffe branches in the United Kingdom, Australia, and Canada sending a small number of missionaries to serve with SIL in Africa, Asia, Latin America, and North America.[79] How did such an unusual organization as WBT-SIL enjoy this level of sustained growth? The answer is that the organization was extraordinarily innovative on some fronts while, at the same time, it maintained an unbending commitment to traditional features of the faith mission paradigm.

Interviews conducted for this book indicate that an overwhelming majority of WBT-SIL candidates were, at some point in their lives, nurtured in socioreligious settings that venerated missionary service as a Christian ideal. Although the evidence is limited, recruits coming of age in the 1930s who joined the organization before about the mid-1940s seem to have been mostly inculcated with missionary idealism in the church and at home. Canadian George Cowan, who joined in 1942, fondly recalled meeting the well-known missionaries to China, Jonathan and Roslyn Goforth, at a Presbyterian church that his father pastored in the 1930s. The overawing presence of the Goforths and the allure of China sparked Cowan's enthusiasm for missions at a tender age.[80] (The closure of China to missionaries in 1950 likely benefited WBT-SIL's growth. There is, however, no specific evidence to support this hypothesis.) Eugene Nida, Ken-

---

76. Cameron Townsend to J. Robert Story, general secretary, Unevangelized Fields Mission, Australia, January 19, 1960, TA 18589.

77. Cameron Townsend to Graham, December 12, 1962, TA 20743.

78. Hibbard to Cameron Townsend, November 16, 1965, TA 24153.

79. Ethel E. Wallis and Mary A. Bennett, *Two Thousand Tongues to Go: True-Life Adventures of the Wycliffe Bible Translators throughout the World Today* (New York: Harper and Brothers, 1959), 258–74; Phyllis Thompson, *Matched with His Hour: The Story of the British Home Base of the Wycliffe Bible Translators* (London: Word Books, 1974).

80. George Cowan, interview by author, August 20, 2007, Santa Ana, California.

neth Pike, and Marianna Slocum, all of whom joined before 1941, also traced their missionary calls to influences at church and home.[81] With the rise of the evangelical youth movement and the emergence of progressive fundamentalism in the mid-1940s, inducements to consider a missionary vocation increasingly originated outside the confines of home and church. Most members who joined from the late 1940s attributed their missionary calling to attendance at Bible school or college. Missionary rallies and campus missionary clubs were also important influences. When asked what moved him to become a missionary, SIL translator Richard Blight recollected his days as a student at Wheaton College. Blight was especially inspired during a campus-wide revival that broke out in 1949.[82] Blight was also at Wheaton with other passionate, mission-minded students, and two of his contemporaries, Jim Elliot and Roger Youdarian, were later enshrined as martyrs when they were speared to death in Ecuador in 1956.[83] WBT-SIL was the beneficiary of a mid-twentieth-century evangelical social milieu that was awash with a rising tide of enthusiasm for missions.

What attracted WBT-SIL candidates specifically to Wycliffe? The mission's particular focus on languages and linguistics was one factor, especially for academically gifted missionary recruits. College attendance in the United States doubled in the decade following World War II.[84] At the war's end, only 40 percent of students were completing high school and a mere 16 percent were enrolling in college. By 1980, 75 percent were graduating from high school and about 45 percent were entering college.[85] The education boom immediately following the war was due in part to returning servicemen taking advantage of funds available under the Servicemen's Readjustment Act (better known as the GI Bill). Camp Wycliffe, with its University of Oklahoma connection, became a government-approved institution for students under the GI Bill. WBT-SIL certainly benefited from this nationwide upsurge in education. By 1977, nearly ten thousand students had taken coursework at SIL in Norman, Oklahoma.[86] Robert Longacre and Mary Ruth Wise, both outstanding career SIL linguists,

81. Eugene A. Nida, "My Pilgrimage in Mission," *International Bulletin of Missionary Research* 12, no. 2 (April 1988): 62; Eunice V. Pike, *Ken Pike: Scholar and Christian* (Dallas: Summer Institute of Linguistics, 1981), 7; Marianna Slocum, interview by author, June 5, 2008, Dallas, Texas.

82. Richard Blight, interview by author, July 2, 2009, Dallas, Texas.

83. Elisabeth Elliot, *Through Gates of Splendor* (New York: Harper, 1957); Steve Saint, *End of the Spear* (Carol Stream, IL: Tyndale House, 2005).

84. George M. Marsden, *The Soul of the American University: From Protestant Establishment to Established Nonbelief* (New York: Oxford University Press, 1994), 390.

85. Diane Ravitch, *The Troubled Crusade: American Education, 1945–1980* (New York: Basic Books, 1983), 324.

86. Frank E. Robbins, "Training in Linguistics," in *The Summer Institute of Linguistics: Its Works and Contributions*, ed. Ruth M. Brend and Kenneth L. Pike (The Hague: Mouton, 1977), 61.

are typical examples of both this postwar surge to pursue educational opportunities and the academic attraction of SIL. Their comments during interviews summarize the sentiment of more than a few WBT-SIL recruits. Longacre, a member since 1946, "fell in love with linguistics at first sight."[87] Wise, who joined in 1951, recollected her college roommate returning from Camp Wycliffe and "talking to me about linguistics and translation . . . Latin and grammar and all that, it [was] wonderful." Wise said that to "proselytize would not be my thing," but she relished her studies at SIL, and on her first furlough garnered an MA in linguistics from the University of Michigan. "Languages," she emphasized, "are fun, the most wonderful things." She eventually earned her PhD in linguistics, as did Longacre.[88] Following World War II, WBT-SIL drew upon an increasing number of young evangelicals eager to pursue higher education and to use their academic talents in a missionary vocation.

Bible translation was the single most important factor attracting recruits to WBT-SIL. The organization's goal of translating Scripture was given as the chief reason for joining the mission with unfailing regularity during interviews. This comes as little surprise, owing to the Bible's prestige among evangelicals.[89] WBT-SIL missionary Florence Gerdel, who joined in 1946, expressed the sentiment of her fellow missionaries when she exclaimed, "What could be more important in the whole world than giving people the Bible?"[90] For Nancy Lanier, a member since 1952, it was "the importance of the Word."[91] Jack Henderson, another long-serving Wycliffe missionary, was present at a mid-1940s Word of Life rally where the evangelist Jack Wyrtzen spoke of "the problem of Bible-less tribes." Henderson recounted that this was what "really impressed" him to join Wycliffe.[92] Already primed for missionary careers and imbued with a passion for the Bible, prospective evangelical candidates often leapt at the opportunity to serve with Wycliffe when they discovered its overarching goal of Scripture translation.

Evidence suggests that, up to at least the late 1970s, actual cash flowing to the organization originated largely from individual missionary sources of support.

87. Robert Longacre, interview by author, June 29, 2010, Dallas, Texas.

88. Mary Ruth Wise, interview by author, June 30, 2009, Dallas, Texas.

89. David W. Bebbington, *Evangelicalism in Modern Britain: A History from the 1730s to the 1980s* (New York: Routledge, 2002), 12–14; George M. Marsden, *Fundamentalism and American Culture: The Shaping of Twentieth-Century Evangelicalism, 1870–1925* (New York: Oxford University Press, 1980), 223–24.

90. Florence Gerdel, interview by author, June 15, 2008, Dallas, Texas.

91. Nancy Lanier, interview by author, July 31, 2009, Catalina, Arizona.

92. Jack Henderson, interview by author, September 24, 2009, Waxhaw, North Carolina. (N.B. Henderson recalled that he attended this rally in either 1944 or 1945.)

According to former Wycliffe president Bernard May, funds collected by individual missionaries accounted for approximately 90 percent of organizational income.[93] Extant records tend to confirm May's estimate. For example, of the $4.2 million collected by WBT-SIL in 1966, donations to individual members accounted for $3.5 million, or 83 percent, of the total.[94] Direct contributions by friends and churches to missionaries under the faith model (a system in which no salaries were paid, thus obliging individuals to seek out their own sources of financial support) were clearly a very significant source of income. However, this reckoning does not account for noncash proceeds such as donated aircraft and government sponsorship of SIL programs and operations. The organization's financial fortunes thus rested on two pillars. WBT-SIL missionaries relied exclusively upon the faith model for their personal remuneration. This was a method with a long and cherished tradition among conservative evangelicals, and it was by far the larger of the two sources of income. Where WBT-SIL was most innovative, as partly detailed in the previous chapter with the International Goodwill airplane project, was in developing corporate sources of income and noncash support for large projects. As the organization expanded, it maintained the faith model for its individual missionaries while at the same time, with Townsend leading the charge, developing entirely new and creative approaches to publicizing and financing the organization's efforts. Both methods of funding contributed in important ways to WBT-SIL's ongoing expansion, and therefore each must be surveyed in its own right.

The faith mission method of garnering funds had deep roots in WBT-SIL. Unlike many other faith missions, such as the Sudan Interior Mission and the China Inland Mission, WBT-SIL did not pool funds for equal distribution among its missionaries.[95] The only nod in the direction of supporting underfunded members was the use of excess corporate funds to "top off" an individual missionary's low support. But aside from this, the pattern in Wycliffe was for missionaries to depend exclusively on their personal support base, and not on the organization or fellow missionaries. With full confidence in the faith mission approach, Townsend unhesitatingly sent recruits abroad without the promise of sufficient financial support.[96] Well into the 1950s, it was not unusual for WBT-SIL missionaries to depart for the foreign field without adequate means of sustaining themselves. Calvin Hibbard, Townsend's secretary for over

93. Bernard May, personal communication to author, November 14, 2011.

94. *Translation*, September–October 1967, 18.

95. Harold Lindsell, "Faith Missions and Money," *Bibliotheca Sacra* 119 (January 1962): 33; Percy to Watters, May 26, 1959, BGA, Records of the IFMA, collection 352, box 13, folder 7.

96. Bruce Moore, interview by author, July 1, 2009, Dallas, Texas; Cameron Townsend to Lambert Anderson and Doris Anderson, July 22, 1952, TA 7546.

forty years, nicely summed up his chief's advice to newly minted missionaries. In Hibbard's words, Townsend would say to new translators, "Let your people know you're going, be sure to let them know when you've arrived, and they will realize, 'Hey, these guys are down there, we better help them!'"[97] Adelle Elson, who joined Wycliffe in 1942, recalled that Townsend's main concern was placing new recruits on the field. Once they had arrived, he believed, the funds would naturally follow. "I think that was his strategy," Elson submitted, "and it worked."[98] In reality, there were times when it did not work so well, but Townsend remained adamant that his missionaries should not look to the corporation for financial assistance. "THE LORD DOES NOT FAIL," he emphasized to George Cowan in 1946 when some Wycliffe missionaries attempted to draw upon organizational resources. "I pity the worker who depends on the organization," Townsend intoned. Townsend maintained an unshakable belief in this version of the faith mission model for individual missionary support. As for undersupported staff, "all I can do is refer them to their Boss," he submitted, meaning their only alternative was to rely on God himself.[99] WBT-SIL chose to follow its founder unswervingly on this point, even as he later departed radically from the faith model for organizational projects.

The faith model was an effective instrument for WBT-SIL missionaries to garner support from evangelicals from a wide spectrum of institutions. For independent missionaries, one of the most difficult places from which to extract backing was mainline Protestantism. The primary obstacle was that the mainline denomination's mission board absorbed most of the local churches' missionary budgets. Furthermore, there was simply no mechanism or convention for supporting faith missionaries. One solution that bypassed denominational structures was for a Sunday school class to take up an occasional collection for a Wycliffe missionary. At other times, it might be another group within the church, such as the local women's missionary society. This was the case for Marianna Slocum, who remained a member of the First Presbyterian Church of Ardmore, Pennsylvania, for many years after joining Wycliffe in 1940. The church did not officially underwrite Slocum's support, but a semiregular collection was taken by the women's missionary society. In addition, other members of the church supported Slocum on an individual basis.[100] Wycliffe missionaries James and Gloria Wroughton, who joined in 1945 and 1950, respectively, likewise obtained income from what they referred to as a "liberal Methodist church." A

97. Calvin Hibbard, interview by author, August 6, 2007, Waxhaw, North Carolina.
98. Adelle Elson, interview by author, August 6, 2007, Waxhaw, North Carolina.
99. Cameron Townsend to Cowan, November 13, 1946, TA 904247.
100. Marianna Slocum, interviews by author, June 5 and 15, 2008, Dallas, Texas.

wealthy family in the church regularly donated funds to the Wroughtons over a fifty-year span.[101] Wycliffe missionaries also cultivated financial backing from the far right. Frank and Ethel Robbins drew support from a GARB church, even though the firebrand Robert Ketcham delivered a broadside against Wycliffe at the church on the same weekend they first visited the congregation in 1960. In this instance, the local pastor, his GARB affiliation notwithstanding, remained committed to supporting Wycliffe.[102] WBT-SIL faith missionaries were in effect free agents, and they were therefore able to garner support from evangelicals of various stripes ensconced within these otherwise inaccessible settings.

One of the most effective features of the faith model was that it often engendered tremendous loyalty. It was quite common for donors to contribute on a regular basis for decades. A not unusual example comes from Benjamin and Adelle Elson, whose small Sunday School Union church took on their support at $35 a month in 1942 and gave in ever-increasing sums over the years right up to their interview with this author in 2007.[103] The personal nature of the relationships was a powerful factor in sustaining these long-standing alliances. In the mainline denominations, missionaries had to rely on the overall financial health of the denomination at large. But Wycliffe missionaries built up enduring sources of support on a personal basis at the grassroots level, and were able to establish a devoted following that was not dependent on a single institution. Wycliffe missionaries and their constituents at home made common cause in pursuit of a vision to take the Bible to every language in the world, and the faith model of missions played a central role in these relationships.

Convincing skeptical Christian leaders that WBT-SIL was, at heart, a faith mission with evangelistic aspirations was a key factor in the organization's success at home. To accomplish this aim, Townsend pressed both friends and foes alike to visit SIL operations on the foreign field, where he could demonstrate the work at first hand. In December of 1944, Townsend wrote George Cowan, giving specific instructions for an upcoming visit to the SIL Mexico branch by the Toronto preacher Oswald J. Smith and evangelist Jack Wyrtzen. Townsend was resolute that Smith and Wyrtzen should receive VIP treatment and come away with a thorough introduction to WBT-SIL methods. "P-l-e-a-s-e-!" Townsend begged Cowan, "be sure that both men get properly indoctrinated with Wycliffe methods."[104] These field visits were not without bodily risks for visitors, but

101. James Wroughton, interview by author, June 20, 2008, Dallas, Texas; Gloria (Grey) Wroughton, interview by author, June 20, 2008, Dallas, Texas.

102. Frank Robbins, interview by author, September 2, 2008, Dallas, Texas.

103. Adelle Elson, interview by author, August 6, 2007, Waxhaw, North Carolina; Benjamin Elson, interview by author, August 6, 2007, Waxhaw, North Carolina.

104. Cameron Townsend to Cowan, December 15, 1944, p. 2, TA 3736.

this too could work to Wycliffe's advantage. In 1964, pilot Floyd Lyon had the privilege of carrying aboard a JAARS aircraft W. A. Criswell, the well-known pastor of the Southern Baptist Convention's largest church, the First Baptist Church of Dallas. Deep in the Peruvian jungle the aircraft's engine experienced a catastrophic failure, but Lyon managed a successful emergency landing on a tributary of the Ucayali River. Both men escaped harm, but the terribly shaken Criswell cut short his trip to Peru and returned forthwith to the safer environs of Dallas. The following Sunday, Criswell delivered a stirring message trumpeting the virtues of Wycliffe and collected a $3,000 missionary offering on the mission's behalf.[105] As in Criswell's case, these field visits were often quite effective in shaping opinions toward SIL's work. After evangelist Jack Wyrtzen's 1952 visit to observe SIL's operation in Mexico, he devoted five consecutive Saturday evening radio messages to trumpeting the virtues of WBT-SIL.[106] Shortly after Wycliffe's break with IFMA, James Ostewig, director of the very conservative New Tribes mission in Bolivia, said his firsthand observations of SIL convinced him of the legitimacy of WBT-SIL's policies.[107] These visits were an effective instrument in WBT-SIL's toolbox that converted many a doubter into a believer. Not always, but very often, once critics became intimately familiar with the work of WBT-SIL at close range, they tended to soften their criticism. These survey trips were expensive, time-consuming, and sometimes dangerous, but they were effective in building up support for the organization.

WBT-SIL plainly upheld key elements of the faith missionary enterprise, and this traditional posture resonated with its evangelical public. At other times, especially at Townsend's insistence, the organization engaged in solicitation and publicity that bore little resemblance to the more modest faith mission style. It developed entirely new avenues for presenting missionary activity to both Christian and non-Christian publics.

Into the late 1950s, the organization's leaders felt that publicity efforts remained inadequate. This concern was more an indication of their ambition for undertaking deputation and promotion on a grand scale than a reflection of any lack of industry. In the organization's earliest days, cofounder L. L. Legters had set the pace for hard-driving deputation. In 1934, Legters bemoaned the fact that he had "spoken only 474 times" in the past year, his survey trip to Mexico

105. Criswell to Cameron Townsend, January 31, 1975, TA 31896; George M. Cowan, personal communication to author, July 7, 2007; George Cowan, interview by author, August 20, 2007, Santa Ana, California; Loos to Cameron Townsend, September 2, 1964, TA 21969; September 18, 1964, TA 21943; October 12, 1964, TA 21922; Cameron Townsend to Loos, August 20, 1964, TA 21970; September 10, 1964, TA 21944; Cameron Townsend to Cowan, November 23, 1964, TA 21663.

106. Cowan to Nyman Sr., September 26, 1952, p. 1, TA 8294.

107. Key to Cameron Townsend, May 28, 1960, TA 18324.

with Townsend having slowed his frenzied pace.[108] In 1949, Wycliffe produced *Oh for a Thousand Tongues*, one of the earliest, if not the first ever, missionary promotional films. Even more extraordinary for its time, the film was produced in full color.[109] *Oh for a Thousand Tongues* was put together with the help of Moody Institute of Science's Irwin Moon, creator of the "Sermons from Science" series, and it was narrated by the warm and familiar voice of popular radio evangelist Charles Fuller.[110] This film, the first of hundreds, featured the work of SIL in Mexico and Peru, and was shown in hundreds if not thousands of churches and at other venues across America well into the 1960s. More than a few members point to this film as their first introduction to WBT-SIL. Former Wycliffe president George Cowan's log, detailing over three thousand speaking engagements, also reveals tireless efforts to promote Wycliffe. Among Cowan's entries from the 1950s and 1960s are reports of sharing the podium with person-alities such as Billy Graham, Jack Wyrtzen, and Dawson Trotman, and speaking at InterVarsity Christian Fellowship, Campus Crusade, and Youth for Christ rallies.[111] Clearly, WBT-SIL was mounting a significant promotional effort on the home front, but Townsend had much bigger plans in mind.

The tedious travail of drumming up funds and publicizing WBT-SIL's work in one church after another was not Townsend's forte. Wycliffe's founder pre-ferred to direct his energies into flamboyant public relations events. An excel-lent example of his penchant for the unusual was his transforming the marriage ceremony of George Cowan and SIL translator Florence Hansen into a pub-licity stunt. Townsend cleverly arranged for their 1943 wedding to take place during a Church of the Open Door missionary rally. At Townsend's urging, Cowan gave a rousing missionary message only minutes before dashing back on to the platform to take his marriage vows.[112] This inclination for the striking publicity event over more mundane deputation work was one of Townsend's outstanding characteristics, and it would help to shape the public's image of the organization.

Alert to the possibilities of exploiting television to further his ambitions, Townsend endeavored to arrange a spot for Wycliffe on Ralph Edwards's na-tionally televised show.[113] Edwards's *This Is Your Life* was a human-interest pro-

---

108. Legters to PMA, October 8, 1934, p. 4, TA 901852.

109. "Prayer Bulletin," WBT, August 1950, BGA, Records of the IFMA, collection 352, folder 6–5.

110. Cameron Townsend, "Charles Fuller and Wycliffe Bible Translators," April 3, 1968, pp. 2–3, TA 42694.

111. George M. Cowan, "Speaking Log," copy in author's possession.

112. George Cowan, interview by author, August 20, 2007; Cameron Townsend to Nyman Sr., October 19, 1943, TA 3406; October 25, 1943, TA 3398.

113. Grossman to Cameron Townsend, February 13, 1957, TA 13578; Nyman Sr. to Cameron

gram, where each week both celebrities and ordinary citizens were interviewed before a live audience by Edwards. The enterprising Townsend landed a place for Wycliffe on the June 5, 1957, episode, during which Wycliffe's Rachel Saint appeared with two of SIL's converts.[114] Saint was the sister of the Missionary Aviation Fellowship pilot Nate Saint, one of the five "Auca martyrs" speared to death in January 1956 by a group of Waorani (Auca) in Ecuador.[115] Saint was accompanied on Edwards's television show by Dayuma, a Waorani converted to Christianity through her missionary efforts in 1956. Joining them from the jungles of Peru was the Shapra chief Tariri Nóchomata Yátarisa, who had been converted through the efforts of SIL missionary-translators Dorothy Cox and Loretta Anderson in 1953.[116] The television appearance was a broadcast success, and the recorded episode was again carried as a fall rerun on September 8, 1957. The response to the two showings was largely upbeat, with only a few critics voicing disapproval. One individual phoned the organization's home office to complain about that "fouled up Wycliffe Bible Translators" run by that "confused Townsend."[117] The Peruvian government and press were not impressed either, complaining that the television program proffered an image of Peru as still largely savage. In response to these complaints, Peru's ambassador to the United States requested that Tariri not make a scheduled appearance during Billy Graham's upcoming New York Crusade.[118] More encouraging reports arrived from other quarters, such as Peter Kyle McCarter, the acting president of the University of Oklahoma, who told Kenneth Pike that the university faculty, after viewing the show, was "very proud" of its association with SIL.[119] On the whole, the television program proved to be a resounding success for WBT-SIL.

With this achievement to his credit, it comes as little surprise to find Townsend setting up a Pavilion of 2000 Tribes at the 1964–1965 World's Fair in New York City. In November 1962, he secured board approval to proceed with plans for Wycliffe to erect an exhibit at the upcoming fair, with the caveat that

---

Townsend, February 13, 1957, TA 13051; Cameron Townsend to Edwards, December 3, 1956, TA 11945; January 23, 1957, TA 13079; Cameron Townsend to Grossman, January 23, 1957, TA 13081.

114. Cameron Townsend to John W. Newman, May 10, 1957, TA 12912.

115. The term "Auca" is considered an epithet meaning "savage"; thus "Huaorani" or "Waorani" is preferred.

116. Doris Cox to Cameron Townsend, September 17, 1953, TA 41251; Russell T. Hitt, *Jungle Pilot: The Gripping Story of the Life and Witness of Nate Saint, Martyred Missionary to Ecuador* (Grand Rapids: Discovery House Publishers, 1997); Cameron Townsend to Saint, May 10, 1957, TA 12916; Ethel Emily Wallis, *The Dayuma Story: Life under Auca Spears* (New York: Harper and Row, 1960); Ethel Emily Wallis, *Aucas Downriver* (New York: Harper and Row, 1973).

117. William G. Nyman Jr. to Cameron Townsend, October 5, 1957, TA 14215.

118. Cowan to Robert Wyatt, October 28, 1958, TA 15608.

119. McCarter to Cameron Townsend, June 18, 1957, TA 12770.

the undertaking should not place the corporation in debt.[120] The estimated budget for building the pavilion and running the fair operation came to $392,000, a rather sizable sum considering WBT-SIL's total annual budget for 1963 was $2.4 million.[121] There were no reserves in the corporate accounts for the project, so Townsend was obligated to look elsewhere for funds. Proving once again that he was rarely at a loss for ideas, he secured a $100,000 bank loan by convincing twenty wealthy acquaintances to underwrite $5,000 tranches of the debt.[122] As Townsend saw it, this plan bypassed the injunction against plunging the corporation into debt. He also believed that the bank note would easily be repaid from cash flows generated by charging admission to the pavilion. Presumably the underwriters would only have to make good on their $5,000 promissory notes if fair receipts fell short, something Townsend considered an utter impossibility. He insisted that Wycliffe would collect no less than $200,000 in ticket sales at fifty cents apiece, even if only one out of every two hundred fairgoers visited the pavilion.[123] On October 4, 1963, Townsend signed a contract with the fair organizers, and the very next day he landed his twentieth underwriter for the bank loan.[124]

In his approach to the fair, Townsend took full advantage of the fact that the midcentury realignments within evangelicalism went hand in glove with larger cultural forces at work in American society. The aftereffects of World War II and the beginnings of the Cold War reawakened many Americans to the idea of American exceptionalism and to a renewed sense of America as the keeper of the world's moral compass. For example, President Harry S. Truman gave voice to this outlook in the early phase of the Cold War when he stated that "to save the world from totalitarianism," it was imperative "for the whole world [to] adopt the American system."[125] For America to fulfill this challenging role, influential elites, from military generals to religious leaders, insisted that the country had to pay more than lip service to halting what was perceived as its declining moral character. The neo-evangelical theologian Carl Henry warned in his 1946 *Remaking the Modern Mind* of the perils of an imminent cultural col-

120. WBT-SIL board of directors meeting, minutes, October 29, 1962, WSA; Cameron Townsend to Graham, November 1, 1962, p. 2, TA 20763.

121. "Estimated Cost Sheet for World's Fair," *Translation*, Spring 1963, 6, TA 41709.

122. Copy of "Guaranty," October 1963, TA 41713; Cameron Townsend to Key, October 5, 1963, p. 1, TA 21328; C. A. Black, business manager, C. Davis Weyerhaeuser Co., to Lawrence Routh, October 15, 1963, TA 21597.

123. Cameron Townsend to Key, December 6, 1963, TA 21300.

124. Cameron Townsend to Key, October 5, 1963, p. 1, TA 21328.

125. Quoted in Niall Ferguson, *Colossus: The Rise and Fall of the American Empire* (New York: Penguin Books, 2004), 80.

lapse should the nation fail to shore up its increasingly shaky Judeo-Christian pillars.[126] Henry's work was part of a much broader offensive to restore what was perceived as a dangerous decline in the country's historically Christian culture. The US Air Force's "Character Guidance" program is a fitting illustration of this nationwide drive to renovate America's moral fiber by instilling the values of Christian morality in military personnel,[127] and exemplifies an overall shift in America's social consciousness that would see religiosity in America at its apogee around 1960. When progressive fundamentalists set sail out of separatist and militant fundamentalism, they benefited from the same cultural winds that were carrying large swathes of American society in a more religiously orientated direction. With the fair project, Townsend took full advantage of this cultural mood.

The idea of progress was also taking on greater prominence in the American mind in the wake of the Depression, and even more so after World War II. The atomic age portended potential annihilation, but it also held out the promise of ever-increasing scientific development and economic prosperity. This general trend was especially notable from the late 1930s, as evidenced by corporate America's concerted effort to demonstrate its capacity for nearly unlimited innovation at the 1939 and 1964 New York World's Fairs. Robert Moses, New York City's planning representative for the 1939 World's Fair and the president of the 1964 equivalent, claimed that the 1964 fair would be "an Olympics of Progress" and "an endless parade of wonders of mankind."[128] The proliferation of consumer goods sustained this assertion, and corporate America contended that the future held out the promise of even more abundance and advancement. At the 1964 fair the automobile manufacturer General Motors boasted that future modes of transport would lead to the colonization of not only the most inhospitable areas of the earth but also the ocean floor and outer space.[129] Obscured by all this triumphal propaganda were the social and ecological costs, as well as the underlying complexity of technological production. These facts were conve-

---

126. Carl F. H. Henry, *Remaking the Modern Mind* (Grand Rapids: Eerdmans, 1946).

127. C. T. Lanham, "The Moral Core of Military Strength" (speech to the National Small Business Men's Association, February 16, 1949), 4, quoted in James Gilbert, *Redeeming Culture: American Religion in an Age of Science* (Chicago: University of Chicago Press, 1997), 96.

128. "Your Day at the New York World's Fair, 1964–1965," brochure, Organization Day Office, World's Fair Headquarters, July 26, 1963, quoted in Michael L. Smith, "Representations of Technology at the 1964 World's Fair," in *The Power of Culture: Critical Essays in American History*, ed. Richard Wightman Fox and T. J. Jackson Lears (Chicago: University of Chicago Press, 1993), 223.

129. Roland Marchand and Michael L. Smith, "Corporate Science on Display," in *Scientific Authority and Twentieth-Century America*, ed. Ronald G. Walters (Baltimore: Johns Hopkins University Press, 1997), 173.

niently ignored. Thus the two World's Fairs did not seek so much to educate the public as to engage in boosterism. "People go to a World's Fair," explained General Electric's J. E. Weldy in 1964, "because they are seeking excitement, and that is the only reason they go."[130] James Gardner, an exhibit designer, confirmed Weldy's outlook: "With entertainment you can couple a little bit of education, but not very much, because people don't go to a World's Fair to study." If it was difficult to educate people, there remained the fair's potential for influencing attenders' attitudes since, as Gardner claimed, they arrived "full of anticipation and excitement. . . . They are," he pointed out, "psychologically ready for you to influence them."[131] Images designed to influence, or even manipulate, public opinion were aspects of popular culture that Townsend was prepared to employ in his efforts to publicize WBT-SIL.

In an expansive mood as the fair approached, Townsend gave free rein to his passion. The entrance to the Pavilion of 2000 Tribes led to an exhibit of photographer Cornell Capa's black-and-white stills of SIL's fieldwork and of some Amazonian indigenous peoples. The Hungarian American Capa was a well-known photographer whose work had been published in the immensely popular *Life* magazine. Townsend and Capa had met in Lima in the 1950s, and they subsequently struck up an enduring relationship. Even though Capa held no strong religious convictions, he nonetheless became a WBT-SIL enthusiast.[132] Displayed in the pavilion's auditorium was a 10' x 100' mural portraying Chief Tariri's transformation "From Savage to Citizen," as it was triumphantly entitled. Townsend had commissioned artist Douglas Riseborough to paint the pantoscopic mural for $15,000, and the painter exercised artistic license in depicting the life of Tariri. Violence, nudity, and bloodshed, along with severed and shrunken heads, were all graphically displayed in full color. SIL's Loretta Anderson, who was well acquainted with Tariri and his people from having lived among them for many years, regarded Riseborough's depiction of the Shapra and Tariri as not "true to life." In fact, she refused to show snapshots of the mural to Tariri, fearing his "wrath." She also worried that if he ever saw the mural, he would "be furious." Anderson complained to Riseborough that the Shapra never went naked, did not kill women, and did not dismember their enemies as depicted in the mural. For Anderson, and some of her SIL colleagues

---

130. J. E. (Jiggs) Weldy, "Exhibit Designs and Techniques That Attract the General Public," in *Key Facts for Advertisers on the NYWF 1964–1965: Third Report* (New York: Association of National Advertisers, 1962), quoted in Marchand and Smith, "Corporate Science on Display," 18.

131. James Gardner, "Exhibit Designs and Techniques That Attract the General Public," in *Key Facts for Advertisers*, 25–26, quoted in Marchand and Smith, "Corporate Science on Display," 169–70.

132. Cornell Capa, Hefley interview, c. 1970, TA 43753.

in Peru to whom she had shown pictures, the mural was a fraudulent portrayal of Shapra violence.[133] Riseborough freely admitted taking "many liberties" as a means "to strengthen the symbolism" and to create "an emotional impact" that would "shock the audience into attention." As he saw it, the mural was not only about the "savagery of Tariri's world," but was also "a symbol of the evil in man throughout the world."[134] Whether or not the average fair attender made the connection between the mural's presentation of Shapra violence and universal human depravity is questionable. This did not worry Townsend in the least. He had no difficulty whatsoever fitting Tariri into the role Riseborough had cast for him, and he unabashedly extolled the virtues of the mural by proclaiming that the artist "is going to produce one of the greatest paintings of this century."[135] In pursuit of the World's Fair project, Townsend once again exhibited an extraordinary degree of pragmatism, coupled with a readiness to engage in artifice rather than settle for a less dramatic reality.

Riseborough's presentation of the Shapra also invoked the idea of progress and its correlation with Christianity. Thus it held a natural appeal for Townsend, and his ideological disposition was on full display when he addressed Wycliffe's supporters on the subject of the fair in a newsletter: "The tremendous picture, 1000 sq. ft. of inspired painting by David Riseborough[,] shows in five symbolic panels the transition of a headhunting chief of the Amazon jungle from witchcraft and boa worship to modern medicine and the Word of God. In the final great scene the artist portrays the chief cutting the umbilical cord that holds the oncoming generation of tribesmen to their hopeless past, freeing them with the 'Sword of the Spirit' that they might ascend the stairs of learning, with Christianity protecting them from the dangers of modern civilization."[136] Of course, this outlook was also in keeping with the overall tenor of the fair itself. The Pavilion of 2000 Tribes was calibrated to the ideological temper prevailing at the fair, where the idea of progress and scientific achievement were widely and loudly proclaimed. Circling the globe with American technological prowess was a common theme, and this fitted well with Wycliffe's presentation. The 1964–1965 World's Fair came at a moment in American history when the idea of progress and Christian civilization were enjoying their last and almost uncontested moment together in the sun. Within a few short years, as the next chapter details, WBT-SIL would come under heavy criticism from a number of quarters for this very kind of sentiment and portrayal of indigenous peoples,

133. Anderson to Riseborough, c. late 1963, TA 21479.

134. Riseborough to Cameron Townsend, July 3, 1963, TA 21503.

135. Cameron Townsend to Frank Sherrill, January 24, 1963, TA 21638.

136. Cameron Townsend, "A Message about the Pavilion of 2000 Tribes at the New York World's Fair," August 31, 1964, TA 22214.

but the early to mid 1960s was ideally suited for Townsend to offer the public his vision for humanity.

"The 'Pavilion of 2000 Tribes' is a success in every way except financially," Townsend announced in August 1964.[137] In fact, the fair project had been threatening the organization's financial health as far back as late 1963. Kenneth Watters, the corporation's ever-vigilant treasurer, confessed to Townsend in October 1963 that "I am scairt [sic], and this project could break Wycliffe's back if . . . we don't come up with some solution here pretty soon."[138] Throwing caution to the wind, Townsend shifted into a no-holds-barred solicitation mode, and he pressed his fair administrators to do the same. Under terrible pressure to find cash, Wycliffe's fair manager Harold Key admitted that his own attitude was slipping into a method of "full solicitation without full information."[139] Yet, a year later, the financial situation had not improved, partly because charging the fifty-cent admission had proved to be a serious miscalculation. Fairgoers were exiting the pavilion complaining that they had paid to hear a sermon. Eventually the admission fee was dropped in favor of a freewill offering. This action did increase receipts, but even though over six hundred thousand fairgoers visited the mural, while an additional half million passed through the pavilion's outer exhibit hall, the attempt to recoup the fair's expenses with collections failed miserably.[140] Organizational leaders contemplated dropping out of the fair, but Townsend demurred. If need be, he was ready to mortgage or even sell the organization's Santa Ana, California, headquarters building if it would keep the fair operation solvent.[141] In a desperate move to raise cash, Townsend sold "shares" in the project under a "Share-the-Fair" campaign to his own Wycliffe missionaries and Wycliffe's supporters at $100 each.[142] When the WBT-SIL board attempted to restrain Townsend, he reacted as he had in the past, by threatening to resign. He also lectured the board that there were no "moral" or "religious" grounds for dis-

137. Cameron Townsend, "A Message about the Pavilion of 2000 Tribes at the New York World's Fair."

138. Watters to Cameron Townsend, October 29, 1963, p. 3, TA 21457.

139. Key to Cameron Townsend, November 10, 1963, TA 21584.

140. Benjamin Elson, interview by author, August 6, 2007, Waxhaw, North Carolina; Elson to Cameron Townsend, September 29, 1964, p. 3, TA 21932; Cameron Townsend to Routh, January 27, 1965, TA 22968.

141. Cameron Townsend to Pittman, August 29, 1964, TA 921782; Cameron Townsend to Elson, September 2, 1964, TA 21778; Cameron Townsend to WBT-SIL board of directors, September 9, 1964, TA 21950.

142. Elson to Cameron Townsend, September 29, 1964, p. 2, TA 21932; Cameron Townsend to Key, August 17, 1964, TA 21788; Cameron Townsend to "Wycliffe Family," September 2, 1964, TA 21779; Cameron Townsend to Robert F. Wildrick, October 14, 1964, TA 21707.

daining solicitation. "Paul solicited," he pressed, and "D. L. Moody solicited," and therefore it must be legitimate to do so.[143] Rather than exercise restraint, Townsend later suggested that "something could likely be done to improve our salesmanship."[144] The board, in characteristic fashion, relented, and the pavilion remained open into 1965.[145]

The fair project was a financial catastrophe, and the strain it produced altered the organization's faith mission approach. Despite all efforts to raise additional funds, the financial crisis eventually reached the point where the underwriters of the bank loan were forced to make good on their $5,000 guarantees, with at least one complaining that Townsend had "pulled the wool over our eyes."[146] Lawrence Routh, an electrical contractor who had helped to develop an operational base for JAARS in Waxhaw, North Carolina, was charged with pressuring the somewhat reluctant underwriters.[147] When all was said and done, Townsend had landed WBT-SIL $200,000 in debt, while dropping any pretense of persevering with the faith method for organizational funding.[148] The upshot of his excursions beyond the boundaries of the faith model for securing funds was the establishment of a new laymen's volunteer organization that was free to pursue a more direct approach to fund-raising outside the confines of WBT-SIL. Routh once again rode to the rescue. In the wake of the World's Fair financial calamity, he undertook Operation 2000, which consisted of a series of banquets held around the country designed to clear Wycliffe's debt and to fund future Bible translation projects.[149] Operation 2000 functioned as a third party under lay auspices separate from WBT-SIL proper; hence Routh was able to engage in a rather direct style of solicitation. The program provided a natural setting, argued Wycliffe's Dale Kietzman, in which to deploy the "faith promise" approach to fund-raising developed by Oswald J. Smith. This well-known mission advocate and pastor of the People's Church of Toronto encouraged donors to pledge, "in dependence on God," a specified amount over and above their regular church tithe.[150] There was a

143. Cameron Townsend to WBT-SIL board of directors, September 7, 1964, TA 21773.

144. Cameron Townsend to Routh, January 27, 1965, TA 22968.

145. Elson to Cameron Townsend, September 29, 1964, TA 21932.

146. Lorin Griset, quoting Amos Baker, Hefley interview, c. 1970, TA 43774.

147. George M. Ive to Routh, November 9, 1964, TA 22162; Routh to Sherrill, November 6, 1964, TA 22143; Routh to Watters, November 6, 1964, TA 22168; Routh to Baker, November 11, 1964, TA 22164; Sherrill to Routh, November 5, 1964, TA 22144.

148. "Comparative Statement of Fair Project," March 31, 1965, TA 41700.

149. Elson to Cameron Townsend, September 29, 1964, p. 2, TA 21932; Routh to Sherrill, November 6, 1964, TA 22143; Routh to William G. Kelly, October 26, 1964, TA 22189; Routh to Wycliffe board of directors executive committee, 1964, TA 22086.

150. James C. Hefley, *God's Free-Lancers: The Story of Wycliffe Associates—Men and Women*

definite technique involved, and one had to master the subtleties of drawing members of the audience into making the pledge on the one hand without offending them on the other. How difficult was it to successfully carry out this delicate technique? Smith himself once remarked to Wycliffe's Harold Goodall that "there is only one man in 10,000 who knows how to take up a Faith Promise Offering."[151] In 1967, Operation 2000 developed into a separate organization known as Wycliffe Associates (WA), which was designed as a lay organization that involved prosperous Christian businesswomen and businessmen, such as Routh, in providing construction and other services to WBT-SIL, as well as operating the nationwide banquet series on a continuing basis. Wycliffe Associates provided a platform for more direct funding appeals outside the core WBT-SIL organization, thus advantageously allowing the mission to maintain its faith status.

To provide for more engaging missionary speakers at banquets and other venues, WA drew upon the public relations expertise of Claude Bowen, a Chicago-based Dale Carnegie franchisee. Carnegie was a popular promoter of "self-improvement" methods and author of the often reprinted *How to Win Friends and Influence People* (1936). Bowen trained both SIL's public relations men and Wycliffe speakers in Carnegie's techniques. Thus the WA banquets were a blend of Smith's finely tuned solicitation methods and Carnegie's strategies for structuring public presentations. All this was designed to hold banquet attenders in rapt attention, while at the same time overcoming any skepticism that would hinder them from making a financial commitment.[152] The WA approach was transformational in that it combined increasingly bold faith-funding methods with the psychology of modern marketing techniques.

In the wake of the World's Fair, individual missionaries continued to follow the faith mission creed of full information, no solicitation, while organizationally Wycliffe maintained a somewhat modified approach that permitted mildly worded appeals for funding large projects.[153] Conversely, Wycliffe Associates employed a rather direct fund-raising style under the rubric of "faith promise" that, with its religious phrasing, obscured the shift away from the older

---

Using Their Skills to Help Wycliffe Missionaries around the World (Orange, CA: Wycliffe Associates, 1983), 35.

151. Smith to Goodall, June 9, 1966, TA 24554.

152. Claude Bowen, informal interview with author, October 2007, Chicago, Illinois; John Alsop, interview by author, September 4, 2008, Dallas, Texas; Benjamin F. Elson, "Executive Director's Report," December 3, 1975, p. 2, TA 31940.

153. WBT corporate conference, minutes, June 4, 1965, WSA; WBT executive committee, minutes, March 17, 1966, WSA.

and more reticent faith mission style of the past. Thus, from the latter half of the 1960s, the WBT-SIL-WA combination utilized a variety of approaches to developing financial support. These new channels for soliciting funds became even more important in the 1970s, as the organization continued to expand. As with the dual-organization structure, the multifaceted approach to funding allowed WBT-SIL missionaries, the WBT-SIL organizational fund-raisers, and WA lay advocates to calibrate the style and nature of their appeals to an almost infinite variety of audiences, thus tremendously enlarging the organization's potential donor base. If statistics are any indication, the organization's methods of developing resources both human and financial were successful, even though the World's Fair project itself proved unsuccessful financially. From the 1,122 members and $2.2 million in receipts of 1961, WBT-SIL expanded to some 2,500 missionaries (mostly from the United States, the United Kingdom, Australia, and Canada) working in twenty-three countries and just over $6.7 million in revenue by 1971.[154]

WBT-SIL not only survived but also thrived during the midcentury restructuring of North American evangelicalism. In part, this happened because the progressive fundamentalists won the day, and the organization found itself in a growing company of cooperative evangelicals from about 1960. When Wycliffe joined the Interdenominational Foreign Mission Association (IFMA) in 1949, the organization's practices were not yet widely known and the rupture between the classical fundamentalists and the new evangelicals lay some years in the future. WBT-SIL's 1959 departure from IFMA did not signal that it had changed its stripes, but rather it indicated that the expanding rift between the two groups had widened sufficiently to force a choice on the organization. After holding out hopes for maintaining harmonious relations across the full spectrum of evangelicals, Wycliffe leaders finally concluded, as Townsend had before them, that WBT-SIL was better served by breaking with the fundamentalists in IFMA. On the other hand, the organization's success also hinged on creative action. With Townsend showing the way, Wycliffe pragmatically adapted itself to the vagaries of both the broader American cultural milieu and the evangelical subculture to build support for the fieldwork of SIL. The organization married the time-honored faith mission ethos to a public relations strategy built on the idea of progress and willingness to employ marketing techniques that proffered exciting images of Christian transformation. In other respects, mainly on the point of serving Catholics, no publicity at all best served the organization. By pursuing bold engagement with popular culture while at the same time holding fast to aspects of the traditional faith mission model, WBT-SIL created a

---

154. *Translation*, October–December 1971, 15; *Translation*, July–September 1971, 14.

remarkably diverse approach to publicizing its activities. Thus, partly as a result of its own progressive outlook in a cultural context where such attitudes were in the ascendant, and partly by dint of its own efforts to align its promotional efforts with the sentiments of various publics, WBT-SIL was phenomenally successful in establishing a generous base of support at home in North America that undergirded its growing operations abroad.

CHAPTER 6

Staying the Course

By the 1970s, WBT-SIL had become a well-organized and amply funded global operation. It was also one of the largest, if not the largest, private organizations involved in language development among the world's most isolated indigenous peoples, and it therefore attracted an outsized share of attention from anthropologists. Beginning in the early 1970s, anthropologists became increasingly critical of WBT-SIL. Allegations reverberated throughout the decade and beyond that the organization was both an agent of US imperialism and a destroyer of indigenous cultures. Some critics also claimed to have uncovered a conspiracy in the dual-organization structure. At a moment when WBT-SIL was enjoying the fruits of its hard-won victories—having carved out for itself a respected place among American evangelicals, linguistic scholars, and foreign government officials—it was once again confronted with opponents who could potentially do it irreparable harm. As the criticism in anthropological circles mounted and as nationalist elements within Latin American countries agitated to eject SIL, the organization maneuvered to maintain its position; but with its evangelical character and missionary purpose, there were limits on just how much change was possible. In fact, a casual observer of WBT-SIL in the early 1980s would have had difficulty distinguishing any real material change at all in the organization's basic strategies. This begs the question: Why, when all was said and done, did the attacks mounted against WBT-SIL in the 1970s and early 1980s prove largely ineffective? The main thrust of the present chapter is directed toward answering this question.

The period extending from the late 1960s to the early 1970s was one of particularly good fortune for WBT-SIL. In the early 1970s, the organization crossed the threshold of 2,500 members and its missionary-linguists were laboring in over twenty countries to translate the Bible into some five hundred languages.[1] SIL Peru director James Wroughton could well have been speaking for the organization at large when he reported to the WBT-SIL board of directors in 1967 that "the branch is approaching peak development" in several areas.[2] That same year a campaign to reach "every tribe by '85" was launched. Confidence was not in short supply. The initiative to begin a New Testament translation in every language lacking the Christian Scriptures by 1985 was based on the expectation that Wycliffe could recruit an additional 6,500 personnel.[3] In nearly every respect, as WBT-SIL entered the 1970s, its strategies were proving successful, and the organization was anticipating a bright future now that it had secured for itself a reputation among its varied constituencies.

The optimism displayed by the organization's top leadership in the mid-1960s was tempered by the combined effects of WBT-SIL's rapid expansion and Townsend's unconstrained exploits and loose management style, all of which in due course led to an administrative crisis. As early as 1963, Philip Grossman, the chairman of the executive committee of the board of directors, was fretting over problems associated with the expansion of the home division based in Santa Ana.[4] Lines of authority, especially those running to and from the general director, were in disarray. Events surrounding Townsend's World's Fair project were a significant source of frustration.[5] The fair project, Kenneth Pike complained to Townsend in 1966, "took up all our push and let all our other avenues wither pretty badly." He worried too that the strains of the fair effort had left the organization's home office in Santa Ana "in a near state of total collapse."[6] Pike was not the only WBT-SIL leader frustrated with the disorderly state of affairs at a time when the organization was increasingly in need of a steady hand on the tiller. George Cowan's patience had reached the breaking point over Townsend's unilateral decision making and circumventions of the board. Wycliffe's ordinarily self-possessed president uncharacteristically protested that "it is inconceivable that a responsible Board of Directors should be by-passed in actions which will have repercussions throughout the entire membership and affect our total world-wide image and public relations."[7] Over the previous few

1. Eunice V. Pike, "Historical Sketch," in *The Summer Institute of Linguistics: Its Works and Contributions*, ed. Ruth M. Brend and Kenneth L. Pike (The Hague: Mouton, 1977), 1; *Translation*, July–September 1971, 14.

2. Wroughton to WBT-SIL board of directors, March 6, 1967, TA 25811.

3. *Translation*, April–June 1970, 12–13.

4. Grossman to Cameron Townsend, January 18, 1963, TA 21555.

5. The World's Fair project is discussed in chapter 5.

6. Kenneth L. Pike to Cameron Townsend, March 30, 1966, TA 24176.

7. Cowan to Cameron Townsend, September 25, 1966, TA 23972.

decades, WBT-SIL leaders had mostly allowed Townsend to have his way. By the mid-1960s, it was becoming clear that the organization had become too large for the founder's unstructured and loose management style, and WBT-SIL's leaders were suffering the consequences of an underdeveloped organizational structure.

Late in 1964 the WBT-SIL board (which remained mostly identical to the executive leadership team)[8] commissioned Spenser Bower of the Christian Services Fellowship, a management consultancy firm, to study the organization's management practices.[9] Bower's 1966 report suggested greater administrative centralization, and it also proposed the elimination of the general director position in favor of an executive director, the primary aim of which was to establish tighter administrative control over the actions of the chief executive. Bower's recommendations met with the board's approval. In June 1966 the WBT-SIL board appointed Benjamin Elson, then deputy general director, to the post of executive director of WBT-SIL. Having invested Elson with administrative authority over the day-to-day operations of the organization, and also having come to the realization that the seventy-year-old Townsend was perhaps beyond his prime, the board endeavored to persuade the general director to give up his post by offering him the role of "honorary founder."[10] In their exertions to impose order on the organization's operations, WBT-SIL's leaders concluded that the time had come for Townsend to give up some of his executive authority.

"Please squelch the suggestion of an honorary title for me," Townsend snapped at Elson in February 1967. "I wouldn't accept it." He was also bitterly opposed to Bower's recommendations that would circumscribe his range of action. "Someone," he contended, "has to be a counterbalance to bureaucracy with daring vision that is thoroughly submissive to God."[11] Still motivated by his particular brand of muscular Keswick theology, where the old refrain of "let go and let God" was turned inside out, Townsend believed submission meant yielding to God's call for audacious action.[12] From his perspective, the current leadership lacked the dynamism that only he could supply. Throughout the first half of 1967 Townsend battled to maintain his freedom of action. Defending himself at the 1967 corporate conference, he inveighed against bureaucracy. While he admitted that "our executives and other officers . . . are absolutely essential" and "there is no way of getting along without bureaucrats," he veered

---

8. *Translation*, Summer–Fall 1964, 15.

9. SIL board of directors meeting, minutes, June 2–4, 1964, WSA.

10. George M. Cowan, Hefley interview, c. 1970, pp. 1–2, TA 43763; WBT board of directors meeting, minutes, May 30–June 4, 1966, pp. 1–2, TA 42533.

11. Cameron Townsend to Elson, February 21, 1967, TA 25090.

12. The influence of Keswick theology and Townsend's variation on the theme are discussed in chapter 2.

close to condescension when, pressing his argument, he pointed to the World's Fair as an example of something that would never have come to fruition "without a General Director with a little bit of vision."[13] Townsend was obviously not about to go quietly into the night simply because Bower's report suggested he do so, or because WBT-SIL's leaders wished to conduct business without his erratic ways and extravagant projects thwarting their designs for a more orderly operation.

When Townsend argued that he was the organization's chief architect of bold publicity and outsized fund-raising, the weight of the evidence was certainly on his side, and he was not bashful about reminding those who sought to undermine his authority of this fact. "Who of you executive officers loaded down with bureaucratic responsibilities," he asked Elson, "could have secured recognition for our organization from USAID for excess government property?"[14] In 1965 Townsend had lobbied US legislators to place SIL on the United States Agency for International Development's (USAID) list of approved non-government organizations.[15] This came at a time when US foreign aid to Latin America was at an all-time high.[16] The increased funding was due in large part to the launching of the Alliance for Progress, a program of social engineering intended as an anticommunist prophylactic.[17] One of the Alliance's main goals was improving adult literacy.[18] SIL was therefore an ideal partner, since it had a proven track record in this area. The efforts of Townsend (and of those who followed in his footsteps in the 1970s) to obtain USAID backing eventually paid off quite handsomely. In May and June of 1973 alone, by way of example, SIL was approved to receive surplus equipment valued at $570,000, and for the entire year of 1973 SIL was the recipient of approximately $1 million in goods.[19] USAID eventually moved into direct funding of SIL's bilingual

13. WBT corporate conference, minutes, May 23, 1967, pp. 1–2, TA 42337.

14. Cameron Townsend to Elson, February 21, 1967, TA 25090.

15. Cameron Townsend to US Senator Fred R. Harris, June 25, 1965, TA 22717; Cameron Townsend to US Senator Milton R. Young, June 28, 1965, TA 22395; Cameron Townsend to US Senator Edmund M. Muskie, September 10, 1965, TA 22352; Cameron Townsend to US Senator Daniel K. Inouye, September 15, 1965, TA 22335.

16. Peter H. Smith, *Talons of the Eagle: Dynamics of U.S.–Latin American Relations* (New York: Oxford University Press, 1996), 151.

17. Jeffrey F. Taffet, *Foreign Aid as Foreign Policy: The Alliance for Progress in Latin America* (New York: Routledge, 2007), 11–13.

18. Federico G. Gil, "The Kennedy-Johnson Years," in *United States Policy in Latin America: A Quarter Century of Crisis and Challenge, 1961–1986*, ed. John D. Martz (Lincoln: University of Nebraska Press, 1988), 11–12.

19. Edward Boyer to Harold L. Beaty, September 24, 1973, p. 2, TA 30028; Alan R. Pence to Boyer, March 22, 1974, TA 31165.

education programs, with contributions totaling over a million dollars by the early 1980s.[20] Developing contacts with USAID was a classic case of Townsend employing his diplomatic and public relations talents to harvest funds from unlikely quarters, and with overwhelming success. He was correct in pointing out that he did more than any other single individual in WBT-SIL to fill the organization's coffers.

Townsend was also quite bold in playing on the sympathies of businessmen eager to extend America's influence abroad. J. Howard Pew of the Sun Oil Company was a frequent donor from the 1950s to the late 1970s. Pew, a conservative Presbyterian, wrung his hands over the baleful effects that communism and socialism could have on free enterprise.[21] The Pew Foundation's early donations ranged from $5,000 to $20,000, but Townsend longed for greater sums, so he audaciously pressed Pew for "$30,000 or $40,000" in August 1960.[22] The foundation demurred and as much as suggested to Townsend that he had overplayed his hand.[23] Undaunted by this mild rebuke, Townsend brandished the Red Menace card before the Pew board. "I believe that Russia will go to any expense necessary to enable Castro to turn Cuba into a showcase of progress that will attract Latin Americans toward the communist orbit." "What are we as a nation," he challenged, "going to do to safeguard our Western Hemisphere against Kruschev's [*sic*] and Castro's aims?" Of course, he had a proposal in mind: another aircraft for WBT-SIL's operation in Brazil, the dedication of which would feature Brazil's former president Juscelino Kubitschek who, he averred, was a "most outstanding leader of democracy." "All this and more," he offered, could be had "for only $35,000!"[24] Pew took the bait and board member Frederick B. Hufnegel Jr. even agreed to head the committee for the Brazil Helio Courier aircraft project.[25] Perhaps the most infamous character—at least in the eyes of critics—from WBT-SIL's constellation of wealthy backers was Nelson Bunker Hunt, a Texas oilman and multibillionaire who, in collusion with his

20. Morris Carney, interview by author, June 15, 2006, Waxhaw, North Carolina; May to Edward Warnock, April 18, 1977, TA 34508; Matane Paulias, Papua New Guinea ambassador to the United States, to WCT, June 14, 1977, TA 34133; Robbins to Cowan, December 11, 1978, pp. 3–5, TA 35643.

21. George M. Marsden, *Reforming Fundamentalism: Fuller Seminary and the New Evangelicalism* (Grand Rapids: Eerdmans, 1987), 155.

22. Cameron Townsend to Allyn R. Bell Jr. and Frederick B. Hufnegel Jr., July 17, 1960, p. 1, TA 18224.

23. Bell to Cameron Townsend, August 2, 1960, p. 1, TA 18223.

24. Cameron Townsend to Hufnegel, September 28, 1960, p. 3, TA 18182.

25. "Gift Airplane to Brazil," *Chamber of Commerce News* (Philadelphia), November 30, 1961, TA 43396; Hufnegel to Cameron Townsend, July 16, 1962, TA 20997; Cameron Townsend to WBT-SIL members, April 18, 1961, TA 19888.

brother William Herbert Hunt, allegedly attempted to corner the soybean and silver commodities markets in the late 1970s. Like Pew, Nelson Bunker Hunt was an ardent anticommunist and supporter of right-wing political causes.[26] When SIL established a campus in Dallas, Hunt donated $1.5 million, a sum sufficient to have a building named after his mother.[27] Townsend and other organizational leaders were clearly willing to affiliate WBT-SIL with right-wing political interests as a means of attracting large financial donations. It must be emphasized that there is no indication that WBT-SIL was ever in any way influenced by these associations. It could actually be argued to the contrary, that these donors made a rather poor choice with their investments, since SIL was committed to serving governments from across the entire political spectrum. What these associations did do, as will be seen below, was raise the ire and suspicion of left-wing antagonists.

At the very moment when WBT-SIL's upper leadership was attempting to diminish Townsend's power, the general director unexpectedly bumped up against the limits of his influence. In October 1966, Paul Witte, a Roman Catholic and a former student of SIL's University of Oklahoma program, expressed his desire to join the organization as a Bible translator.[28] Townsend, who had recently been pressing WBT-SIL members in Colombia to attend Catholic mass on occasion, was thrilled with the prospect of Witte joining the organization.[29] Here was his chance to demonstrate that SIL was truly nonsectarian. Townsend understood that success in this venture would require bypassing the board of directors in order to win the favor of the membership at large. In a pair of open letters dispatched between late 1966 and early 1967, Townsend argued his case. "Sometimes we get candidates who are gifted and dedicated," he wrote in his Christmas 1966 circular, "loving the Lord and His Word with all their hearts, but whom the Board cannot accept because they have been ruled to be incompatible to us due to some viewpoint they hold in fact or theory. . . . People who have been close to them find that some at least were perfectly compatible but we failed to harness them because they didn't fall into our cut and dried rule of compatibility."[30] He kept up the drumbeat, and in an April 1967 letter

26. Jerome Tuccille, *Kingdom: The Story of the Hunt Family of Texas* (Ottawa: Jameson Books, 1984); Harry Hurt III, *Texas Rich: The Hunt Dynasty from the Early Oil Days through the Silver Crash* (New York: Norton, 1981).

27. Clark W. Breeding to Cameron Townsend, April 3, 1978, TA 35252; "The International Linguistics Center: Answering Basic Human Needs Around the World," brochure, Wycliffe Bible Translators and Summer Institute of Linguistics, Dallas, Texas, n.d., in author's possession.

28. Witte to WBT, October 26, 1966, TA 23910.

29. Cameron Townsend to WBT membership, February 10, 1965, TA 50828.

30. Cameron Townsend to WBT-SIL branches, December 7, 1966, p. 1, TA 924340.

he reasoned that Roman Catholicism was just another denomination. "Can we honestly tell officials . . . that we are non-sectarian within the Christian framework if we rule out true Christians just because of the denomination to which they belong?"[31] Despite his relentless urgings, opposition to Witte joining WBT mounted.[32] A survey of opinion taken in SIL's Ecuador branch in 1967 revealed that 75 percent of members agreed that "membership in a heretical organization [Roman Catholicism] is sufficient reason to bar a candidate from WBT."[33] In June 1967 the matter was taken up by the WBT-SIL conference, the highest body of authority in the organization, and Townsend failed in his bid to secure Witte's membership.[34] The conference passed a motion stating that "we reaffirm our full confidence in the existing legislation and general procedures relating to the processing of applicants." In addition, the motion stated that "applicants who maintain views widely divergent from the doctrines of evangelical Christianity shall not be accepted for membership on the grounds of doctrinal incompatibility."[35] WBT-SIL members had learned to serve and befriend Catholics, but embracing them as fellow members proved too radical. Townsend's fellow missionaries not only handed him a defeat, but they also stated clearly that WBT-SIL was and would remain evangelical in its religious character.

Even before Townsend's defeat at the 1967 conference, the recently appointed executive director Benjamin Elson was asserting his authority. This was plainly visible when Elson countered Townsend's open letters on the Witte issue with his own five-page communiqué in May 1967, in which he opposed the general director.[36] For the most part, though, Townsend was simply eased out of administrative affairs as Elson expanded his range of control. By 1970 Townsend was complaining that he was no longer receiving board meeting minutes without requesting them, and he was falling into the habit of dropping despondent lines to confidants. In one such letter to Richard Pittman, he grumbled that "Ben doesn't tell me much news & I don't get with the others much so I don't have much to pass on."[37] Townsend's occasional periods of melancholy would likely have had detrimental effects, not only on his well-being but also on the organization, had the board and conference not unhesitatingly backed his ambitious gambit of establishing a foothold for SIL in the USSR (discussed

31. Cameron Townsend to WBT-SIL members, April 10, 1967, p. 2, TA 24964.

32. Frank Robbins, interview by author, September 2, 2008, Dallas, Texas.

33. Ecuador branch conference, minutes supplement, 1967, p. 1, TA 39985.

34. The WBT-SIL conference was made up of elected members from each of SIL's branches around the world.

35. WBT policy board, minutes, May 17–June 1, 1967, p. 36, WSA.

36. Elson to WBT-SIL membership, May 4, 1967, TA 25762.

37. Cameron Townsend to Pittman, January 30, 1970, TA 27406.

below). Increasingly distanced from the operational aspects of running the organization, and expending most of his energies on annual visits to the Soviet Union and reminding a rising generation of new leaders to "stay on course," the seventy-five-year-old Townsend finally resigned from his general director post without fanfare and accepted the title of "founder" at the 1971 WBT-SIL conference.[38]

The 1971 conference proved significant for another reason. WBT-SIL's evangelical missionaries sometimes found it difficult to suppress their evangelistic impulses. An event that occurred in Peru in the late 1960s is illustrative. Rosa Corpancho, a public relations officer at the University of San Marcos in Lima and a strong advocate for SIL, was also very well connected with governmental and educational elites in Lima. Thus she was ideally placed to hear complaints that SIL's research and publication seemed to be taking a backseat to Bible translation. Calvin Hibbard, Townsend's personal secretary, conveyed the essence of Corpancho's concerns from Peru in July 1969. Corpancho, Hibbard wrote, implored him to "please get the members of the Institute together and tell them that they must not emphasize so much your spiritual, missionary work, but rather the scientific nature of the institute." SIL in Peru was, by her reckoning, "slipping into a general missionary approach."[39] As this episode exemplifies, there remained within the organization the ever-present threat of evangelistic activism undermining SIL's commitment to scholarship. To sustain SIL's focus on linguistic research and academic production therefore required vigilance by Kenneth Pike and the organization's cadre of professional linguists.[40] The issue of scholarly production came to a head at the 1971 conference, and, with Pike leading the charge, the delegates voted to "reaffirm our historical commitment to producing and publishing technical linguistic papers and monographs as an essential and substantial part of our task."[41] Pike had conquered his own anti-intellectual tendencies in the 1930s and, with the help of Eugene Nida, had set SIL on a scholarly course.[42] During his long career in WBT-SIL, Pike

38. Cameron Townsend, "Let's Stay on Course," May 20, 1976, TA 50136; WBT-SIL conference, minute extracts, May 24–June 2, 1971, S-14, WSA.

39. Hibbard to Richard Rolland and E. C. Members, July 22, 1969, pp. 1–2, TA 27032.

40. Kenneth L. Pike, with Hugh Steven, *Pike's Perspectives: An Anthology of Thought, Insight, and Moral Purpose* (Langley, BC: Credo Publishing, 1989), 58–61; Frank E. Robbins, "Training in Linguistics," in *The Summer Institute of Linguistics: Its Works and Contributions*, ed. Ruth M. Brend and Kenneth L. Pike (The Hague: Mouton, 1977), 65; Gary F. Simons, "The Call to Academic Community," in *Language and Life: Essays in Memory of Kenneth L. Pike*, ed. Mary Ruth Wise, Thomas N. Headland, and Ruth M. Brend (Arlington: University of Texas at Arlington and SIL International, 2003), 86–87.

41. WBT-SIL conference, minute extracts, May 24–June 2, 1971, S-7, WSA.

42. These events are discussed in chapter 2.

continually encouraged students and SIL translators to give equal attention to the heart and the mind.[43]

In addition to the 1971 reaffirmation, Pike was greatly aided in his efforts to buttress the scholarly nature of SIL by the development of the Dallas-based International Linguistics Center (ILC) in the early 1970s. SIL maintained its own linguistic school on the ILC campus, and it also established a cooperative academic program with the nearby University of Texas at Arlington (UTA). The SIL-UTA cooperative program, which began with the fall semester in September 1972, provided for the sharing of faculty between the two schools and for students to pursue graduate degrees in linguistics.[44] The creation of a permanent campus dedicated to the SIL side of the dual organization was an important factor in sustaining the organization's academic character.

The leadership of WBT-SIL had, by the early 1970s, effectively brought the organization under greater administrative control and managed Townsend's transition from general director to honorary founder. However, none of Townsend's basic policies were altered. In fact, the strategies developed by the founder were routinely emphasized. A fine example is George Cowan's 1977 message "Restating the Foundations," wherein he dilated on trusting God for the impossible, pioneering Bible translation, and service to all.[45] On the other hand, by the early 1970s WBT-SIL was a better-organized and more bureaucratic organization than Townsend would have preferred. The loosely structured mission he launched in the 1930s had become an example of what mission historian Andrew Walls referred to as "Missions Incorporated." "In some broken-backed nations," Walls noted, these large and highly developed missions "now have the most flexible, powerful, and efficient organization in the country."[46] "Managerial missiology," as two other observers of the modern parachurch missions put it, has "developed a sophisticated missions apparatus with complex lines of communications, patterns of fund raising and multiple layers of administration."[47] Whether one commended or bemoaned this state

43. Kenneth L. Pike, *With Heart and Mind: A Personal Synthesis of Scholarship and Devotion*, 2nd ed. (Duncanville, TX: Adult Learning Systems, [1962] 1996).

44. Sarah C. Gudschinsky, "Literacy," in Bend and Pike, *The Summer Institute of Linguistics*, 53; Longacre to Clark W. Breeding, June 1, 1977, TA 34475; "Memorandum of Agreement" between SIL and the University of Texas at Arlington, March 27, 1972, TA 43236; Robbins, "Training in Linguistics," 61.

45. George M. Cowan, "Restating the Foundations: A Message to the 1977 International Conference of the Wycliffe Bible Translators," September 1979, TA 34365.

46. Andrew F. Walls, *The Missionary Movement in Christian History: Studies in the Transmission of Faith* (Maryknoll, NY: Orbis, 1996), 238.

47. James F. Engel and William Dyrness, *Changing the Mind of Missions: Where Have We Gone Wrong?* (Downers Grove: InterVarsity, 2000), 89, 50.

of affairs, it certainly described WBT-SIL as it entered the decade of the 1970s. It was an evangelical mission with a worldwide reach and was comfortable in the corridors of power.

Opposition from the Left

As WBT-SIL labored to build up its operations in Latin America, Asia, Africa, and the Pacific region, at home it established relationships with American business magnates, some of whom spent lavishly to further their political and economic views. The organization also joined hands with the US government through the USAID program. However, by forging these relationships WBT-SIL had unintentionally painted itself as a target for critics, such as one who asserted in 1973 that the "WBT world-wide 'evangelical advance'" was nothing less than "a religious manifestation of U.S. cultural and economic imperialism."[48] By the early 1970s, WBT-SIL was coming to be seen by a growing number of critics as a symbol of American expansionism.

The cultural mood in the early years of the Cold War had a chilling effect on the Left. In the apt phrasing of one social historian, "The fifties was a dry season for the American Left."[49] By 1968, with the appearance of what has been referred to as the "New Left," this was no longer the case. The counterculture movement, the civil rights movement, campus riots, and the Vietnam War protests together signaled that the American consensus of the 1950s was shattered.[50] The ferment of the 1960s was global in nature. In Europe political, social, and economic strife was symbolized by the Paris riots and strikes of 1968. Outside the West there was a rising tide of anticolonialism and nationalism. Perhaps the most visible manifestations of the tumult outside the West were the Cuban Revolution in 1959 and the formal decolonization of Africa. In 1960 alone, for example, no fewer than seventeen African nations gained independence from their European colonizers. This was also a period when America's Cold War foreign policy was generating its fair share of resentment. As the Vietnam War escalated, the United States was increasingly seen by the Left as an imperial power, and certainly not as the altruistic bearer of democracy and freedom. The commonplace sentiment on the Left at home and abroad concerning US

48. Laurie Hart, "Story of the Wycliffe Translators: Pacifying the Last Frontiers," *Latin America and Empire Report* 7, no. 10 (December 1973): 17.

49. Peter Clecak, "The Movement of the 1960s and Its Cultural and Political Legacy," in *The Development of American Culture*, ed. Stanley Coben and Lorman Ratner (New York: St. Martin's Press, 1983), 261.

50. Clecak, "Movement of the 1960s," 264–70.

foreign policy by about 1968 was summarized by Democrat Senator William J. Fulbright, who complained that under President Johnson America displayed an "arrogance of power."[51] The years around 1968 marked a watershed moment when left-right political polarization took on a renewed significance.

In the late 1960s, the discipline of anthropology was swept by the same intellectual currents that were spurring the New Left to action. What followed was a paroxysm of self-flagellation and a frenzied effort to right the wrongs of the past. The anthropologist Kathleen Gough, in a landmark 1968 article in *Current Anthropology*, charged that "anthropology is a child of Western Imperialism."[52] Another anthropologist, William S. Willis Jr., argued in the same year that anthropologists' study of primitive cultures amounted to a form of "intellectual exploitation . . . that parallels the economic exploitation by imperialists." Willis also indicted anthropologists for having been "'penny' imperialists in making modest profits from studying dominated colored peoples."[53] This leftward intellectual turn found anthropologists poised to attack anything that smacked of imperialism. In her "new proposal," Gough regretted the "American rejection of Marxist and 'rebel' literature . . . since the McCarthy period." She issued a call for critical anthropological studies of the oppressors and the phenomenon of Western imperialism.[54] Gough also pressed for an examination of "revolution," which, she imagined, "now begins to appear as *the* route by which underdeveloped societies may hope to gain freedom from Western controls."[55] The substance of Gough's argument was that anthropologists should cast a critical eye on the hegemonic and antirevolutionary powers, mainly the United States, that were thwarting the incipient social transformation of underdeveloped nations. Long-standing enmity among many anthropologists toward Christian missions ensured that the missionary enterprise also came under scrutiny.[56] Leading anthropologist Stanley Diamond claimed in 1974 that "the universalism of Christianity is no more than a symptom of imperial control

51. Thomas G. Patterson, J. Garry Clifford, and Kenneth J. Hagan, *American Foreign Relations: A History Since 1895*, vol. 2, 4th ed. (Lexington, MA: Heath, 1995), 407.

52. Kathleen Gough, "New Proposals for Anthropologists," *Current Anthropology* 9, no. 5 (December 1968): 403–35.

53. William S. Willis Jr., "Skeletons in the Anthropological Closet," in *Reinventing Anthropology*, ed. Dale Hymes (New York: Pantheon, [1969] 1972), 126.

54. Gough, "New Proposals for Anthropologists," 406.

55. Gough, "New Proposals for Anthropologists," 405.

56. John W. Barton, "Some Reflections on Anthropology's Missionary Positions," *Journal of the Royal Anthropological Institute* 13, no. 1 (March 2007): 209–17; Robert J. Priest, "Missionary Positions: Christian, Modernist, Postmodernist," *Current Anthropology* 42, no. 1 (February 2001): 29–68; Claude E. Stipe et al., "Anthropologists versus Missionaries: The Influence of Presuppositions (and Comments and Reply)," *Current Anthropology* 21, no. 2 (April 1980): 165–79.

by Western civilization of the cultural space of other peoples."[57] Both Western nations and missionaries, according to the emerging anthropological critique, were obstructing the aspirations of revolutionary forces in the "third world."[58]

The concerns of the Left also registered in the upper echelons of liberal Protestantism. At the World Council of Churches (WCC) 1968 Assembly in Uppsala, Sweden, according to the editor of the assembly's report, Norman Goodall, "the most obvious and widely acknowledged feature . . . was its pre-occupation—at times, almost obsession—with the revolutionary ferment of our time, with questions of social and international responsibility, of war and peace and economic justice."[59] The WCC fused rhetoric with action in January 1971 by sponsoring the Barbados Symposium, where a dozen social scientists, mostly Latin American anthropologists, deliberated on the problems affecting "politically powerless and disenfranchised tribal peoples."[60] The signatories of the Declaration of Barbados concluded that "the suspension of all missionary activity is the most appropriate policy on behalf of both Indian society as well as the moral integrity of the churches involved," and if missionaries persisted in their objectives, they "must be held responsible by default for crimes of eth-nocide and connivance with genocide."[61] Conversion of indigenous peoples to Christianity under the influence of Western missionaries was, according to the authors of the declaration, tantamount to cultural destruction.

SIL was mentioned only sporadically in the symposium's report, but when it was singled out, it came in for rebuke. Stefano Varese, a contributor from Peru's Ministry of Education, contended that "SIL is spreading among members of the native communities a spirit and value which are markedly individualistic and capitalistic in the purest Weberian sense of the term."[62] From Varese's perspective, SIL's efforts were antithetical to Latin American communal social values,

57. Stanley Diamond, *In Search of the Primitive: A Critique of Civilization* (New Brunswick, NJ: Transaction Books, 1974), 31.

58. The term "third world" to designate less developed nations came into wide usage during the Cold War, but in the post–Cold War era its usage has declined due to the rise of multicultur-alism. B. R. Tomlinson, "What Was the Third World?" *Journal of Contemporary History* 38, no. 2 (April 2003): 307–21.

59. Norman Goodall, ed., *The Uppsala Report, 1968* (Geneva: World Council of Churches, 1968), xviii.

60. "Declaration of Barbados for the Liberation of the Indians," in *The Situation of the Indian*, ed. Walter Dostal (Geneva: World Council of Churches, 1972), 376.

61. "Declaration of Barbados," 376–81. N.B. The term "ethnocide" indicates the destruction of a people's culture only, as opposed to "genocide," which aims to physically annihilate a particular people based on language, race, or cultural identity.

62. Stefano Varese, "Inter-Ethnic Relations in the Selva of Peru," in Dostal, *The Situation of the Indian*, 138.

and the organization's program was inherently imperialistic, since it presumed to impose Western values on non-Western peoples.

In December 1973 the American anthropologist Laurie Hart vilified WBT-SIL in an article entitled "Story of the Wycliffe Translators: Pacifying the Last Frontiers." Hart's piece was published in the North American Congress on Latin America's (NACLA) journal *Latin America and Empire Report*.[63] NACLA was formed by a small band of New Left students with the support of some mainline Protestant groups. The upstart organization was given free working space in Manhattan by the Presbyterian (USA) office of the Interchurch Center. The Presbyterians also financed the printing of NACLA's newsletter (the precursor to its journal). In addition, NACLA received grants from the United Methodist Church and from the National Council of Churches' Division of Youth Ministries.[64] As the title of her article implied, Hart viewed SIL's project as nothing less than aiding and abetting internal colonialism, since the organization's strategy constituted a process for placing the indigenous peoples into a "decultured" state so that they could be psychologically reconstituted as citizens of the dominant culture. All this was odious to Hart and her New Left corevolutionaries at NACLA. She decried the "pacification" of the indigenous peoples through the inculcation of Christian doctrine, and charged that if missionaries really cared for these peoples they would "support resistance," "work to incorporate the isolated defensive struggles," and engage in the "long-term fight against the system of exploitation."[65] Evangelical religion, with its focus on "millennial expectation" and "submission," was for Hart anathema, since it presumably dampened the will of the indigenous peoples to foment revolution. Hart's criticism of WBT-SIL was, just as Kathleen Gough had called for in 1968, unmistakably grounded in Marxist revolutionary ideology.

The twenty-three-year-old budding anthropologist David Stoll fired the next round at WBT-SIL. Stoll's "Onward Christian Soldiers" appeared in the March 26, 1974, edition of the *Michigan Daily*, a University of Michigan campus newspaper. The work of SIL had come to Stoll's attention while he was pursuing his bachelor's degree at the university. The article was essentially a recapitulation of Hart's 1973 NACLA piece, and he confessed his debt to her work. Yet Stoll's critique was far more personal in that it was directed, in part, at Kenneth Pike, whom Stoll had encountered at the university. Repeating the ethnocide charge, Stoll found it "shameful" and "inexcusable" that the university was, by

63. Hart, "Story of the Wycliffe Translators," 16–31.

64. "History," North American Congress on Latin America, accessed June 9, 2017, https://nacla.org/history.

65. Hart, "Story of the Wycliffe Translators," 29.

its association with the president of SIL, complicit in the destruction of indigenous cultures.[66] After the article's publication, Pike invited Stoll to examine SIL at first hand in Latin America in order to acquire a better understating of its work.[67] Stoll took Pike's advice and, as a result, launched his academic career as an outspoken critic of WBT-SIL.

The first book-length condemnation of WBT-SIL arrived on the scene in 1981 as *Is God an American?*, a collection of essays by North American and European anthropologists.[68] The essayists in this anthology represented what anthropologist John Bodley has defined as "idealist" anthropologists who argued that indigenous peoples should be allowed to maintain their way of life rather than having to surrender to modernizing forces. "Realist" anthropologists, on the other hand, assumed that indigenous peoples would inevitably succumb to the inexorable march of progress and the state-making process.[69] In the broadest sense, *Is God an American?* was an idealist criticism of what was seen as a realist-orientated SIL. The authors found WBT-SIL guilty of two principal offenses: collusion with US imperialism and ethnocide. According to one contributor, Luis A. Pereira, SIL was serving the interests of "the northern oppressor" in the "guise of the Good Shepherd." He contended that SIL was carrying out a strategy of pacification among the Indians that tried "to turn hatred into fatalistic adjustment, adjustment to regimes which in turn exist only at the mercy of, and for the benefit of, Big Brother from the north."[70] The French Canadian Bernard Arcand found it "especially disturbing" that SIL would introduce "Christian mythology" as an "alternative" into the indigenous peoples' preexisting cultural matrix. For Arcand, this was both "ludicrous" and "criminal."[71] The authors of this scathing critique were nearly unanimous in their judgment that WBT-SIL was the handmaiden of a US Cold War foreign policy that aimed to thwart communist revolutions and keep Latin American states under US domination. The organization's purported contributions toward this end were the dampening of indigenous peoples' revolutionary impulses through cultural destruction and the inculcation of supposedly gullible Indians

66. David Stoll, "Onward Christian Soldiers," *Michigan Daily*, March 26, 1974, 2; Pike's tenured position at the University of Michigan is discussed in chapter 3.

67. Hibbard to Robbins, May 7, 1982, TA 938931.

68. Søren Hvalkof and Peter Aaby, eds., *Is God an American? An Anthropological Perspective on the Missionary Work of the Summer Institute of Linguistics* (London: Survival International; Copenhagen: International Work Group for Indigenous Affairs, 1981).

69. John H. Bodley, *Victims of Progress*, 5th ed. (New York: AltaMira Press, 2008), 251–82.

70. Luis A. Pereira, "Go Forth into Every Part of the World and Make All Nations My Disciples," in Hvalkof and Aaby, *Is God an American?*, 111.

71. Bernard Arcand, "God Is an American," in Hvalkof and Aaby, *Is God an American?*, 77.

with evangelical religion as a means of pacification. By way of conclusion, the editors of the book stated that by aligning itself with the interests of the United States, SIL had itself become the "Indians' problem."[72]

In 1982 Stoll published a book-length analysis of WBT-SIL entitled *Fishers of Men or Founders of Empire?*[73] Unlike other critics of WBT-SIL, he acknowledged the inevitability of outside forces impacting indigenous peoples. But this admission did little to diminish his antipathy for SIL. "Even if some form of contact with the world market was inevitable," he averred, "SIL's hidden church-planting agenda, with its sweeping disrespect for religious tradition and subservient attitude toward bad government was not."[74] The dual-organization strategy also invited critique. Stoll was particularly exercised over the elastic rhetoric that accompanied the dual strategy, and he referred to it as "a versatile fiction."[75] He also dilated on this topic in *Is God an American?*, claiming that it "violate[d] the evangelical standard of honesty." WBT-SIL was, Stoll declared, willing to "sanctify semantic Machiavellianism as basic Christianity."[76] From his perspective, Townsend had "constructed a new and sanctified semantic universe, a cult of divine expediency derived from evangelical meanings but essentially privy to Wycliffe itself."[77] More than any other critic, Stoll exploited the real and imagined contradictions of the dual-organization discourse in mounting his arguments against WBT-SIL.

Some critics also considered the academic side of the organization a mere pretense. Belgian anthropologist André-Marcel d'Ans alleged that SIL's scientific character was simply a "fraud." "I can state that the Institute's so-called 'scientific' articles are based on poorly collected data and a confused and obscure methodology," asserted d'Ans.[78] The methodology d'Ans referred to was Kenneth Pike's "tagmemic" theory of grammar, and it is true that when Noam Chomsky's "generative" theory of grammar arrived on the scene, it more or less sealed the fate of tagmemics in the field of descriptive linguistics.[79] In 1982 Stoll argued that SIL remained committed to Pike's method of grammar anal-

72. Søren Hvalkof and Peter Aaby, "No Tobacco, No Hallelujah," in Hvalkof and Aaby, *Is God an American?*, 185.

73. David Stoll, *Fishers of Men or Founders of Empire? The Wycliffe Bible Translators in Latin America* (Cambridge, MA: Cultural Survival, 1982), 12.

74. Stoll, *Fishers of Men*, 17.

75. Stoll, *Fishers of Men*, 12.

76. David Stoll, "Words Can Be Used in So Many Ways," in Hvalkof and Aaby, *Is God an American?*, 24.

77. Stoll, "Words Can Be Used," 31.

78. André-Marcel d'Ans, "Encounter in Peru," in Hvalkof and Aaby, *Is God an American?*, 147.

79. Kenneth L. Pike, "Reminiscences by Pike on Early American Anthropological Linguistics," in Wise, Headland, and Brend, *Language and Life*, 46–47.

ysis because Chomsky's was a far more "demanding" theory, implying that SIL translators were unable to master this presumably more complex method of grammatical analysis.[80] According to some of its critics, SIL's scientific character was mostly a ruse; furthermore, they contended that the organization's linguists were incapable of grappling with advancing theoretical developments in linguistics.

In constructing their arguments, the critics did not have to dig very deep for supporting evidence. In fact, WBT-SIL was partly a victim of its own publicity. Laurie Hart quoted directly from a 1973 article carried in the organization's official publicity organ *Translation*.[81] The piece explained to the public that the purpose of SIL's Brazilian bilingual education program was "to integrate [the Indians] into the Brazilian way of life and instill in them a sense of responsibility." For "such a complete psychological restructure" to be successful, "the students needed to cultivate a more helpful attitude toward integration while appreciating their own language and culture." At least one Indian student was apparently bewildered by the overwhelming and seemingly contradictory implications of the education program's goals, and the reluctant pupil sought to be excused from classes. "You can choose between your own way of life or the life of the *civilizado*," an SIL missionary counseled the young student, adding that "each has its price and recompense. For your way the price is lack of progress, hunger, and death, and the recompense is life without the pain of change. For the *civilizado* way, the price is work and maintaining what you've achieved. Your recompense is that you will have more."[82] Here was nothing less than an obvious attempt to reconstruct indigenous culture and communal economic organization along specifically individualist and capitalistic lines. WBT-SIL's own rhetoric and actions seemed to sustain the charge that it sought to replace the traditional social order with what looked very much like the Western, if not specifically the American, way of life.

The *Translation* piece reflected the essence of SIL's philosophy of culture change. In 1959 Kenneth Pike had staked out SIL's position on the future for indigenous peoples and their languages. "Eventually, of course," Pike asserted, "in most of the areas where we work, the indigenous converts must be absorbed into the national culture, with the national language."[83] Townsend, in a 1972 work entitled *They Found a Common Language*, offered glowing praise for the Soviet Union's goal of eliminating linguistic fragmentation as part of its attempt

80. Stoll, *Fishers of Men*, 251.

81. Hart, "Story of the Wycliffe Translators," 20–21.

82. Isabel Murphy, "The Chosen Ones," *Translation*, September–October 1973, 6.

83. Kenneth L. Pike, "Our Own Tongue Wherein We Were Born," *Bible Translator* 10, no. 2 (April 1959): 15.

to unify its numerous "republics." "Out of the hodgepodge of one hundred tongues," Townsend wrote, "has come one predominant and useful language."[84] WBT-SIL accepted the assumption that in the process of state modernization indigenous peoples were destined for integration, and would eventually lose their native languages. SIL's realist anthropological stance on culture change left the organization exposed to the charges emanating from its idealist critics.

Reaction and Response by WBT-SIL

The intellectual transformation taking place in the discipline of anthropology from the late 1960s registered in SIL only when the organization was criticized specifically. In the dramatic phrasing of the long-serving SIL anthropologist Thomas Headland, Laurie Hart's 1973 NACLA article "exploded like a hand grenade tossed into the organization."[85] Responses to the criticism varied, but there was widespread agreement that SIL should take action to limit the damage. The condemnations of WBT-SIL sparked efforts to refashion the organization into a more international and inclusive one, in hopes that this would diminish SIL's distinctly Western, and especially American, character. After reading the NACLA report in 1974, the SIL Ecuador director concluded that "somehow we've got to get the focus off hurry-hurry, flash-bang efficient U.S. way of doing things."[86] Biennial conference proceedings in the 1970s were regularly punctuated with discussions and work papers on how to integrate nationals into SIL's work. The 1973 session featured a paper entitled "The Involvement of Citizens of All Countries in the Work of SIL." Four years later, in 1977, a paper entitled "Dewesternization in WBT/SIL" was read and discussed.[87] In the middle years of the 1970s, there was a growing concern within the organization over how to include nationals in SIL's work as a means of lowering its Western-orientated profile.

Efforts to train indigenous translators and place them in SIL projects proved frustrating for a number of reasons. In 1973 the SIL Brazil branch reported a "lack of general success" in its efforts because local Christians were unwilling to provide financial support to national missionaries.[88] The long tradition in

84. W. Cameron Townsend, *They Found a Common Language: Community through Bilingual Education* (New York: Harper and Row, 1972), 13.

85. Headland, personal communication to author, February 8, 2012.

86. John Lindskoog to Clarence Church, March 14, 1974, p. 1, TA 31172.

87. "The Involvement of Citizens of All Countries in the Work of SIL," corporation conference study paper, May 1973, WSA; David Thomas, "Dewesternization in WBT/SIL," corporation conference work paper, 1977, TA 934486.

88. "Brazil Branch Report to the 1973 Biennial Conference," p. 5, WSA.

Anglo-American evangelicalism of sending missionaries and providing for their financial support was a foreign concept in predominantly Catholic Latin America. More problematic was the lack of formal education among the small tribal groups where SIL concentrated its efforts.[89] The high level of technology employed by SIL was also an obstacle for nationals. A report from Peru noted that SIL's "technology and standards are . . . far advanced over that of the countries we are working in." And, it was frankly admitted, few expatriate missionaries were ready to adapt their "technology to . . . practical levels."[90] The WBT-SIL missionary enterprise was too costly and too technologically advanced for most non-Western peoples to participate in on anything resembling an equal footing.

The obstacles to integrating nationals into Bible translation projects in Latin America were not present in Africa. British WBT-SIL member John Bendor-Samuel established the work of SIL in Africa beginning in the early 1960s. There were far more educated Christians in sub-Saharan Africa than among the more isolated Latin American indigenous peoples, and Bendor-Samuel pushed for a vigorous approach to national involvement. He also maintained that the African context was ripe for SIL to collaborate with churches rather than with governments, since the cleavage between church and state prevailing in much of Latin America was not present in most of sub-Saharan Africa.[91] Townsend, who never set foot on the African continent, clung to his belief that Bible translation was primarily a Western missionary activity and that turning it over to the nationals was the equivalent of "passing the buck."[92] The founder was also resolute that SIL, as a nonsectarian organization, should work only under government sponsorship, not with churches. Richard Pittman was the leading figure in establishing SIL in the Asia and Pacific regions, and as a Townsend protégé he remained committed to his mentor's methods of only working under government contracts, and principally utilizing expatriate missionaries. Townsend argued strenuously for his time-tested approach to be used on a worldwide basis until his death in 1982.[93] With the weight of opinion behind Townsend's classical strategy, Bendor-Samuel's hopes for cooperating with churches and incorporating Africans into SIL as full members were largely thwarted at the time.

89. "Brazil Branch Report to the 1973 Biennial Conference," p. 4, WSA.

90. Paul Wyse, "Some Observations on National Involvement in Support Affairs in Peru," item (D), November 1976, pp. 2–3, TA 41094.

91. John Bendor-Samuel, interview by author, February 21, 2006, Nairobi, Kenya.

92. Cameron Townsend, "No, Lord: We Won't Pass the Buck," 1975, TA 42677.

93. Cameron Townsend to Elson, February 22, 1971, TA 28429; Cameron Townsend to WBT-SIL board of directors, 1976, TA 32598; Cameron Townsend to WBT-SIL members, March 23, 1977, TA 33851; Cameron Townsend, "Founder's Reminders to Biennial Conference," 1977, TA 42282.

Townsend was not without persuasive arguments for his position. Ever the advocate for the religious independence of indigenous peoples, he was wary of incorporating nationals into WBT-SIL, where they would likely lose a good measure of self-determination. In the words of long-serving SIL member Earl Adams, Townsend "was very strong in his conviction, (and practice) that we expats are guests in the countries where we serve. If nationals were to become members, they would be subject to the 'control' and disciplinary procedures of the [Western] membership. That should never be. We serve them but never manage them in the ways that members are managed."[94] WBT-SIL's founder was clearly concerned that bringing nationals into SIL would naturally lead to situations where expatriate missionaries would exercise control over non-Western members. He lamented in May of 1975 that "I've seen letters during the past few months which to me reveal a spirit of imperialism, of Wycliffe bossing as to who should do the translation work." Townsend complained about "Wycliffe laying down the rules and regulations, and Wycliffe is a foreign organization in these lands. And that is imperialism."[95] He could not tolerate such relationships, for they contradicted his conviction that nationals should remain independent of WBT-SIL control, and he also feared that his own colleagues would not treat nationals as equals.

The solution Townsend offered was for SIL to encourage the nationals to form, and assist them in forming, their own translation organizations that would presumably be free of external control.[96] He did not want to have SIL, a foreign organization, controlling national organizations. Therefore, the national organization "would naturally make its own decisions regarding standards for membership, discipline, funding, etc." Specifically, "WBT-SIL would help [the local organization] in various ways as long as we [SIL] were in the country, but we would not get ourselves into a position where foreign members were outvoting and thus bossing nationals and vice versa."[97] Uppermost in Townsend's mind was how to avoid the appearance of SIL manifesting a colonial attitude, and he thought cross-cultural tensions would arise with a mixed membership, leading to accusations of paternalism. To avoid conflict, he believed it best for nationals and expatriates to maintain separate organizations.

John Bendor-Samuel remained a champion of African involvement in Bible translation throughout his long WBT-SIL career, which began in 1953 and was

---

94. Earl Adams, email to author, March 28, 2006.
95. Cameron Townsend, policy statement, May 4, 1976, p. 1, TA 50742.
96. Cameron Townsend, report at bicentennial conference, May 1977, TA 50123.
97. Cameron Townsend to WBT-SIL members, March 23, 1977, p. 1, TA 33851.

only ended by the unfortunate circumstances of a 2011 automobile accident. SIL work was first established on the African continent in Ghana by Bendor-Samuel in 1962. In July 1980, the Ghana Institute of Linguistics, Literacy and Bible Translation (GILLBT) took responsibility for the work SIL had initiated in 1962. GILLBT was established as a national organization affiliated with WBT-SIL, and its formation set a pattern that would continue to emerge in Africa and beyond. For example, in Kenya, Bible Translation and Literacy (BTL) was formed without an antecedent SIL branch having first been established in the country. As a National Bible Translation Organization, or NBTO, as these affiliate institutions were referred to in WBT-SIL circles, BTL was assisted in its first few years of development by an expatriate SIL team constituted as the Kenya Working Group, and BTL finally accepted full charge of Bible translation for SIL in Kenya in 1987. The NBTO solution to national involvement blossomed over the next three decades, and these organizations eventually became important players in the global Bible translation movement.

Whereas the attempts to integrate nationals directly into the organization were mostly unsuccessful in the 1970s, the criticism of SIL was effective in provoking SIL leaders to place greater emphasis on anthropology. SIL had built its academic reputation almost exclusively within the discipline of linguistics. For example, linguistic publications outnumbered ethnographic descriptions and anthropological articles by a margin of about five to one before the mid-1970s.[98] At the 1971 biennial conference, the SIL anthropology coordinator Dale Kietzman complained of anthropology's "second rating" in the organization. "We have no specific standard of [anthropological] training, and we provide none," he pointed out.[99] Kietzman recognized that SIL's flank was exposed, since it lacked the same level of sophistication in anthropology that it had attained in linguistics.

The criticism of WBT-SIL prompted SIL's handful of anthropologically trained translators to reassess the effects of the organization's language development and Bible translation programs. In the mid-1970s, contrary to previous statements on the matter, SIL anthropologists began to argue that language development projects could actually increase the likelihood of cultural survival. At the 1976 International Congress of Americanists in Paris, Kietzman asserted that the promotion of vernacular languages and mother-tongue literacy was important in "maintaining ethnic pride and reinforcing tribal mores," which

---

98. Alan C. Wares, ed., *Bibliography of the Summer Institute of Linguistics*, vol. 1, *1935–1975* (Dallas: Summer Institute of Linguistics, 1979).

99. Dale W. Kietzman, "Report of the Coordinator of Anthropology and Community Development," 1971, p. 2, WSA.

in turn had a direct effect on "maintaining group identity and unity."[100] SIL anthropologists also took pains to explain how the organization's advocacy of indigenous territorial rights was an important factor in these people's survival. SIL's first full-time anthropologist, James Yost, in a paper presented at a 1978 meeting of the Society for Applied Anthropology in Merida, Mexico, described how SIL's action to secure a land reserve for the Waorani of Ecuador was a key factor leading to a marked increase in their rate of survival.[101] Paternalism was yet another aspect of SIL's work that the organization's anthropologists labored to counter. Toward this end, Yost argued "that the Waodani [should] be allowed to adapt to [the] expanded physical, social, ideological and technological environment as they would prefer to adapt to it, not as outsiders would prefer to see them adapt to it."[102] External criticisms were an important factor pushing SIL to reinterpret the nature and effects of its language development and Bible translation projects in terms more compatible with the idealist perspective of secular anthropologists.

However, as an evangelical missionary organization, SIL had limits on how far it could shift its programs or philosophy with respect to culture change. SIL anthropologist William Merrifield, in a paper read at the 1977 annual meeting of the American Anthropological Association (AAA), affirmed that SIL remained "committed to culture change, and without apology."[103] The basis for SIL's philosophy rested on the assumption that a "biblically-based ethic has universal relevance to the extent that it mirrors the nature of the Creator."[104] Merrifield cautioned that SIL's religious beliefs should not be taken to suggest that the organization practiced coercion, since not "everyone was expected to receive with alacrity the invitation to become a Christian."[105] Presentation of choice, Merrifield emphasized, was the key to SIL's outlook. "We believe," he stressed,

---

100. Dale W. Kietzman, "Factors Favoring Ethnic Survival," in *Actes du XLIIe Congrès International des Américanistes* (Paris, 1976), 2:535, extract on file at GIAL, Dallas, Texas.

101. James A. Yost, "Community Development and Ethnic Survival: The Wao Case" (paper presented to the Society for Applied Anthropology, April 1978, Merida, Yucatan, Mexico), 2–3, 9, on file at the SIL International Language and Culture Archives, and available at http://www.sil .org/resources/archives/527.

102. Yost, "Community Development and Ethnic Survival," 9. "Waodani" is a variant spelling of "Waorani."

103. Quote from William R. Merrifield, "On the Ethics of Christian Mission" (paper presented at the seventy-sixth annual meeting of the American Anthropological Association, November 29 to December 3, 1977, Houston, Texas), 3, copy in author's possession, later published as William R. Merrifield, "On the Ethics of Christian Mission," in *Current Concerns of Anthropologists and Missionaries,* ed. Karl Franklin (Dallas: International Museum of Cultures, 1987).

104. Merrifield, "On the Ethics of Christian Mission," 4.

105. Merrifield, "On the Ethics of Christian Mission," 6.

"that people are unable to choose unless they are presented with alternatives."[106] In fact, "using force to prevent a change," Merrifield argued elsewhere, could itself "be simply a form of repression."[107] What mattered most from SIL's perspective was that social or cultural adaptation should be constructive in nature. In a 1976 exposition of SIL's official philosophy of culture change, the organization embraced the United Nations Universal Declaration of Human Rights for determining "positive" cultural change. Destructive or "negative" features, such as bathing a sick child in urine as a medicinal curative or revenge killings, were routinely discouraged. Encouraged were those aspects of culture that led to the "well-being" of the society and that fostered "security" for its people.[108] In this important articulation of SIL's philosophy of culture change, the authors emphasized that there was a great deal of commonality between SIL's understanding of Christian ethics and the United Nations Declaration of Human Rights, and even the AAA's own statement of ethics.[109] Trusting in the fundamental morality of its position, SIL unswervingly stood by its Christian-based philosophy of indigenous culture change.

As the 1970s unfolded, there was little to suggest that SIL had altered its basic strategies. Anthropology had gained some measure of prominence—after 1974, new translators were required to take at least one university course in cultural anthropology—and SIL anthropologists preached the gospel of cultural sensitivity. They had also undertaken a project to recast SIL's philosophy of culture change in more idealist terms. Yet the organization had made little headway in its effort to include nationals as fellow members, and it remained steadfast and unapologetic in its stance on the desirability of "positive" cultural change. The twin goals of Bible translation and Christian conversion also endured. Critics were therefore both dismayed and mystified at SIL's staying power. In March 1980, the *Latinamerica Press* expressed its bewilderment that, even after years of anthropologists' calls for SIL's expulsion and promises by governments to eject the organization, the mission nonetheless "shows no signs of faltering."[110] During the 1970s and early 1980s, SIL left only three countries permanently.

106. Merrifield, "On the Ethics of Christian Mission," 8.

107. Philip Baer and William R. Merrifield, *Two Studies of the Lacadones of Mexico* (Norman: Summer Institute of Linguistics of the University of Oklahoma, 1971), 355.

108. Eugene Loos, Patricia Davis, and Mary Ruth Wise, "Culture Change and the Development of the Whole Person: An Exposition of the Philosophy and Methods of the Summer Institute of Linguistics," in *Bilingual Education: An Experience in Peruvian Amazonia*, ed. Mildred L. Larson and Patricia M. Davis (Washington, DC: Center for Applied Linguistics, [1976] 1981), 358–61.

109. Loos, Davis, and Wise, "Culture Change," 386.

110. June Carolyn Erlick, "Indian Control Law Coming Up for Debate in Colombian Congress," *Latinamerican Press* 12, no. 11 (March 13, 1980): 1, TA 43940.

The fall of South Vietnam precipitated SIL's evacuation; Nepal refused to renew its contract; and it was ejected from Panama, although members continued to gain entry by obtaining thirty-day visas.[111] Why, then, with persistent calls from the political and academic Left, did the organization continue to prosper in the late 1970s and beyond?

This question will be answered in two parts. By examining more closely the criticism against SIL from within the intellectual setting in which it arose, we will demonstrate the degree to which a specific and transient historical setting shaped the critical anthropologists' analysis of WBT-SIL. Second, we will take the measure of the criticism against WBT-SIL on its own merits. Was any of the criticism in fact deserved, and if so, in what way? It is expected that this twofold analysis will allow us to explain WBT-SIL's resilience.

The Criticism in Context

In the 1920s and 1930s, an often unstated objective of many anthropologists was a critique of middle-class mores, liberal democracy, and capitalism.[112] In the period between the late 1960s and the early 1980s, many anthropologists were possessed of a similar sentiment, which was exemplified by their yearning for social liberation and their embrace of the counterculture movement. The "need for a body of revolutionary theory which deals with the question of consciousness, culture, and social action so evident in today's world," wrote anthropologist Mina Davis Caulfield in 1969, "is a need which I feel for my *own* liberation."[113] The influence of the sexual revolution and counterculture movements on anthropology was unmistakable at the 1970 AAA annual meeting in San Diego. The anthropologist Herbert S. Lewis later recalled that by "overwhelming voice vote the membership of the AAA gave its blessing to sexual relations of any kind between consenting adults, and the smell of pot was in the air."[114] The criticism

111. Bendor-Samuel to SIL board of directors, June 15, 1984, WSA; Cameron Townsend to Billy Graham, May 17, 1979, TA 36300; "Twenty Bible Translators Expelled by Panama," *Charlotte News*, July 7, 1981, 4C, TA 44847; David Watters, *At the Foot of the Snows: A Journey of Faith and Words among the Kham-Speaking People of Nepal* (Seattle: Engage Faith Press, 2011), 216.

112. George E. Marcus and Michael M. J. Fischer, *Anthropology as Cultural Critique: An Experimental Moment in the Human Sciences* (Chicago: University of Chicago Press, 1986), 111–19, 128–31.

113. Mina Davis Caulfield, "Culture and Imperialism," in Hymes, *Reinventing Anthropology*, 209.

114. Herbert S. Lewis, "The Radical Transformation of Anthropology: History Seen through the Annual Meetings of the American Anthropological Association, 1955–2005," *Histories of Anthropology Annual* 5 (2009): 213.

of WBT-SIL was situated within an intellectual milieu where anthropologists were once again challenging traditional social and moral values.

Political scientist Robert A. Gorman made the apropos observation in 1982 that "New Leftism sounds the revolutionary alarm. It is tactical, not theoretical." "Theory," Gorman went on to explain, "is an afterthought, an epiphenomenon conditioned by praxis."[115] Therefore, when New Left political activism found its way into the discipline of anthropology, it tended to usurp detached and objective inquiry. The effects of the politicization of anthropology were readily apparent in the works critical of WBT-SIL. A case in point is Bernard Arcand's chapter in *Is God an American?*, which reads more like tabloid journalism than serious scholarship. WBT-SIL missionaries, he claimed, typically hailed "from rural America" and were therefore "considered backward, ugly farmers by other Americans." In part, Arcand was unable to treat WBT-SIL missionaries in a serious fashion because, as he stated at the outset, "Religious beliefs are not very interesting. I could never work up much enthusiasm for the idea that some people consider the sun a deity, while others wait for a messiah."[116] David Stoll's analysis likewise repeatedly miscarried. When a lack of evidence impeded an argument, he simply settled for guilt by association. In one instance he struck a conspiratorial tone by obliquely suggesting that the meetings SIL Asia area director Richard Pittman held with President Ramón Magsaysay of the Philippines in 1952, and with South Vietnamese president Ngo Dinh Diem in 1956, had some shadowy connection with the CIA. The only evidence Stoll provided was to claim that both presidents were "under the tutelage of Colonel Edward Lansdale of the Central Intelligence Agency" at the time of the meetings.[117] Stoll's examination of WBT-SIL, while often penetrating and detailed, is nonetheless marred by its excessively polemical character and by the author's penchant for intrigue. Caught up in the revolutionary ferment of the day, anthropologists critical of WBT-SIL displayed a pronounced tendency to lapse into an anti-intellectual frame of mind in order to achieve their ends.

SIL scholars found themselves in decidedly unsympathetic company in 1976 at the Forty-First Congress of Americanists in Paris. SIL's Mary Ruth Wise, who held a PhD in linguistics from the University of Michigan (1968), took the podium on September 3 to read a paper on SIL's philosophy of culture change and development. When she began to explain the role of Bible translation in SIL's programs, the audience raucously erupted. The moderator was unable to

---

115. Robert A. Gorman, *Neo-Marxism: The Meanings of Modern Radicalism* (Westport, CT: Greenwood Press, 1982), 274.

116. Arcand, "God Is an American," 77.

117. Stoll, *Fishers of Men*, 87.

quell the outburst, and Wise was forced to leave the platform before finishing her paper. In a subsequent session, Wise brought along two Peruvian bilingual teachers, Gerardo Wiplo Deicat, an Aguaruna, and Leonardo Witantcout, a Ticuna, to discuss their relationships with SIL and to speak on indigenous issues. Witantcout fared only marginally better than had Wise when he argued that the Indians themselves had the right to choose elements of Western culture if they so desired; if indigenous peoples wished to give up polygamy, it was within their prerogative to do so. Shouts of protest immediately erupted from the floor that there was nothing wrong with polygamy.[118] Clearly, liberation from prevailing social mores trumped scholarly objectivity. The harsh reality was that SIL's Christian moral underpinnings were held in contempt by a number of anthropologists.

Anthropologists' eagerness to condemn Western society and Christian missionaries was sometimes matched by their propensity to extol or even self-identify with indigenous culture. Whereas Bernard Arcand was bored by religion, American anthropologist and fellow *Is God an American?* contributor Richard Chase Smith was fascinated by the subject. "We visited the center of the Amuesha universe [and] communed with a group of stones which had the power to hold this earth together," Smith quoted from his ethnographic field notes taken in Peru. "I could feel the power radiating from them. There was something alive about them." At some later point, after SIL had purportedly driven a "Christianizing wedge" into Amuesha society, thereby altering their traditional religious practices, Smith mourned over "how very sad [the stones] must feel now, abandoned, broken, and forgotten."[119] There was a marked tendency among some of WBT-SIL's opponents to characterize primitive society as inherently superior to Western civilization. SIL was therefore looked upon as an unwelcome, and even retrograde, intrusion into indigenous society.

It would be useful to examine the trajectory of anthropology in the 1980s. Smith was not the first, nor the most distinguished, anthropologist to abandon scholarly objectivity and drift into uncritical veneration of indigenous society. In 1983 anthropologist Derek Freeman uncovered considerable evidence that the celebrated anthropologist Margaret Mead had mischaracterized adolescent sexuality in Samoan society. It was rare before about 1970 to find anthropologists conducting field research where fellow anthropologists had previously

---

118. William R. Merrifield, "Report of Paris Meeting: 41st International Congress of Americanists," September 2–9, 1976, TA 33224; Mary Ruth Wise, interview by author, June 30, 2009, Dallas, Texas; William Cameron Townsend, "Report on Congress of Americanists," Paris, October 3, 1976, TA 50130.

119. Richard Chase Smith, "The Summer Institute of Linguistics: Ethnocide Disguised as a Blessing," in Hvalkof and Aaby, *Is God an American?*, 123.

labored. In this case, it proved devastating, since Freeman offered up compelling evidence that Mead's research of the 1930s was marred by her preconceived notions of the nature of "primitive" society, and by her desire to portray primitive society as superior to that of the socially and morally repressive West.[120] Freeman concluded his work with a call for "a more scientific anthropology."[121] It was a timely plea. By the early 1980s, the excesses of the late 1960s and 1970s had produced a sense of confusion within anthropology. In the apt phrasing of anthropologist Herbert Lewis, "The rebellions within anthropology . . . were over-determined."[122] The influence of postmodernism within the discipline beginning in the mid-1980s ensured that Freeman's hopes were more often met with uncertainty than with confidence. "In anthropology and all other human sciences at the moment," observed anthropologist George E. Marcus in 1986, "'high' theoretical discourse—the body of ideas that authoritatively unify a field—is in disarray."[123] The confidence so recently displayed by many anthropologists was giving way to greater circumspection. An appropriate example is Stanley R. Barrett's book *The Rebirth of Anthropological Theory* (1984), wherein he observed "that social behavior is both complex and contradictory." Barrett argued that "virtually every value, norm, decision, and act has alternative (or alternatives) that are potentially its negation." Barrett concluded that "there is no mechanism, whether theoretical, methodological, moral, or pragmatic, to determine which alternative beliefs or actions open to man are intrinsically superior and preferable."[124] Søren Hvalkof and Peter Aaby's *Is God an American?* and David Stoll's *Fishers of Men* were products of a particularly volatile decade in anthropology, but they were also exemplars of a genre that was soon to lose some of its luster as anthropologists began to reckon with the excesses of the recent past and to adjust to the unsettling intellectual currents of the immediate future.

While anthropologists were busy putting their house in order, published attacks on WBT-SIL were mainly left to investigative journalists such as Gerald Colby and Charlotte Dennett, who together published a nine-hundred-page tome purporting to link Nelson Rockefeller and Cameron Townsend as

120. Derek Freeman, *Margaret Mead and Samoa: The Making and Unmaking of an Anthropological Myth* (Cambridge, MA: Harvard University Press, 1983).

121. Freeman, *Margaret Mead and Samoa*, 294–302.

122. Lewis, "Radical Transformation of Anthropology," 208.

123. George E. Marcus, "Ethnography in the Modern World System," in *Writing Culture: The Poetics and Politics of Ethnography*, ed. James Clifford and George E. Marcus (Berkeley: University of California Press, 1986), 166.

124. Stanley R. Barrett, *The Rebirth of Anthropological Theory* (Toronto: University of Toronto Press, 1984), 5.

coconspirators in exploiting Latin America's natural resources.[125] Despite the extraordinary length of *Thy Will Be Done: The Conquest of the Amazon*, its authors did not furnish any evidence that the two men had ever met.[126] Reviewers in the national press frequently found fault with Colby and Dennett's work.[127] A *Washington Post* reviewer, commenting on the strained attempt to link Rockefeller and SIL, suggested that "the authors would have done better to jettison the ill-fitting missionary sub-plot altogether."[128] Of particular relevance is David Stoll's 1996 review. He censured Colby and Dennett for engaging in "power-structure research," which, he charged, "turns everything into a function of deals between powerful white males." Indicative of just how far Stoll had traveled from the 1970s and early 1980s was his suggestion that SIL's cooperative and uncritical stance toward Latin American governments might actually have benefited indigenous peoples. Stoll noted that by serving the state, SIL missionaries "could give hard-pressed native people medicine and schools they would otherwise not have had, not to mention," he acknowledged, "the Bible translations that some have appreciated."[129] Stoll's defense of SIL is a fitting example of an anthropologist discarding a politicized ideological outlook for a more dispassionate appraisal of the evidence regarding the organization.

The Criticism: An Evaluation

Shifting intellectual currents in anthropology ensured that published polemics against SIL began to dwindle after the early 1980s. Despite the transience and politicized nature of the criticism, were the arguments lodged against the organization nonetheless merited? For example, was SIL a scholarly pretender or, conversely, was its scholarship of a higher caliber than the critics contended? Perhaps the most obvious evidence in SIL's favor on this point was its long-

125. Gerald Colby, with Charlotte Dennett, *Thy Will Be Done: The Conquest of the Amazon; Nelson Rockefeller and Evangelism in the Age of Oil* (New York: Harper Perennial, 1995).

126. There is evidence suggesting that Townsend and Rockefeller might have met. According to James Wroughton, a retired SIL government relations officer, the two men crossed paths at the 1945 Peace Conference in Chapultepec, Mexico. Seven years later, in 1952, Townsend sent Wroughton to call on Rockefeller at his hotel in Lima, but the oil magnate had no time for SIL. Wroughton to Rockefeller, June 28, 1952, TA 8404; Wroughton, telephone interview by author, March 6, 2009.

127. Robert Lloyd to Arthur Lightbody, media reviews of *Thy Will Be Done*, confidential memo, February 6, 1996, copy in author's possession.

128. Pamela Constable, "Imperialism in the Rain Forest," *Washington Post*, May 21, 1995, final edition, X06.

129. David Stoll, "Missionaries as Foreign Agents," *American Anthropologist* 98, no. 3 (September 1996): 637.

standing cooperative program at the University of Oklahoma.[130] Likewise, the University of Texas at Arlington (UTA) would not likely have embraced SIL if the organization's professionally trained linguists were incapable of holding their own academically. Then too, Stoll's inference that SIL linguists were ill equipped to engage with Chomsky's generative grammar was a particularly fragile assertion. In the 1970s, SIL maintained cooperative summer programs not only at UTA but also at the University of Washington (Seattle) and the University of North Dakota, as well as at universities in Canada, England, and Australia. Depending upon the institution in question, SIL faculty taught from no fewer than three differing theoretical perspectives, that is, transformational (generative) grammar, stratificational grammar, and Pike's tagmemics.[131] Moreover, SIL linguists had carried out research from a Chomskyan generative perspective from as early as 1966.[132] To be sure, with its large corps of non-professional linguists, not every missionary-translator matched SIL's cadre of professional linguists in academic attainment or quantity of production. Yet it remains true that the organization enjoyed a fine reputation as an institution of applied linguistics, and its better-trained linguists were capable of engaging with a variety of theoretical models.

The charge of ethnocide proved equally untenable. Provoked by David Stoll's "Onward Christian Soldiers" article and Laurie Hart's NACLA piece, Catherine A. Callaghan, an associate professor of linguistics at Ohio State University, recommended in 1975 that the AAA ethics committee investigate SIL on the charge of ethnocide.[133] In his rebuttal of the AAA's ethics case, Kenneth Pike went on record with a concise articulation of WBT-SIL's strategy of serving indigenous peoples from within the framework of state modernization. In his discussion of "cultural pluralism," Pike declared that "we believe that the separate cultural entities in the modern world need to be provided an opportunity for self-realization within the larger society to lead to national coherence-in-diversity within which each group ultimately supports the other."[134] In making the case for SIL, Pike did not avoid the evangelical character of the organization nor evade the subject of Bible translation. Indeed, he argued that with the on-

---

130. Chapter 2 details the SIL–University of Oklahoma cooperative linguistics program.

131. Brend and Pike, *The Summer Institute of Linguistics*, 8, 63, 96–97.

132. John Daly, "Generative Syntax of Mixteco" (PhD diss., Indiana University, 1966); Bruce A. Sommer, "Kunjen Syntax: A Generative View" (PhD diss., University of Hawaii, 1970); Klaus Wedekind, "An Outline of the Grammar of Busa (Nigeria)" (PhD diss., University of Kiel, 1972).

133. Callaghan to James Spradley, AAA, committee on ethics, Macalester College, April 17, 1975, PSC.

134. Kenneth L. Pike to Alan R. Beals, recommendation subcommittee on ethics, AAA, May 21, 1975, p. 6, PSC.

slaught of "secularism" and the inevitable introduction of the "presuppositions of western civilization," translated Scriptures provided indigenous people with an anchor for "hope, dignity and courage, without which neither culture or [the] individual may survive."[135] With the submission of Pike's report to the AAA, SIL's reputation hung in the balance with the most important scholarly anthropological organization in North America, if not the world.

In November 1975, the reviewing subcommittee of the AAA's committee on ethics issued its report, in which the reviewers stated that "further investigation of the matter . . . is unlikely to be fruitful." In fact, the committee applauded SIL for the timely "remedial measures" it took after its workers had, on one occasion, inadvertently introduced a foreign disease into an indigenous community. "The organization [SIL] is almost unique among anthropological organizations in its concern with disease prevention and medical treatment."[136] The subcommittee's report was unanimously accepted by the full AAA ethics committee and, at the Eighty-Fifth AAA meeting of May 1976, the organization's executive board also unanimously placed its seal of approval on the report.[137] The AAA not only exonerated SIL of the ethnocide charge, but also acknowledged SIL as a bona fide anthropological organization and, perhaps most notably, offered its tacit approval of SIL's Christian-based philosophy of culture change.

The concept of ethnocide was itself a dubious one. In a sense, the notion of ethnocide was the product of an overdetermined anthropological idealism that presupposed a hypothetical primitivism that did not reflect the actual experience of indigenous peoples in a globalizing world. SIL translator and anthropologist Thomas Headland, who arrived among the Agta people of the Philippines in 1962 expecting to find an isolated primitive people, was both chagrined and surprised when he one day happened to hear a G-string-attired Agta singing, in English, the familiar American chorus, "Oh, come to the church in the wildwood." "So much for the isolated people at the end of the world," Headland somewhat plaintively recollected in 1990.[138] In 1975, some Waorani in Ecuador invited anthropologist James Yost to inspect an airstrip they had recently constructed at their own initiative. Yost discovered that this effort was undertaken "to bring them outside goods and an outside teacher."[139] Ideal-

---

135. Kenneth L. Pike to Beals, May 21, 1975, p. 6, PSC.

136. Recommendations subcommittee for Case 75-2 to committee on ethics of the AAA, November 19, 1975, p. 1, PSC.

137. Edward J. Lehman, AAA executive director, to Kenneth L. Pike, September 20, 1976, PSC.

138. Thomas N. Headland, "Paradise Revisited," *Sciences* 30, no. 5 (September–October 1990): 45.

139. James A. Yost, "Twenty Years of Contact: The Mechanism of Change in Wao ('Auca') Culture," in *Cultural Transformations in Ethnicity in Modern Ecuador*, ed. Norman E. Whitten (Urbana: University of Illinois Press, 1981), 688.

ist anthropologists might have wished to keep primitive cultures in a pristine state, but manufactured products and new ideas were fast becoming coveted commodities. To withhold these goods, Yost observed, led only to "frustration and desperation." As with Headland, Yost had begun his missionary career with idealist tendencies. He was therefore originally opposed to the Waorani learning Spanish, but when the people themselves expressed a desire to learn Spanish, he was forced to alter his position.[140] Indigenous peoples could and did make choices of their own accord as they managed their expanding range of social interactions. To claim that SIL was guilty of ethnocide was tantamount to suggesting that indigenous peoples were hapless receptacles into which SIL poured its ideology; in actuality, these peoples often made choices based upon their own estimation of the value of what was on offer.

Furthermore, there is mounting evidence that indigenous language development and Bible translation functioned less as tools of cultural imperialism than as potential instruments of indigenous liberation. In the first place, when Western missionaries undertook to spread Christianity in the vernacular, they placed themselves in a rather vulnerable position since their success depended on the indigenous peoples learning to read the language. In turn, once they acquired literacy and the Bible, indigenous peoples possessed resources for asserting both their political and religious independence. The Gambian historian and Yale Divinity School professor Lamin Sanneh, speaking in part from personal experience, argued in an important 1987 article that when "armed with a written vernacular Scripture, converts to Christianity invariably called into question the legitimacy of all schemes of foreign domination—cultural, political and religious."[141] Sanneh likewise concluded in *Translating the Message* (1989) that "missionary translation was instrumental in the emergence of indigenous resistance to colonialism."[142] Among the many examples Sanneh provided as evidence supporting his thesis was the close connection between Zulu language development and Bible translation by missionaries, and the emergence of a Zulu cultural awakening.[143] Other scholars have confirmed Sanneh's claims. A sociological study of religion in El Salvador, where American evangelicals expended considerable missionary resources in the mid-twentieth century, revealed weak to nonexistent correlations between right-wing North American politics and evangelicalism, and Salvadorian Protestantism. "The diffusion of Protestantism

140. Yost, "Community Development and Ethnic Survival," 8–9.

141. Lamin Sanneh, "Christian Missions and the Western Guilt Complex," *Christian Century* 104, no. 11 (April 8, 1987): 333.

142. Lamin Sanneh, *Translating the Message: The Missionary Impact on Culture* (Maryknoll, NY: Orbis, 1989), 123.

143. Sanneh, *Translating the Message*, 167.

in El Salvador," concluded the authors of this study, "may be a cultural challenge, but it is not overtly political." "Rather," the researchers concluded, "Protestantism has provided a strategy for emotional husbandry and personal survival in one of the most difficult environments for the poor in this hemisphere."[144] David Stoll is yet another witness of the connection between missionary language development and indigenous agency. While Stoll still maintained that "SIL can be criticized on many scores," he nevertheless forthrightly noted in 1990 that "much of the leadership of the current native rights organization in the Peruvian Amazon comes out of its [SIL's] bilingual schools."[145] The introduction of vernacular Bible translations and literacy by missionaries, while seen as tools of cultural imperialism by critics of the Western missionary enterprise, often led to the erosion of the missionaries' supposedly hegemonic power and, as well, to the political and cultural empowerment of previously illiterate indigenous peoples.

The charge that SIL was an instrument of US imperialism suffers much the same fate as the ethnocide accusation upon closer inspection of the evidence. The extent to which SIL was esteemed in nations where it served is exemplified by the response to its impending ejection from Peru. During the 1975–1976 transition from the presidency of General Juan Velasco Alvarado to that of General Francisco Morales Bermúdez, SIL came under fire from several quarters.[146] Anti-SIL professors from the linguistics department of San Marcos University called for the organization's explusion.[147] There were also demands for SIL's departure coming from the Confederación Nacional Agaria, a left-of-center organization of small-scale farmers, which hoped to appropriate SIL facilities.[148] Adding to the anti-SIL ferment were rumors, originating from Colombia, that SIL was a front for the Central Intelligence Agency.[149] In March 1976, SIL received word that its contract with Peru would be allowed to lapse and that it would have to depart by the end of the year.[150] As the Peru branch of SIL made preparations in April 1976 for handing over its operations to various Peruvian ministries, branch director Lambert Anderson prayed for "the Lord to do a miracle, [one] that would be something that would be completely outside

---

144. Kenneth M. Coleman et al., "Protestantism in El Salvador: Conventional Wisdom versus the Survey Evidence," in *Rethinking Protestantism in Latin America*, ed. Virginia Garrard-Burnett and David Stoll (Philadelphia: Temple University Press, 1993), 134.

145. David Stoll, *Is Latin America Turning Protestant? The Politics of Evangelical Growth* (Berkeley: University of California Press, 1990), 330.

146. Lambert Anderson to SIL Colombia branch, July 23, 1975, TA 32095.

147. Anderson to Cameron Townsend, January 5, 1976, p. 2, TA 33107.

148. Anderson to Cameron Townsend, April 17, 1976, TA 933011.

149. Anderson to Robbins, January 29, 1976, TA 33525.

150. Anderson to Cameron Townsend, March 22, 1976, TA 33473.

of anything" he could expect. Soon thereafter, on May 4, he received a letter backing SIL signed by the entire linguistics department faculty of the prestigious University of Trujillo.[151] This letter was only a single incident in a larger flood tide of support. Announcements in several of Peru's leading newspapers publicizing SIL's imminent departure were the occasion for advocates of SIL to rise up in defense of the organization. The April 25 editions of Lima papers *La Prensa* and *Expresso* both carried a "declaracion" in support of SIL, which was signed by sixty-six public figures, including academicians, politicians, government ministers, lawyers, businessmen, doctors, air force commanders, navy admirals, and army generals. Even the well-known Peruvian novelist Mario Vargas Llhosa signed the "declaracion" in support of SIL.[152] SIL opponents had suddenly run afoul of influential friends cultivated by SIL government-relations men and Townsend himself over the past three decades. Anderson also noted that the Concilo Evangélico del Peru (Evangelical Council of Peru) declared on the radio their wish for SIL to remain in Peru. Support was also registered at the other end of Peru's social strata when twenty-five indigenous leaders, from five different tribal groups where SIL worked, came knocking on the Peruvian president's door in Lima, with over fifteen hundred signatures in hand endorsing SIL.[153] This outpouring of support was a testament to the effectiveness of SIL's diplomatic efforts over the years and to the widespread support the organization enjoyed at all levels of society.

It is noteworthy that the attempt to unseat SIL came during the disorder that accompanied the toppling of the left-leaning Velasco regime by the right-of-center junta of General Bermúdez in August 1975. If SIL had been widely considered an imperialist instrument, it surely would have been expelled during the Velasco presidency, for it was a period when Peru went so far as to join the Non-Aligned Movement, establish diplomatic relations with the Soviet Union, and purchase Soviet military weaponry, all in an effort to demonstrate its independence from the United States.[154] When General Velasco took power in 1968, he announced that Peru "must stop being a colony of the United States," and he pledged the "definitive emancipation of our homeland."[155] It would appear

---

151. Anderson to Cameron Townsend, May 4, 1976, TA 32996.

152. Anderson to Cameron Townsend, April 26, 1976, TA 33004; annotated copy of *Expresso* article with signatories, TA 41103; "Declaracion Sobre El Instituto Linguistico De Verano," *Expresso*, April 25, 1976, TA 56260; "Piden Siga Funcionando Instituto Lingüístico de Verano en el Perú," *La Prensa*, April 25, 1976, TA 56259.

153. Anderson to Cameron Townsend, May 17, 1976, TA 32987.

154. Ronald Bruce St. John, *The Foreign Policy of Peru* (Boulder, CO: Lynne Rienner Publishers, 1992), 193, 199.

155. "Manifiesto del Gobierno Revolucionario," *Peruvian Political Party Documents*, folder

that SIL's antagonists on the left overplayed their hand by attempting to remove the organization. Once Bermúdez consolidated his power, SIL's contract was quickly reinstated. Branch director Anderson sent out an elated memo in July 1976 relating that "the premier who signed the resolution against us last April 15 suddenly, three months and one day later, was himself deposed."[156] Summing up the year's events in his November report to the executive committee, Anderson noted that a new five-year contract was in the making, which gave SIL even more freedom of action than the previous contract.[157] SIL loyally served governments regardless of political coloring, which was a significant factor in the organization's long-term success abroad.

Mexico was another place where SIL's reputation stood it in good stead. Even after losing its long-standing official contract in Mexico in 1979, SIL continued to operate under a gentlemen's agreement. In 1981 Townsend, accompanied by three seasoned SIL Mexico branch administrators, Robert Goerz, Benjamin Elson, and John Alsop, met with President López Portillo. Townsend thanked the president for awarding him the Aztec Eagle, the highest distinction bestowed upon foreigners, just two years before. Townsend then pled SIL's case, and the president forthwith directed the trio to his private secretary, who was instructed to provide assistance so that the organization could continue working in Mexico.[158] Although SIL's contract was not formally renewed and obtaining visas remained problematic, this incident demonstrates how personal relationships, which are so very important in Latin America, maintained an open door for the organization under conditions where it might otherwise have been denied any access at all.

SIL's linguistic, literacy, and community development efforts garnered for the organization a steady stream of accolades and awards. Two examples among many were the Philippine government's honoring of SIL with the Ramon Magsaysay Award for International Understanding in 1973 and the Bolivian government's awarding SIL its Medal of Honor for work in bilingual education in 1980.[159] The steady stream of tributes paid to SIL and the lengthening list of

6, reel 1, quoted in Hal Brands, *Latin America's Cold War* (Cambridge, MA: Harvard University Press, 2010), 80.

156. Anderson to Gerald K. Elder, July 20, 1976, TA 32877.

157. Lambert Anderson, "Branch Director's Report to the E.C.," November 30, 1976, TA 41097; Anderson to Cameron Townsend, March 28, 1978, TA 35261; "Peruvian Branch of SIL Gets Official Support," *Linguistic Reporter* 19, no. 6 (March 1977): 1, TA 42762.

158. Cameron Townsend, "Two Presidents . . . and the Chamulas," in Townsend et al., *Being Vectored In: The Harmonics of International Relations* (n.p.: Summer Institute of Linguistics, 1989), 144.

159. Margaret Hickey, chairman, advisory committee on voluntary foreign aid, Department

awards collected by Townsend during the 1970s offer additional support for the contention that SIL was generally looked upon with favor by the governments of the states it served.[160]

At the international level, the anti-SIL polemics faltered because of a recurring tendency to exaggerate the hegemonic role of the United States while at the same time underestimating Latin American agency. On this point, recent postrevisionist Cold War historiography provides a helpful corrective. The Duke University historian Hal Brands offers compelling evidence that Latin American governments were far more capable of managing the heavy hand of US influence in the region than many scholars have previously supposed.[161] For example, Brands reveals that the widespread presence of antirevolutionary and anticommunist sentiment among Latin American military governments was not simply a US-inspired phenomenon. National Security Doctrine (NSD), which was a body of theory concerned with imposing internal state control as a means to counter revolution, was in fact more a legacy of French military training prior to World War II than a US-inculcated idea. Indeed, the presence of NSD in many cases predated the Kennedy administration's counterinsurgency efforts in the region.[162] Brands fittingly points out that Venezuela received far more US military assistance than did Peru in the 1970s; yet it was Peru that experienced two coups in less than a decade whereas Venezuela's military government became less interventionist in internal affairs.[163] Many Latin American governments also took the US debacle in Vietnam as a sign of weakness, and this led to a more assertive diplomacy on their part in the 1970s, as amply attested by the Velasco regime's overtures toward the Soviet Union.[164] The United States was certainly a powerful force in the region, but anthropologists critical of WBT-SIL exaggerated its hegemonic power over Latin American nations.

Had critical anthropologists examined Townsend's efforts to establish SIL in the Soviet Union in the 1970s, they would have been confronted with yet more evidence undermining their accusations that SIL was in collusion with US hegemonic ambitions. In the late 1960s, the septuagenarian Townsend cast

---

of State, Agency for International Development, Washington, DC, to Edward R. Boyer, October 1, 1973, TA 30015; "Press Release for 1973 Ramon Magsaysay Award for International Understanding," TA 43167; *The Ramon Magsaysay Awards: 1973–1975* (Manila: Carmelo and Bauermann Printing Corp., 1982), 104–19; "Awards and Commendations," SIL International, accessed June 10, 2017, http://www.sil.org/literacy/awards.htm.

160. "Honors Received by Cameron Townsend," n.d., TA 43129.

161. Brands, *Latin America's Cold War*.

162. Brands, *Latin America's Cold War*, 79.

163. Brands, *Latin America's Cold War*, 80.

164. Brands, *Latin America's Cold War*, 131–34.

about for the "toughest place to go," as Wycliffe's president, George Cowan, later put it.[165] The Iron Curtain loomed as the ideal challenge for this intrepid missionary-diplomat. With the support of the WBT-SIL conference and board, Townsend planned his last major undertaking.[166] A bit of arm twisting among his diplomatic contacts in Mexico eventually secured him an invitation to the Soviet Union under the auspices of the Russian Academy of Sciences in the fall of 1968.[167] In many ways Townsend's venture in the Soviet Union was the Mexico experiment all over again. He and Elaine formed relationships with linguists at the Academy of Sciences in Moscow and toured the Caucasus region as bilingual education specialists. During their expedition of 1973–1974, they even towed a camper trailer behind an enormous Chrysler New Yorker sedan, driving from Armenia to Leningrad;[168] in similar fashion, he and Elvira had driven around Mexico forty years earlier. Townsend returned to the USSR every year until 1979.

Just how pragmatic Townsend was willing to be to pursue his aims is evident in his glowing appraisal of the Soviet Union's experiment in socialism. From Moscow in 1968 he crafted a letter to his old friend Lázaro Cárdenas, the former president of Mexico. "Perhaps," Townsend wrote, "the simple fact that they [the Russian linguists in the Academy of Sciences] have received us as friends will serve as proof that everything in the USSR is not as bad as it has been painted in the capitalistic press of my country."[169] In his estimation, Soviet-style socialism was remarkably similar to New Testament Christianity. "Soviet philosophy and Christian principle have quite a bit in common," he wrote in his 1975 publicity book, *The USSR as We Saw It*. To present an optimistic picture of the Soviet Union, Townsend downplayed some of the more unpleasant aspects of Soviet history. He allowed that Aleksandr Solzhenitsyn and others had "suffered at the hands of tough atheists," but he almost casually brushed this off; after all, he had not observed any persecution, so it "must be a thing of the past."[170] In 1977 he complained in writing to Ambassador Anatoly F. Dobrynin that he was

165. George M. Cowan, Hefley interview, c. 1970, p. 14, TA 43764.

166. WBT-SIL conference, minute extracts, May 24–June 2, 1971, S-14, WSA.

167. Cameron Townsend to Boris A. Kazantsev, Consejero de la Embajda de la Unión Repúblicas Socialistas Soviéticas, Mexico City, July 29, 1968, TA 26021; William Cameron Townsend, "Though I Be Nothing . . . I Can Do All Things through Christ: Report on First Trip to USSR," April 1969, TA 50045.

168. William Cameron Townsend and Elaine Mielke Townsend, *The USSR as We Saw It: From Armenia to Russia; Many Languages, Much Progress, Sincere Friends* (Waxhaw, NC: International Friendship, 1975).

169. Cameron Townsend to Cárdenas, October 1968, p. 2, TA 25970.

170. William Cameron Townsend and Elaine Mielke Townsend, *USSR as We Saw It*, 42–43.

"so tired of the constant propaganda" emanating from the United States "about persecution of Christians and dissenters in the USSR."[171] Likewise, most of the blame for poor US-Soviet relations was laid at the feet of the United States. Townsend remarked to Dobrynin in 1976 that he was "embarrassed that détente has been opposed by so many of my fellow citizens."[172] Here was nothing less than a complete about-face from his earlier Red Scare tactics. Townsend was hardly a reliable Cold War warrior or an unalloyed proponent of US foreign policy. What critics failed to understand was the sincerity with which WBT-SIL and Cameron Townsend took the policy of "service to all."

On the other side of the ledger, Townsend's contradictory position on communism, ranging from outright anticommunist remarks to glowing pro-Soviet statements, is just one example of many that lends credibility to Stoll's contention that WBT-SIL's rhetoric sometimes breached the "evangelical standard of honesty." Stoll was not alone in presuming that evangelicals should hew closer to the facts than the somewhat elastic versions of the truth deployed by WBT-SIL. It was the dubious nature of dual-organization rhetoric, we recall, that ultimately led charter board member Eugene Nida to resign in 1953.[173] Townsend had long taught his troops that a partial truth was not equivalent to falsehood. "Was it honest," he asked rhetorically in 1975, "for the Son of God to come down to earth and live among men without revealing who He was?"[174] If Jesus had not always felt compelled to tell the whole truth, then, in Townsend's way of thinking, WBT-SIL was under no obligation to do so either. WBT-SIL took on a measure of its founder's pragmatism, and was therefore, at least on occasion, willing to obfuscate rather than clarify its actions as a means of accomplishing its goals.

If the organization is to be faulted for slipping into a pragmatic frame of mind, it is also true that WBT-SIL offered social goods that both the state and indigenous peoples often desired. WBT-SIL most certainly engaged unabashedly in nation-building exercises that sought to incorporate indigenous peoples into the state, and it also aspired to change these indigenous peoples spiritually, socially, and psychologically. The debate between SIL and secular anthropologists was over differing assumptions about the moral legitimacy of these objectives. At the end of the day, WBT-SIL won the debate because it was offering social goods that both the state and indigenous peoples often desired, or alternatively rejected on their own terms. At the most basic level, critical

171. Cameron Townsend to Dobrynin, March 3, 1977, TA 33872.

172. Cameron Townsend to Dobrynin, April 7, 1976, p. 2, TA 32642.

173. Nida's resignation from SIL is detailed in chapter 4.

174. William Cameron Townsend and Richard S. Pittman, *Remember All the Way* (Huntington Beach, CA: Wycliffe Bible Translators, 1975), 61.

anthropologists had little of tangible value to offer indigenous peoples. Anthropologist Robert Jay recollects an event that transpired near the conclusion of his field research in a Malay village in 1963. "I was approached," Jay confessed in 1969, "by a small delegation of villagers, who said to me, 'You are a professor in an American university who has studied our village for a whole year. You must have learned a lot about us in that time that could help us with our problems here. Will you please tell us some of what you know?'" Jay frankly admitted that he was "taken aback," adding that "I had only been thinking of my knowledge as of interest only to my colleagues, and had gathered material toward that end, not material selected out of any sense of what any of the villagers might want."[175] The critics, for all the heat and noise they generated, had little of tangible value to offer indigenous peoples save for an ideological perspective that was useful only as a fulcrum for political agitation or revolutionary fervor. Alternatively, those who could begin to alleviate the very real ills that plagued indigenous peoples, such as malnutrition, poor health, and powerlessness due to a lack of education and illiteracy, had the upper hand. A willingness to invest finances and endure long careers in remote areas serving the needs of the poor made for a force difficult to dislodge. Therefore, it was WBT-SIL's contributions of substance to nations and indigenous communities that ultimately checked the critics.

The accusations that WBT-SIL was a collaborator in US imperialist ambitions and that it was guilty of ethnocide do not hold up very well under close scrutiny. That WBT-SIL weathered the storms of the 1970s was due in no small part to the weak foundations upon which the criticisms were constructed. By wrongly equating the Western missionary enterprise with cultural imperialism, many anthropologists' interpretations of missionary intentions miscarried. The most significant effect the critics had on WBT-SIL was in pressing the organization to shift its philosophy of culture change from a decidedly realist perspective to what might be referred to as a moderate idealist perspective. In actual practice, however, there was little fundamental alteration in its programs. As the critics began to turn their gaze elsewhere, WBT-SIL was left to pursue much the same set of strategies and goals that it had from its inception.

However, the accusations and attacks leveled at the organization during the 1970s and early 1980s did leave a mark. The embrace between SIL and governments in some places later turned into something closer to cooperation between divorced parties in a formerly happy marriage. Such was the case with Mexico, where the government contract was never reinstated, and new branch head-

---

175. Robert Jay, "Personal and Extrapersonal in Anthropology," in Hymes, *Reinventing Anthropology*, 378.

quarters were established in Catalina (Tucson), Arizona, to support SIL personnel, who worked in the country under various kinds of visas and permits.[176] SIL linguists and anthropologists bore the brunt of unremitting animosity that continued down to recent times in some areas of academia. One place where they persistently experienced rough treatment was at meetings of the AAA, not by the organization itself, but mostly by individual anthropologists. Animus was regularly directed toward SIL scholars at meetings of the International Congress of the Americanists, as well.[177] Internally, WBT and SIL expended a tremendous amount of time and energy haggling over the dual identity, which so often figured in the various conspiracy theories directed against the organization. To address the issue, a "WBT and SIL Image Conference" was convened in 1981. The opening statement that was to guide the proceedings read: "In these days of Is God an American, we cannot afford to have a fuzzy image." A committee on opposition was formed and a study of the opposition was initiated, but neither clarification nor restructuring of the dual organization was forthcoming.[178] The weight of history and institutional habit proved too heavy, and it was another two decades before Wycliffe and SIL became fully separated.[179] The deeper and more lasting effects of the barrage of criticism in the 1970s and 1980s, and the more sporadic criticism in later years, are more easily sensed from inside the organization than documented from without. There remains, down to the present day, an undercurrent of wariness that sometimes manifests itself as suspicious reflexes when the organization comes under scrutiny from unknown or untrusted quarters.

WBT-SIL circa 1982

Cameron Townsend was laid to rest at the Jungle Aviation and Radio Service (JAARS) headquarters in Waxhaw, North Carolina, in April 1982. In that year, WBT-SIL's missionary presence extended to forty countries in five major geographic regions (North America, Latin America, Asia, Africa, and Oceania), where 4,500 members of the organization labored in or in support of over 761 indigenous language projects. In keeping with this pattern of growth, the organization's reported income had risen from $6.7 million in 1971 to $44 mil-

176. Elson to Cameron Townsend, December 11, 1980, TA 37171; February 12, 1981, TA 38373; March 3, 1981, TA 38350.

177. Headland, email to author, August 7, 2014.

178. Thomas Moore, "Report to the Administration on Opposition" (unpublished report, October 1989), p. 55, Pittman Special Collection, Language and Culture Archives, Dallas, Texas.

179. These events are discussed in the epilogue.

lion in 1982.[180] By all appearances, Townsend's legacy was secure. The JAARS headquarters was a fitting resting place for this inventive missionary and champion of international goodwill. Missionary aircraft buzzed around in the sky overhead, and situated next to Townsend's final resting place was a museum dedicated to former Mexican president Lázaro Cárdenas and the nation of Mexico. It was here too in Waxhaw that Townsend had once dreamt of building an "International Friendship City."[181] Such grand visionary schemes perished with the founder, and WBT-SIL was thereafter mostly content to build upon the foundations he laid. While there would be no more projects akin to the World's Fair venture or the International Goodwill airplane project, the organization nevertheless remained fully committed to Townsend's basic strategies. In a 1982 progress report, members were reminded of Townsend's "five principles": trusting God for the impossible, the linguistic approach, service to all, pioneering in unwritten languages, and giving people the Bible.[182] These five principles served as points of light leading the organization into the future.

"It used to be said of faith mission builders," WBT-SIL's arch-critic David Stoll wrote in 1981, "that they were men greatly used of God: Cameron Townsend used God, faith became his handmaiden."[183] Stoll came uncomfortably close to the truth here in describing Townsend's particular inflection of Keswick theology. In the 1930s Townsend and L. L. Legters had turned the older, more restrained faith mission approach on its head with their enthusiastic and confident style that assumed that success was tantamount to God's approval of their venture. Wycliffe president George Cowan kept up the tradition of "trusting God for the impossible" in Townsend's stead. In a 1982 article, written for Wycliffe's in-house organ *In Other Words*, Cowan disputed the old Keswick refrain of "let go and let God." "Some think that faith is doing nothing and letting God do everything," he wrote. But this was not at all the case in the Wycliffe world, where the goals that Townsend articulated were considered the objects of one's faith. "Faith goals," Cowan contended, "is not a contradiction in terms but a call to trust and obey, to work toward certain objectives."[184] In

180. *Translation*, July–September 1971, 14; *Translation*, October–December 1971, 15; "The World of Wycliffe," progress report, a special edition of *In Other Words* 8, no. 4 (Summer 1982): 1, on file at GIAL.

181. Draft map by Townsend of envisaged International Friendship City, c. 1969, TA 46447; WCT to Cuauhtémoc Cárdenas (son of Lázaro Cárdenas), May 11, 1973, TA 46446.

182. "The Five Principles," progress report, a special edition of *In Other Words* 8, no. 4 (Summer 1982): 18, on file at GIAL.

183. Stoll, "Words Can Be Used," 31.

184. George M. Cowan, "Faith and Goals: A Contradiction of Terms?" *In Other Words* 8, no. 3 (April 1982): 4, on file at GIAL.

the same issue, former pilot and incoming Wycliffe president Bernard May enthused that "there's no need to slow down." "Our Lord has gone before us," May emphasized, "and as long as he says that way is clear, there's no need to throttle back."[185] Townsend had long ago taught his disciples to think of WBT-SIL's strategies as God-given; therefore, it was quite proper to operationalize one's faith by pursuing the organization's ends. "Faith mission," in the Wycliffe vernacular, meant grasping the future with both hands.

At the International Linguistics Center in Dallas, Kenneth Pike's presence ensured that SIL held fast to its scholarly commitment. Although Pike retired as president of SIL in 1979, he continued lecturing and writing for nearly two more decades.[186] Thus another generation of evangelical students was encouraged to apply both their "hearts and minds" to the missionary task.[187] One was a young graduate student pursuing a degree in anthropology in the early 1970s, whose introduction to Pike changed the course of her life. "Weary after the culture wars of the 1960s, I had no hope or direction left and only a little faith," explained a mature Elinor Abbot in 1996, adding that "the anti-intellectualism of much of the religious response to the secular challenge left me alienated and discouraged." A friend passed to her some of Pike's writings, and Abbot "found Pike's synthesis of scholarship and devotion to God was genuine[,] . . . and the encounter was life-changing and eye-opening for me."[188] Abbot joined WBT-SIL in the 1970s and was one of SIL's early anthropologists. Pike also relentlessly pushed students and missionary-translators to "publish or perish."[189] Pike's call was heeded, and scholarly production proceeded apace. As of 1982, SIL's bibliography listed 9,513 entries, a good number of which were published in refereed journals.[190] The measure of Pike's own scholarly success was exemplified in 1985 when he was elected to the prestigious National Academy of Sciences.[191] In the early 1980s, scholarly pursuits remained alive and well in SIL.

Townsend's insistence on humanitarian service remained undiminished in

185. Bernard May, "Climbing on Course: Living at Cruising Speed," *In Other Words* 8, no. 3 (April 1982): 8, on file at GIAL.

186. Thomas N. Headland, "A Tribute to the Life of Kenneth L. Pike," in Wise, Headland, and Brend, *Language and Life*, 13.

187. Headland, "A Tribute," 16.

188. Abbot to the John Templeton Foundation, October 6, 1996, in "Letters about Kenneth Lee Pike: Written in Support of His Nomination for the Templeton Prize for Progress in Religion," p. 20, PSC.

189. Kenneth L. Pike, with Hugh Steven, *Pike's Perspectives*, 1.

190. *Bibliography of the Summer Institute of Linguistics* (Dallas: Summer Institute of Linguistics, 1992).

191. Thomas N. Headland, "Kenneth Lee Pike: A Biographical Memoir," in *Biographical Memoirs*, vol. 84 (Washington, DC: National Academies Press, 2004), 4.

SIL as he departed the scene. In 1979 the United Nations Educational, Scientific and Cultural Organization (UNESCO) recognized SIL's contribution to indigenous peoples by awarding the institute the International Reading Association Literacy Prize.[192] Perhaps Kenneth Pike's nomination in 1982 for the Nobel Peace Prize was the most significant indicator that SIL had lived up to the ideal of service to humanity.[193] In part, these accolades for SIL were the result of the organization's concern for the "whole person" as opposed to the narrower aim of Christian conversion.[194] This perspective remained a hallmark of WBT-SIL. In its 1981 statement on the mission's philosophy and methods, SIL maintained that it was the organization's "conviction that every human being has the need and the right to fulfillment as a whole person."[195] Serving humanity endured as an essential component of the organization's overall strategy as it entered the 1980s.

Measured by interview responses, what Wycliffe missionaries were probably most proud of was that by the time of Townsend's passing in 1982, 160 New Testament translations had been completed by WBT-SIL missionary-translators and their indigenous cotranslators. However, research conducted over the previous decade revealed that the task before the organization was much larger than previously thought. In 1982, WBT-SIL estimated that some three thousand language groups were still without mother-tongue Scriptures.[196] "There is," wrote Bernard May to Wycliffe supporters, "much, much more to be done."[197] For the remainder of the 1980s, WBT-SIL had the goal of recruiting three thousand additional members and publishing five hundred more translations of the New Testament.[198] Pioneer Bible translating remained at the center of the organization's efforts.

Cameron Townsend was a visionary, not an administrator. It was therefore left to his lieutenants to impose greater administrative order on WBT-SIL. As they went about this process, the organization's leaders were careful to preserve Townsend's guiding principles. The marriage of the founder's strategies with ample funding proved a powerful and durable combination. In a sense, it was

192. "Serving People around the World: Progress Report, 1979" (Huntington Beach, CA: Summer Institute of Linguistics, 1979), 5, copy on file at GIAL.

193. "To Honor Kenneth Lee Pike on the Occasion of His 70th Birthday: Papers of His Nomination for the Nobel Peace Prize for the Year 1982," compiled by Adam Makkai, executive director of the Linguistic Association of Canada and the United States (June 1982), on file at the PSC.

194. Discussed in chapter 5.

195. Loos, Davis, and Wise, "Culture Change," 368.

196. "The World of Wycliffe," 1.

197. May, WBT to "Dear Friends," letter printed in *In Other Words* 8, no. 4 (Summer 1982), on file at GIAL.

198. "Faith Goals for the 1980s," *In Other Words* 8, no. 4 (Summer 1982): 16, on file at GIAL.

the organization's power that distressed its critics. They feared its capacity to do exactly what it set out to accomplish: effecting indigenous social, religious, and psychological change. This brought the organization into conflict with anthropologists over the ethical legitimacy of these objectives. In the main, it was the revolutionary intellectual milieu of the 1960s and 1970s that invested anthropologists with the confidence that they held the moral high ground. The convulsions that wracked anthropology in many places during the 1960s and 1970s were of sufficient intensity to blind WBT-SIL's critics to the fact that the organization was generally supplying desired social and religious goods. Once the intellectual mood shifted in the early 1980s, the criticism directed at WBT-SIL by anthropologists began to dissipate. In light of the evidence presented here, WBT-SIL's critics often mischaracterized the organization. This was particularly the case with the ethnocide charge. Had there been material grounds for this accusation, it is almost certain that the AAA, when the discipline of anthropology was at its most politicized and radicalized moment, would have uncovered damning evidence. The generally favorable response to SIL's projects by governments and indigenous peoples also suggests that the criticism was mostly undeserved. The critical campaign mounted against WBT-SIL by anthropologists miscarried in the long run because it was transient and mostly unjustified. Most importantly, however, the criticism failed to do lasting damage because it was a point of view not widely shared by the peoples and the nations served by WBT-SIL.

Conclusion

It is a near certainty that the dual-structured WBT-SIL was, more than any other twentieth-century mission, a compound of both the Enlightenment-style voluntary mission and the Romantic-style faith mission. Therefore, when the Christian missionary impulse was refracted through the multidimensional character of this dual organization, WBT-SIL was bound to cause confusion since it maintained elements of a typical faith mission while at the same time boldly breaking with convention. On the side of tradition, WBT-SIL missionaries eschewed direct solicitation, and instead opted to garner their personal financial support "in faith." Thus, at home in North America, and later in other Western nations, WBT-SIL members presented themselves as faith missionaries and projected a familiar missionary image to the evangelical public. Since the reading of the translated Scriptures was expected to result in conversions to Christianity, the organization's primary religious aim was in keeping with that of most faith missions. Likewise, the mission remained evangelical in its religious temperament. Viewed from the perspective of these factors, WBT-SIL maintained the most salient characteristics of a classical faith missionary enterprise. On the other hand, when operating abroad under the banner of SIL, members tended to mask their missionary identity to one degree or another and, significantly, did not preach, baptize converts, or found churches under SIL auspices. Faith mission constraints on funding fell by the wayside at the organizational level, as occurred with the International Goodwill airplane project and Cameron Townsend's fund-raising exploits during the World's Fair project. The organization's emphases on literacy and education, not to mention cooperating with governments and serving Roman Catholics, were all in one way or another departures from the norms of mid-twentieth-century faith mission practice. This merging of traditional faith mission qualities with decidedly uncharacteristic features provoked criticism from nearly all sides while also creating an entirely new style of mission that ultimately proved remarkably successful on most fronts.

The restructuring of the faith mission model carried out by Townsend was an exercise that necessarily involved the articulation of new ideas in the spiritual vernacular. In other words, it was essential to invoke a higher authority for the renovations in mission thought and practice that he envisaged. Keswick theology, or Victorious Life Testimony, was an important motive force in faith missions, but submission to the rigors of missionary life and selfless devotion to the missionary task were also vital elements of Keswick spirituality. Townsend, along with L. L. Legters and Howard Dinwiddie, transformed the Keswick mantra of "let go and let God" into something closer to "take hold and do for God." One looks in vain for Townsend passively enduring impediments obstructing his goals or patiently waiting on funds to arrive "in faith." On the contrary, Townsend was entirely self-possessed in assuming that he knew exactly what God wished him to accomplish. Impelled by his entrepreneurial temperament and fortified by this restyled Keswick spirituality, WBT-SIL's founder turned the faith mission template inside out. As WBT-SIL set out to "trust God for the impossible," the generally more modest and measured conduct of conventional faith missions, exemplified by the Central American Mission and the Missionary Aviation Fellowship, gave way to a more dynamic and less restrained pursuit of the organization's aims.

It would be difficult to find among Townsend's North American evangelical contemporaries any other figure that shared the same level of confidence in the potential for human progress. Townsend's mind-set, marked by a strong belief in the enlightening effects of biblical literacy and basic education, shared much in common with the early twentieth-century exponents of sociopolitical Progressivism. Townsend was so deeply committed to the idea of progress, in a popular sense, that it colored just about every endeavor he embarked upon, from the social uplift of indigenous peoples to designs for international goodwill. The founder's pervasive optimism created in WBT-SIL an organizational culture that was less susceptible to the pessimistic and unconstructive qualities that were so often features of fundamentalist organizations. Rather than expending energy shoring up the ramparts of a separated fundamentalist citadel, WBT-SIL missionaries directed their efforts outward in a more public-spirited fashion. This is not to suggest that WBT-SIL followed the path trodden by the Social Gospelers, for few if any members of the organization would have conflated human progress with Christianity. In WBT-SIL, however, missionary activity was understood as more than the mere gathering up of souls for eternity. Conversion to Christianity was also valued for its putative power to expand the cognitive horizons of indigenous peoples so that they could better come to terms with modernity, and thus enjoy a richer life in the present. WBT-SIL's progressive sociopolitical outlook was a key factor in the successful realization of the founder's varied strategies, such as service to all, bilingual education, and international goodwill.

In pursuit of his aims, Townsend emphasized cooperation with governments of all political persuasions and advocated a respectful stance toward all religious perspectives. By following in the founder's footsteps, WBT-SIL ended up serving just about everyone from Catholics to communists. Whereas less daring evangelicals worried that these strategies might lead the faithful down the road to perdition, Townsend demonstrated that it was possible to cooperate with secularists and to serve nonevangelicals without necessarily diluting one's evangelical faith. Moreover, what Townsend understood, but many of his detractors struggled to comprehend, was that benevolent service could draw the levers of power and means of influence closer to hand. As a master of the art of persuasion, Townsend schooled his people in the art of soft power rather than in the use of the blunt instruments employed by militant fundamentalists. Whether for merely objective purposes or out of authentic compassion—and most typically some combination of both—WBT-SIL broke the prevailing evangelical taboos to serve those who were otherwise considered adversaries or even enemies of the faith.

WBT-SIL's pragmatic adaptation to varied circumstances did not pass without consequences for the organizational mind-set. The mission's readiness to equivocate bordered at times on what might be called "situational ethics." When the entire truth threatened the organization's plans, a partial truth was at times considered sufficient. WBT-SIL charted new frontiers where old verities could hinder if not halt its progress. For radically new ideas such as those Townsend was experimenting with to take root, perhaps it was obligatory to create favorable circumstances for their maturation. Only when it was observed that these innovative approaches were effective in practice was it possible to pull back the veil completely. There was, though, the ever-present danger of slipping into a strategy of the ends justifying the means, and this indubitably happened on more than one occasion. In pursuit of what was seen as the greater good, WBT-SIL tore a page from the Good Book and followed the scriptural injunction to be wise as serpents but innocent as doves in an effort to accomplish its aims.

Ultimately the strategy of "service to all" succeeded because WBT-SIL had something of value to offer developing nations beyond its religious objectives. It was WBT-SIL's willingness to serve nearly anyone regardless of religious or political convictions that undermined the arguments of the organization's secular opponents. Anthropologists critical of Christian missions made a rather poor choice in singling out WBT-SIL as the organization upon which to construct their antimission arguments. On the surface, WBT-SIL appeared as a likely candidate for censure; after all, it was one of the largest private organizations at work among the world's indigenous peoples, it publicly espoused a Christian-based philosophy of culture change, and it was supposed by its critics to be populated by narrow-minded fundamentalists. Thus critics assumed that SIL cared little for indigenous peoples' aspirations, and that it was more concerned with Christianizing and Westernizing these peoples than anything else. Without a doubt the World's Fair mural of the early 1960s, which depicted Chief Tariri's transformation "from savage to citizen," would have sent shivers down the spine of just about any anthropologist of the 1970s. SIL's anthropological realist outlook on culture change, which survived into the mid-1970s, obscured the fact that it was actually providing social and religious goods that were often appreciated and desired. The criticism directed at SIL by anthropologists has never ceased completely. However, as the leftward revolutionary upheaval within the discipline of anthropology began to abate after the 1980s, some critical anthropologists conceded that SIL, for all its purported sins, perhaps did more good than harm while others simply chose to ignore the organization altogether. Much of the literature of the 1970s and early 1980s that was critical of WBT-SIL, especially the early writings of David Stoll and the essays published in the Søren Hvalkof and Peter Aaby volume, was the product of a politically volatile period in the discipline of anthropology, and these works should therefore be handled with a measure of skepticism.[1]

WBT-SIL's apolitical service also undercuts assumptions that the organization was of a piece with US right-wing politics. Billy Graham's tenure on the WBT-SIL board of directors, Vice President Richard Nixon's christening of an SIL aircraft, the wooing of anticommunist and procapitalist donors, and Townsend's anticommunist rhetoric must all be set alongside WBT-SIL's service to governments from across the political spectrum. With his grand visions for fostering international goodwill, including in the USSR, WBT-SIL's founder was largely free of political provincialism. The apolitical character of Townsend's hopes for international peace differs sharply from that of other midcentury evangelicals. Carl F. H. Henry, the neo-evangelical theologian, immediately

---

1. Søren Hvalkof and Peter Aaby, eds., *Is God an American? An Anthropological Perspective on the Missionary Work of the Summer Institute of Linguistics* (London: Survival International; Copenhagen: International Work Group for Indigenous Affairs, 1981); David Stoll, "Onward Christian Soldiers," *Michigan Daily*, March 26, 1974; David Stoll, *Fishers of Men or Founders of Empire? The Wycliffe Bible Translators in Latin America* (Cambridge, MA: Cultural Survival, 1982).

comes to mind, along with his fellow faculty members at Fuller Seminary. Even as Henry and his neo-evangelical brethren set out to reform fundamentalism, they remained steadfastly conservative in their domestic political convictions and staunchly anticommunist in their international outlook.[2] Townsend, on the other hand, was too pragmatic and idealistic to be straitjacketed into any narrow political ideology. From the time he took up Mexico's cause against North American oil companies in the 1930s to his glowing reports of life in the Soviet Union in the 1970s, Townsend demonstrated that he was prepared to ally himself and his organization with just about any regime in order to gain a foothold for SIL. WBT-SIL certainly played upon the sentiments of the Right in the United States for financial support, but this in no way dictated the organization's political stance outside North America. Under Townsend's direction, WBT-SIL became adept at advantageously adapting itself to varying social and political contexts both at home and abroad. If this pragmatic approach meant serving regimes hostile to the United States, such as Peru from 1968 to 1975, then SIL was prepared to do so. WBT-SIL was hardly an ideological hostage of the Right in the United States.

The strategy of service to all was made possible by the dual-organization construct. On a practical level, the dual structure offered WBT-SIL the flexibility to adapt both its programs and its publicity to widely differing constituencies. By incorporating as a humanitarian and scientific organization, SIL made itself a convenient partner for governments. The nonreligious nature of SIL, or at least the appearance thereof, fostered close cooperation between the organization and government ministries, particularly in nations where secularizing forces were attempting to disentangle the church from the state. Concomitantly, the Wycliffe side of the organization presented to the North American evangelical public a recognizable faith mission image, and it drew heavily upon the traditions and ethos of the faith mission legacy to build support. While the dual nature of WBT-SIL was perhaps confusing at times, the public relations and programmatic benefits of the dual strategy outweighed the complications it sometimes generated.

Separation of the religious and scientific aspects of the organization also contributed to the flourishing of scholarship in SIL. Unlike most Bible colleges, which existed solely within the evangelical subculture, SIL was obliged to maintain a level of scholarly attainment that met nationally recognized university standards. With its scientific reputation at stake, SIL rose to the challenge. The academic status that SIL achieved, along with its secular veneer, gave it the

---

2. George M. Marsden, *Reforming Fundamentalism: Fuller Seminary and the New Evangelicalism* (Grand Rapids: Eerdmans, 1987), 60–63.

opportunity to develop linguistic programs in cooperation not only with the University of Oklahoma and the University of Texas at Arlington but also with many other academic institutions and universities around the world. Intra-organizationally, the SIL side also created something of an academic haven that helped to insulate it from the strains of anti-intellectualism that occasionally threatened to undermine scholarly activity, especially when such endeavors seemed far removed from the immediate goal of Bible translation. It is not difficult to imagine that scholarship would have suffered if the organization had been constituted in a unitary fashion under the religiously orientated Wycliffe Bible Translators.

The distinctly linguistic nature of SIL was an important factor in yet another respect. Some of the most heated debates in mid-twentieth-century North American evangelicalism were sparked by differences of opinion on matters of doctrine and theology. In WBT-SIL, theology ranked well behind linguistics in scholarly importance, as is evidenced by the dearth of seminarians and theologians in the organization. Moreover, doctrinal discussions remained internal affairs and never became public spectacles. The Wycliffe side satisfied the Christian public by publishing the organization's conservative doctrinal statement, while behind the scenes quietly allowing for some latitude in theological position, so long as such deviations remained within broadly evangelical boundaries. By not quibbling over doctrinal punctilios publicly, the organization largely avoided explosive polemics over such matters. WBT-SIL was therefore never near the center of the doctrinal controversies that sporadically rocked North American evangelicalism throughout the twentieth century. While WBT-SIL did come under attack from the evangelical right for its intrepid policy toward Catholics and for its service to governments, these strategies seemed to have had less devastating effects than the hotly contested theological debates that fractured so many other organizations and relationships. This relegation of theology in WBT-SIL to a secondary status, coupled with an overwhelming attention to linguistics, eliminated a considerable source of potential tension both within WBT-SIL and from without.

By successfully navigating the precarious landscape of post–World War II evangelicalism, WBT-SIL provides an important counterexample to the current historiography on the emergence of neo-evangelicalism in which Fuller Seminary and its faculty loom large.[3] SIL's fruitful engagement with secular

---

3. John D'Elia, *A Place at the Table: George Eldon Ladd and the Rehabilitation of Evangelical Scholarship* (New York: Oxford University Press, 2008); Gary Dorrien, *The Remaking of Evangelical Theology* (Louisville: Westminster John Knox, 1998), 49–101; Marsden, *Reforming Fundamentalism*; Rudolph Nelson, *The Making and Unmaking of an Evangelical Mind: The Case of Edward Carnell* (New York: Cambridge University Press, 1987); Garth M. Rosell, *The Surprising Work of*

academia—Kenneth Pike's tenure at the University of Michigan being an outstanding example—clearly makes for a study in contrasts with the troubled development of Fuller Seminary. While it is true that SIL experienced its own internal debates over the role and status of scholarship, scriptural inerrancy, and mission strategy, these controversies never became comparable with the clashes afflicting Fuller. As the case of WBT-SIL attests, there was an equally significant but rather different scholarly advance paralleling that of Fuller. Indeed, in SIL, evangelicals can rightly claim to have created one of the world's foremost institutions of applied linguistics, and it therefore deserves a prominent place in the historiography of evangelical institutions of higher learning.

This examination of WBT-SIL in its North American setting reveals that the postwar divide between the fundamentalists and the new evangelicals was mirrored in the faith mission community. The fact that the conservative Interdenominational Foreign Mission Association (IFMA) took an increasingly unfavorable view of WBT-SIL while the progressive Evangelical Foreign Missions Association (EFMA) welcomed it in the late 1950s is indicative of this cleavage. Therefore the faith missions of IFMA, including some of the largest, such as the Africa Inland Mission (AIM) and the Sudan Interior Mission (SIM), should not unconditionally be classified as "moderate" or "progressive," as Joel Carpenter specified in his study of the emergence of progressive fundamentalism.[4] The mission historian Klaus Fiedler also underestimated the degree to which the fundamentalist-evangelical divide was reflected in the cleavage between IFMA and EFMA before the early 1960s.[5] An important corrective to Carpenter's and Fiedler's views is Edwin L. Frizen's study of IFMA, an overlooked and important source that details the separatist instincts of IFMA and its oppositional stance toward the new evangelicalism before the early to mid 1960s.[6] Therefore, Frizen's history of IFMA and the account presented here of the Wycliffe-IFMA controversy both indicate that the faith missions belonging to this conservative and separatist association were clearly not as moderate as some historians have contended.

Another factor in WBT-SIL successfully avoiding internal splinters was its distinctive organizational structure. In the first place, the extensive overlap

---

God: Harold John Ockenga, Billy Graham, and the Rebirth of Evangelicalism (Grand Rapids: Baker Academic, 2008), 201–6.

4. Joel A. Carpenter, *Revive Us Again: The Reawakening of American Fundamentalism* (New York: Oxford University Press, 1997), 83–84.

5. Klaus Fiedler, *The Story of Faith Missions: From Hudson Taylor to Present Day Africa* (Irvine, CA: Regnum, 1994), 14, 27–28.

6. Edwin L. Frizen Jr., *75 Years of IFMA, 1917–1992: The Nondenominational Missions Movement* (Wheaton, IL: Interdenominational Foreign Mission Association, 1992).

between the board of directors and executive management eliminated potential conflicts between two seats of power. Populating the board of directors with an overwhelming majority of WBT-SIL leaders ensured that it had its finger on the pulse of the organization, whereas a truly external board would probably have known less about the day-to-day workings of the mission. Board decisions were therefore, more or less by design, in alignment with the objectives of the executive leadership. In the second place, the principle of democracy, where the ultimate power over the organization was vested in the membership through elected delegates to the biennial conference, served to create a sense of ownership while at the same time widely diffusing power. Under this democratic organizational structure, neither the board of directors nor upper management could forcibly act contrary to the desires of the broader membership. In the third place, the founder's subordinate position (theoretically) to the board of directors tempered somewhat Townsend's power, by forcing him to win the favor of a majority of the membership to effect any significant change of direction. Townsend's failed bid to include Roman Catholics in the WBT-SIL membership ranks as the most visible instance of the membership curtailing his power to act. WBT-SIL's unconventional structure at once distributed power widely and created a sense of shared responsibility for the organization. Although greater administrative control was imposed from the mid to late 1960s, this basic organizational structure remained in place into the 1980s. In effect, WBT-SIL was less a top-down organization than a close-knit familial association, excepting when its *paterfamilias* Cameron Townsend threw his weight around, and this democratic structure contributed to the unity of the membership and to the fact that the organization never experienced a significant rupture or split of any consequence.

A democratic organizational structure did not, however, prevent WBT-SIL from evolving into a modern parachurch mission. Edward Irving's 1824 sermon lamenting the businesslike mission structures of his day would pertain as well to WBT-SIL in the 1970s. The very fact that the organization hired a management consultant in the early 1960s indicates just how far WBT-SIL had come toward merging the faith mission approach with modern management practices. Likewise, the rather direct funding appeals launched under the banner of Wycliffe Associates were a long way from orphanage founder George Müller's hand-to-mouth faith style of obtaining funds. The rise of the sophisticated missionary organization is what led Andrew Walls to refer to these large, powerful, and technocratic missions as "Missions Incorporated."[7] By not only adapting but

---

7. Andrew F. Walls, *The Missionary Movement in Christian History: Studies in the Transmission of the Faith* (Maryknoll, NY: Orbis, 1996), 238.

also avidly pursuing efficiency and technological innovation, WBT-SIL was a trendsetter in the refashioning of the traditional faith mission into a modern parachurch enterprise.

Lastly, can WBT-SIL legitimately be lumped together with other American missionary institutions as a disseminator of "fundamentalist Americanism," as was claimed in 1996 by the authors of *Exporting the American Gospel*?[8] Recall that the "belief system" of "fundamentalist Americanism" was defined by those authors as a composite of "biblical inerrancy, dispensationalism, and millenarianism, along with strong doses of Americanism."[9] Moreover, it was argued that this potent form of conservative evangelicalism not only "encouraged authoritarianism" but was also marked by "an aggressive tendency to identify U.S. interests with God's interests" and by "an intolerance of peoples from different cultures."[10] Among North American evangelical missions, it would be difficult to find an organization that was further removed from this brand of fundamentalism than WBT-SIL. While the connections drawn between American political power and global Protestant fundamentalism by Brouwer, Gifford, and Rose are not under scrutiny here, it is unmistakable that they were, as was the case with other scholars, led astray in their assessment and classification of WBT-SIL by having based their assumptions on David Stoll's *Fishers of Men or Founders of Empire?* That book, as has been shown here, was guilty of misrepresentation.

What, then, can be said of WBT-SIL within the context of mid-twentieth-century North American evangelicalism? By practicing engagement from the 1930s on rather than separation, and affirmation rather than confrontation, WBT-SIL had more in common with the progressive fundamentalists than with the classical fundamentalists. Indeed, Townsend founded the mission on a nonseparatist and nonmilitant approach. To be sure, these points were debated in 1947 and 1948, but no change of course toward militancy or separatism ever transpired. Moreover, the classical fundamentalists' affection for premillennial dispensationalism was not mirrored in the WBT-SIL mind. After a few rounds of debate in the early 1950s, even some flexibility was permitted on the most essential of fundamentalism's doctrines, scriptural inerrancy, by crafting a somewhat ambiguous statement on biblical inspiration. In essence, the 1955 statement simply marked a return to the wider interpretation of inspiration that had been the status quo on the topic since the organization's founding. Then too there was WBT-SIL's concern not only with born-again conversion but also

---

8. Steve Brouwer, Paul Gifford, and Susan D. Rose, *Exporting the American Gospel: Global Christian Fundamentalism* (New York: Routledge, 1996), 18, 185.

9. Brouwer, Gifford, and Rose, *Exporting the American Gospel*, 265.

10. Brouwer, Gifford, and Rose, *Exporting the American Gospel*, 270.

with education, social justice, and international goodwill. Perhaps more than anything else, WBT-SIL's 1959 departure from IFMA attested to the organization's nonfundamentalist status. It can therefore be stated with confidence that WBT-SIL never truly bore the marks of a fundamentalist institution, since it lacked the cluster of tendencies that defined fundamentalism. The mission was, on the whole, from its earliest days, not so much fundamentalist in character as broadly evangelical in nature, and it remained so into the 1980s.

WBT-SIL's influence on North American evangelicalism is more difficult to assess. The dual-organization structure certainly limited its impact on evangelicalism, since the Wycliffe side of the mission presented a rather traditional image to the churchgoing public. Moreover, the organization was not active in promoting revival in America nor was it self-consciously involved in the project to reform fundamentalism. As with SIL's academic achievements, which were directed into linguistics and not the rehabilitation of evangelical theology, the organization's missionary aims were less concerned with spiritual life at home than abroad. Yet, by recruiting, training, indoctrinating, and deploying hundreds and then thousands of progressive-minded missionaries, WBT-SIL became an important participant in post-WWII evangelicalism. The organization not only sustained rapid growth to become the largest North American evangelical mission by the early 1960s, but it accomplished this feat despite its status as one of the most unusual missions in its radical strategies. For these two reasons, if for nothing else, WBT-SIL certainly deserves a larger place in the historiography of twentieth-century North American evangelicalism than it has yet been afforded.

Sensitized to the plight of Guatemala's indigenous peoples at a tender age, Cameron Townsend conceived of social justice for these peoples in terms of biblical literacy and upward mobility. To accomplish his aims, he turned the Keswick-style spirit of personal submissiveness and patient waiting on God into an aggressive and confident acting upon what God presumably desired for his chosen vessels to accomplish. To overcome the obstacles presented by a growing nationalism in the developing world, Townsend conceived the dual organization. The dual structure was a novelty that irritated friends and foes alike, but proved its worth in creating conceptual space for the flowering of new modes of action and thought. In the years before World War II, when many faith missions were exhibiting such fundamentalist characteristics as separatism and anti-intellectualism, the organization steered toward a position where these qualities could be mostly curtailed or even dispensed with while yet retaining at least some of the cardinal features of a faith mission. This movement away from traditional faith mission structures carried WBT-SIL far from conventional mission practice into cooperating with governments and serving Roman

Catholics. Essential to this transformational project was WBT-SIL's pragmatic and progressive organizational mind-set. The mission was by design able to take full advantage of the nationalistic and anticlerical realities of Latin America, thereby providing a platform from which to assist indigenous peoples in their transition to modernity and from which to carry out mother-tongue Bible translation projects. Likewise at home in North America, WBT broke with traditional faith mission reticence in order to appeal to a consumer-orientated marketplace. While there is no doubt that on occasion WBT-SIL shaded the truth, the organization never abandoned its dual commitment to humanitarian service and the provision of a translated New Testament for every known language community in the world. In the final analysis, the organization prospered because it remained true to the vision of Cameron Townsend. In the footsteps of the founder, WBT-SIL adapted its programs and public image to a variety of contexts at home and abroad by becoming "all things to all men," while at the same time placing service to indigenous peoples and non-Western nations above sectarian or political interests "for the gospel's sake."

Epilogue

The development of Wycliffe Bible Translators (WBT) and the Summer Institute of Linguistics (SIL) in the 1980s was accompanied by both continuity and change. While a full accounting of the organization in the post-1980 period is beyond the scope of this volume, what follows is a very brief survey of the main contours of the organization's development (now, more properly, organizations', plural), down to the recent past. Unless otherwise specified in footnotes, all the information presented here was drawn from publicly available sources, such as organizational web pages, annual reports, and publicity materials.

The expansion of the WBT and the SIL (the latter now organized as SIL International) continued apace in the decades after the passing of William Cameron Townsend in 1982. From its inauspicious beginnings in 1934, the WBT and SIL combination flourished to become an international "family" of related organizations with a combined staff of over 5,500 members, representing more than sixty nationalities, and with a combined annual income of approximately $237 million in 2012. In 1980 Wycliffe Bible Translators International (WBTI) was formed, and as of 2013, there were forty-five self-governing national Wycliffe organizations around the world. Over the last couple of decades, the Jungle Aviation and Radio Service (JAARS) extended its repertoire of services beyond aviation and radio communication to include computer technology and software development. Wycliffe Associates (WA) maintained its nationwide series of fund-raising banquets, and it also continued to provide technical and construction services to both SIL and WBT through the efforts of lay volunteers. In 1993, the Seed Company (TSC), an entirely new organization, was formed as an affiliate of Wycliffe to accelerate the number of new Bible translation projects. TSC collaborates with local churches and mother-tongue translators to develop and fund projects to produce Bible translations for their own people. Finally, and most recently, SIL's linguistic training program at the International Linguistics Center was reconstituted as the Graduate Institute of Applied Linguistics (GIAL) in 1999.

One of the more notable changes in the organizational structure was the uncoupling of WBT and SIL, a process that was begun in the 1980s but not completed until 2008, with the appointment of separate chief executives and nonoverlapping boards of directors for each organization. In yet another departure from the past, the composition of the boards was altered to include a majority of nonmember directors from outside of WBT and SIL. These actions were taken largely in response to the shifting center of gravity of Christianity from the West to the East and South. History proved that SIL's John Bendor-Samuel was correct when, in the 1970s, he argued that in the future partnerships with churches and non-Western Christians would play an increasingly larger role in Bible translation.[1] However, it proved difficult for SIL, with its nonsectarian and quasi-secular nature, to relate closely with religious bodies. On the other hand, the religiously orientated WBTI, with its growing roster of national Wycliffe member organizations around the world, was much better positioned to develop partnerships with Christian organizations and churches. Wycliffe therefore moved beyond its traditional recruiting and fund-raising roles to include Bible translation. As for SIL, it continued to relate primarily to governments, nongovernment organizations (NGOs), and universities. These structural changes raise some important questions. Will the two organizations, now fully independent of one another, drift apart? Will the old head-versus-heart dichotomy rear its head, thus dissolving the long-standing symbiotic relationship between the two sides of the organization that maintained the twin emphases of activism and scholarship in creative tension? Only time will tell if the move to separate will ultimately prove beneficial or detrimental.

In February 2011, WBTI began doing business under a new name, Wycliffe Global Alliance (WGA). According to the organization's leadership, the new name better conveyed the twenty-first-century nature of WBTI in that it was no longer a Western-centric enterprise, but rather a worldwide network of partner organizations that focused on Bible translation. To emphasize the international character of the organization, it relocated its corporate headquarters to Singapore. Another indicator of organizational change, one that Townsend would have cheered but did not live to see, was the formation of Wycliffe Russia in the post–Soviet Union era. At the time of this writing, WGA is composed of

1. John Bendor-Samuel's push for national involvement in Bible translation is briefly discussed in chapter 6.

forty-five autonomous WBT national organizations, with an additional sixty non-WGA partner organizations, all participating in Bible translation around the world.

The development of SIL over the past three decades built upon the foundations laid by Kenneth Pike and Eugene Nida. SIL International has carried out linguistic research in no fewer than 2,590 languages spread across nearly one hundred countries. The organization's bibliography continues to expand, and as of 2013 more than forty thousand books, journal articles, dissertations, scholarly papers, Scripture publications, vernacular publications, and unpublished materials (including audio and video) produced by SIL personnel in almost 2,000 languages were listed. From 1982 down to the present day, 209 SIL members earned doctorates and another 920 garnered master's degrees.[2] Linguistic research and language documentation remain core competencies of SIL, and the results of these efforts are made available in SIL's *Ethnologue: Languages of the World*, one of the most important reference works on the 7,105 known living languages spoken around the world. In 1993 SIL was granted special consultative status by the United Nations Economic and Social Council (ECOSOC) and the United Nations Educational, Scientific and Cultural Organization (UNESCO). In 2007, SIL was appointed by the International Organization for Standardization (ISO) as the registration authority for maintaining an international database of the world's languages under the provisions of ISO 639–3. SIL's contributions in the areas of language development and literacy also continued to evoke appreciation. A singular example was the Philippine government's issuing a series of postal stamps in 2003 commemorating SIL's contributions to that nation over the previous five decades. The returns on investment of Pike and Nida's efforts to secure and maintain SIL's scholarly status continued to compound.

In the late 1990s, SIL began seeking regional accreditation for its linguistic school based at the International Linguistics Center campus in Dallas, Texas. Upon discovering that accreditation could only be conferred upon a separate institution, SIL established the Graduate Institute of Applied Linguistics (GIAL) in 1999. As of 2013, GIAL offered graduate-level majors in applied linguistics, language and culture studies, and world arts, with concentrations in Bible translation, descriptive linguistics, cross-cultural service, literacy, sociolinguistics, language survey, and Scripture engagement. SIL also continued to maintain partnership programs at a number of other academic institutions, such as the University of North Dakota (UND). In 2011 SIL and UND marked sixty years

---

2. These figures were kindly supplied by Carlos Rolando González, SIL International Academic Personnel Coordinator.

of partnership in linguistics training. Outside of North America, SIL offered degree programs in cooperation with universities in no fewer than sixteen countries.

As it was from the day Townsend first set foot in Mexico, Bible translation today remains the motive force behind the Wycliffe and SIL family of organizations. As of 2012, taken together, these organizations have had a hand in the translation of 830 complete New Testaments and thirty-five complete Bibles. Also as of 2012, under the umbrella of Wycliffe Global Alliance, over one hundred organizations from around the globe were involved in 1,537 translation projects. What began with a starry-eyed visionary in the 1930s had matured into nothing less than a worldwide Bible translation movement.

By the turn of the twenty-first century, it was becoming increasingly evident that the Christianity exported by Western missionaries from the beginning of the age of exploration was not dying out with the demise of imperialism. Rather, the Christian religion was rapidly expanding in the postcolonial era, thus confounding conventional wisdom that fully expected the "white man's religion" to dwindle as the stranglehold of the Western powers was loosened in former colonial possessions. In his landmark 2002 work entitled *The Next Christendom*, the historian Philip Jenkins appositely notes that "Amazing as it may appear to a blasé West, Christianity exercises an overwhelming global appeal, which shows not the slightest sign of waning."[3] The assumption that the Christian faith in the South and East would decline was based on the erroneous idea that Christianity was solely a Western religion, when in fact in its first several centuries of existence it was more robust and of greater extent in Asia and North Africa than it was in Europe.[4] As the British historian Andrew Walls and the Gambian historian Lamin Sanneh have argued, Christianity is eminently translatable.[5] "Cross-cultural transmission," Walls wrote, "is integral to Christian faith."[6] The spread of Christianity, Walls also pointed out, is serial rather than progressive, moving through phases in a process of transmission, appropriation, and eventually regression. Therefore, the modern missionary period was simply another "episode . . . in an ongoing story." And if this is

---

3. Philip Jenkins, *The Next Christendom: The Coming of Global Christianity* (New York: Oxford University Press, 2002), 39.

4. Jenkins, *The Next Christendom*, 15.

5. Lamin Sanneh, *Translating the Message: The Missionary Impact on Culture* (Maryknoll, NY: Orbis, 1989); Andrew F. Walls, *The Missionary Movement in Christian History: Studies in the Transmission of Faith* (Maryknoll, NY: Orbis, 1996); Andrew F. Walls, *The Cross-Cultural Process in Christian History: Studies in the Transmission and Appropriation of Faith* (Maryknoll, NY: Orbis, 2002).

6. Walls, *Missionary Movement*, 257.

true—the evidence certainly suggests that it is—then Walls is correct to state that "the idea of territorial Christianity . . . lies irretrievably broken."[7] The translatability of Christianity, and hence Bible translation itself, strongly suggests that the WBT and SIL combination was, and remains, a central player in the rapid expansion of Christianity in the South and East. "If it were necessary," wrote the well-known historian Mark Noll in his 1997 history of Christianity, "to find a single turning point symbolizing the movement of Christianity from the North to the South, a good candidate might be the founding of Wycliffe Bible Translators in 1934."[8] Cameron Townsend's vision of a Bible in every language fired the imaginations of hundreds and then thousands of missionaries, donors, and indigenous peoples (whose absence from the process would have made Bible translation impossible) to make that dream a reality. The crucial role played by the WBT and SIL combination in the globalization of Christianity invites closer examination. This volume, along with those of William Svelmoe and Todd Hartch, has only scratched the surface of what will hopefully eventuate in a more comprehensive and detailed examination of the organization's part in, to borrow from Andrew Walls, the "transmission and appropriation" of the Christian faith in the twentieth century.

7. Walls, *Missionary Movement*, 258.

8. Mark A. Noll, *Turning Points: Decisive Moments in the History of Christianity* (Grand Raipds: Baker, 1997), 308.

Interviews

John Alsop, September 4, 2008, Dallas, Texas
Loretta Anderson, September 28, 2009, Waxhaw, North Carolina
Herman Aschmann, July 20, 2006, Dallas, Texas
Elmer Ash, September 22, 2009, Waxhaw, North Carolina
Ruth Ash, September 22, 2009, Waxhaw, North Carolina
Lester Bancroft, September 17, 2009, Waxhaw, North Carolina
Margaret Bancroft, September 17, 2009, Waxhaw, North Carolina
Doris Bartholomew, August 4, 2009, Catalina, Arizona
John Bendor-Samuel, February 21, 2006, Nairobi, Kenya
Faith Blight, July 2, 2009, Dallas, Texas
Richard Blight, July 2, 2009, Dallas, Texas
Morris Carney, June 15, 2006, Waxhaw, North Carolina
George Cowan, August 20, 2007, Santa Ana, California
Ellis Diebler, June 14, 2006, Waxhaw, North Carolina
Martha (King) Diebler, June 14, 2006, Waxhaw, North Carolina
T. Wayne Dye, July 22, 2014, Dallas, Texas
Adelle Elson, August 6, 2007, Waxhaw, North Carolina
Benjamin Elson, August 6, 2007, Waxhaw, North Carolina
Alda Fletcher, September 24, 2009, Waxhaw, North Carolina
George Fletcher, September 24, 2009, Waxhaw, North Carolina
Grace Fuqua, September 3, 2008, Dallas, Texas
Florence Gerdel, June 5, 2008, and June 15, 2008, Dallas, Texas
George Hart, June 14, 2006, Waxhaw, North Carolina
Cecil Hawkins, July 10, 2009, Dallas, Texas
Jack Henderson, September 24, 2009, Waxhaw, North Carolina

Donald Hesse, August 29, 2008, Dallas, Texas
Lois Jean Hesse, August 29, 2008, Dallas, Texas
Calvin Hibbard, August 6, 2007, Waxhaw, North Carolina
Hilda Hoogshagen, July 31, 2009, Catalina, Arizona
Searle Hoogshagen, July 31, 2009, Catalina, Arizona
Esther Jenkins, September 29, 2009, Waxhaw, North Carolina
Rister Jenkins, September 29, 2009, Waxhaw, North Carolina
Nancy Lanier, July 31, 2009, Catalina, Arizona
John Lind, July 27, 2009, Wilcox, Arizona
Royce Lind, July 27, 2009, Wilcox, Arizona
Robert Longacre, June 29, 2010, Dallas, Texas
Betty Loos, June 25, 2009, Dallas, Texas
Eugene Loos, June 25, 2009, Dallas, Texas
Edward Loving, September 17, 2009, Waxhaw, North Carolina
Aretta Loving, September 17, 2009, Waxhaw, North Carolina
Arthur Lynip, June 17, 2006, Waxhaw, North Carolina
Bernard May, September 18, 2009, Waxhaw, North Carolina
Dorothy Minor, September 10, 2008, Dallas, Texas
Eugene Minor, September 10, 2008, Dallas, Texas
Bruce Moore, July 1, 2009, Dallas, Texas
Evelyn Pike, July 19, 2006, Dallas, Texas
Frank Robbins, September 2, 2008, and September 9, 2008, Dallas, Texas
Eugene Scott, September 21, 2009, Waxhaw, North Carolina
Marie Scott, September 21, 2009, Waxhaw, North Carolina
William Sischo, July 29, 2009, Catalina, Arizona
Marianna Slocum, June 5, 2008, and June 15, 2008, Dallas, Texas
Donald Smith, September 18, 2009, Waxhaw, North Carolina
Emily Stairs, June 29, 2009, Dallas, Texas
Glen Stairs, June 29, 2009, Dallas, Texas
Viola Stewart, June 29, 2009, Dallas, Texas
Martha (Duff) Tripp, September 29, 2009, Waxhaw, North Carolina
Robert Tripp, September 29, 2009, Waxhaw, North Carolina
Vivian (Forsberg) Van Wynan, September 7, 2009, Dallas, Texas
Katherine Voightlander, July 29, 2009, Catalina, Arizona
Mary Walker, July 29, 2009, Catalina, Arizona
Kenneth Watters, July 21, 2006, by telephone
Mary Ruth Wise, June 30, 2009, Dallas, Texas
Gloria (Grey) Wroughton, June 20, 2008, Dallas, Texas
James Wroughton, June 20, 2008, Dallas, Texas

SIL University Affiliations (1990)

Universidad Nacional de Santiago del Estero, Argentina
Université Nationale du Benin, Benin
Université Nationale de Ouagadougou, Burkina Faso
University of Yaoundé, Cameroon
Trinity Western University, Canada
Universidad Católica de Valparaiso, Chile
Guizhou University, China
Université Marien Ngoua, Congo
Université d'Abidjan, Côte d'Ivoire
Université de la Sorbonne, France
Universidad Mariano Gálvez, Guatemala
Cenderwasih University, Indonesia
Hasanuddin University, Indonesia
Pattimura University, Indonesia
University of Nairobi, Kenya
Universidade Eduardo Mondlane, Mozambique
L'Université de Niamey, Niger
Universidad de Lima, Peru
University of the Philippines, Manila
University of Juba, Sudan
Mahidol University, Thailand
Payap University, Thailand
Thammasat University, Thailand
Makerere University, Uganda
University of Reading, United Kingdom

University of North Dakota, USA
University of Oregon at Eugene, USA
University of Texas at Arlington, USA

Note: The character of these affiliations varied but constituted one or more SIL members teaching at the institution, engagement with SIL in cooperative research projects, or sponsorship of SIL linguistic research. (Compiled by SIL's Richard Pittman and Calvin Hibbard, TA 43212.)

Bibliography

Primary Sources

Archives

Billy Graham Center Archives, Wheaton, Illinois (BGA)

Central American Mission Archives, Dallas, Texas (CAA)

Graduate Institute of Applied Linguistics, Dallas, Texas (GIAL)

L. Tom Perry Special Collections, Harold B. Lee Library, Brigham Young University, Provo, Utah

Mexico Branch of the Summer Institute of Linguistics Archives, Catalina, Arizona (MBA)

Pike Special Collection, SIL International Language and Culture Archives, Dallas, Texas (PSC)

Pittman Special Collection, SIL International Language and Culture Archives, Dallas, Texas

SIL International Language and Culture Archives, Dallas, Texas (LCA)

University of Oklahoma Archives, Western History Collection, Norman, Oklahoma (UOA)

William Cameron Townsend Archives, JAARS Center, Waxhaw, North Carolina (TA)

Wycliffe Bible Translators and SIL International Corporate Archives, Dallas, Texas (WSA)

Books

Baer, Philip, and William R. Merrifield. *Two Studies of the Lacadones of Mexico.* Norman: Summer Institute of Linguistics of the University of Oklahoma, 1971.

Barrett, Stanley R. *The Rebirth of Anthropological Theory.* Toronto: University of Toronto Press, 1984.

Beekman, John, and John Callow. *Translating the Word of God, with Scripture and Topical Indexes.* Grand Rapids: Zondervan, 1974.

Bibliography of the Summer Institute of Linguistics. Dallas: Summer Institute of Linguistics, 1992.

Blanshard, Paul. *American Freedom and Catholic Power.* Boston: Beacon, (1949) 1950.

Brouwer, Steve, Paul Gifford, and Susan D. Rose. *Exporting the American Gospel: Global Christian Fundamentalism.* New York: Routledge, 1996.

Buckingham, Jamie. *Into Glory: The Miracle Filled Story of the Jungle Aviation and Radio Service—Taking Wycliffe Bible Translators to the Earth's Remotest Regions.* Plainfield, NJ: Logos International, 1974.

Capa, Cornell, and Dale Kietzman, eds. *Language and Faith.* Santa Ana, CA: Wycliffe Bible Translators, 1972.

Carnegie, Dale. *How to Win Friends and Influence People.* Rev. ed. New York: Pocket Books, (1936) 1981.

Carnell, Edward J. *The Case for Orthodox Theology.* Philadelphia: Westminster, 1959.

Clifford, James, and George E. Marcus, eds. *Writing Culture: The Poetics and Politics of Ethnography.* Berkeley: University of California Press, 1986.

Colby, Gerald, with Charlotte Dennett. *Thy Will Be Done: The Conquest of the Amazon; Nelson Rockefeller and Evangelism in the Age of Oil.* New York: Harper Perennial, 1995.

Cook, Harold R. *Missionary Life and Work: A Discussion of Principles and Practices of Missions.* Chicago: Moody Press, 1959.

Cowan, George M. *The Word That Kindles: People and Principles That Fueled a Worldwide Bible Translation Movement.* Chappaqua, NY: Christian Herald Books, 1979.

Daniels, Josephus. *Shirt-Sleeve Diplomat: Ambassador to Mexico, 1933–1942.* Chapel Hill: University of North Carolina Press, 1947.

Diamond, Stanley. *In Search of the Primitive: A Critique of Civilization.* New Brunswick, NJ: Transaction Books, 1974.

Dollar, George W. *The Fight for Fundamentalism.* Orlando: Daniels Publishing, 1983.

————. *A History of Fundamentalism in America.* Greenville, SC: Bob Jones University Press, 1973.

Dostal, Walter, ed. *The Situation of the Indian in South America.* Montevideo, Uruguay: Tierra Nueva, 1972.

Eakin, Lucille. *Nuevo Destino: The Life Story of a Shipibo Bilingual Educator.* Dallas: SIL Museum of Anthropology, 1980.

Elliot, Elisabeth. *Shadow of the Almighty: The Life and Testament of Jim Elliot.* New York: Harper and Brothers, 1958.

————. *Through Gates of Splendor.* New York: Harper, 1957.

Engel, James F., and William Dyrness. *Changing the Mind of Missions: Where Have We Gone Wrong?* Downers Grove: InterVarsity, 2000.

Garvin, Paul L., ed. *Method and Theory in Linguistics.* The Hague: Mouton, 1970.

Graham, Billy. *Just as I Am: The Autobiography of Billy Graham.* New York: Harper Paperbacks, 1997.

Grimes, Joseph E. *The Thread of Discourse.* The Hague: Mouton, 1975.

Gutt, Ernst-August. *Relevance Theory: A Guide to Successful Communication in Translation.* Dallas: SIL International, 1992.

————. *Translation and Relevance: Cognition and Context.* Oxford: Basil Blackwell, 1991.

Hall, Clarence W. *Miracle in Cannibal Country.* Costa Mesa, CA: Gift Publications, 1980.

Henry, Carl F. H. *Confessions of a Theologian: An Autobiography.* Waco: Word, 1986.

————. *Remaking the Modern Mind.* Grand Rapids: Eerdmans, 1946.

————. *The Uneasy Conscience of Modern Fundamentalism.* Grand Rapids: Eerdmans, 1947.

Hitt, Russell T. *Jungle Pilot: The Gripping Story of the Life and Witness of Nate Saint, Martyred Missionary to Ecuador.* Grand Rapids: Discovery House Publishers, 1997.

Hocking, Ernest William. *Re-Thinking Missions: A Laymen's Inquiry after One Hundred Years.* New York, 1932.

Huxley, Matthew, and Cornell Capa. *Farewell to Eden.* New York: Harper and Row, 1964.

Hvalkof, Søren, and Peter Aaby, eds. *Is God an American? An Anthropological Perspective on the Missionary Work of the Summer Institute of Linguistics.* London: Survival International; Copenhagen: International Work Group for Indigenous Affairs, 1981.

Hymes, Dell, ed. *Reinventing Anthropology.* New York: Pantheon, (1969) 1972.

Kane, J. Herbert. *Faith, Mighty Faith: A Handbook of the Interdenominational*

Foreign Mission Association. New York: Interdenominational Foreign Mission Association, 1956.

Larson, Mildred L. *Meaning-Based Translation: A Guide to Cross-Language Equivalence.* New York: University Press of America, 1984.

Larson, Mildred, and Lois Dodds. *Treasure in Clay Pots: An Amazon People on the Wheel of Change.* Dallas: Person to Person Books, 1985.

Lindsell, Harold. *The Battle for the Bible.* Grand Rapids: Zondervan, 1976.

Longacre, Robert E. *An Anatomy of Speech Notions.* Lisse, Netherlands: Peter de Ridder Publications, 1976.

———. *Discourse, Paragraph, and Sentence Structure in Selected Philippine Languages.* Santa Ana, CA: Summer Institute of Linguistics, 1968.

———. *The Grammar of Discourse.* New York: Plenum Publishing, 1983.

Marcus, George E., and Michael M. J. Fischer. *Anthropology as Cultural Critique: An Experimental Moment in the Human Sciences.* Chicago: University of Chicago Press, 1986.

McGavran, Donald A. *The Bridges of God: A Study in the Strategy of Missions.* London: World Dominion Press, (1955) 1957.

———. *Understanding Church Growth.* 3rd ed. Grand Rapids: Eerdmans, (1970) 1990.

Merrifield, William R., ed. *Five Amazonian Studies on World View and Culture Change.* Dallas: International Museum of Cultures, 1985.

Moennich, Martha. *That They May Hear: Wycliffe Bible Translators.* Chicago: Chicago Gospel Tabernacle, 1944.

Nelson, Shirley. *The Last Year of the War.* Rev. ed. Wheaton, IL: Northcote Books, (1979) 1989.

Nida, Eugene A. *Bible Translating: An Analysis of Principles and Procedures, with Special Reference to Aboriginal Languages.* New York: American Bible Society, 1947.

———. *Fascinated by Languages.* Philadelphia: John Benjamins, 2003.

———. *God's Word in Man's Language.* New York: Harper and Brothers, 1952.

———. *Morphology: The Descriptive Analysis of Words.* Ann Arbor: University of Michigan Press, 1949.

———. *Religion across Cultures: A Study in the Communication of the Christian Faith.* New York: Harper and Row, 1968.

———. *Toward a Science of Translating.* Leiden: Brill, 1964.

Nida, Eugene A., and William D. Reyburn. *Meaning across Cultures.* Maryknoll, NY: Orbis, 1981.

Pike, Eunice V. *Ken Pike: Scholar and Christian.* Dallas: Summer Institute of Linguistics, 1981.

———. *Not Alone.* Chicago: Moody Bible Institute, 1964.

————. *The Uttermost Part*. Chicago: Moody Press, 1971.

————. *Words Wanted*. Huntington Beach, CA: Wycliffe Bible Translators, 1958.

Pike, Kenneth L. *Language in Relation to a Unified Theory of the Structure of Human Behavior*. 2nd rev. ed. The Hague: Mouton, 1967.

————. *Linguistic Concepts: An Introduction to Tagmemics*. Lincoln: University of Nebraska Press, 1982.

————. *Mark My Words*. Grand Rapids: Eerdmans, 1971.

————. *Phonetics: A Critical Analysis of Phonetic Theory and a Technic for the Practical Description of Sounds*. Ann Arbor: University of Michigan, 1943.

————. *Stir, Change, Create: Poems and Essays in Contemporary Mood for Concerned Students*. Huntington Beach, CA: Wycliffe Bible Translators, 1967.

————. *Talk, Thought, and Thing: The Emic Road toward Conscious Knowledge*. Dallas: Summer Institute of Linguistics, 1993.

————. *With Heart and Mind: A Personal Synthesis of Scholarship and Devotion*. 2nd ed. Duncanville, TX: Adult Learning Systems, (1962) 1996.

Pike, Kenneth L., with Hugh Steven. *Pike's Perspectives: An Anthology of Thought, Insight, and Moral Purpose*. Langley, BC: Credo Publishing, 1989.

Rains, John C., and Thomas Dean, eds. *Marxism and Radical Religion: Essays toward a Revolutionary Humanism*. Philadelphia: Temple University Press, 1969.

Ramon Magsaysay Awards: 1973–1975, The. Manila: Carmelo and Bauermann Printing, 1982.

Rauschenbusch, Walter. *Christianity and the Social Crisis*. New York: Macmillan, 1907.

Roosevelt, Theodore. *The Works of Theodore Roosevelt: National Edition*. Edited by Hermann Hagedorn. Vol. 27. New York: Charles Scribner's Sons, 1926.

Saint, Steve. *End of the Spear*. Carol Stream, IL: Tyndale House, 2005.

Sebeok, Thomas A., ed. *Current Trends in Linguistics*. The Hague: Mouton, 1974.

Slocum, Marianna, with Grace Watkins. *The Good Seed*. Orange, CA: Promise Publishing, 1988.

Slocum, Marianna, and Sam Holms, eds. *Who Brought the Word?* Santa Ana, CA: Wycliffe Bible Translators, 1963.

Steven, Hugh. *The Man with the Noisy Heart: The John Beekman Story*. Chicago: Moody Press, 1979.

Stoll, David. *Fishers of Men or Founders of Empire? The Wycliffe Bible Translators in Latin America*. Cambridge, MA: Cultural Survival, 1982.

Summer Institute of Lingustics. *Walking Upright on Foreign Soil*. Waxhaw, NC: Summer Institute of Linguistics, 1995.

Townsend, W. Cameron. *Lazaro Cardenas: Mexican Democrat.* 2nd ed. Waxhaw, NC: International Friendship, 1979.

———. *The Truth about Mexico's Oil.* Los Angeles: Inter-American Fellowship, 1940.

Townsend, Cameron, et al. *Being Vectored In: The Harmonics of International Relations.* N.p.: Summer Institute of Linguistics, 1989.

———. *Bridge Builders.* Waxhaw, NC: Summer Institute of Linguistics, 1994.

———. *Fifty Gold Buckles.* Waxhaw, NC: JAARS, 1985.

———. *Giving a Heading: The Symphonics of International Relations.* N.p.: Summer Institute of Linguistics, 1990.

———. *The Wycliffe Sapphire.* Huntington Beach, CA: Wycliffe Bible Translators, 1991.

Townsend, William Cameron, and Elaine Mielke Townsend. *The USSR as We Saw It: From Armenia to Russia; Many Languages, Much Progress, Sincere Friends.* Waxhaw, NC: International Friendship, 1975.

Townsend, William Cameron, and Richard S. Pittman. *Remember All the Way.* Huntington Beach, CA: Wycliffe Bible Translators, 1975.

Wallis, Ethel Emily. *Aucas Downriver.* New York: Harper and Row, 1973.

———. *The Cakchiquel Album.* Costa Mesa, CA: Gift Publications, 1981.

———. *The Dayuma Story: Life under Auca Spears.* New York: Harper and Row, 1960.

———, ed. *Tariri: My Story; From Jungle Killer to Christian Missionary.* New York: Harper and Row, 1965.

Wallis, Ethel E., and Mary A. Bennett. *Two Thousand Tongues to Go: True-Life Adventures of the Wycliffe Bible Translators throughout the World Today.* New York: Harper and Brothers, 1959.

Wares, Alan C., ed. *Bibliography of the Summer Institute of Linguistics.* Vol. 1, *1935–1975.* Dallas: Summer Institute of Linguistics, 1979.

Whorf, Benjamin Lee. *Language, Thought, and Reality: Selected Writings of Benjamin Lee Whorf.* Edited by John B. Carroll. Cambridge, MA: MIT Press, 1956.

Wilson, Woodrow. *The Papers of Woodrow Wilson.* Edited by Arthur S. Link et al. Princeton: Princeton University Press, 1966–1994.

Wise, Mary Ruth. *Identification of Participants in Discourse: A Study of Aspects of Form and Meaning in Nomatsiguenga.* Norman, OK: Summer Institute of Linguistics, (1968) 1971.

Wonderly, William L. *Bible Translations for Popular Use.* N.p.: United Bible Societies, 1968.

Journal Articles

Beekman, John. "Idiomatic versus Literal Translations." *Notes on Translation* 18 (November 1965): 1–15.

———. "Propositions and Their Relations within a Discourse." *Notes on Translation* 37 (1970): 6–23.

Forsberg, Vivian. "Understanding Metaphors." *Notes on Translation* 68 (March 1978): 29–32.

Gough, Kathleen. "New Proposals for Anthropologists." *Current Anthropology* 9, no. 5 (December 1968): 403–35.

Grimes, Joseph E. "Positional Analysis." *Language* 43 (1967): 437–44.

Gudschinsky, Sarah C. "Discourse Analysis of a Mazatec Text." *International Journal of American Linguistics* 25, no. 3 (July 1959): 139–46.

Hart, Laurie. "Story of the Wycliffe Translators: Pacifying the Last Frontiers." *Latin America and Empire Report* 7, no. 10 (December 1973): 16–31.

Headland, Thomas N. "Paradise Revisited." *Sciences* 30, no. 5 (September–October 1990): 45–50.

Kietzman, Dale W. "Conversion and Culture Change." *Practical Anthropology* 5 (September–December 1958): 203–10.

———. "The Missionary Role in Culture Change." *Practical Anthropology* 1 (1953–1954): 71–75.

Kietzman, Dale W., and William A. Smalley. "The Missionary Role in Culture Change." *Practical Anthropology*, supplement (1960), 85–90.

Lauriault, James. "Some Problems in Translating Paragraphs Idiomatically." *Bible Translator* 8 (October 1957): 166–69.

Lindsell, Harold. "Faith Missions and Money." *Bibliotheca Sacra* 119 (January 1962): 28–37.

Longacre, Robert E. "Items in Context: Their Bearing on Translation Theory." *Language* 34, no. 4 (October–December 1958): 482–91.

———. "Some Fundamental Insights of Tagmemics." *Language* 41, no. 1 (February 1965): 65–76.

———. "String Constituent Analysis." *Language* 36, no. 1 (January–March 1960): 63–88.

Loos, Eugene E. "Capanahua Narration Structure." In *Studies in Literature and Language* 4 (supplement) (Austin: University of Texas, 1963), 697–742.

Loriot, James, and Barbra Hollenbach. "Shipibo Paragraph Structure." *Foundations of Language* 6 (1970): 43–66.

Nida, Eugene A. "My Pilgrimage in Mission." *International Bulletin of Missionary Research* 12, no. 2 (April 1988): 62–65.

————. "A New Method in Biblical Exegesis." *Bible Translator* 3, no. 3 (July 1952): 97–111.

————. "The Relevance of Bible Translating." *Babel* 7, no. 2 (1961): 51–52.

————. "Science of Translation." *Language* 45, no. 3 (September 1969): 483–98.

Pike, Kenneth L. "Christianity and Culture: III. Biblical Absolutes and Certain Cultural Relativisms." *Journal of the American Scientific Affiliation* 31, no. 3 (September 1979): 139–45.

————. "Grammatical Prerequisites to Phonemic Analysis." *Word* 3, no. 3 (December 1947): 155–72.

————. "Our Own Tongue Wherein We Were Born." *Bible Translator* 10, no. 2 (April 1959): 3–16.

Stoll, David. "Missionaries as Foreign Agents." *American Anthropologist* 98, no. 3 (September 1996): 636–38.

————. "The Summer Institute of Linguistics and Indigenous Movements." *Latin American Perspectives* 9, no. 2 (Spring 1982): 84–99.

Wonderly, William. "Information-Correspondence and the Translation of Ephesians into Zoque." Part I. *Bible Translator* 3 (July 1952): 138–42.

————. "Information-Correspondence and the Translation of Ephesians into Zoque." Part II. *Bible Translator* 4 (January 1953): 14–21.

Dissertations

Daly, John P. "Generative Syntax of Mixteco." PhD diss., Indiana University, 1966.

Pickett, Velma B. "The Grammatical Hierarchy of Isthmus Zapotec." PhD diss., University of Michigan, 1959.

Pike, Kenneth L. "A Reconstruction of Phonetic Theory." PhD diss., University of Michigan, 1941.

Sommer, Bruce A. "Kunjen Syntax: A Generative View." PhD diss., University of Hawaii, 1970.

Waterhouse, Viola G. "The Grammatical Structure of Oaxaca Chontal." PhD diss., University of Michigan, 1958.

Wedekind, Klaus. "An Outline of the Grammar of Busa (Nigeria)." PhD diss., University of Kiel, 1972.

Winn, Wilkins Bowdre. "A History of the Central American Mission as Seen in the Work of Albert Edward Bishop, 1896–1922." PhD diss., University of Alabama, 1963.

Wise, Mary Ruth. "Identification of Participants in Discourse: A Study of Aspects of Form and Meaning in Nomatsiguenga." PhD diss., University of Michigan, 1968.

Secondary Sources

Books

Abercrombie, David, R. E. Asher, and Eugénie J. A. Henderson, eds. *Towards a History of Phonetics.* Edinburgh: Edinburgh University Press, 1981.

Abrams, Douglas Carl. *Selling the Old Time Religion: American Fundamentalists and Mass Culture, 1920–1940.* Athens: University of Georgia Press, 2001.

Adams, Richard Newbold. *Crucifixion by Power: Essays on Guatemalan National Social Structure, 1944–1966.* Austin: University of Texas Press, 1970.

Ammerman, Nancy Tatom. *Bible Believers: Fundamentalists in the Modern World.* New Brunswick, NJ: Rutgers University Press, 1987.

Anhalt, Diana. *A Gathering of Fugitives: American Political Expatriates in Mexico, 1948–1965.* Santa Maria, CA: Archer Books, 2001.

Atherton, William. *In God's Time and Ours: Philippine Branch History; A Narration, 1953–1983.* Manila: Summer Institute of Linguistics, 2003.

Baldwin, Deborah. *Protestants and the Mexican Revolution: Missionaries, Ministers, and Social Change.* Urbana: University of Illinois Press, 1990.

Barnet, Richard J. *Intervention and Revolution: The United States in the Third World.* New York: World Publishing, 1968.

Baughman, James L. *The Republic of Mass Culture: Journalism, Filmmaking, and Broadcasting in America Since 1941.* 3rd ed. Baltimore: Johns Hopkins University Press, 2006.

Bays, Daniel H., and Grant Wacker, eds. *The Foreign Missionary Enterprise at Home: Explorations in North American Cultural History.* Tuscaloosa: University of Alabama Press, 2003.

Beale, David O. *In Pursuit of Purity: American Fundamentalism Since 1850.* Greenville, SC: Unusual Publications, 1986.

Beaver, R. Pierce, ed. *American Missions in Bicentennial Perspective.* South Pasadena, CA: William Carey Library, 1977.

Bebbington, David W. *The Dominance of Evangelicalism: The Age of Spurgeon and Moody.* Downers Grove: InterVarsity, 2005.

———. *Evangelicalism in Modern Britain: A History from the 1730s to the 1980s.* New York: Routledge, 2002.

———. *Patterns in History: A Christian Perspective on Historical Thought.* Vancouver, BC: Regent College Publishing, 1990.

Becker, Marjorie. *Setting the Virgin on Fire: Lázaro Cárdenas, Michoacán Peasants, and the Redemption of the Mexican Revolution.* Berkeley: University of California Press, 1995.

Bingham, Rowland V. *Seven Sevens of Years and a Jubilee: The Story of the Sudan Interior Mission.* New York: Evangelical Publishers, 1943.

Black, Matthew, and William A. Smalley, eds. *On Language, Culture, and Religion: In Honor of Eugene A. Nida.* The Hague: Mouton, 1974.

Bodley, John H. *Victims of Progress.* 5th ed. New York: AltaMira Press, 2008.

Bonk, Jonathan J. *Missions and Money: Affluence as a Missionary Problem.* Rev. ed. Maryknoll, NY: Orbis, 2006.

Boone, Kathleen C. *The Bible Tells Them So: The Discourse of Protestant Fundamentalism.* Albany: State University of New York Press, 1989.

Bosch, David J. *Transforming Mission: Paradigm Shifts in Theology of Mission.* Maryknoll, NY: Orbis, 1991.

Boyer, Paul. *When Time Shall Be No More: Prophecy Belief in Modern American Culture.* Cambridge, MA: Harvard University Press, 1992.

Brandenburg, Frank. *The Making of Modern Mexico.* Englewood Cliffs, NJ: Prentice-Hall, 1964.

Brands, Hal. *Latin America's Cold War.* Cambridge, MA: Harvard University Press, 2010.

Brantlinger, Patrick. *Dark Vanishings: Discourse on the Extinction of Primitive Races, 1800–1930.* Ithaca, NY: Cornell University Press, 2003.

Brend, Ruth M. *Advances in Tagmemics.* London: North-Holland Publishing, 1974.

Brend, Ruth M., and Kenneth L. Pike. *The Summer Institute of Linguistics: Its Works and Contributions.* The Hague: Mouton, 1977.

————, eds. *Tagmemics.* Vol. 1: *Aspects of the Field.* Trends in Linguistics 1. The Hague: Mouton, 1976.

————, eds. *Tagmemics.* Vol. 2: *Theoretical Discussion.* Trends in Linguistics 2. The Hague: Mouton, 1976.

Brereton, Virginia Lieson. *Training God's Army: The American Bible School, 1880–1940.* Bloomington: Indiana University Press, 1990.

Britton, John A. *Revolution and Ideology: Images of the Mexican Revolution in the United States.* Lexington: University of Kentucky Press, 1995.

Brower, Reuben A., ed. *On Translation.* Cambridge, MA: Harvard University Press, 1959.

Buss, Dietrich G., and Arthur F. Glasser. *Giving Wings to the Gospel: The Remarkable Story of Mission Aviation Fellowship.* Grand Rapids: Baker, 1995.

Bynon, Theodora, and F. R. Palmer. *Studies in the History of Linguistics.* New York: Cambridge University Press, 1986.

Carey, James C. *Peru and the United States, 1900–1962.* Notre Dame: University of Notre Dame Press, 1964.

Carpenter, Joel A. *Revive Us Again: The Reawakening of American Fundamentalism.* New York: Oxford University Press, 1997.

Carpenter, Joel A., and Kenneth W. Shipps, eds. *Making Higher Education Christian: The History and Mission of Evangelical Colleges in America.* Grand Rapids: Eerdmans, 1987.

Carpenter, Joel A., and Wilbert R. Shenk, eds. *Earthen Vessels: American Evangelicals and Foreign Missions, 1880–1980.* Grand Rapids: Eerdmans, 1990.

Carson, D. A. *Exegetical Fallacies.* 2nd ed. Grand Rapids: Baker, 1996.

Clayton, Lawrence A. *Peru and the United States: The Condor and the Eagle.* Athens: University of Georgia Press, 1999.

Cleland, Robert Glass. *The History of Occidental College: 1887–1937.* Los Angeles: Ward Ritchie Press, 1937.

Cline, Howard F. *Mexico: Revolution to Evolution, 1940–1960.* New York: Oxford University Press, 1962.

Coates, Ken S. *A Global History of Indigenous Peoples: Struggle and Survival.* London: Palgrave Macmillan, 2004.

Coben, Stanley, and Lorman Ratner, eds. *The Development of American Culture.* New York: St. Martin's Press, 1983.

Commager, Henry Steel. *The American Mind: An Interpretation of American Thought and Character Since the 1880's.* New Haven: Yale University Press, 1950.

Considine, John J. *New Horizons in Latin America.* New York: Dodd, Mead, 1958.

Cooper, John Milton, Jr. *Pivotal Decades: The United States, 1900–1920.* New York: Norton, 1990.

―――, ed. *Reconsidering Woodrow Wilson: Progressivism, Internationalism, War, and Peace.* Baltimore: Johns Hopkins University Press, 2008.

Coronado, Jorge. *The Andes Imagined: Indigenismo, Society, and Modernity.* Pittsburgh: University of Pittsburgh Press, 2009.

Cumberland, Charles C. *Mexico: The Struggle for Modernity.* New York: Oxford University Press, 1968.

Dahl, Jens. *IWGIA: A History.* Copenhagen: IWGIA, 2009.

Dahlquist, Anna Marie. *Burgess of Guatemala.* Langley, BC: Cedar Books, 1985.

―――. *Trailblazers for Translators: The Chichicastenango Twelve.* Pasadena, CA: William Carey Library, 1995.

Dame, Lawrence. *Maya Mission.* Garden City, NY: Doubleday, 1968.

Dark, K. R., ed. *Religion and International Relations.* New York: St. Martin's Press, 2000.

Debo, Angie. *Geronimo: The Man, His Time, His Place.* Norman: University of Oklahoma Press, 1976.

D'Elia, John. *A Place at the Table: George Eldon Ladd and the Rehabilitation of Evangelical Scholarship.* New York: Oxford University Press, 2008.

Dinneen, Francis P., SJ, and E. F. Konrad Koerner, eds. *North American Contributions to the History of Linguistics.* Philadelphia: John Benjamins, 1990.

Dorrien, Gary. *The Remaking of Evangelical Theology.* Louisville: Westminster John Knox, 1998.

Drennan, Robert D., and Carlos A. Uribe, eds. *Chiefdoms in the Americas.* New York: University Press of America, 1987.

Edwards, Fred E. *The Role of the Faith Mission: A Brazilian Case Study.* South Pasadena, CA: William Carey Library, 1971.

Eskridge, Larry, and Mark A. Noll, eds. *More Money, More Ministry: Money and Evangelicals in Recent North American History.* Grand Rapids: Eerdmans, 2000.

Ferguson, Niall. *Colossus: The Rise and Fall of the American Empire.* New York: Penguin Books, 2004.

Fiedler, Klaus. *The Story of Faith Missions: From Hudson Taylor to Present Day Africa.* Irvine, CA: Regnum, 1994.

Flehinger, Brett. *The 1912 Election and the Power of Progressivism: A Brief History with Documents.* New York: Bedford/St. Martin's, 2003.

Fousek, John. *To Lead a Free World: American Nationalism and the Cultural Roots of the Cold War.* Chapel Hill: University of North Carolina Press, 2000.

Fox, Richard Wightman, and T. J. Jackson Lears. *The Power of Culture: Critical Essays in American History.* Chicago: University of Chicago Press, 1993.

Frank, Douglas. *Less Than Conquerors: How Evangelicals Entered the Twentieth Century.* Grand Rapids: Eerdmans, 1986.

Freeman, Derek. *Margaret Mead and Samoa: The Making and Unmaking of an Anthropological Myth.* Cambridge, MA: Harvard University Press, 1983.

Friedman, Lawrence J., and Mark D. McGarvie, eds. *Charity, Philanthropy, and Civility in American History.* Cambridge: Cambridge University Press, 2003.

Frizen, Edwin L., Jr. *75 Years of IFMA, 1917–1992: The Nondenominational Missions Movement.* Wheaton, IL: Interdenominational Foreign Mission Association, 1992.

Fuller, Daniel P. *Give the Winds a Mighty Voice: The Story of Charles E. Fuller.* Waco: Word, 1972.

Gaddis, John Lewis. *We Now Know: Rethinking Cold War History.* New York: Clarendon, 1997.

Garrard-Burnett, Virginia. *Protestantism in Guatemala: Living in the New Jerusalem.* Austin: University of Texas Press, 1998.

Garrard-Burnett, Virginia, and David Stoll, eds. *Rethinking Protestantism in Latin America.* Philadelphia: Temple University Press, 1993.

Garthoff, Raymond L. *Détente and Confrontation: American-Soviet Relations from Nixon to Reagan.* Washington, DC: Brookings Institution, 1985.

George, Calvin. *The History of the Reina-Valera 1960 Spanish Bible.* Kearney, NB: Morris, 2004.

Gilbert, James. *Redeeming Culture: American Religion in an Age of Science.* Chicago: University of Chicago Press, 1997.

Girling, John L. S. *America and the Third World: Revolution and Intervention.* Boston: Routledge and Kegan Paul, 1980.

Gorman, Robert A. *Neo-Marxism: The Meanings of Modern Radicalism.* Westport, CT: Greenwood Press, 1982.

Graham, Richard, ed. *The Idea of Race in Latin America, 1870–1940.* Austin: University of Texas Press, 1990.

Greene, Betty. *Flying High: The Amazing Story of Betty Greene and the Early Years of Mission Aviation Fellowship.* Camp Hill, PA: Christian Publications, 2002.

Hankins, Barry. *God's Rascal: J. Frank Norris and the Beginnings of Southern Fundamentalism.* Lexington: University Press of Kentucky, 1996.

Hannah, John D. *An Uncommon Union: Dallas Theological Seminary and American Evangelicalism.* Grand Rapids: Zondervan, 2009.

Hansen, Roger D. *The Politics of Mexican Development.* Baltimore: Johns Hopkins University Press, 1971.

Harris, Harriet A. *Fundamentalism and Evangelicals.* New York: Oxford University Press, 1998.

Harris, Marvin. *The Rise of Anthropological Theory: A History of Theories of Culture.* New York: Thomas Y. Crowell, 1968.

Harris, Roy, and Talbot J. Taylor. *Landmarks in Linguistic Thought: The Western Tradition from Socrates to Saussure.* New York: Routledge, 1989.

Hartch, Todd. *Missionaries of the State: The Summer Institute of Linguistics, State Formation, and Indigenous Mexico, 1935–1985.* Tuscaloosa: University of Alabama Press, 2006.

Hassler, Gerda, ed. *History of Linguistics 2008: Selected Papers from the 11th International Conference on the History of the Language Sciences.* Philadelphia: John Benjamins, 2011.

Hatch, Nathan, and Mark Noll, eds. *The Bible in America: Essays in Cultural History.* New York: Oxford University Press, 1982.

Headland, Thomas N., Kenneth L. Pike, and Marvin Harris, eds. *Emics and*

Etics: The Insider/Outsider Debate. Newberry Park, CA: Sage Publications, 1990.

Hefley, James C. *God's Free-Lancers: The Story of Wycliffe Associates—Men and Women Using Their Skills to Help Wycliffe Missionaries around the World.* Orange, CA: Wycliffe Associates, 1983.

————. *Peril by Choice: The Story of John and Elaine Beekman, Wycliffe Bible Translators in Mexico.* Grand Rapids: Zondervan, 1968.

Hefley, James C., and Marti Hefley. *Uncle Cam: The Story of William Cameron Townsend, Founder of the Wycliffe Bible Translators and the Summer Institute of Linguistics.* Waco: Word, 1974.

Hefner, Robert W., ed. *Conversion to Christianity: Historical and Anthropological Perspectives on a Great Transformation.* Berkeley: University of California Press, 1993.

Henry, James O. *For Such a Time as This: A History of the Independent Fundamental Churches of America.* Westchester, IL: Independent Fundamental Churches of America, 1983.

Hodges, Donald C. *The Latin American Revolution: Politics and Strategy from Apro-Marxism to Guevarism.* New York: Morrow, 1974.

Hofstadter, Richard. *Anti-intellectualism in American Life.* New York: Knopf, 1970.

Hollinger, Dennis P. *Individualism and Social Ethics: An Evangelical Syncretism.* New York: University Press of America, 1983.

Hurt, Harry, III. *Texas Rich: The Hunt Dynasty from the Early Oil Days through the Silver Crash.* New York: Norton, 1981.

Hutchison, William R. *Errand to the World: American Protestant Thought and Foreign Missions.* Chicago: University of Chicago Press, 1993.

Hymes, Dell, and John Fought, eds. *American Structuralism.* The Hague: Mouton, 1981.

Jenkins, Philip. *The Next Christendom: The Coming of Global Christianity.* New York: Oxford University Press, 2002.

Kessler, J. B. A., Jr. *A Study of the Older Protestant Missions and Churches in Peru and Chile: With Special Reference to the Problems of Division, Nationalism, and Native Ministry.* Goes, Netherlands: Oosterbaan & Le Cointre, 1967.

Klaiber, Jeffrey. *The Catholic Church in Peru, 1821–1985: A Social History.* Washington, DC: Catholic University of America Press, 1992.

————. *Religion and Revolution in Peru, 1824–1976.* Notre Dame: University of Notre Dame Press, 1977.

Koerner, E. F. K. *Towards a Historiography of Linguistics: Selected Essays.* Amsterdam: John Benjamins B. V., 1978.

Koerner, E. F. K., and R. E. Asher, eds. *Concise History of the Language Sciences: From the Sumerians to the Cognitivists.* New York: Pergamon Press, 1995.

Kraus, C. Norman. *Dispensationalism in America: Its Rise and Development.* Richmond, VA: John Knox, 1958.

Krauze, Enrique. *Mexico: Biography of Power; A History of Modern Mexico, 1810–1996.* New York: HarperCollins, 1977.

Kuklick, Henrika, ed. *A New History of Anthropology.* Malden, MA: Blackwell, 2008.

LaFeber, Walter. *America, Russia, and the Cold War: 1945–1984.* New York: Knopf, 1985.

Larsen, Timothy, ed. *Biographical Dictionary of Evangelicals.* Downers Grove: InterVarsity, 2003.

Larson, Mildred L., and Patricia M. Davis, eds. *Bilingual Education: An Experience in Peruvian Amazonia.* Washington, DC: Center for Applied Linguistics, 1981.

Latourette, Kenneth Scott. *Christianity in a Revolutionary Age: A History of Christianity in the 19th and 20th Centuries.* Vol. 5, *The Twentieth Century Outside Europe.* Grand Rapids: Zondervan, 1969.

Lazere, Donald, ed. *American Media and Mass Culture: Left Perspectives.* Berkeley: University of California Press, 1987.

Lewis, Donald M., ed. *Christianity Reborn: The Global Expansion of Evangelicalism in the Twentieth Century.* Grand Rapids: Eerdmans, 2004.

Lewis, Jack P. *The English Bible from the KJV to NIV: A History and Evaluation.* 2nd ed. Grand Rapids: Baker, 1991.

Livingstone, David N., D. G. Hart, and Mark A. Noll. *Evangelicals and Science in Historical Perspective.* New York: Oxford University Press, 1999.

Long, Lynne, ed. *Translation and Religion: Holy Untranslatable.* Buffalo: Multilingual Matters, 2005.

Mainwaring, Scott, and Alexander Wilde, eds. *The Progressive Church in Latin America.* Notre Dame: University of Notre Dame Press, 1989.

Malley, Brian. *How the Bible Works: An Anthropological Study of Evangelical Biblicism.* New York: AltaMira Press, 2004.

Marsden, George M., ed. *Evangelicalism and Modern America.* Grand Rapids: Eerdmans, 1984.

———. *Fundamentalism and American Culture: The Shaping of Twentieth-Century Evangelicalism, 1870–1925.* New York: Oxford University Press, 1980.

———. *Reforming Fundamentalism: Fuller Seminary and the New Evangelicalism.* Grand Rapids: Eerdmans, 1987.

————. *Religion and American Culture*. 2nd ed. Belmont, CA: Thompson Wadsworth, 2001.

————. *The Soul of the American University: From Protestant Establishment to Established Nonbelief*. New York: Oxford University Press, 1994.

Martin, David. *Tongues of Fire: The Explosion of Protestantism in Latin America*. Cambridge, MA: Blackwell, 1990.

Martin, Dorothy. *100 . . . and Counting: The Story of the CAM's First Century*. Dallas: CAM International, 1990.

Martin, William. *A Prophet with Honor: The Billy Graham Story*. New York: Morrow, 1991.

Marty, Martin E., and R. Scott Appleby, eds. *Accounting for Fundamentalisms: The Dynamic Character of Movements*. Fundamentalism Project, vol. 4. Chicago: University of Chicago Press, 1994.

————. *Fundamentalisms and Society: Reclaiming the Sciences, the Family, and Education*. Fundamentalism Project, vol. 2. Chicago: University of Chicago Press, 1993.

————. *Fundamentalisms and the State: Remaking Polities, Economies, and Militance*. Fundamentalism Project, vol. 3. Chicago: University of Chicago Press, 1993.

————. *Fundamentalisms Comprehended*. Fundamentalism Project, vol. 5. Chicago: University of Chicago Press, 1995.

————. *Fundamentalisms Observed*. Fundamentalism Project, vol. 1. Chicago: University of Chicago Press, 1991.

Martz, John D., ed. *United States Policy in Latin America: A Quarter Century of Crisis and Challenge, 1961–1986*. Lincoln: University of Nebraska Press, 1988.

Masterson, Daniel. *The History of Peru*. Westport, CT: Greenwood Press, 2009.

————. *Militarism and Politics in Latin America*. New York: Greenwood Press, 1991.

McCutcheon, Russell T., ed. *The Insider/Outsider Problem in the Study of Religion: A Reader*. New York: Cassell, 1999.

Meyer, Michael C., and William L. Sherman. *The Course of Mexican History*. 3rd ed. New York: Oxford University Press, 1987.

Mörner, Magnus, ed. *Race and Class in Latin America*. New York: Columbia University Press, 1970.

Morrisey, Will. *The Dilemma of Progressivism: How Roosevelt, Taft, and Wilson Reshaped the American Regime of Self-Government*. New York: Rowman and Littlefield, 2009.

Nelson, Rudolph. *The Making and Unmaking of an Evangelical Mind: The Case of Edward Carnell*. New York: Cambridge University Press, 1987.

Niezen, Ronald. *The Origins of Indigenism: Human Rights and the Politics of Identity.* Berkeley: University of California Press, 2003.

Noll, Mark A. *Between Faith and Criticism: Evangelicals, Scholarship, and the Bible in America.* San Francisco: Harper and Row, 1986.

———. *The New Shape of World Christianity: How American Experience Reflects Global Faith.* Downers Grove: IVP Academic, 2009.

———. *The Scandal of the Evangelical Mind.* Grand Rapids: Eerdmans, 1994.

———. *Turning Points: Decisive Moments in the History of Christianity.* Grand Rapids: Baker, 1997.

Noll, Mark A., David W. Bebbington, and George A. Rawlyk, eds. *Evangelicalism: Comparative Studies of Popular Protestantism in North America, the British Isles, and Beyond, 1700–1990.* New York: Oxford University Press, 1994.

Noss, Philip A., ed. *A History of Bible Translation.* Rome: Edizioni Di Storia E Letteratura [American Bible Society], 2007.

Olsen, Bruce. *Missionary or Colonizer?* Chappaqua, NY: Christian Herald Books, 1977.

Orlinsky, Harry M., and Robert G. Bratcher. *A History of Bible Translation and the North American Contribution.* Atlanta: Scholars Press, 1991.

Paher, Stanley W. *Death Valley's Scotty's Castle: The Story behind the Scenery.* Las Vegas, NV: K. C. Publications, 1993.

Patterson, Thomas G., J. Garry Clifford, and Kenneth J. Hagan. *American Foreign Relations: A History Since 1895.* Vol. 2. 4th ed. Lexington, MA: Heath, 1995.

Pearce, Roy Harvey. *Savagism and Civilization: A Study of the Indian and the American Mind.* Rev. ed. Berkeley: University of California Press, 1983.

Pike, Eunice V. *Ken Pike: Scholar and Christian.* Dallas: Summer Institute of Linguistics, 1981.

Pike, Fredrick B. *The Modern History of Peru.* New York: Praeger, 1967.

Pike, Kenneth L. *Kenneth L. Pike: Selected Writings.* Edited by Ruth M. Brend. The Hague: Mouton, 1972.

Polenberg, Richard. *One Nation Indivisible: Class, Race, and Ethnicity in the United States Since 1938.* New York: Viking, 1980.

Pollack, J. C. *The Keswick Story: The Authorized History of the Keswick Convention.* Chicago: Moody Press, 1964.

Price, Charles, and Ian Randall. *Transforming Keswick: The Keswick Convention Past, Present, and Future.* Waynesboro, GA: Paternoster, 2000.

Randall, Ian M. *Evangelical Experiences: A Study of the Spirituality of English Evangelicalism, 1918–1939.* Carlisle, UK: Paternoster, 1999.

Ravitch, Diane. *The Troubled Crusade: American Education, 1945–1980.* New York: Basic Books, 1983.

Riding, Alan. *Distant Neighbors: A Portrait of the Mexicans.* New York: Vintage Books, 1986.

Robert, Dana L. *American Women in Mission: A Social History of Their Thought and Practice.* Macon, GA: Mercer University Press, 1996.

Robin, Ron. *The Making of the Cold War Enemy: Culture and Politics in the Military-Intellectual Complex.* Princeton: Princeton University Press, 2001.

Robins, R. H. *A Short History of Linguistics.* 2nd ed. New York: Longman, 1979.

Rosell, Garth M. *The Surprising Work of God: Harold John Ockenga, Billy Graham, and the Rebirth of Evangelicalism.* Grand Rapids: Baker Academic, 2008.

Sampson, Geoffrey. *Schools of Linguistics.* Stanford: Stanford University Press, 1980.

Sanneh, Lamin. *Translating the Message: The Missionary Impact on Culture.* Maryknoll, NY: Orbis, 1995.

Scanlon, A. Clark. *Church Growth through Theological Education in Guatemala.* Eugene, OR: Institute of Church Growth, 1962.

Schrecker, Ellen, ed. *Cold War Triumphalism: The Misuse of History after the Fall of Communism.* New York: New Press, 2004.

Scott, James C. *Seeing Like a State: How Certain Schemes to Improve the Human Condition Have Failed.* New Haven: Yale University Press, 1998.

Sharp, Daniel A., ed. *U.S. Foreign Policy and Peru.* Austin: University of Texas Press, 1972.

Shenk, Wilbert R. *Changing Frontiers of Mission.* Maryknoll, NY: Orbis, 2003.

Simpson, Lesley Bird. *Many Mexicos.* 4th ed. Berkeley: University of California Press, 1974.

Smalley, William A. *Translation as Mission: Bible Translation in the Modern Missionary Movement.* Macon, GA: Mercer University Press, 1991.

Smith, Peter H. *Talons of the Eagle: Dynamics of U.S.–Latin American Relations.* New York: Oxford University Press, 1996.

Stanley, Brian, ed. *Christian Missions and the Enlightenment.* Grand Rapids: Eerdmans, 2001.

———. *Missions, Nationalism, and the End of Empire.* Grand Rapids: Eerdmans, 2003.

Steven, Hugh. *Doorway to the World: The Memoirs of W. Cameron Townsend, 1934–1947.* Wheaton, IL: Harold Shaw, 1999.

———. *Manuel.* Old Tappan, NJ: Revell, 1970.

———. *Manuel: The Continuing Story.* Langley, BC: Credo Publishing, 1987.

————, ed. *A Thousand Trails: Personal Journal of William Cameron Townsend, 1917–1919.* Langley, BC: Credo Publishing, 1984.

————. *Translating Christ: The Memoirs of Herman Peter Aschmann, Wycliffe Bible Translator.* Pasadena, CA: William Carey Library, 2011.

————. *Wycliffe in the Making: The Memoirs of W. Cameron Townsend, 1920–1933.* Wheaton, IL: Harold Shaw, 1995.

————. *Yours to Finish the Task: The Memoirs of W. Cameron Townsend, 1947–1982.* Huntington Beach, CA: Wycliffe Bible Translators, 2004.

Stine, Philip C. *Bible Translation and the Spread of the Church: The Last 200 Years.* New York: Brill, 1990.

————. *Let the Words Be Written: The Lasting Influence of Eugene A. Nida.* Atlanta: Society of Biblical Literature, 2004.

St. John, Ronald Bruce. *The Foreign Policy of Peru.* Boulder, CO: Lynne Rienner Publishers, 1992.

Stoll, David. *Is Latin America Turning Protestant? The Politics of Evangelical Growth.* Berkeley: University of California Press, 1990.

Svelmoe, William Lawrence. *A New Vision for Missions: William Cameron Townsend, the Wycliffe Bible Translators, and the Culture of Early Evangelical Faith Missions, 1896–1945.* Tuscaloosa: University of Alabama Press, 2008.

Swanson, Jeffrey. *Echoes of the Call: Identity and Ideology among American Missionaries in Ecuador.* New York: Oxford University Press, 1995.

Taffet, Jeffrey F. *Foreign Aid as Foreign Policy: The Alliance for Progress in Latin America.* New York: Routledge, 2007.

Thompson, Phyllis. *Matched with His Hour: The Story of the British Home Base of the Wycliffe Bible Translators.* London: Word Books, 1974.

Thuesen, Peter J. *In Discordance with the Scriptures: American Protestant Battles over Translating the Bible.* New York: Oxford University Press, 1999.

Trollinger, William Vance, Jr. *God's Empire: William Bell Riley and Midwestern Fundamentalism.* Madison: University of Wisconsin Press, 1990.

Tuccille, Jerome. *Kingdom: The Story of the Hunt Family of Texas.* Ottawa: Jameson Books, 1984.

Tucker, Gene M., and Douglas A. Knight, eds. *Humanizing America's Iconic Book: Society of Biblical Literature Centennial Addresses, 1980.* Chico, CA: Scholars Press, 1982.

Turner, John G. *Bill Bright and Campus Crusade for Christ.* Chapel Hill: University of North Carolina Press, 2008.

Waard, Jan de, and Eugene A. Nida. *From One Language to Another: Functional Equivalence in Bible Translating.* New York: Nelson, 1986.

Wallis, Ethel Emily. *Lengthened Cords: How Dawson Trotman—Founder of the*

Navigators—Also Helped Extend the World-Wide Outreach of the Wycliffe Bible Translators. Glendale, CA: Wycliffe Bible Translators, 1958.

Walls, Andrew F. *The Cross-Cultural Process in Christian History: Studies in the Transmission and Appropriation of Faith.* Maryknoll, NY: Orbis, 2002.

———. *The Missionary Movement in Christian History: Studies in the Transmission of Faith.* Maryknoll, NY: Orbis, 1996.

Walters, Ronald G., ed. *Scientific Authority and Twentieth-Century America.* Baltimore: Johns Hopkins University Press, 1997.

Warren, Kay B. *The Symbolism of Subordination: Indian Identity in a Guatemalan Town.* Austin: University of Texas Press, 1978.

Weber, Timothy P. *Living in the Shadow of the Second Coming: American Premillennialism, 1875–1925.* New York: Oxford University Press, 1979.

Weyl, Nathaniel, and Sylvia Weyl. *The Reconquest of Mexico: The Years of Lázaro Cárdenas.* New York: Oxford University Press, 1939.

Whitfield, Stephen J. *The Culture of the Cold War.* Baltimore: Johns Hopkins University Press, 1991.

Willmer, Wesley K., David J. Schmidt, with Martyn Smith. *The Prospering Parachurch: Enlarging the Boundaries of God's Kingdom.* San Francisco: Jossey-Bass, 1998.

Wilson, Richard A., ed. *Human Rights, Culture, and Context: Anthropological Perspectives.* London: Pluto, 1997.

Wise, Mary Ruth, Thomas N. Headland, and Ruth M. Brend, eds. *Language and Life: Essays in Memory of Kenneth L. Pike.* Arlington: University of Texas at Arlington and SIL International, 2003.

Wuthnow, Robert. *The Restructuring of American Religion: Society and Faith Since World War II.* Princeton: Princeton University Press, 1988.

Yates, Timothy. *Christian Missions in the Twentieth Century.* New York: Cambridge University Press, 1996.

Journal Articles

Banks, Robert. "The Intellectual Encounter between Christianity and Marxism: A Contribution to the Pre-History of a Dialogue." In "Conflict and Compromise: Socialists and Socialism in the Twentieth Century," special issue, *Journal of Contemporary History* 11, no. 2 of 3 (July 1976): 309–31.

Brend, Ruth Margaret. "Tagmemic Theory: An Annotated Bibliography, Appendix I." *Journal of English Linguistics* 6 (March 1972): 1–16.

Burton, John W. "Some Reflections on Anthropology's Missionary Positions." *Journal of the Royal Anthropological Institute* 13, no. 1 (March 2007): 209–17.

Carson, D. A. "The Limits of Dynamic Equivalence in Bible Translation." *Notes on Translation* 121 (1987): 1–14.

Coote, Robert T. "The Uneven Growth of Conservative Evangelical Missions." *International Bulletin of Missionary Research* 6, no. 3 (July 1982): 118–23.

Friedman, Max Paul. "Retiring the Puppets, Bringing Latin America Back In: Recent Scholarship on United States–Latin American Relations." *Diplomatic History* 27, no. 5 (November 2003): 621–36.

Goodenough, Ward H. "Anthropology in the 20th Century and Beyond." *American Anthropologist*, n.s., 104, no. 2 (June 2002): 434–35.

Hale, Charles A. "Frank Tannenbaum and the Mexican Revolution." *Hispanic American Historical Review* 75, no. 2 (May 1995): 215–46.

Headland, Thomas N. "Kenneth Lee Pike (1912–2000)." *American Anthropologist* 103, no. 2 (June 2001): 505–9.

Helfrich, H. "Beyond the Dilemma of Cross-Cultural Psychology: Resolving the Tension between Etic and Emic Approaches." *Culture and Psychology* 5, no. 2 (June 1999): 131–53.

Hill, Harriet. "The Vernacular Treasure: A Century of Mother-Tongue Bible Translation." *International Bulletin of Missionary Research* 30, no. 2 (April 2006): 82–88.

Huntington, Samuel P. "American Ideals versus American Institutions." *Political Science Quarterly* 97, no. 1 (Spring 1982): 1–37.

Jaquette, Jane S., and Abraham F. Lowenthal. "The Peruvian Experiment in Retrospect." *World Politics* 39, no. 2 (January 1987): 281–82.

Lewis, Herbert S. "The Radical Transformation of Anthropology: History Seen through the Annual Meetings of the American Anthropological Association, 1955–2005." *Histories of Anthropology Annual* 5 (2009): 200–228.

Nunn, Frederick M. "Professional Militarism in Twentieth-Century Peru: Historical and Theoretical Background to the Golpe de Estado of 1968." *Hispanic American Historical Review* 59, no. 3 (August 1979): 391–417.

Osterling, Jorge P., and Héctor Martínez. "Notes for a History of Peruvian Social Anthropology, 1940–1980." *Current Anthropology* 24, no. 3 (June 1983): 343–44.

Pike, Fredrick B. "Church and State in Peru and Chile Since 1840: A Study in Contrasts." *American Historical Review* 73, no. 1 (October 1967): 42–47.

———. "The Modernized Church in Peru: Two Aspects." *Review of Politics* 26, no. 3 (July 1964): 307–18.

Pineo, Ronn. "Recent Cold War Studies." *History Teacher* 37, no. 1 (November 2003): 79–86.

Priest, Robert J. "Missionary Positions: Christian, Modernist, Postmodernist." *Current Anthropology* 42, no. 1 (February 2001): 29–68.

Sanneh, Lamin. "Christian Missions and the Western Guilt Complex." *Christian Century* 104, no. 11 (April 8, 1987): 330–34.

Shelley, Bruce. "The Rise of Evangelical Youth Movements." *Fides et Historia* 18 (January 1986): 47–63.

Smalley, William A. "Language and Culture in the Development of Bible Society Translation Theory and Practice." *International Bulletin of Missionary Research* 19, no. 2 (April 1995): 64–67.

Stipe, Claude E., et al. "Anthropologists versus Missionaries: The Influence of Presuppositions (and Comments and Reply)." *Current Anthropology* 21, no. 2 (April 1980): 165–79.

Tomlinson, B. R. "What Was the Third World?" *Journal of Contemporary History* 38, no. 2 (April 2003): 307–21.

Tuck, Stephen. "New American Histories." *Historical Journal* 48, no. 3 (September 2005): 811–32.

UNESCO. "The Use of Vernacular Languages in Education." *Monographs on Fundamental Education* 8 (Paris: UNESCO, 1953).

Waterbury, John, "Hate Your Policies, Love Your Institutions." *Foreign Affairs* 82, no. 1 (January–February 2003): 58–68.

Williams, Edward J. "The Emergence of the Secular Nation-State and Latin American Catholicism." *Comparative Politics* 5, no. 2 (January 1973): 261–77.

Dissertations

Geisinger, Sandra Staples "'Go Ye into All the World and Preach the Gospel . . .': An Ethnographic Study of How Evangelical Christian Missionaries Work with National and Indigenous Peoples in Ecuador." PhD diss., Columbia University, Teachers College, 1995.

Hamilton, Michael S. "The Fundamentalist Harvard: Wheaton College and the Continuing Vitality of American Evangelicalism, 1919–1965." PhD diss., University of Notre Dame, 1994.

Loucks, Clarence Melvin. "The Theological Foundations of the Victorious Life: An Evaluation of the Theology of the Victorious Christian Life in Light of the Present and Future Aspects of Biblical Sanctification." PhD diss., Fuller Theological Seminary, School of Theology, 1984.

Index

American Bible Society, 104; and SIL, 98–100, 121
Anderson, Lambert, 215, 216, 217
Anderson, Loretta, 178–79
Anthropology: idealist vs. realist, 198–99, 201, 205, 213–14; and philosophy of culture change, 200–201, 204–6, 212–13, 221; politicization of, 195–96, 207–10; secular critique of WBT-SIL, 185, 196–201, 211, 213, 226, 230
Arcand, Bernard, 198, 208, 209
Aschmann, Herman, 83–84, 86

Beekman, John, 102, 106; translation theory of, 96–100
Bendor-Samuel, John, 202, 203–4, 239
Bible House of Los Angeles, 16, 17
Bible translation: challenges of pioneer, 83–86; and doctrine of inspiration/inerrancy debate, 87–96; linguistics and, 29–30, 61–62, 68–69, 71, 81, 83; as mission strategy of WBT-SIL, 1, 11, 31, 36, 42, 47, 81–89, 102–4, 107–8, 121–23, 162, 169, 225, 241; national participants in, 201–4; theories of, 96–100, 104, 106–7
Bilingual education, 188–89; and integration of indigenous peoples, 29, 39, 42, 124–25, 144–45, 200, 215
Blight, Richard, 163, 168

Bloomfield, Leonard, 73–74; *Language*, 56–57
Burgess, Paul, 26–27, 31, 35

Camp Wycliffe, 10, 29, 37, 46, 49, 83, 151, 168; academics at, 52, 55, 56, 58, 59–64, 80; separationist tendencies of, 64–70. *See also* Summer Institute of Linguistics
Cárdenas, Lázaro, 42–44, 45–46, 137
Catholicism, Catholic Church: in Guatemala, 18–19, 23; in Mexico, 38, 41, 43–44, 122; participation in SIL at Norman, 66, 67, 70; and SIL in Peru, 7, 9, 119, 123, 143–48; and WBT-SIL, 161, 164, 165–66, 190–91, 232
Central American Mission (CAM), 7, 27, 228; and Cameron Townsend, 11, 20, 21–23, 24, 26,32, 33, 36
Christian Aviators' Missionary Fellowship (CAMF). *See* Missionary Aviators' Fellowship
Cowan, George, 167, 174, 186, 223
Cuesta, José Martín, 143, 144

Davis, Ralph T., 153, 158, 160
Descriptive linguistics, 1, 47, 56, 199, 240; and Bible translation, 36, 37. *See also* Structural linguistics
Dinwiddie, Howard, 31, 32–34, 48, 228

269